THE
1930S

THE 1930s

William H. Young
with Nancy K. Young

American Popular Culture Through History
Ray B. Browne, Series Editor

GREENWOOD PRESS
Westport, Connecticut · London

Library of Congress Cataloging-in-Publication Data

Young, William H., 1939–
    The 1930s / William H. Young with Nancy K. Young.
      p. cm. (American popular culture through history)
    Includes bibliographical references and index.
    ISBN 0–313–31602–3 (alk. paper)
    1. United States—Civilization—1918–1945. 2. Popular culture—United
States—History—20th century. 3. Nineteen thirties. I. Young, Nancy K., 1940–
II. Title. III. Series.
    E169.1.Y59   2002
    973.9—dc21   2002016105

British Library Cataloguing in Publication Data is available.

Library of Congress Catalog Card Number: 2002016105
ISBN: 0–313–31602–3

First published in 2002

Greenwood Press, 88 Post Road West, Westport, CT 06881
An imprint of Greenwood Publishing Group, Inc.
www.greenwood.com

Printed in the United States of America

The paper used in this book complies with the
Permanent Paper Standard issued by the National
Information Standards Organization (Z39.48–1984).

10 9 8 7 6 5 4 3 2 1

To our parents,
Bill and Gwen Young
and
Bruce and Clara Kent
For them,
a defining decade

Contents

Series Foreword *by Ray B. Browne*   ix

Introduction   xi

Timeline of Popular Cultural Events   xv

Part I   Life and Youth During the 1930s   1

1   Everyday America   3

2   World of Youth   17

Part II   Popular Culture of the 1930s   35

3   Advertising   37

4   Architecture and Design   57

5   Fashion   81

6   Food and Drink   95

7   Leisure Activities   119

8   Literature   147

9   Music   169

10   Performing Arts   185

11   Travel and Recreation   231

Contents

12   Visual Arts   257

Cost of Products   279

Notes   283

Further Reading   293

Index   317

Series Foreword

Popular culture is the system of attitudes, behaviors, beliefs, customs, and tastes that define the people of any society. It is the entertainments, diversions, icons, rituals, and actions that shape the everyday world. It is what we do while we are awake and what we dream about while we are asleep. It is the way of life we inherit, practice, change, and then pass on to our descendants.

Popular culture is an extension of folk culture, the culture of the people. With the rise of electronic media and the increase in communication in American culture, folk culture expanded into popular culture—the daily way of life as shaped by the *popular majority* of society. Especially in a democracy like the United States, popular culture has become both the voice of the people and the force that shapes the nation. In 1782, the French commentator Hector St. Jean de Crèvecoeur asked in his *Letters from an American Farmer*, "What is an American?" He answered that such a person is the creation of America and is in turn the creator of the country's culture. Indeed, notions of the American Dream have been long grounded in the dream of democracy—that is, government by the people, or popular rule. Thus, popular culture is tied fundamentally to America and the dreams of its people.

Historically, culture analysts have tried to fine-tune culture into two categories: "elite"—the elements of culture (fine art, literature, classical music, gourmet food, etc.) that supposedly define the best of society—and "popular"—the elements of culture (comic strips, best-sellers, pop music, fast food, etc.) that appeal to society's lowest common denominator. The "educated" person approved of elite culture and scoffed at popular culture. This schism first began to develop in western Europe in the fifteenth century when the privileged classes tried to discover and develop differences in societies based on class, money, privilege, and lifestyles. Like many aspects of European society, the debate between elite and popular cultures came to the United States. The upper class in America, for example, supported museums and galleries that would exhibit the finer things in life, that would "elevate" people. As the twenty-first century emerges, however, the distinctions between popular culture and elitist culture have blurred. The blues songs (once denigrated as "race music") of Robert Johnson are now revered by musicologists; architectural students study buildings in Las Vegas, Nevada, as examples of what Robert Venturi called the "kitsch of high capitalism"; sportswriter Gay Talese and heavyweight boxing champ Floyd Patterson were copanelists at a 1992 State University of New York–New Paltz symposium on literature and sport. The examples go on and on, but the one commonality that emerges is the role of popular culture as a model for the American Dream, the dream to pursue happiness and a better, more interesting life.

To trace the numerous ways in which popular culture has evolved throughout American history, we have divided the volumes in this series into chronological periods—historical eras until the twentieth century, and decades between 1900 and 2000. In each volume, the author explores the specific details of popular culture that reflect and inform the general undercurrents of the time. Our purpose, then, is to present historical and analytical panoramas that reach both backward into America's past and forward to her collective future. In viewing these panoramas, we can trace a very fundamental part of American society. The "American Popular Culture Through History" series presents the multifaceted parts of a popular culture in a nation that is both grown and still growing.

Ray B. Browne
Secretary-Treasurer
Popular Culture Association
American Culture Association

Introduction

Any study of the 1930s must begin not with January 1930, but with October 1929—Thursday, October 24, to be precise. That autumn day saw the collapse of the stock market—the traditional indicator of the nation's economic health—and signaled the onset of the Great Depression. Those grim years shaped the 1930s, and because popular culture is a reflector of its times, advertising, books, magazines, movies, music, radio, theater, and all the other outlets for mass entertainment responded.

On a similar note, the decade itself may have technically concluded on December 31, 1939, but it really ended, symbolically, four months earlier, on September 1, 1939. That was the date of the German invasion of Poland. When Nazi armies smashed across the Polish border, the false peace of the late 1930s was forever laid to rest, and World War II began in earnest. It also marked the end of American innocence, a refusal to believe that the nation could be lured into yet another European conflict. Some of the spirit of the thirties, however, hung on until October 27, 1940, and the final day of the New York World's Fair. When "The World of Tomorrow" shut its gates for the last time, the world was already at war, and the fair itself closed bankrupt. It was a fitting conclusion to a spectacle drenched in optimism, but one that turned away from reality. Whatever date is chosen, the thirties must be seen as a remarkable decade, full of energy and despair, contradictions and confirmations, humor and pathos.

This work focuses on the general content of mass entertainment. It discusses the movies, the discovery of the teenager as a marketable entity, the increase in leisure time and travel, the innumerable dance fads and the dominance of swing, the rise of the radio comedians—and all the other fads and phenomena that made the 30s so memorable.

The economic history of the era has been recorded many times and well. President Herbert Hoover, searching for a term to describe what had happened to the nation's economy, chose the word "depression." Perhaps it was not a good choice. "Depression" suggests misery, a quiet dulling of the spirit, something that wears a person down without dramatic symptoms. Had he said "panic" or "crisis," he might have spoken more wisely. In addition, panics and crises can be approached spectacularly but effectively, whereas "depression" presents no dramatic resolution. President Hoover, however, provided no answers; he had little in mind at all.

As the Depression grew more grim, Hoover attempted to change his public image. He attended baseball games. He suggested comedian Will Rogers should provide jokes that would make people laugh about the crisis. He asked crooner Rudy Vallee to sing songs on the radio that would cause people to forget their troubles. These were stopgaps that had little effect, but they do illustrate a primitive understanding on Hoover's part that popular culture was bound to be part of the solution.

When examining the era through the long lens of history, it is tempting to romanticize the 1930s in one of two ways. First, the decade was a terrible time, filled with constant, unimaginable human suffering, a period of unceasing chaos. The second approach invokes a kind of false nostalgia: that the decade provided people an opportunity to pull together, that it was a time of bonding, that things were not as bad as some imagined. Both positions have elements of truth, thus reinforcing the idea that, by any measure, it was one of the most tumultuous eras in the nation's history.

This volume is liberally supplied with photographs that sample some of the many flavors of the 1930s. The bulk of the illustrations reflect the work of the Farm Security Administration. Among other tasks, this federally financed group took on the assignment of documenting American life; it dispatched photographers who took thousands of pictures during the 1930s. The result is a remarkable collection of images, both urban and rural, of the United States throughout the decade. The Library of Congress now holds that collection, so it is accessible to the public; what is found on these pages is but a small part of those riches.

Throughout the book, particular emphasis is placed on movies that were popular during the decade. Well over half the population went to the movies regularly, thereby giving motion pictures unprecedented influence. With their combination of visual imagery and spoken narrative, movies were uniquely suited to reach and affect audiences, simultaneously making them both primary movers and reflectors of public opinion. Considerable space has been devoted to the close relationships that exist between films and the other popular arts. Dozens of Hollywood features, some well known and some obscure, are provided as examples of the cultural crossover that occurs in any broad examination of popular media.

By and large, popular culture mirrors the concerns and attitudes of many different people at a particular time. When those concerns and attitudes shift, popular culture likewise changes, continuing in its role of interpreter and presenter. Given human nature, the images and language of popular culture tend to be generally positive, forward-looking, and upbeat, even when referring to serious, problem-filled situations or events. The 1930s were no exception. The economy might be in disarray, another world war could be looming, but instead of being mired in a slough of despondency, the artifacts of popular culture assured the nation that "Happy Days Are Here Again" because "We're in the Money." The movies danced to *42nd Street*, records asked "Who's Afraid of the Big, Bad Wolf?" radio found future stars with *Major Bowes and His Original Amateur Hour*, and Scarlett O'Hara could say, "I'll think about it tomorrow."

ACKNOWLEDGMENTS

A work of this size and scope cannot be written without the assistance of many individuals. We are indebted to director Chris Millson-Martula and his able staff at the Lynchburg College Library in Lynchburg, Virginia. They were always gracious and helpful, no matter how demanding and time-consuming the request. Ariel Meyers was outstanding in her role of locating interlibrary loan titles; some of the works were obscure at best, but she found them, and always with good humor. Sue Cook at the National Gallery, Virginia Dunn at the Virginia State Library, and Ben DeWhitt at the National Archives smoothed some steps for accessing government documents. Jan Grenci and her associates at the Library of Congress made looking at thousands of pictures a pleasure, and she patiently walked us through the procedures for getting a picture reproduced from their voluminous files. Tom Giddings, Jessica Gisclair, Jimmy Roux, Bobbi Schuler, Berkey Vicks, and Mary and Roger Zimmermann were generous with recordings, movies, books, magazines, and other materials from the period, as well as some timely computer assistance. The unerring eye of Dawn Hensley Fisher was responsible for catching typos and awkward constructions. Finally, Greenwood Press deserves an appreciative nod; this project was first in the able hands of Debby Adams and Rob Kirkpatrick. Liz Leiba and Beth Wilson then worked with the manuscript. The astute advice and gracious comments of all four carried it all to conclusion. Of course, any errors of commission or omission are ours and ours alone.

Timeline of Popular Cultural Events

1930

U.S. population stands at approximately 123 million. Unemployment is about 4.5 million, almost 9 percent of the total workforce, for the year.

Men selling apples at a nickel apiece begin to appear on street corners.

The Chrysler Building opens on May 27 in New York City; it is briefly the world's tallest skyscraper.

Miniature golf becomes a fad, and dance marathons regain popularity.

Commercial air travel between New York and Los Angeles is initiated in October. United Airlines hires the first stewardesses.

Bobby Jones wins the Grand Slam of golf and announces his retirement on November 17.

Grant Wood's *American Gothic* is unveiled at the Art Institute of Chicago in the fall.

The impact of the movies is felt in fashion: the cool, sophisticated looks of Greta Garbo, Joan Crawford, Jean Harlow, and Marlene Dietrich gain popularity.

Little Caesar, a gangster epic starring Edward G. Robinson, opens, and *Anna Christie* allows audiences to hear Greta Garbo talk.

1931

Unemployment swells to 16 percent; 8 million are out of work. For the first time ever in America, more people are leaving the country than are entering it.

On May 1, the Empire State Building opens in New York City; it is the world's tallest skyscraper.

In October, Chester Gould's *Dick Tracy* makes its debut in newspaper comic strips.

Babe Ruth and Lou Gehrig hit forty-six home runs apiece for the New York Yankees.

Birds Eye frozen vegetables appear, along with Hostess Twinkies and Snickers candy bars.

"Life Is Just a Bowl of Cherries" reflects American disdain for the Depression, Bing Crosby's rendition of "Where the Blue of the Night Meets the Gold of the Day" establishes his fame as a crooner, and Kate Smith's "When the Moon Comes Over the Mountain" sells so well she is named America's "Songbird of the South."

Pearl Buck's *The Good Earth* dominates the best-seller lists.

Two new afternoon radio serials, based on popular comic strips, come on the air: *Buck Rogers* and *Little Orphan Annie.*

Dracula reflects the growing popularity of horror films and makes Bela Lugosi a star. It is followed by *Frankenstein*, which establishes the fame of Boris Karloff.

1932

Unemployment reaches almost 24 percent; 14 million are without jobs. Wages are 60 percent less than in 1929. Franklin D. Roosevelt promises a "new deal" at the Democratic convention in June; he defeats incumbent Herbert Hoover for the presidency in the November elections.

In February, the first winter Olympics are held at Lake Placid, New York, sparking an interest in skiing.

In March, the infant son of Charles and Anne Lindbergh is kidnapped, setting off sensational press coverage. His body is found in May.

Despite the Depression, Radio City Music Hall, a part of the ongoing Rockefeller Center, opens in New York City at Christmastime.

The song "Brother, Can You Spare a Dime?" sums up the disillusionment that accompanies the worsening Depression.

The Jack Benny Program and *The Fred Allen Show* premiere on network radio.

The first Big Little Book comes out; it features *Dick Tracy.*

Shirley Temple makes her film debut; she is three years old.

Walt Disney receives a special Academy Award for his creation of Mickey Mouse.

1933

In February, Congress votes to repeal Prohibition. By early December, enough states approve the measure that the Twenty-first Amendment (Repeal) is passed.

Franklin D. Roosevelt assumes the presidency in March. He faces 25 percent unemployment, with 15 million workers affected. Family income has dropped almost 40 percent since the onset of the Depression.

In March, President Roosevelt begins his "Fireside Chats" on radio, drawing record audiences.

In May, the Century of Progress Exposition opens in Chicago; architecturally, it features a mix of Modernism and traditional revival styles.

Erle Stanley Gardner writes his first Perry Mason mystery, *The Case of the Velvet Claws*.

Bridge becomes the most popular card game; the sales of expert Ely Culbertson's *Contract Bridge Blue Book*, first published in 1931, soar.

"Who's Afraid of the Big Bad Wolf?" a song from Walt Disney's cartoon *The Three Little Pigs*, expresses the hope following Roosevelt's inauguration.

42nd Street and *Gold Diggers of 1933* are the definitive Depression musicals; *King Kong* and *The Invisible Man* demonstrate how movie special effects can create great entertainment.

The first All-Star baseball game is played; the American League wins.

1934

Unemployment drops slightly to about 22 percent; 11 million are out of work.

The National Recovery Administration's emblem, a blue eagle and the slogan "We Do Our Part," is seen in factories, stores, and shops everywhere.

On May 28, the Dionne quintuplets are born in Ontario; the event brings unprecedented press coverage and public interest.

On September 18, Bruno Hauptmann is arrested for kidnapping Charles Lindbergh's infant son.

In December, Benny Goodman's *Let's Dance* show brings big-band swing nightly to radio.

John Dillinger, "Baby Face" Nelson, "Pretty Boy" Floyd, and Bonnie and Clyde are shot and killed by law officers, effectively ending the reign of colorful gangsters.

Frank Capra's *It Happened One Night*, one of the Depression era's "screwball comedies," sweeps the Academy Awards.

Hervey Allen's *Anthony Adverse* leads the best-seller lists for fiction.

The Chrysler Airflow, the first mass-produced car to incorporate streamlined design, is introduced.

1935

Unemployment dips to about 21 percent; 10 million are out of work. One out of four households receives some kind of relief.

On January 1, the trial of Bruno Hauptmann begins for the kidnapping and murder of the Lindbergh baby. He is convicted of all charges by mid-February.

In April, *Your Hit Parade* begins on NBC radio, tracking the most popular records of the week, and a new comedy series, *Fibber McGee and Molly*, also debuts on the network.

On May 24, the first major league baseball game played under lights occurs in Cincinnati.

George Gershwin's folk opera *Porgy and Bess* opens on Broadway in October.

Bingo is allowed in movie theaters and becomes a craze, as do chain letters.

The board game Monopoly becomes an overnight sensation.

The Marx Brothers challenge high culture in *A Night at the Opera*.

Cole Porter's "Begin the Beguine," as recorded by Artie Shaw, is a big hit.

1936

Unemployment drops to 17 percent—about 8 million workers. In November, President Roosevelt swamps challenger Alf Landon, 523 electoral votes to 8, losing only Vermont and Maine.

On April 3, Bruno Hauptmann is executed for kidnapping and killing the infant son of Charles Lindbergh, ending one of the most sensational investigations and trials in U.S. history.

The Douglas DC-3 begins production in June. The airplane quickly sets the standards for luxury and safety in air travel.

Famed director Cecil B. De Mille begins hosting *Lux Radio Theater* in June; it becomes a major dramatic show, with scripts based on popular movies of the time.

In August, the Summer Olympics are held in Berlin; Jesse Owens humiliates Hitler and the Nazis, along with their racist theories, by winning four gold medals in track events.

Margaret Mitchell's *Gone with the Wind* sells over a million copies by December and eclipses all competition.

The biggest news story is the abdication by King Edward VIII of England for "the woman I love," Wallis Warfield Simpson, on December 11.

Dancer Fred Astaire finds himself a major singing star with four hits: "Let's Face the Music and Dance," "Let Yourself Go," "The Way You Look Tonight," and "Pick Yourself Up." The songs all come from his movies with Ginger Rogers.

Over 5000 artists paint thousands of murals in post offices, train stations, courthouses, and other buildings across the country as part of the Federal Arts Program.

1937

Unemployment drops to 14 percent; 7 million workers are without jobs. Toward the end of the year, the stock market again declines, and the nation moves toward a recession.

In March, teenagers jitterbug in the aisles of New York's Paramount Theater to the swing of Benny Goodman.

The German dirigible *Hindenburg* crashes at Lakehurst, New Jersey, on May 6; the disaster is reported live on radio.

On May 9, *The Chase and Sanborn Hour* introduces ventriloquist Edgar Bergen and Charlie McCarthy on NBC radio.

Aviatrix Amelia Earhart disappears over the Pacific Ocean on July 2.

Beginning in November, Arturo Toscanini and the NBC Symphony Orchestra bring classical music to a large radio audience.

Howard Johnson begins franchising restaurants, opening the market to chain eateries and fast food.

Gone with the Wind continues to outsell all other books.

Walt Disney's *Snow White and the Seven Dwarfs*, all-color and all-animated, opens.

1938

With a recession, unemployment jumps to 19 percent, or 9 million jobless. Defense spending increases, however, and the country begins to pull out of its decline.

The growing popularity of jazz and swing gives rise to a concert by Benny Goodman's band in New York's Carnegie Hall on January 16.

On June 22, Joe Louis knocks out Max Schmeling to retain his heavyweight crown and avenge an earlier loss to the German boxer.

The June issue of *Action Comics* features the adventures of a brand-new character, Superman.

Howard Hughes flies around the world in three days, nineteen hours, and fourteen minutes in July. "Wrong Way" Corrigan flies to Dublin instead of California (as he planned) that same month.

Orson Welles, as a Halloween prank, frightens many Americans with his radio adaptation of H.G. Wells's *War of the Worlds*.

Dale Carnegie's *How to Win Friends and Influence People* enters its second year as a leader among nonfiction books.

The Andy Hardy films begin, with Mickey Rooney in the title role.

Singer Frank Sinatra makes his radio debut on small stations in the New York area.

1939

U.S. population at the end of the decade stands at approximately 130 million; it has grown about 7 percent during the decade, well below past averages. Unemployment dips to 17 percent, or 8 million jobless.

Swallowing goldfish becomes a campus fad in March.

On April 9, singer Marian Anderson draws 75,000 to an open-air concert in Washington, D.C., after being barred from Constitution Hall by the Daughters of the American Revolution.

On April 30, the New York World's Fair opens, despite depressing international news, and Germany is excluded. The extravaganza is billed as "The World of Tomorrow." The opening ceremonies are televised, and TV monitors are a big hit at the fairgrounds.

On September 1, Germany invades Poland; World War II begins.

After a year of promotion, the film version of *Gone with the Wind* opens on December 15, overshadowing all other movie events.

Nylon stockings go on sale in the face of a silk shortage.

The Glenn Miller Orchestra has hits with "Little Brown Jug," "Sunrise Serenade," and "In the Mood."

Reporter Edward R. Murrow broadcasts nightly from London for CBS; more and more airtime is devoted to war news.

PART I

LIFE AND YOUTH DURING THE 1930S

THE 1930S

1

Everyday America

BACKGROUND

Some months prior to the April opening of the New York's World Fair, a time capsule was buried. Made of Cupaloy, an almost indestructible alloy of copper, chrome, and silver, the shiny tube was eight feet long, eight inches in diameter, weighed 800 pounds, and was sponsored by Westinghouse. In theory, it will not be opened for 5000 years, or not until 6939. The capsule was sunk fifty feet into the earth at Flushing Meadow; detailed instructions on locating it, along with an inventory of its holdings, were left with 3650 libraries and museums around the world in hopes that, 5000 years hence, someone could still find it.

The time capsule is fascinating for what it contains: seeds, coins and paper money, a can opener, a safety pin, swatches of cloth and plastics, a sample of cement, a microfilm essay about life on earth during the 1930s that runs to some 10 million words and features over 1,000 pictures, a sound newsreel, and many other artifacts deemed worthy of inclusion. Those who made the choices were closely attuned to popular culture. A Mickey Mouse cup, playing cards and a set of bridge rules, some rhinestone jewelry from Woolworth's, a reproduction of Grant Wood's painting *American Gothic*, the sheet music for "Flat Foot Floogie" (a pop hit of the day), a copy of *Gone with the Wind*, and several popular newspapers and magazines are among the items. Topping them all off is the 1938–1939 Sears, Roebuck catalog, a hefty document that should fill in any gaps about American consumer culture for that future person who unearths the capsule.[1]

Throughout the decade, the media provided a full curriculum of mass education unequaled in previous human history. Fashion, sports, celebrities, manners, and mores—all were represented in the daily outpouring of popular culture that has come to define the United States. It was in color, it had sound, and it was available for next to nothing. It was the marriage of technology and culture, and everyone was invited to the wedding. Certainly the Cupaloy time capsule itself was a reflection of that bonding, and the theme of the fair—"The World of Tomorrow"— extolled the utopian possibilities provided by modern science.

FRANKLIN D. ROOSEVELT

Overshadowing everyone and everything during the decade was the figure of Franklin Delano Roosevelt. He swept into national prominence in 1932, first at the Democratic national convention, where he promised a "New Deal" for Americans weary of the Great Depression. He then soundly defeated an outclassed Herbert Hoover for the presidency in November. For many, Hoover's lack of fresh thinking about solutions for the growing economic crisis was in sharp contrast to Roosevelt's unending stream of ideas and suggestions.

Roosevelt had his "Hundred Days" (the term used to signify his first 100 days in office, when much significant legislation was passed) and his Brain Trust; he had Eleanor, possibly the best-known First Lady in history; he had his dapper cigarette holder, tilted up at an jaunty angle for endless photo opportunities; and he even had Fala, his impossibly cute Scottish terrier. No previous president had ever mastered the media as did Roosevelt. Hoover was stiff and uncomfortable before microphones and cameras; Roosevelt reveled in the attention. Not only was he president, he was a celebrity of the first rank, the equal of any movie or radio star. His Fireside Chats on national radio were eagerly listened to, drawing larger audiences than the top-rated network shows. He showed up in theater newsreels, in magazine spreads, and almost daily in the papers. Roosevelt did not just make news, he himself was news, the embodiment of the popular culture celebrity.

A major event that gripped the nation was an attempted assassination of Roosevelt on February 15, 1933. A disgruntled anarchist, Giuseppe Zangara, who said in his defense only that "I hate all presidents," and "too many people are starving to death," fired six shots at Roosevelt in Miami, Florida. Although the president-elect was unhurt, two bullets struck Chicago's mayor, Anton Cermak, his traveling companion. Several weeks later, Cermak died from his wounds.

Public outrage was immediate and justice was equally swift. Zangara was indicted on the same day as the attack; he pleaded guilty; and he was electrocuted by the state of Florida on March 20, just five weeks

Franklin D. Roosevelt delivering one of his famous "Fireside Chats."
More than any president before him, Roosevelt understood the power
of radio. (Photograph courtesy of the Library of Congress.)

after the crime. Americans devoured radio and newspaper accounts of the crime throughout February and March, hearing and reading about the would-be assassin's life, Mayor Cermak's weakening condition, and Roosevelt's reactions to the event. It was a media circus that allowed people to momentarily forget the Depression.

Buoyed by an outpouring of sympathy along with his electoral mandate, the president enjoyed a tempestuous first term. The public loved it; he was returned to office in 1936 with an overwhelming majority. But despite all his energy, Roosevelt could not seem to cure the nation's economic ills. His second term was marked by severe labor disorders, especially sit-down strikes and the growth of unions. A 1937 Gallup Poll showed 70 percent of Americans favored the existence of unions, but most opposed the sit-down tactics. The presidential honeymoon soured as labor disputes grew uglier and the nation slid into a full-scale recession.

Nevertheless, Roosevelt remained a figure of endless media coverage and public interest. Nothing he said or did escaped the unblinking eye of the camera and the poised pen of the reporter. Despite his political setbacks in the later 1930s, the threat of war convinced a majority of Americans to return him to office for an unprecedented third term in 1940. The cigarette holder might not be quite so jaunty in 1939, but Roosevelt was still a celebrity in all respects.

THE GREAT DEPRESSION

The Great Depression was a defining event in American life; perhaps only the Civil War was more stressful and touched proportionally more people. National income fell by 50 percent. Economic stresses brought about rising divorce and separation rates. Fewer children were being born, and the size of the typical American family shrank to the smallest of any decade. Couples postponed marriage; 290,000 fewer people got married in 1932 than in 1920. Those who did marry delayed having children. Frequently they continued living at home or doubled up with friends. As a result, the birthrate fell below the replacement level for the first time ever, and a more liberal attitude toward birth control manifested itself. Clinics sprang up that offered advice about contraception, a subject that was "hush-hush" just a few years earlier.[2]

By 1932, one out of every five American workers was unemployed, and others were underemployed, attempting to adjust to partial schedules and reduced hours. Without jobs, without income, the shame of unemployment drove many from their spouses, and child neglect became a problem. Lack of supervision, disease, and malnutrition were among the leading factors in such cases. For older children, there was a kind of silver lining in all this: they stayed in school longer, continuing their educations instead of hunting for nonexistent jobs. Others opted to leave home and hit the road; uncounted thousands of young people lived hand-to-mouth lives, wandering the country and hoping for the best in the midst of hard times.

As the Depression worsened in the early thirties, the volume of manufactured goods dropped sharply, as did national payrolls. The response was to lay off workers, slash dividends, reduce inventories, cut remaining wages, forgo improvements, and reduce production. Twenty-six thousand businesses folded in 1930, 28,000 in 1931, and almost 32,000 in 1932. These discouraging numbers meant that unemployment rose from 429,000 in 1929 to 15 million in 1933. That was the face of everyday America in the depths of the Great Depression.

Construction of new housing dropped by 95 percent between 1928 and 1933. Those already in homes could ill afford to maintain them. Home repairs dropped by 90 percent and housing prices declined, wiping out holdings and equity. This disaster hit the middle class particularly hard; many of the poor already rented, but it was the first experience with poverty for those struggling to purchase or hold on to their own homes. In 1931 there were 200,000 foreclosures. In 1932 the number soared to 250,000, and by 1933, half of all home mortgages were technically in default.[3]

People borrowed on their tangible and intangible assets. Life insurance, mortgages, and household possessions were all used as collateral, but often these were not enough. Without the means to pay rent or maintain mortgage payments, more and more citizens lost their homes. Evictions grew ominously in the early years of the decade. In New York City alone, some 15,000 people were considered homeless in 1931; the city lacked the resources to house them, and they wandered the streets in search of shelter of any kind.[4]

RURAL HARDSHIPS

The suffering was not confined to cities. In 1900, 41 percent of Americans lived on farms; in 1930, the figure had plummeted to about 25 percent—and was still falling. The small, traditional family-owned farm was particularly threatened. Agricultural income collapsed, dropping a full 50 percent in those terrible years. Farms were abandoned or lost to banks; in 1932, over 200,000 farms, homes, and businesses were foreclosed. In order to stave off disaster, people left their own properties and turned to sharecropping and tenant farming. As banks and other lenders attempted to take over farms in default, "penny auctions" erupted. Buyers would get a farm's goods for pennies, return them to the owner, and turn the cash over to the bank as payment for the mortgage. The foreclosures continued almost unabated into the mid-1930s.

Nor did nature cooperate with the struggling farmers. These were the years of the Dust Bowl, a time when rural land dried up, turning into a fine dust. "Black rollers" were moving clouds of precious topsoil, dislodged from the earth, billowing across the countryside just like a thunderstorm. Sometimes they were accompanied by a few drops of "black rain," water mixed with dust that left a smear of mud wherever it landed. Occasionally the storms lasted several days, the blowing soil piling up in drifts against buildings and along fences. Highways were obliterated, buried under inches or even feet of sandy dust. If the "roller" came from the north, it had black dirt from Colorado and Nebraska; if it blew up from the south, it contained the red sand of Texas and Oklahoma. No matter the source, throughout the Depression, American agriculture was worse off than any other sector of the economy. Basically, however, the farm crisis was invisible to American popular culture because there was no real rural popular culture.

A breadline. For the unemployed, times were harsh in the early 1930s. Here, people are waiting for free food at the base of New York's Brooklyn Bridge. (Photograph courtesy of the Library of Congress.)

URBAN HARDSHIPS

In the cities, the crisis was far more visible. An old word from the nineteenth century re-entered the national vocabulary: breadline. Unable to afford groceries or meals, many city dwellers found themselves standing in breadlines, waiting for a handout. Run primarily by charitable organizations, soup kitchens (another resurrected term) and other suppliers of free food attracted long lines of people anxious for a bit of nourishment. Although there are virtually no verified cases of starvation during the Depression, many individuals and families went to bed hungry each night.

Certainly an image of the Depression that remains prevalent is that of a man standing on a street corner selling apples for a nickel apiece. This icon evolved through a mixture of commercial marketing and public desperation. In 1929 and 1930, the state of Washington had a surplus of apples. The International Apple Shippers Association, through fliers and word of mouth, persuaded many men—and a few women—the enterprise was not only respectable but a means of seventy-two Northwest apples for $1.75. The association, by virtue of some shrewd publicity, convinced these would-be entrepreneurs that they could make—after expenses—$1.85 a day by hawking apples on a busy corner. "Buy an apple a day and ease the Depression away!" was the slogan, and it became a scheme that had thousands of takers in most larger American cities.

Apple Mary

The apple-selling movement lasted only about a year, and as more and more vendors became disillusioned about easy money, it faded away. But it was not forgotten. In 1934, cartoonist Martha Orr convinced Publishers' Syndicate to carry a new comic strip she had developed for national newspaper distribution. She called her creation *Apple Mary*, and it featured a rather dowdy older woman who sold apples from a street cart. The strip told serialized stories that were very much in the soap opera mold, and her heroine was wise in the ways of solving the problems of the lovelorn. *Apple Mary* was nevertheless set firmly in its time, with unemployment and poverty a major part of the strip's visual and story components. Since the '30s was the golden age of newspaper comics, it was fitting that such a strip made its debut.

Apple Mary lasted in its original format until 1938. Its topicality was limited, and as the Depression waned, the idea of an apple seller had decreasing relevance. Nothing, however, ever really dies in popular culture; it simply metamorphoses into something that will gain a larger audience. And so *Apple Mary* became *Apple Mary and Dennie*, and then *Mary Worth's Family*, with the kindly older widow continuing the soap opera plotting but without the nuisance of the apple cart.

In 1933, film director Frank Capra made a movie called *Lady for a Day*. It deals with a rather disreputable woman named Mary (played by May Robson), who is loosely based on a character called Madame La Gimp, created by writer Damon Runyon in a short story of the same name (collected in the Runyon anthology *Guys and Dolls*, 1931). Both Madame La Gimp and Mary are down on their luck, reduced to doing whatever will bring in a few coins. For Mary, that includes selling apples. The success of *Lady for a Day* led to a sequel, *Lady by Choice* (1934). This latter effort was directed by David Burton and stars Carole Lombard—but not as Mary; that honor again belongs to May Robson. Although real apple vendors were around only for a year or so during the Depression, the power of their image was such that popular culture, specifically the comics and the movies, kept them at their trade far longer than anyone would have expected.[5]

Despite the elevation of the nickel apple into a symbol for the Depression, most of the jobless found more profitable pursuits. The idea of

A Depression-era American family in their living room.
From furnishings to fashions, this was a typical scene;
the children are reading the newspaper comics.
(Photograph courtesy of the Library of Congress.)

shoeshines held some appeal; by 1932 thousands of novice bootblacks were trying their hand at it. Others took up door-to-door sales, making the Fuller Brush Company one of the most profitable firms of the decade. Some passed out handbills or placed ads on car windshields. Still others attempted mining—coal, gold, silver—whatever the earth would give up. The point of all these efforts was the old American quality of self-reliance, to avoid going on the dole. In the 1930s, the thought of accepting public relief still bore a stigma, a carryover from earlier years.

Popular culture, however, offered an escape from unpleasant realities. At the same time, it reinforced family intimacy. Mom, Dad, the kids, sitting around the living room listening to the radio—it was a reassuring image, something that happened in millions of households each and every evening. This sense of being close was not limited to radio: books, newspapers, and magazines, along with motion pictures, also were enormously popular during the decade. In fact, the impact of the movies as family entertainment was probably almost as great as radio's. An average of 60 to 75 million people went to the movies each week, more than 60 percent of the total population.[6]

EMPLOYMENT

Movies and radio to the contrary, by 1932, 40 million Americans, urban and rural, knew poverty of some kind. As a result, women entered the workplace in ever greater numbers. Husbands had to come to the decision to "allow" their spouses to work, suppressing old prejudices about working wives and mothers. The move was based on necessity, not preference. As factory and other male-dominated jobs decreased in number, more and more men joined the ranks of the unemployed. Often, the only jobs available were clerical and domestic ones, occupations traditionally held by women. A shift in employment patterns occurred, with the percentage of men in the workforce declining as the number of women taking jobs increased. But there was a price to pay: all social ills, from juvenile delinquency to divorce, were laid at the feet of working mothers. Further, 75 percent of women believed that if the husband had a paying position, the wife should not work, thereby freeing up jobs for men.[7]

Another employment problem that went beyond gender was race. The already existing inequities between blacks and whites were exacerbated by the Depression. Black skilled workers saw their wages fall much faster than those of similar white employees. The National Recovery Administration (NRA) was a government agency established to provide aid to those in need, but its rules contained a grandfather clause that allowed wage discrepancies that were based on wages earned in the past. For many blacks, NRA meant "Negro Run Around" and "Negroes Rarely Allowed." Black sharecroppers and tenant farmers in the South received some 70 percent less in relief payments than white farmers, a situation that often forced them off the land entirely.[8]

With worsening conditions, the cost of living dropped. But tumbling prices did not help the millions who had less to spend. This was no "economic adjustment"; this was a full-fledged depression. The consumer price index, if measured as 100 in 1929, had declined to 80.8 in 1932. With the economy toppling, banks and other lenders had second thoughts about installment buying. Although Americans had long been

The National Recovery Administration (NRA) emblem.
The "Blue Eagle" was found everywhere. It
demonstrated support for government policies aimed
at ending the Depression. (Photograph of the NRA
poster by the author.)

imbued with the notion to pay cash for virtually everything except housing, the Depression brought about some subtle changes. It was noted
that people did not default on most loans; the banks might go under,
but individuals were usually reliable about repaying debt. As a result,
automobile financing actually grew during the 1930s, and many people
chose this means to acquire new or used cars. Department stores and
other retail establishments likewise extended credit throughout this turbulent decade.

The closing years of the 1930s, however, continued to be marked by
uncertainty and worry. Between 1933 and 1939, at least 10 percent of the
workforce remained jobless. For the naysayers who opposed government
involvement in employment and considered it meddling, the word

"boondoggle" entered the language. Originally intended to mean simple craftwork like woven belts, it came to mean any silly, useless project, and usually implied the government had a hand in it. For the unemployed, however, the jobs provided by the NRA and the Works Progress Administration (WPA), along with all their associated agencies, were genuine lifesavers, not expensive make-work. The NRA Blue Eagle ("We Do Our Part") was an icon of the times, proudly displayed in commercial establishments everywhere. Whether it was pouring concrete in a large city or building a highway through mountainous terrain, 20 percent of the total workforce labored in some capacity in these organizations' programs.[9]

If a young man had fifteen cents in his pocket—a nickel and a dime— he was king of the road. In terms of today's dollars, he had about $1.75 jingling around, and that should see him through his day. He could eat for a nickel and still have a dime left over. The nickel itself took on a certain significance. Five cents in the pocket meant a person was not totally down and out. In 1936, three times more nickels and dimes were minted than in 1934.

MAJOR NEWS STORIES

The Lindbergh Kidnapping

Amid all the economic woes, the public found escape in the problems of others. A prime example was the March 1, 1932, kidnapping of the infant son of Charles and Anne Lindbergh, "the Crime of the Century." Still very much a hero to Americans because of his solo flight across the Atlantic in 1927, Lindbergh had retreated with his wife to rural New Jersey to escape the ceaseless glare of publicity that continued to surround "the Lone Eagle." Unfortunately, the kidnapping had the opposite effect on the couple; the crime made the Lindberghs the most visible parents in the nation, and they would remain that way for several years as the press shadowed their every move and the nation took in every word written about the crime.

The Lindbergh case had all the makings of the worst and best of movie or radio drama: handsome, famous parents; heinous crime; and an equally fascinating cast of secondary players. On May 12, 1932, the infant's body was located, but not until 1934, after a series of cruel hoaxes, was a suspect arrested. Finally, in September, Bruno Hauptmann was charged with the kidnapping, and in January 1935, almost three years after the crime, the trial commenced in the rural town of Flemington, New Jersey. An army of reporters descended on the village, prepared to record all details of the proceedings. A breathless public stayed glued to

Charles Lindbergh arriving to testify in 1935. The 1932 kidnapping of his infant son led to "the Trial of the Century," an event marked by media sensationalism. (Photograph courtesy of the Library of Congress.)

its radios for the latest reports; newspapers issued extra editions chronicling the courtroom scenes. The Depression, the New Deal, and even Roosevelt were put aside for six weeks as evidence was presented. Hauptmann was convicted and eventually executed; the media extravaganza was over, Flemington returned to its quiet ways, and the country, temporarily sated, reverted to more mundane interests.

Admiral Byrd

If a grisly kidnapping was not everyone's cup of tea, the popular media had many other items on its varied menu. Tales of exploration and courage found a receptive audience in the depressed thirties; they were a pleasant change from discouraging economic statistics. Rear Admiral Richard E. Byrd had distinguished himself by flying over the North Pole in 1926 and the South Pole in 1929. Those feats, however, only seemed to urge him on to greater adventure. In 1933 he mounted a land and air expedition to the Antarctic in order to study and map the last unknown continent. So great was public interest in this undertaking that it was partially funded by innumerable private donations from individuals. And in 1933 a commemorative stamp, designed by none other than President Roosevelt himself, was issued to celebrate the undertaking.[10]

Byrd's party set up weather stations at scattered locations on the ice sheet, and he himself settled into an isolated, nine-foot-by-thirteen-foot cabin some 125 miles from the crew's base camp, Little America II. Equipped only with a two-way radio, he sat out the 1934–1935 Antarctic winter in his shack, studying climatic patterns. His weekly broadcasts on CBS Radio enthralled the nation, and he had an immediate best-seller in his book *Alone* (1938), a retelling of the saga on the polar ice. Admiral Byrd returned to Antarctica in 1939, but his solitary stint some five years earlier, man against the elements, had made him one of the genuine heroes of the decade.

THE DIONNE QUINTUPLETS

Another event of the era that rivaled the interest generated by Admiral Byrd had absolutely nothing to do with exploration, politics, or crime. In 1934, on a tiny farm near Callander, Ontario, Elzipe Dionne gave birth to five girls—Annette, Cécile, Emilie, Marie, and Yvonne. The quintuplets were born in a span of thirty minutes, a rare medical occurrence. Immediately dubbed "the quints" by the press and a huge, adoring public, the family was inundated with gifts of all descriptions. People in the United States were particularly taken by this Canadian event; thousands crossed the border to make the drive to the little Ontario village. Despite an almost sideshow-like atmosphere surrounding the humble Dionne home, all five girls survived and grew into normal, healthy children.

Momentarily, however, Callander was transformed. Some 3,000 visitors a day descended on the town, where the fortunate might get a glimpse of the quints when they were on display in the public nursery. For almost a decade, their every activity got reported, the gifts continued unabated, and the Dionne family struggled with its newfound celebrity. The little girls were used to endorse products of every description, their faces peering out from advertisements and billboards. For most Americans, it served as a welcome respite from the day-to-day battles with unemployment and a straitened economy.

EDWARD VIII AND MRS. SIMPSON

As the decade wore down, stumbling from depression to partial recovery and then into recession, one final bright spot captured the public's attention. Nothing consumed more column inches of newspaper space than the abdication and subsequent marriage of King Edward VIII of

England. Americans have always been intrigued with royalty. Almost any king, queen, duke, or duchess of any country will do, but the best is English royalty.

When the handsome bachelor king renounced the throne in December 1936, the world was agog. His reason was a simple one: he wished to marry Wallis Warfield Simpson, an American divorcée, a move that Parliament would not countenance. And so, for "the woman I love" he gave it all up.

Mrs. Simpson and the king had already been the subject of a tremendous volume of gossip, but no one suspected he would abdicate. The American press was relentless in its quest for stories about "Wally and the Prince," and the whole affair did much to usher in the use of telephoto lenses for photographers eager to get a shot of the two aboard the royal yacht.

When the king made his surprise announcement, any remaining media reticence was immediately cast aside. And, in order that the maximum number of people would hear his proclamation, Edward used a radio hookup in Windsor Castle. Like a good celebrity, he understood the immediacy of radio, and the live broadcast connected him to his subjects, along with millions of fascinated Americans. In many ways, the king's words had an impact similar to the "Fireside Chats" that had been so carefully scripted and delivered by President Roosevelt. The two leaders were discovering the power of electronic media.

For the next several months—from Edward's December abdication until his June 1937 marriage to Mrs. Simpson—the press was persistent and its readers insatiable. Following the marriage, the couple continued to be hounded by reporters and photographers. Although the furor eventually died down, the Duke and Duchess of Windsor—the former king and the commoner—continued to be media personalities, forever dogged by the endless publicity generated by their fairy-tale romance.

And so it was that, somehow or the other, the United States survived the Great Depression and its aftermath. Toward the end of the 1930s, in a gesture that probably said as much about an ailing economy as it did anything, President Roosevelt moved the date of Thanksgiving from the last Thursday in November to the fourth Thursday in the month. This official shift had nothing to do with patriotism or reverence for the nation's founding; it was done in order to extend the Christmas shopping season. No one protested, and the nation lurched toward recovery, war, and a new prosperity.

2

World of Youth

BACKGROUND

The Depression and its aftermath had a profound impact on American youth. For the first time, the federal government attempted to identify and assist young people put at risk by the economic calamity. More important, popular culture realized it had been more or less ignoring a whole segment of American society, and moved to rectify the omission. What emerged was the modern teenager, along with a new marketing strategy designed to capitalize on the discovery.

UNEMPLOYMENT AND EDUCATION

The children born in the 1920s were moving into their adolescent years in the 1930s, providing a sizable young adult population. Falling infant mortality rates, along with increased longevity, also contributed to the growing numbers. In addition, attitudes toward the young were undergoing change. For example, the idea of putting children to work at an early age was falling out of favor, particularly when dangerous or difficult jobs were involved. In 1910 almost 20 percent of those aged ten to fifteen held jobs, a remarkably high figure by later standards. By 1930 only about 5 percent of this age group worked. The government, in an effort to stem unemployment among adults, strove to keep young people out of the distressed job market. One result was the 1938 Fair Labor Standards Act, which outlawed most remaining child labor, thereby legally putting virtually all underage children out of work.[1]

The same could not be said about those youth fifteen or over who might desire employment. They were immediately affected by the economic downturns that plagued the 1930s. Unemployment in 1930 was around 4 million, and approximately a quarter of the total was in the fifteen to twenty-four age range. By 1933, the worst year of the Depression, 15 million people lacked jobs. Of those, about 25 percent, or almost 4 million, were youths aged fifteen to twenty-four. Too many employable young people were out of work. In 1938, the nation was wracked by a severe recession, and of the more than 10 million who had no jobs, 20 percent, or over 2 million, were again young workers. Further, an overwhelming majority of jobless youth came from low-income homes, and the problem was intensified for those from African-American families.[2]

Gloomy statistics notwithstanding, an unexpected benefit came about: more and more youth stayed in school for a longer time. But a growing classroom population had its problems, too, since school construction was at a virtual halt. As the Depression worsened, the trend toward a kindergarten through twelfth grade education nevertheless gained appeal. By 1939, about 85 percent of all children aged five to seventeen were in school. Colleges saw similar enrollment changes: in 1930, slightly over a million students attended college; by the end of the decade some 1.5 million students were enrolled in colleges and universities, about 15 percent of the total college-age population.

Despite these growing numbers of children and young adults in school or college, communities were busily reducing expenditures for education in an attempt to save money. Many poorer districts had to shut their schools temporarily, leaving some 300,000 children with no educational facilities during 1932 and 1933. School terms were shortened in one out of every four American communities. In addition, American schools had 25,000 fewer teachers in 1934 than they had in 1930—but they had 1 million more students. Youths who might have been working were instead studying in overcrowded, understaffed classrooms.

With the election of Franklin D. Roosevelt as president in November 1932, political positions on public assistance to both education and the unemployed underwent marked changes. The federal government began to earmark more money for schools, and this aid allowed most closed facilities to reopen. By the late 1930s, a majority of American teenagers were attending high school, and educational spending once again equaled that of the late 1920s.

But additional school funding was no guarantee of employment: in the mid-1930s, the average teenager had to wait two years after high school graduation to land a job. They might be better educated than ever before, but their prospects were still dim. In addition, the government was not anxious to see a deluge of youthful graduates enter the tight job market. The solution was to create training programs for youth, a policy that prolonged the time spent gaining job skills and reduced visible unemployment.

Since a paying job was no longer a viable option for most graduating teenagers, and it took time to establish government alternatives, not all students opted to remain in the classroom. Or, if they did graduate, the combination of unemployment and a creaky relief system did little to instill hope. For many young people, the answer was to pack up and take off. It is estimated that 250,000 young people were roaming America during the bleak years of 1932 and 1933. Most rode the rails or hitchhiked. They came from everywhere and had no set destinations. Some of their wanderlust evolved from the old pioneer spirit, the "Go West, young man!" ethos. Somewhere up ahead lay fame and fortune, and more than a few saw themselves as rugged individualists cut from that pioneer cloth.[3]

They were frequently called runaway youth, or transient youth, and they constituted a mix of ages, backgrounds, and expectations. A significant number of these wanderers were young women; some were unhappy with their jobs—if they had been lucky enough to get one in the first place—because they had usually been prepared for office employment, but instead found themselves doing domestic work or clerking. And so they, too, joined the quarter-million roaming the land.

THE CIVILIAN CONSERVATION CORPS

In the meantime, the wheels of government were turning. In 1933, the Civilian Corps Reforestation Youth Rehabilitation Movement was formed. Since all the New Deal agencies were usually known by their initials, this would have come out as the CCRYRM, an impossible combination of letters. It was promptly changed to the Civilian Conservation Corps, or the easily remembered CCC. The agency was granted an initial sum of $500 million to recruit and organize 250,000 male workers aged seventeen to twenty-seven. For a variety of reasons, mainly sexist ones, the CCC did not admit women. The organization was set up to put men to work doing hard physical labor; in those times, such work was still seen as inappropriate for young women. One of the government's loudly proclaimed goals was to keep those 250,000 young men off relief rolls; an unspoken goal was the desire to keep those same potential workers from competing for scarce jobs.

Overall, the CCC enlisted some 3 million young men and paid them $30 a month, most of which was automatically sent home. The average applicant was twenty years old and came from a large family on relief. In order to attract the biggest possible pool of applicants, no one could work for more than nine months. It was not an easy life: they got up at

A Civilian Conservation Corps volunteer. This
government-run agency provided young men with
both needed job skills and a small wage. (Photograph
courtesy of the Library of Congress.)

6 A.M. and were at work by 8 A.M.; they knocked off at 4 P.M., and it
was lights out by 10 P.M. To make the tour of duty a bit more attractive,
the government did provide recreational facilities. At the end of their
nine-month stint, the men were awarded eighth-grade equivalency cer-
tificates, or even high school diplomas in some cases.

The program provided meaningful employment to 500,000 young men
by 1935, its peak year. Across the country, 1468 CCC camps dotted the
landscape, and their inhabitants significantly improved the natural areas
in which they were located. These volunteers built roads into wilderness

tracts, established parks and other outdoor facilities for the public, and planted over 200 million trees and shrubs. It is estimated that the CCC set park and related recreational development in the United States ahead by at least a decade.[4]

THE NYA AND THE WPA

The success of the CCC did not go unnoticed. Under the banner "Youth Must Be Served!" and with a $50 million appropriation from Congress, the National Youth Administration (NYA) was established in 1935. Once again, the American government was targeting young people for federal assistance, especially those identified as "troubled youth," and it allowed women in its ranks. The goals of this agency were two-fold: to keep kids in school, by offering them quasi apprenticeships so they would be more employable upon graduation, and to prevent them from competing in the tight job market. In addition, the NYA had transient camps and resident programs to teach homemaking and vocational skills to those who had dropped out of school or in other ways needed special attention.

Available to those eighteen to twenty-five and on relief, the NYA limited participation to a maximum of seventy hours a month. By March 1938, over 480,000 persons were enrolled in its programs and, unlike the CCC, almost half of them were women. By the end of the decade, estimates suggest that the CCC and the NYA together assisted several million young adults and probably allowed many older persons to find otherwise unavailable jobs.[5]

Another federal agency, the Works Progress Administration (WPA), likewise benefited large numbers of young people. Its Recreation Division employed upwards of 49,000 individuals to create and maintain recreational sites. Not every youth, however, could expect to get a government-funded job. In larger cities, groups of teenagers began congregating in what came to be called "cellar clubs." Usually based on ethnic or racial ties, these clubs had no connection to the WPA or any other government agency, but they briefly enjoyed a certain vogue; they were independent and used vacant sites for clubhouses and clubrooms. The Youth Service Division of the WPA, realizing their popularity, attempted to work with these groups in order to steer them clear of dangerous activities. Where federal money was concerned, many, particularly members of Congress, worried about government involvement with young persons; they wanted to be sure that any appropriations instilled traditional values in the participants.[6]

Young women enrolled in vocational training. These participants were part of the National Youth Administration (NYA [note the sign in the background]). (Photograph courtesy of the Library of Congress.)

YOUTH AND POLITICS

Part of Congress's concern grew out of student interest in radical groups. Among adults, there was widespread fear that demagogues would subvert their children. The success Nazis and Fascists had in recruiting and militarizing young people in Europe was taken as an object lesson. Students in both high schools and colleges tried to make sense of their times, with the result that social science and history courses gained popularity. Marxist study and discussion groups, such as the Young Socialists and the Young Communists, saw rising memberships, much to the chagrin of many conservative observers. In addition, as the threat of world war loomed ever larger in the late 1930s, students openly demonstrated for peace. National youth organizations lobbied in Washington for noninvolvement in foreign conflicts. From England came the Oxford Pledge Movement, an antiwar organization aimed at young people. It quickly spread to American colleges during the mid-1930s, and led to demonstrations on several campuses.

In 1935, a group of students at Princeton founded the VFW, or the Veterans of Future Wars—not to be confused with the national Veterans of Foreign Wars organization. It had started somewhat tongue-in-cheek,

A 1939 poster supporting athletics for youth.
This poster, part of a campaign by the Works
Progress Administration, was done by
participants in the Federal Arts Project.
(Photograph courtesy of the Library
of Congress.)

but the concept struck a responsive chord among draft-age students. In 1936 the group campaigned on about 120 campuses for immediate government payments to all prospective soldiers. The movement revealed both a realization of impending war and a growing isolationism. It even spread to women's schools, with the founding of Gold Star Mothers of Future Wars. It may have been a lark for some, but the grim knowledge that war was a very real possibility underlay it all; young people knew they would be on the front lines.

Of course, the fears that American teenagers would soon be storming the barricades proved groundless. As is the case with so many movements, teens were simply curious; it was a flirtation with new ideas, but most quickly returned to traditional values. Even the wanderers out on the highways and railroads eventually came home. There would be no revolution. And not all the organized activities directed at America's young were political or ideological. Many were simply a means of providing adolescents worthwhile ways of spending their time. In rural areas, several hundred thousand farm youths belonged to 4-H clubs (the name stands for *Head*, *Hands*, *Heart*, and *Health*), an organization sponsored by the Agriculture Department. The clubs displayed steady growth throughout the decade.

Similarly, the Boy Scouts of America, which had been incorporated in 1910, did well during the Depression. By the early 1930s, membership had surpassed 1 million. In fact, they were so popular that the Cub Scout program for younger boys was launched in 1930. Not to be outdone, the Girl Scouts of America also were actively recruiting. They had formed the Brownies for younger girls in 1916, but the group did not become an integral part of organized scouting until 1938. In addition, the Girl Scouts inaugurated their annual cookie sale in 1936; they found it an effective fund-raiser, and it soon became an established part of the American scene.

THE TEENAGER

This movement toward highly organized activities for young people was in clear response to the times. Traditionally, adolescents were not viewed as teenagers; they were seen as young adults. The more government policies systematically kept this age group from active employment, the more the concept of teenagers as identifiable members of a separate and unique generation, complete with its own culture, took hold. Previously, when the term "teenagers" was used at all, it generally referred to the offspring of wealthy families, usually of high school age. It seldom applied to working-class kids who were already employed in factories and department stores. They were expected to work, and the pleasures of a prolonged childhood were not part of their world.

The Depression, however, changed perceptions about being young in the United States. With millions of adolescents denied jobs, and encouraged by advertising and popular media, teenagers had, by the mid-1930s, established a growing subculture that had little to do with family or approaching adulthood. Since school attendance had bloomed, and most youth stayed in school at least through twelfth grade, their most constant companions were other teenagers. They soon learned to look to one another and not to adults for advice, information, and approval, and their behavior began to reflect this new reality.

⁓ With the onset of the swing dance craze, female teenagers were increasingly called "bobby-soxers," a name derived from the white ankle-length socks then worn by millions of girls. These were the teens who jitterbugged the night away, dancing in the aisles of New York's Paramount Theater to the Benny Goodman band in 1937. They were also the girls who swooned when a skinny crooner named Frank Sinatra began singing with trumpeter Harry James and his orchestra. Flustered adults immediately complained that teen lifestyles had become "too exciting," and that young people would never achieve anything on their present course. Belatedly, self-styled "experts" urged parents to keep their teenage children away from radio, movies, and swing music. But the die had long since been cast; by the end of the decade, teenagers were a force in American life that would never again be denied.

TEENAGE CULTURE

Advertisers and merchandisers could not have been more delighted with the emergence of this new market in an otherwise weak economy. They targeted school supplies and clothing directly at teens, not their parents. The makers of products once aimed at housewives changed their entire advertising strategies. Fleischmann's Yeast was not just for baking anymore; it now promised to clear pimply complexions. Postum, a beverage once promoted as a substitute for the evils of caffeine and coffee, suddenly promised young people vitality and pep, not just a relaxing night's sleep. Planter's peanuts were no longer a light snack; if a teen offered friends some Planter's, the gesture guaranteed popularity. Advertising had found a new audience.

Popularity and acceptance: those were the themes played upon by merchandisers for the burgeoning teenage market. As the Depression waned, movies, books, magazines, and radio—along with advertising, of course—began to create an image of the American teen that revolved around the ability to enjoy a social life; it included a car, a telephone, an allowance, stylish clothes, and endless entertainment. Personal freedom became all-important for this newly discovered generation.

As is always the case, teenagers developed their own slang. Among the favorites for the '30s were "Yowsah!" (a variant on "yes," "yessuh!" or "yeah!"), "Booshwash!" (also spelled "bushwa" and meaning "baloney!" "bunk!" or anything patently untrue), and "cheesy" (of inferior quality—"full of holes"). Some terms came from the movies and radio, but the more arcane examples often simply evolved on their own. And as quickly and mysteriously as they appeared, they just as quickly disappeared, replaced by new words and phrases initially known to only a few.

Another vocabulary evolved to describe teenage rituals. Dating replaced "calling" (the practice of the male formally visiting the young woman's residence by prior invitation), and the arrangements were made by the young people themselves, not by intrusive adults. The privacy allowed by cars brought about "parking," or snuggling up in a car with a date, usually after dark and in a secluded place. "Necking" (kissing) and "petting" (caressing) carried over from the '20s. Since increasing numbers of couples were putting off marriage given the bleak economic outlook, "going steady," or dating only one special person, emerged as a way of describing a couple's protracted courtship. If sexual activity was involved, the term was "going all the way."

Despite the claims of independence and autonomy, however, the long-term goals of the new teenage culture were simple and traditional: girls were destined to be mothers and homemakers, while boys would become fathers and breadwinners. It was a black-and-white world of convention: boys would be boys and girls would be girls, and no gender-bending.

Popular culture taught that males learned productive skills, and activities like camps and organized sports would teach them. Team play was an important attribute for future wage earners, because competition was what they would encounter in the business world. Young women, on the other hand, learned to respect family life, including how to maintain a home and how to raise healthy, happy children. Although an occasional article suggested a girl might aspire to a profession like medicine or the law, as a rule any lifelong careers were viewed as man's domain; clearly, the woman's place was in the home. Even with increased numbers of young women in college, the strictures remained in place. Special skills like art, music, and sewing could be nurtured, but they were individual choices, not something practiced in a group setting.[7]

MAGAZINES

Male-oriented publications such as *American Boy* and *Boy's Life* reinforced character building. This was imparted through inspiring stories, usually adventure tales that depicted their heroes as experienced in the use of guns and masters of survival skills. Bravery was to be admired, but real men never took risks lightly; they had responsibilities to others. Not surprisingly, firms like Remington firearms and Daisy air rifles underwrote a significant amount of advertising in these periodicals.

Boys' magazines also published numerous articles on moneymaking opportunities that ranged from delivering newspapers to printing one's own business cards. The advertisers were often companies that offered tools and instructions for developing profitable skills. Always the stress was on being practical and looking to a future that included a meaning-ful job or profession.

Conversely, publications for girls, like *American Girl* and *Everygirls*, taught that life improved after marriage and children. Community serv-ice was an option, but domestic skills such as cooking and housekeeping came first. Careers were discussed, but only vaguely, and never in direct competition with male goals. More important was knowing proper eti-quette and understanding how dating and courtship worked in Ameri-can society. "Mr. Right" grew as an important concept, along with the need to wait to marry until "he" came along.

Both boys' and girls' magazines avoided any frank discussions of sex. Their goal was to prepare adolescents to become responsible adults, not to address teenage sexuality. Unspoken, but suggested through content, was the idea that adolescents who followed their ambitions and interests would have little energy left for sexual experimentation. Two adult mag-azines, *Parents* and *Ladies' Home Journal*, did encourage parents to face the reality of their children's sexual development. They advised father-son and mother-daughter talks that stressed responsibility and the need to prepare for a productive future. In fact, the *Journal*, along with a hand-ful of other women's magazines and a few newspapers, regularly ran advice columns on how to deal with modern youth. The advice for girls was always the same: practice caution and restraint—the man was strong, the woman was weak, and the man must protect the woman. No comparable literature existed for adolescent boys, although they did have *Spicy Detective*, *Esquire*, and the notorious "8-pagers," or "Tijuana Bibles" (crude, cheaply printed little cartoon booklets that depicted porno-graphic situations), for titillation.

MOVIES

A side of youthful behavior that began to receive attention during the 1930s was juvenile delinquency. Petty crime, running in gangs, and as-sociations with known criminals were the warning signals, and these questionable activities attracted both academics and film producers. A spate of books and pamphlets on juvenile delinquency were issued by well-meaning government agencies and private publishers, but not be-fore the release of less learned movies featuring both child and adult actors that claimed to show the detrimental effects of city life on young people.

For much of the decade, the movies had been undecided on how to portray teenagers, particularly those in trouble. As a result, adolescents are in films of the period, but seldom in meaningful roles that clearly identify them with any teenage culture. Finally, even Hollywood acknowledged this emerging generation and came out with *Dead End* (1937), a film that argued for the primacy of environment in shaping the lives of young people. Its message seemed to be, "Kids are basically good, but . . . if a child is raised in a slum and cannot escape it, then that child may well be doomed to a life of crime." *Dead End* is the cinematic adaptation of Sidney Kingsley's successful, long-running play about slum life. Humphrey Bogart, in a role that helped propel him into the first rank of movie stars, plays an adult gangster who has returned to his old haunts; it co-stars the Dead End Kids, a group of young actors who portray every shade of youthful hoodlum.

What might have been censored with an adult cast was given great leniency in *Dead End* and its numerous successors; after all, these pictures were presenting scientific findings. Such films were advertised as "educational," although they also promised lots of action and excitement. They purported to demonstrate how economic and social forces combine to wear down a neighborhood and turn its innocent children into hardened criminals.

The success, both box-office and critical, of *Dead End* opened the floodgates to a stream of similar films. *Angels with Dirty Faces* came out in 1938. Jimmy Cagney, along with Humphrey Bogart, reprised some of his earlier gangster roles in this popular movie. Again present are the Dead End Kids, perhaps the real stars of these pictures (the best-known and longest-lasting performers in the group were Huntz Hall and Leo Gorcey). Their characterizations of troubled youths may contain elements of Hollywood fantasy, but their on-screen disrespect for law, adults, and general middle-class mores doubtless reinforced audience stereotypes about slum kids. Although they usually played for laughs, underlying their performances was an attitude that teenagers were prisoners of environment, that breaking out of poverty and juvenile delinquency was virtually impossible.

Initially, the movies were envisioned as hard-hitting studies of juvenile delinquency, but they gradually eroded into youthful shenanigans and finally into slapstick comedy. Regardless of the messages they might be sending the audience, however, fans loved the Dead End Kids and the censors tolerated them.

RADIO

By any estimate, film was one of the most successful forms of popular entertainment to reach young people. Kids everywhere went to Saturday matinees and saw the same features, short subjects, newsreels, and serials, reinforcing national modes of behavior. And once these eager moviegoers got home, the radio was waiting. It was the true rival of motion pictures and carried almost as much influence.

It did not take long for the major networks to devote their late afternoon schedules to children's programming. From roughly 4 P.M. until 6 P.M., the soap operas gave way to serials and variety features aimed at the after-school crowd. The serials were continuing fifteen-minute tales of action and adventure, patriotism and heroics, spirit and derring-do. In essence, they were soap operas for kids, especially boys. They took their cue from the innumerable movie serials that had been cranked out from the early days of silent film and on into the sound era.

Typical radio serials involved a young man and his pals. "Pals" could be any age, male or female, but usually did not include the hero's parents—they were nice enough, but they could not qualify as "pals." A friendly uncle, on the other hand, was perfectly appropriate. As the decade progressed, the young male might be replaced by a character from the comic strips or, better, a superhero from comic books. All manner of media crossovers occurred in the realm of these radio series. Popularity meant, possibly, a film serial based on a radio serial, or vice versa. In any case, fantasy gradually replaced the less intense realistic fiction of earlier programming.

Without exception, good was pitted against evil, and good always triumphed. These were morality tales in quarter-hour segments, and they attracted a huge following of listeners from elementary through high school. If a fellow planned his time, he could catch five episodes each of his favorite radio serials during the week, and then see the latest movie serial involving the same characters at a Saturday matinee. And, in an absolutely perfect week, the latest issue of the comic book chronicling the exploits of his best-liked adventure hero could be picked up at the corner newsstand.

The quintessential afternoon serial was *Jack Armstrong, the All-American Boy*. This long-running series, which premiered in 1933, shamelessly touted loyalty, friendship, obedience, service, perseverance, clean living, sportsmanship, and any other qualities American youth should ideally possess. Today, anyone coming across a yellowing script from the series would most likely derisively dismiss it, but to a generation of avid listeners, being like Jack Armstrong did not seem a bad thing.

Jack attends Hudson High School and lets no one forget it. His friends Billy and Betty, and his fabulously wealthy Uncle Jim, are led by his enthusiastic response to the world around him. Incidentally, Betty's a pal, not someone liable to excite sexual tensions, and Uncle Jim is useful, since Jack frequently needs access to expensive technology. No adventure is too exotic, no villain too villainous, and no scientific explanation of how things work too detailed for this remarkable young man. In the

1930s, Jack's mix of pep and curiosity played well, making for endless adventures that attracted a wide audience.

An exciting afternoon of radio was capped by the half-hour *The Lone Ranger*, a show that usually came on just before Mom summoned everyone to dinner. Adapted from a series of books by Fran Striker, *The Lone Ranger* was not just a radio program; the masked hero also appeared in a movie serial, Big Little Books, comic books, and a newspaper comic strip during the 1930s. Kids everywhere knew about the Lone Ranger, his wonder horse Silver, and his faithful Indian sidekick Tonto, who in each episode uttered his mysterious "kemo sabe" (no exact translation exists, because it was made up). The show's stirring theme music was lifted from the overture to Rossini's opera *William Tell*, making it possibly the best-known classical composition of the day.

The later years of the decade saw more and more afternoon serials crowding onto the already-jammed network schedules. On the eve of World War II, the characters were increasingly military: *Captain Midnight, Don Winslow of the Navy, Sky King, Hop Harrigan*, and *Smilin' Jack* stood ready to fight any enemies of the United States. Thus afternoon radio reflected the real world and presented young listeners with exciting ways to cope with it.

Since radio was financed through paid advertising, these afternoon serials had many different sponsors. The soap operas might have their detergents and cleansers; the evening variety shows their cigarettes and automobiles; but the afternoon serials had food: Wheaties for *Jack Armstrong*, Ralston products for *Tom Mix*, Cocomalt for *Buck Rogers*, and Ovaltine for *Captain Midnight*. Most of these sponsors had no problems getting their characters to regularly plug the products—"use [product name] and you can be just like [character name]." To add punch to their pitch, companies offered all manner of "free" gifts, or premiums, that somehow tied in with the series and usually proved irresistible for kids. There were "silver bullets" for *The Lone Ranger*, interplanetary maps for *Buck Rogers*, pedometers and decoder rings for *Jack Armstrong*, and a host of other "valuable prizes" from a long list of shows. It usually took box tops or other proofs of purchase to obtain these treasures, and that was an easy way to track listenership.

In the evening, children listened with their parents to essentially adult shows, so *Amos 'n' Andy* and *Fibber McGee and Molly* had their share of young fans. Another favorite that attracted a younger audience was *The Aldrich Family*, created in 1939. The star was Henry Aldrich, a teenager in the Andy Hardy mold, and it was an immediate hit. Throughout the decade, network radio reached out more and more to the youth market, a move that led, just like the movies, to a greater standardization of culture around the country. Young people dressed alike, watched and listened to the same entertainment, and even ate alike. The mass media were leading the way to a mass culture for and about youth.

COMIC STRIPS

Newspaper comics had a varied offering for young readers, and they were often ahead of both movies and radio in their portrayals of adolescent characters. For instance, *Harold Teen*, a strip created by Carl Ed in 1919, found a fresh generation of readers in the 1930s. The "Flaming Youth" and raccoon coats of the 1920s were gone, and Harold soon reflected the new decade. A film of the same name came out in 1933, but did little at the box office; perhaps it was in advance of its time. Even older than *Harold Teen* was *Freckles and His Friends*, a strip by Merrill Blosser that first appeared in 1915. During the 1920s, Freckles is portrayed as being about eight years old. Suddenly, with the emphasis on teenagers that occurred in the 1930s, Freckles grows to sixteen and gets involved with girls, dating, and all the other rituals of adolescence.

The idea of adolescent boys leading other boys (and occasional adults) in rip-roaring adventures also took firm hold in the comics, a far cry from the humor of *Harold Teen* and *Freckles*. Milton Caniff's *Terry and the Pirates* was an immediate success when it premiered in 1934. Its adventure format, exotic Far East locale, and likable young hero matched up well with the radio serials of the day, and in fact the strip got its own late afternoon network time slot in 1937. *Roy Powers, Eagle Scout*, a rather self-explanatory late-1930s series by Frank Godwin, even managed to bill itself as "the official strip of the Boy Scouts of America." Hardly contemporary, but certainly adventurous, Hal Foster's medieval *Prince Valiant* debuted in 1937. This long-running story of the Knights of the Round Table initially featured a young Prince Valiant who only later matured into adulthood.[8]

OTHER PRINT MEDIA

It is but a small jump from newspaper strips to pulp magazines and comic books. Young readers could thrill to youthful protagonists in cheap periodicals like *Argosy*, *Doc Savage*, *Action Stories*, *The Shadow*, and innumerable other titles. Or they could spend a dime and follow their comic-book heroes in *Detective Comics*, *Superman*, *Batman*, and dozens more. The choice was theirs, and the selections were limitless.

Not every teen adventure featured adolescent boys. In 1930, a book entitled *The Secret of the Old Clock* appeared. A mystery novel featuring a teenage heroine named Nancy Drew, it was ostensibly written by "Carolyn Keene," but actually came from the pen of Mildred Wirt Benson, a ghostwriter employed by the Stratemeyer Syndicate. This organization specialized in mass-producing formularized fiction for youthful readers. It owned a number of ongoing series, and Nancy Drew was a runaway success; sixteen more titles were published during the decade. Each was a mystery novel featuring the teenaged heroine. In the space of two years, four movies were rushed into release: *Nancy Drew, Detective* (1938), *Nancy Drew, Reporter* (1939), *Nancy Drew, Troubleshooter* (1939), and *Nancy Drew and the Hidden Staircase* (1939), the last the only title actually based on one of the novels.

In books and on film, Nancy can do just about anything. She has a sporty little blue roadster and her own nonthreatening pal, Ned Nickerson. Like Jack Armstrong of the radio serials, Nancy has mobility and speed, important components of the adventure genre—and she knows her engines and transmissions as well as any male. Her spirit and inventiveness make her the equal not just of boys her age but also of any adult, an important motif in the growing body of entertainment created for youthful audiences. The success of Nancy Drew inspired a rash of imitators, such as Judy Bolton (1932), the Dana Girls (1934), and Kay Tracey (1934).

HOBBIES AND LEISURE

Despite the books, serials, and movies directed at young people, adults still fretted about how children and teenagers spent their free time. Government leaders, educators, and psychologists agreed that worthwhile hobbies kept susceptible youth out of the clutches of juvenile delinquency. Lists of "good" avocations, such as collecting stamps and autographs, were published, along with corresponding lists of "bad" hobbies, such as collecting comic-strip ephemera or matchbook covers. Thanks to the influence of President Roosevelt, stamp collecting emerged as possibly the most widespread hobby among teenagers, although activities like building model airplanes also gained legions of young fans.[9]

Young boys joined the Junior Birdmen of America during the 1930s. This enterprise was sponsored by the publisher William Randolph Hearst and his newspaper empire. The Birdmen constructed model airplanes, choosing from a vast selection of kits available at local hobby shops. Interest reached the point that city parks were allocating open areas for flight competition. Aviatrix Amelia Earhart even endorsed the Earhart Trophy, an award that recognized excellence among girls in model airplane activities.

The NBC radio network, sensing a possible fad, underwrote the Model Airplane Club of the Air. The show offered hints and advice about constructing models. *The Jimmie Allen Club* also came about, a radio serial

Two boys looking over their stamp collections. Philately—stamp collecting's proper name—soared in popularity during the decade. (Photograph courtesy of the Library of Congress.)

that followed the exploits of Jimmie Allen, the pseudonym of Dudley Steele, a real-life pilot. The radio adventures were a hit, and a club and newsletter followed, along with a cartoon strip that advocated flying for all. Young Hollywood stars like Mickey Rooney and Shirley Temple proudly displayed their Jimmie Allen membership badges, which at the time was high endorsement indeed.

As World War II became more imminent, these loosely run organizations took on a more military air. Members were organized into "flights" and "squadrons." The American Legion formed the Air Cadets of America in 1933. Their goal was to have boys ready to go into pilot training in case of war or national emergency. In all these groups, discipline got stressed, perhaps inspired by Germany and its use of youth in its successful rearmament. So widespread was the craze that newspapers, magazines, radio stations, and department stores sponsored model-building activities.[10]

The most bizarre behavior among young people during the 1930s has been saved until last. In 1935, at staid, prestigious Harvard University, a freshman swallowed a live goldfish, apparently on a dare. Within days, the stunt was being repeated at other colleges, and quickly became a full-fledged fad. No one knows how it got started—and why a gold-fish?—but goldfish swallowing was established on American campuses. In 1938, an M.I.T. student set the unofficial record by swallowing forty-two in succession. There might have been a Depression, there might be a war looming, but in the time-honored tradition of American students, there was still time for silliness.[11]

SUMMARY

The 1930s were both a troubling decade for youth and one filled with promise. The economic realities of the Depression deprived many young people of jobs, but out of adversity grew a more recognizable teenage culture. Increasingly, adolescents turned to each other in order to define their generation; as they did so, the popular media paid them the ulti-mate compliment by celebrating teenagers as a distinct, identifiable group.

PART II

POPULAR CULTURE OF THE 1930S

THE 1930S

3

Advertising

BACKGROUND

The 1920s—the Jazz Age, the Roaring Twenties—were years of advertising excess. The decade even adopted a word to describe its approach to selling: ballyhoo. This nineteenth-century term means to exaggerate blatantly, to win attention in any way possible. Accordingly, advertising in the 1920s pulled out all the stops, clamorously demanding the consumer's notice. But it was all a reflection of the era; the prosperity was seen as secure and unending, an investment in the future. By 1929, advertising revenues had peaked at $3.4 billion, a new record.

ADVERTISING GOALS

It seemed that the most challenging task facing advertisers was showing the public new and different ways to spend its money. Ads were not based on how much people needed goods and services, but on how those items would enhance one's social status, grant benefits, and bring pleasure. With disposable cash, consumers faced an endless array of choices. For the most part, the public uncritically accepted all the ballyhoo; the economy was strong and the government benign, reluctant to intervene. The future looked bright; how could it all end?

Thus the ad agencies of the 1920s introduced halitosis (bad breath), "acidosis" (sour stomach), B.O. (body odor), Tinea Trichophyton (usually referred to as "athlete's foot" or itchy feet), "pink toothbrush" (bleeding gums, caused by pyorrhea), and "film"—on the teeth, on dishes, on bathtubs, on car finishes—plus a host of other ailments and social disgraces that helped define America's ultrasanitary and hygienic culture, themes that would continue to be popular throughout the 1930s. Of course, odors, scratching, and film notwithstanding, the ballyhoo did end—dramatically.

With the Great Crash of 1929, the mission for advertisers changed significantly. Should they reflect the realities of the crisis, or should they be the carriers of messages that in effect denied the economic collapse? For many, the question was answered by their clients. Businesses soon began feeling the economic pressures, and their bloated ad budgets were cut. A ripple effect resulted, and there was a general cutting back at most advertising agencies. After a decade of almost uninterrupted growth, the agencies slashed salaries and eliminated jobs, and the ads themselves were done as cheaply as possible. More important, the public was exposed to a steadily shrinking number of commercial appeals, at least in print. An exception, however, was the thriving medium of radio. As print advertising declined, radio promotions increased, although even radio revenues temporarily decreased in 1932.

The changes, however, were not seen only in business and advertising. Unemployment soared everywhere, and with less money to spend, a popular distrust of advertising grew. People became suspicious, especially of extravagant claims. Their fears were fueled by books like *Your Money's Worth* (1927), *100,000,000 Guinea Pigs* (1933), *Skin Deep* (1934), *Eat Drink and Be Wary* (1935), *The Popular Practice of Fraud* (1935), *Partners in Plunder* (1935), and the magazine *Ballyhoo*. Founded in 1931 and dedicated to deriding most advertising, *Ballyhoo* did well its first two years. The editors refused all paid ads, and instead ran trenchant parodies of the real thing. But the novelty soon wore off, and *Ballyhoo* died a lingering death, finally sputtering out completely in 1939.

CONSUMERISM

In the meantime, consumerism had taken hold for many Americans. Organizations like Consumers Union and Consumers Research enjoyed rapid growth and prosperity throughout the 1930s, their success reflecting public discontent with inflated claims and shoddy products. By the end of the decade, they had memberships of 80,000 and 60,000, respectively. Government, slow to exert any pressures on advertising during the 1920s, also responded to the crisis. The Pure Food, Drug, and Cosmetic Act was passed in 1938. The Federal Trade Commission and the Securities and Exchange Commission, along with the U.S. Post Office Department and the Internal Revenue Service, began to increase their supervisory and regulatory controls over advertising.[1]

Advertisers took heed, and much of the clamor and hoopla of just a few years earlier was toned down. Yet, for all of that, advertising in the Depression seldom reflects the nation's problems. Despair and social upheaval are rarely even hinted at in newspaper or magazine spreads, and the growing volume of radio commercials likewise ignores economic realities. Occasionally, an ad or commercial suggests the need for a good appearance in order to gain or hold a job—which implies the importance of working—or urges forbearance toward those less successful, but they are the exceptions. More frequent would be the advertisement that shows the consumer in his or her preferred environment—the man in his office, the woman in her home—and in the presence of the PRODUCT. Radiant beams of light perhaps play on the product, the focus might be slightly blurred and soft (or in sharp black and white—"soft" ads were feminine; "hard" ads were masculine), but the message is one of consumption.

Despite its refusal to acknowledge the crisis, advertising did change. Ads are more direct—"louder"—than their 1920s counterparts. The hazy view of an optimistic future is replaced with a more hard-edged depiction of the present, but it is a present without the Depression. Thus many, if not most, of the Depression-era messages remain cheery, with automobiles, soft drinks, cigarettes, and foodstuffs dominating. They reflect aspirations, not realities. Because most advertising is passively absorbed, the imagery tends to reinforce already held attitudes; it does not challenge beliefs but instead supports the popular mind.

The rise of self-service supermarkets and huge department stores in which clerks were difficult to find caused consumers to receive less and less direct advice about what to buy at the point of purchase. Instead, they had to rely increasingly on advertising to make their decisions about quality, brand, reputation, and so forth. Advertising therefore became, during the 1930s, both educator and adviser. It was faced with the paradoxical situation of both reassuring the consumer that prosperity is right around the corner and simultaneously urging hard work and sacrifice in order to weather the economic storm because times are tough.

To accommodate this change in approach, ads focus less on the consumer and more on the product. The thrust of a message might be to buoy up sagging spirits and to bolster confidence about price and value. Advertisers attempted to reassure a clientele that felt uncertain about the rapid changes in society and technology. Throughout the 1930s, this shift gained impetus as the certainties of an earlier age came into question.[2]

An unspoken aura of guilt occasionally hangs over Depression-era ad copy. If consumers did not possess or employ a specific product, it can be inferred that they would pay a terrible price. Letting insurance policies lapse would force children to drop out of school and go to work; reluctance to buy a new appliance would lead to social ostracism; failure to practice good hygiene will create a bad first impression; sobbing

FIFTH AVENUE · NEW YORK
The World's Greatest Shopping Street
TRAVEL BY TRAIN

1932 advertisement with the Empire State
Building in the background. In an attempt to
get consumers to use the railroads and shop in
New York City, this poster was widely displayed
during the depths of the Depression.
(Photograph courtesy of the Library
of Congress.)

women and stern-faced men provide true confessions of what happened
when they neglected to buy certain products or perform particular acts.
But this kind of finger-pointing is in the minority; the majority of ads
simply promise a better life and better days ahead, thus reinforcing the
goals and objectives already held by the public.

In the meantime, ad revenues continued their decline, plunging to a
low of $1.3 billion in 1933, about a third of what they had been three

years earlier. As income fell off, the nature of the advertisements themselves changes. Some agency art directors felt that too much detail in an ad was distracting. Bowing to the streamlined ethic of the decade, less becomes more and simplicity is the key to communicating a message. Gone are the wordy parables and long testimonials so beloved by copywriters; although lengthy statements about the product or service remain the norm, they now are couched in terms of how the product or service will benefit the consumer. More direct are those ads that talk openly about price—how low it is, how much a thrifty person can save, what those savings might buy. Even jingles, at least in magazines, disappear, although they had a firm hold in the new medium of radio. As the economy improved after 1933, scattered images of gracious living reappear, and the copy is appreciably shorter.

ADVERTISING COMPONENTS

Not everyone, however, subscribed to simplification in advertisements. Many agencies and clients favored loud, cluttered messages. The graceful Art Deco typefaces of the 1920s were replaced by a plain block style that resembles newspaper headlines. No opportunity is lost in getting the message out to the consumer. Bold type, harsh black-and-white photographs, and a terse, direct prose style that drops nuance and subtlety for the hard sell become characteristic of a large number of print ads during the 1930s. Any nostalgia for the styles of the twenties is lost as advertisers try to cram as much information as they can into a limited space. More and more ads are also notices of contests and giveaways, further cluttering the space. Much of this emphasis on promotions came from the success they had on radio, employing similar techniques. In all, it is a nervous, tense display, perhaps echoing the tenor of the times more than readers were aware. As the decade progressed, agencies continued to cut costs in every way possible, meaning that lush illustration and imaginative graphics were usually among the victims.[3]

Modernity was also brought forth in a significant number of advertisements. There was a rapid integration of innovative new ideas in technology, design, architecture, and the like into the world of style; the "new" was promptly made chic—for example, color-coordinated ensembles in clothing; plumbing fixtures; cars; china; and silverware. Elements of contemporary art, such as expressionism, cubism, abstraction, and impressionism, surface with some regularity on the ad pages of mass-circulation magazines. (See Chapter 12, "Visual Arts.") In contrast to the cluttered ads mentioned above, words are kept to a minimum, allowing the pictures to carry the messages. Emotions are evoked by color choices, shapes are broken down to their basic components. Technology might

Advertisment for five-and-dimes. This poster, done under
the auspices of the Federal Arts Project, suggests the
variety of items available at these popular stores.
(Photograph courtesy of the Library of Congress.)

be suggested by deliberately distorted arrangements of motifs, and delicate illustrations convey a sense of the seasons. It was one more way of suggesting the new and the novel visually. This use of the techniques of modern art was, however, in the minority, and stands as a reaction to the highly realistic illustrations of the 1910s and 1920s.

Market researchers like George Gallup and A.C. Nielsen (of the Gallup Poll and Nielsen Ratings, respectively) discovered that the majority of Depression audiences desired ads that were clear and simple. Using the argument that advertisers should be more responsive to consumer wants and needs, the pollsters and the social scientists also plumbed the public mind. As a result, the use of comic strip characters and cartoon drawings emerged as a favorite. Speech balloons, a device taken from the popular comics, are freely used. To this simplistic approach are added photographs, instead of drawings, for authenticity and impact. Illustrators, working in oil and watercolor, were often retained, but their work was in less demand; as art and design became secondary to the print message, it became common for commercial artists not to be replaced when they left an agency.[4]

For an example of the success to be achieved with cartoon art, one need only look in the pages of a comic book of the era. Generations of American boys have dreaded being "97-lb. weaklings," thanks to the classic ads of Charles Atlas, holder of the title "The World's Most Perfectly Developed Man." This honor was bestowed by Bernarr Macfadden, a physical culturist of considerable note (see Chapter 8, "Literature," for more on Macfadden), on a man named Charles Siciliano, a onetime "weakling" who soon thereafter dubbed himself "Charles Atlas."

Starting in the late 1920s, and blossoming during the 1930s, Atlas, along with promoter Charles Roman, created a mail order business that quietly boomed for the next half-century and became an icon of American popular culture. In an unending series of advertisements, usually found in the back pages of comic books and cheaper pulp magazines aimed at male readers, Atlas showed through rather crude cartoons how weak men are victimized by brawny bullies. But help was just a coupon away: a fellow could send for a booklet that would demonstrate how *Dynamic Tension* (Atlas's secret method of developing muscles and power; today it would be called isometrics) could change one's physique and outlook on life. It was a come-on as old as advertising, but the comic strip situations, especially a classic one in which the victim has sand kicked in his face while at the beach with his girlfriend, in time lured over 6 million men into trying *Dynamic Tension* at thirty dollars for twelve lessons on breathing, exercises, diet, and the like.[5]

If further evidence is needed to establish the importance given comic strips as an advertising forum during the 1930s, one need only look at the campaign for Grape Nuts cereal that was initiated in 1931. Grape Nuts used Suburban Joe as a continuing cartoon character, and their increased sales soon caught the notice of various ad agencies. Shortly thereafter, Lifebuoy Soap, Jell-O, Rinso laundry soap, Wonder Bread, and a host of other products were being touted in mini-dramas presented in a comic strip format. It worked so well that the Sunday comics in a typical newspaper became a mix of straight strips and virtually identical advertising messages. Sometimes it was up to the reader to determine which was which.

For many agencies, however, the Depression was no time to be experimenting with new styles. The realistic, folksy illustrations of Norman

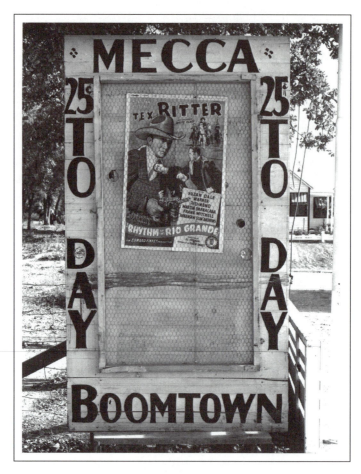

Sign in Summit City, California. Both the movies and advertising were important components of everyday life, as this small billboard demonstrates. (Photograph courtesy of the Library of Congress.)

Rockwell were infinitely preferable to any attempts at Modernism in advertising. As a result, a philosophical split developed: a significant portion of the advertising art of the 1930s is indistinguishable from that of preceding decades, but an equally large segment attempts to employ a more modern, more abstract kind of imagery. By the end of the decade, there was no clear favorite, and the dichotomy between old and new continued.

Even with the difficult choices and grim prospects faced by most advertising firms in the 1930s, there were a few bright spots. One was outdoor advertising, a growing industry during the Depression. The 1920s are often called "The Golden Age of Billboards," but the 1930s continued that exuberance. In 1932, about 320 advertising firms used outdoor ads on a nationwide basis; by 1939, over 500 companies were employing billboards. Outdoor advertising traditionally aims at a broad middle- and lower-middle-class audience. It is direct and realistic, and it has to convey its entire message quickly. Whereas magazines were turning increasingly to photography to display products, billboards and posters clung to the traditional painted and airbrushed illustration. In addition, the use of gentle, nonsatiric humor in outdoor signs expanded throughout the thirties.

BURMA-SHAVE

One of the most unusual ad campaigns in the long history of American outdoor advertising was that launched by Burma-Shave in 1925. Burma-Shave (technically the Burma-Vita Company) was a struggling firm attempting to market a men's brushless shaving cream. They had tried giving out sample jars, but that approach was getting nowhere. Then, using scrap pieces of wood, the Minnesota-based company erected small roadside signs that gave a serial message. As cars raced by, the drivers could read them in order. It was not long before the signs were being professionally manufactured; the messages consisted of simple, light-hearted poems, a sign for each line. By the 1930s, the campaign was in high gear and national, with yearly contests urging consumers to send in verses they had written. And write them they did; the little red Burma-Shave signs could be found alongside virtually every highway in the country. In 1931, motorists might read

HALF A POUND

FOR HALF A BUCK

COME ON SHAVERS

YOU'RE IN LUCK

BURMA-SHAVE

Or, in 1934,

HE HAD THE RING

SHE HAD THE FLAT

BUT SHE FELT HIS CHIN

AND THAT WAS THAT

BURMA-SHAVE

So it went throughout the decade. Some 200 new verses were written and posted by 1940; the campaign continued unabated until 1963 with hundreds of additional poems. In 1938, over 7000 sets of verse were standing, which translates into more than 40,000 individual signs alongside the highway. Throughout the decade, and with the emergence of a true national campaign, Burma-Shave saw its fortunes rise sharply. The end of the "signs by the road" signified the loss of a part of Americana known to everyone who traveled by car in those days.[6]

RADIO ADVERTISING

Not all advertising was in print, of course. People might quote, verbatim, ad copy they saw in a magazine, but it was much more likely they could repeat the jingles and slogans they heard on radio. Either way, it meant they were quoting national brands with big advertising budgets. People sincerely believed that widely promoted products were somehow superior to less ballyhooed ones. Although radio advertising began in earnest in 1922, it did not truly hit its stride until the thirties. With the incredible growth of broadcasting that occurred at the beginning of the decade, radio commercials helped bring about greater homogeneity in national patterns of taste and consumption. Any remaining regional barriers were disappearing as network radio linked the entire nation.

One of the most popular formats for a broadcast ad was the singing commercial. Composed of three parts, the piece would commence with an incidental opening (humorously known as the "cowcatcher"), move to the actual commercial message, and close with a final plug (also called the "hitchhiker"). These ditties were repeated incessantly throughout the day. Listeners, like it or not, grew to know them by heart. Who needed print and pictures when you had words and music?[7]

By advertising nationwide on network radio, manufacturers were able to establish unparalleled brand loyalty. For example, by sponsoring *The Chase and Sanborn Hour* (1929–1948), a little-known coffee rose to become a national leader in sales. Miracle Whip salad dressing was introduced in 1933; its manufacturer, Kraft Foods, wisely pushed it both in major magazine campaigns and on the radio. *The Kraft Music Hall* (1934–1949) was hosted by the popular Bing Crosby for most of its years on the air, and within a decade, Kraft's Miracle Whip had won half the market for sandwich spreads.

In the late afternoons, children everywhere stopped what they were doing to listen to *Jack Armstrong, the All-American Boy*. From 1933 until 1951, Jack and his pals urged kids, "Just buy Wheaties / The best breakfast food in the land!" As a result, General Mills rose to become a leading cereal manufacturer. Rarely, in any medium, has the main character been so identified with a product.

Pepsodent toothpaste likewise found a vast audience with its sponsorship of the enormously popular *Amos 'n' Andy* from 1929 until 1939; just before dropping *Amos 'n' Andy*, the company began to underwrite *The Pepsodent Show Starring Bob Hope*, a relationship that lasted until the days of television. With two of the biggest programs on radio, Pepsodent was soon a major force in the competitive field of dental hygiene. Similar stories could be told about Jell-O, Lucky Strike cigarettes, Ovaltine, Johnson Wax, Pepsi-Cola, Fitch Shampoo, and a host of other products that came to be identified—and purchased—as a result of their association with network broadcasting.

As the 1930s progressed, radio commercials grew ever more blatant. The entire emphasis was on encouraging the listener to buy. Little information might be given about the product being advertised, but through repetition, music, and sound effects, there was no doubt about the brand name. Anyone attempting to assess the decade through commercial radio broadcasting would learn virtually nothing about the Depression. But radio, after all, provided escapism, and that is the way the growing audience wanted it. Further, radio fosters the illusion of intimacy; the announcer is speaking directly to the listener. Although print ads can address themselves to the consumer, it is difficult to establish any relationship with the reader. The ad copy remains removed and somewhat distant, no matter how dramatic the presentation. With radio, on the other hand, the listener gets "to know" the announcer, a fact that broadcasters use to their advantage. Don Wilson (*The Jack Benny Program* and Lucky Strike cigarettes), Harlow Wilcox (*Fibber McGee and Molly* and Johnson's Wax), Harry Von Zell (*Eddie Cantor* and Pabst Blue Ribbon Beer), Ed Herlihy (*Kraft Music Hall* and Kraft foods), Westbrook Van Voorhis (*The March of Time* and *Time* magazine), and dozens of others emerged as celebrities in their own right, often becoming significant parts of the shows as well as spokesmen for the sponsors' products. Radio announcers held prestigious positions in the 1930s, and testified to the importance given commercial messages.

TRADEMARKS

A sure way to enhance sales of new products was to have a memorable label or trademark. For instance, the giant food processor General Mills created a corporate symbol and spokesperson in "Betty Crocker." She was invented in 1921 as a symbol for the company, appearing as a nutrition expert in print media of various kinds. But it was in the 1930s that she became most influential. General Mills found "Betty Crocker" did best on radio, so she soon had a regular show that, not incidentally, touted company products. The producers aimed the show at housewives, with Crocker paying a friendly visit to each listener's home and proffering advice on better homemaking. Listeners wrote letters to her that "she" (an anonymous woman reading from a script in the studio) responded to on the air. Other sponsors followed suit, and radio advisers became a rage. These imaginary personalities thus became the symbolic representatives of large corporations.

Betty Crocker was finally given a face in 1936. Motherly, her hair streaked with a touch of gray, she was emblematic of quality and good American cooking. Her countenance has continued to look out at consumers ever since; some eight makeovers later—sometimes younger, sometimes just a bit older—Betty Crocker still epitomizes motherhood and apple pie, especially if that pie is baked with Gold Medal Flour, a longtime staple in the General Mills pantry.

The popular "Betty Crocker" radio show did address aspects of the Depression. It played on the air five times a week, and the sponsor, General Mills, saw to it that two of the week's broadcasts included menus and recipes oriented to families on relief. It was a gesture of recognition, and a small one at that, but it nonetheless acknowledged that not everyone was participating in the American Dream of work and prosperity.[8]

In 1936, the Minnesota Valley Canning Company went to a large New York advertising firm for advice on lagging sales. Out of that meeting came the Jolly Green Giant, another enduring icon in the annals of American marketing. Consumers liked the smiling giant (the fact that he was green never seemed to bother anyone) holding up equally huge corn and peas, and sales surged. Perhaps his sheer size suggested health and vitality—and he possessed echoes of the beloved Paul Bunyan, another wholly created figure.

MAGAZINE ADVERTISING

American advertisers responded to the great economic upheavals of the 1930s, both in the number of their commercial messages and in their content. Magazines are second only to newspapers in the volume of print advertising. The Depression proved no exception, and economic ups and downs can be tracked by the relative numbers and types of ads appearing in any particular medium. For example, a look at three representative magazines of the decade—the *Saturday Evening Post*, *Good Housekeeping*, and *Life*—can reveal a great deal about advertising, the effects of the Depression, and changing tastes among American consumers.

Saturday Evening Post

Month & Year	Total Pages	Total Ads	Full-Page	Partial-Page
11/22/30	134 pp.	119	48	71
11/21/31	108 pp.	88	41	47
11/19/32	92 pp.	86	34	52
11/25/33	92 pp.	74	24	50
11/24/34	92 pp.	80	27	53
11/23/35	104 pp.	85	38	47
11/21/36	112 pp.	101	47	54
11/20/37	120 pp.	115	36	79
11/26/38	100 pp.	73	30	43
11/25/39	96 pp.	97	26	71

Good Housekeeping

Month & Year	Total Pages	Total Ads	Full-Page	Partial-Page
11/30	320 pp.	346	113	233
11/31	262 pp.	260	73	187
11/32	230 pp.	206	49	157
11/33	238 pp.	223	56	167
11/34	256 pp.	246	60	186
11/35	254 pp.	246	67	179
11/36	260 pp.	277	60	217
11/37	254 pp.	277	59	218
11/38	228 pp.	246	39	207
11/39	222 pp.	232	36	196

Life [*Life* did not begin publishing until November 1936.]

Month & Year	Total Pages	Total Ads	Full-Page	Partial-Page
11/23/36	94 pp.	32	26	6
11/22/37	120 pp.	119	71	48
11/21/38	76 pp.	53	19	34
11/20/39	108 pp.	102	30	72

Both the *Saturday Evening Post* and *Good Housekeeping* were successful, well-established periodicals in 1929, at the onset of the Depression. The *Post*, a weekly, general-interest magazine, could trace its roots back to 1821; the monthly *Good Housekeeping* was aimed more at women, and was founded in 1885. *Life*, on the other hand, was a new weekly, mass-circulation magazine featuring photojournalism that made its debut in November of 1936. It was a daring venture to bring out a new periodical with the country still in economic difficulties, but things looked better in 1936 than they had a year or so earlier. Like the *Post* and *Good House-keeping*, *Life* appealed to a mass audience and carried a large quantity of advertising, something a bit unusual for a magazine so new. If there was any reflection of economic turmoil in American magazines, it should therefore be found in the advertisements appearing on the pages of these successful periodicals.

Between 1930 and 1932, there was a steady overall decline in advertising. That period, of course, corresponds to the bleakest years of the Great Depression, and it stands to reason that current and potential advertisers would be watching their budgets closely. With sharply diminished sales, profits would be down, and thus less could be expended on advertising. This drop shows up in the magazines themselves; both the November 19, 1932, *Saturday Evening Post* and the November 1932 *Good Housekeeping* are about a third shorter than their corresponding 1930 issues. The number of features (articles, stories, columns, etc.) remains about the same in each, which means the loss reflects the missing advertisements.

The *Post* continued its decline into 1933; although *Good Housekeeping* managed a tiny increase in both number of pages and number of advertisements. In 1934, the upturn applied to both magazines, but was gradual. The years 1935 through 1937 marked a partial recovery for the nation, and those years found the two magazines struggling to recapture their earlier statistics. Plus there was the appearance of *Life* in 1936.

Since the November 23, 1936, issue of *Life* was its first, it is difficult to say whether the advertising response to the new magazine was good or not. It would take several issues to establish the magazine's advertising strengths, which it did in short order. While *Good Housekeeping* held even in 1937, even amid fears of a new recession, the *Saturday Evening Post* recorded some modest increases, and the year-old *Life* boasted spectacular gains, more than tripling the number of ads in its premier issue. A recession did indeed hit the nation in 1938–1939, and the lowered page and advertisement figures for all three magazines testify to the new economic woes. Only *Life*, in 1939, was coming back to its earlier numbers.

These statistics reveal how advertisers tighten their belts when the economy stumbles. In good times (1930, 1935, 1936, 1937), the number of expensive full-page advertisements grows. Cheaper partial-page ads are also abundant, since they are less costly. When times become more difficult (1931, 1932, 1933, 1934, 1938), the full-page spreads decline. The number of partial-page ads, although smaller, remains large. Closer examination of the ads themselves shows that many firms had not ceased advertising; they had simply chosen to reduce their purchases of space, cutting their investment from a full page to a fraction of one. On the other hand, many companies that had previously run small ads disappeared altogether during these troubled times.

The world portrayed by the ads, large and small, is almost always an urban or suburban one. Although over a quarter of the nation's population still resided on farms or in what were considered rural areas in the 1930s, the milieu of advertising had long since been urbanized. Skyscrapers represent the office environment; large factories, the manufacturing one; and the home is an apartment, a house on a city street, or a cozy dwelling in the suburbs of a large metropolis.

The consumer, when depicted in ads, is typically a woman—a sophisticated, modern woman who makes most of the purchasing choices for her family. A man's home may be his castle, but a woman manages it; men hold down jobs, and women do the shopping and keep informed about products and services, at least in the world pictured by advertisers. The message given in an overwhelming majority of ads during the 1930s is that men are producers and women are consumers. Naturally, most of the commercial messages direct themselves at women, an approach that results in rampant stereotyping of both sexes.

AUTOMOBILE ADVERTISING

For both the *Post* and *Life*, automobile spreads are an important component of the advertising mix. Americans actually bought more used cars than they did new ones during 1934 and 1935; but they nonetheless continued to purchase new vehicles even in the worst days of the Depression. By the later thirties, sales were up once more, justifying the ad campaigns. Auto manufacturers have traditionally found magazine layouts an effective format for presenting the latest models and mechanical information. Since *Good Housekeeping* was perceived as a woman's magazine, it ran fewer automobile promotions. Body by Fisher, auto heaters and radios, and automotive cleaning supplies can be found on its pages, suggesting that women were seen as being interested in specific aspects of car ownership, such as comfort and appearance.

Throughout the decade, automobile firms stressed reliability over luxury. This was also true of accessories and parts. The fact that things would last was of utmost importance, and that belief was not limited to automobiles. For the duration of the Depression, whatever the product, durability and dependability were consistently stressed. Manufacturers mentioned price openly, since economy was also a concern of strapped consumers. In the automotive field, however, the few luxury cars advertised stayed with the traditional artist's rendering of the vehicle, and reliability and price got little play. It was the uncompromising black-and-white photographs of lower-priced Fords, Chevrolets, and Plymouths that reflected the concerns of many Americans during the 1930s.

Perhaps the ultimate form of realism in advertising is photography. Not only is a photograph cheap in comparison to a commissioned painting, but it also conveys authenticity. In fact, as photography became more prominent in ads, many looked on it as more "real" than a painted illustration. The rise of consumerism and the desire for greater truth in advertising also gave photography a strong boost. By the mid-thirties, about half of all magazine ads were photographs, and the age of the illustrator was on its way out. The fact that photographs can be retouched, manipulated, and distorted seemed not to matter; consumers preferred the sincerity suggested by photography. In reality, all the devices of traditional illustration continue to appear, but in the guise of heightened realism.

With so much space given over to commercial messages, it is difficult to say what kinds of products dominated in print advertising. Cars and automotive supplies are present in abundance, but so are household items like General Electric clocks, Bendix Home Laundries, Hoover vacuum cleaners, and Zenith radios. Liquor ads make a statement about the end of Prohibition and the propriety of home consumption of alcohol. A number of ads in the magazine sample tout various brands of beer and whiskies after 1933 and the repeal of prohibition. All the liquor advertisements are directed toward men; times may have been improving, but distillers seemed unwilling to cross any gender lines. This is especially true of *Good Housekeeping*; no ads for alcohol can be found on its pages during the period surveyed.

Since cars and liquor are consistently strong performers in any tally of advertising, it can be concluded that ad agencies perceived certain types of magazines as appropriate venues for their marketing. They were careful, however, to choose those titles appealing to adult males with incomes sufficient to support lifestyles that included alcohol and new

Ad for the 1936 Ford V-8. Although car sales lagged during most of the 1930s, automobile advertising continued to urge consumers to purchase the newest, latest models. (Photograph courtesy of the Library of Congress.)

cars. In short, both the *Saturday Evening Post* and *Life* were seen as middle-class publications aimed predominantly at middle-class males, but *Good Housekeeping* was not. Popular magazines might be a mass medium, but they were also niche markets on an individual basis.

The American breakfast is an example of advertising's cumulative impact on national taste. Dry cereal appeared in the late nineteenth century, but the choice was limited: shredded wheat and corn flakes were about all that was available; bacon and eggs, plus other meats and potatoes, were still considered the mainstays of the morning meal. Through ceaseless advertising, the public became aware of new cold cereals, such as Wheaties, Grape-Nuts, Pep, and Cheerios. Margarine began to make inroads on the monopoly enjoyed by butter for use on toast, as did white bread over various darker grains. Florida and California competed mightily for the burgeoning orange juice market, and bananas emerged as standard fare. Ovaltine and Bovril competed as coffee substitutes, and vitamin supplements were being pushed by the end of the decade. All of this change can be tracked on the advertising pages of national magazines.

ADVERTISING AND RACE

In order to pitch their messages at a certain emotional level, a number of American products, especially foods, have long used African Americans as part of their labeling: Cream of Wheat (hot cereal), Aunt Jemima (pancake mix), and Uncle Ben (rice products) are probably the best known. The racial stereotyping is obvious, right down to the demeaning use of "Uncle" and "Aunt." This carries over directly from the days of slavery and "Uncle Tom" and "Uncle Remus," drawing uncomfortable connections between race and servitude. For example, Rastus, the beaming chef on the Cream of Wheat label, clearly creates an image of master and servant. Throughout the 1930s, print ads show him serving white children steaming bowls of their favorite hot cereal. Certainly, images like these supported much of the racial stereotyping so rampant in the United States during the first half of the twentieth century.

Worse than the silent countenance of Rastus, however, is the written speech attributed to Aunt Jemima. Rastus simply smiles upon the onlooker; Aunt Jemima addresses the consumer directly. For instance, in the November 1939 *Good Housekeeping*, she says, "Don't you fret, Honey! Jus' feastify dem wif my pancakes!" And that same month, in the *Saturday Evening Post* she implores the reader to "Thrill yo' appetite wif' my down South treat!" adding in the November 20, 1939, *Life* to "Get bofe packages from yo' grocerman." The agency writers who created such bits of hackneyed dialect thereby perpetuated the destructive image of the African American who speaks a minstrel-show form of English. In large-circulation, middle-class magazines, such egregious stereotyping was commonplace during the 1930s.

Even products like chewing gum were sometimes advertised in demeaning ways. In a 1933 cartoon ad, Beech-Nut gum shows several white adventurers (adult male, adolescent boy, and girl) getting captured by buffoonish black cannibals in what is supposed to be Africa. Only by dint of Beech-Nut gum and some silly magic tricks—the latter available free, for only five outside wrappers—do they gain their freedom. The trio becomes honored tribal magicians in the process. This image of white superiority over bloodthirsty but ultimately childlike tribesmen is a sad commentary on the state of racial awareness and sensitivity in 1930s advertising.[9]

It was but a small step from these degrading advertisements to the stereotyped antics of Eddie Anderson as "Rochester" on Jack Benny's radio show, or the steady stream of dialect jokes on the tremendously popular *Amos 'n' Andy*. (See Chapter 10 "Performing Arts.") This media cross-reinforcement of deeply set cultural racism continued well beyond the thirties.

ADVERTISING AND SMOKING

Another pernicious aspect of popular American advertising during the Depression years was the heavy promotion of smoking. The aforementioned magazines all ran tobacco ads. Even in the early 1930s, *Good Housekeeping* has ads for Camel cigarettes touting the pleasures of smoking for women. As a rule, the person pictured with a cigarette is an attractive socialite; if upper-class women could openly smoke, then why not all women? For men and women alike, cigarettes signified urbanity, sophistication. They required little time and attention, in contrast with, say, a pipe, and they were convenient. In fact, cigarettes were *streamlined*—they fit the imagery of the time. The *Saturday Evening Post* and *Life*, on the other hand, continue with a more traditional approach: men enjoying a male prerogative, often by themselves or in the company of other men.

In 1937, a national survey found that 95 percent of men would smoke openly on the street, but only 28 percent thought women should have the same privilege. Those interviewed could find some support for their attitudes: throughout the 1930s, most religious magazines continued to rail against women smoking at all. Tobacco use nevertheless continued its climb among both men and women throughout the decade. As another demonstration of the power of advertising, 66 percent of all men under forty smoked during the 1930s, and 26 percent of women under forty enjoyed cigarettes. More revealing, however, is another set of figures: 40 percent of men *over* forty smoked, but only 9 percent of women *over* forty smoked. Obviously, smoking was a generational custom, one that was promoted to the fashionable young and was fueled by the ceaseless ad campaigns that urged increased tobacco consumption.[10]

As the propriety of women's smoking grew, cigarette manufacturers were faced with the problem of appealing to everyone. Should ads target both men and women, or should they be gender-based, with separate campaigns for each sex? For instance, the Marlboro brand was advertised from 1924 to 1954 as a sophisticated woman's cigarette. During the 1930s,

Marlboros had an "ivory tip" and a red "beauty tip"; the latter was pushed because it showed no lipstick smears. In addition, Marlboros were touted as being "Mild as May," hardly a slogan to appeal to a male audience. If sales are an accurate indicator, their approach had little effect, and Marlboros languished in the lower ranks of popularity until they became a "man's cigarette" in 1954. Conversely, Lucky Strikes claimed that they could help one avoid overeating: "When tempted, reach for a Lucky instead!" Even more feminized was the slogan "Reach for a Lucky instead of a sweet!" This ploy apparently worked; Lucky Strike was one of the leading brands of the decade. Another successful campaign was that mounted by Chesterfields. They ran illustrations of women happily staring at men smoking and saying, "Blow Some My Way." This imaginative piece of prose first appeared in 1926 and was revived in 1931. With the growing proportion of younger women taking up smoking in the 1930s, these advertisements had obviously struck a chord.

One of the more memorable cigarette ad series began in 1933, when the Philip Morris brand was launched. The company decided on a distinctive advertising strategy: a page boy who would cry, in a loud voice, "Call-l-l for Philip Mor-r-riss-s-s-s!" The voice belonged to Johnny Roventini, a page at the New Yorker Hotel. The ad premiered in April 1933. Because it relied on sound more than image, it was perfect for radio. Roventini came into the studio dressed in a black page boy hat, red jacket, and black pants, and gave his famous cry. Almost overnight, Philip Morris gained a sizable market share and America had a new advertising icon.

SUMMARY

Advertising is not a mirror of society. It presents objects and people in situations that may cause recognition by the audience, but any reflection of the time is distorted, and deliberately so. The purpose of an ad is to sell a product or service, not to comment on the passing social scene. It may reflect aspirations to or visions of "the good life," but it is hardly an accurate portrayal of the times.

Through the use of familiar motifs and stereotypes, American advertising in the 1930s rose to the difficult challenges of the Depression. It told consumers they would survive the crisis and could go on consuming, that hard work and the genius of American capitalism would lead to better times, and that advertising would be a guide along the way.

THE 1930S

4

Architecture and Design

BACKGROUND

The architectural and design word of the 1930s was Modernism, and it was expressed in either Art Deco or Streamline Moderne. The terms Moderne, Art Moderne, and Modernistic are frequently used interchangeably, and each refers to an idiom that incorporates items as diverse as buildings, steamships, automobiles, radio cabinets, fabric patterns, perfume bottles, and kitchen china. In the turmoil of the 1930s, conventional art was seen as stagnant, and Modernism was embraced as the new symbol of the age.

Art Deco, Streamlining, and Modernity

The chief characteristic of most modern design during the '30s is the lack of ornament. Lines—both straight and curving, but always uncluttered—dominate. In many ways, the architects and designers of the period were in rebellion against the ornamentation of the Victorian and Edwardian eras, when applied decoration was carried to excess. This rebellion included many of the characteristic motifs of Art Deco, a "modern" style that had grown out of the *L'Exposition Internationale des Arts Decoratifs et Industriels Modernes,* a lavish 1925 exhibition held in Paris. American architects and designers eagerly embraced much of Art Deco—the familiar chevrons and jagged lightning bolts, the setback skyscrapers with their fantastical upper stories, the use of glass and mirrors and plastics on a scale previously unimagined. But as the 1930s progressed, these flourishes were dismissed as mere indulgences. A new style was emerging, and it would be called Streamline Moderne.

The streamline aesthetic was just that: smooth surfaces devoid of any adornments. It could be summed up in the ovoid, or teardrop, shape; that simple form was the essence of streamlining, and it meant motion with a minimum of friction. It signified the age of the smooth-running, efficient machine.

Whereas Art Deco tends to be steeped in classical traditions, especially in its use of ornamentation, the Streamline movement attempts a clean break with the past. The two approaches do share an affinity for geometric form, and that helps to explain why many people confuse one with the other. Art Deco was not so much a radical approach to design as it was a substitution of machinelike decoration for more traditional motifs. It evoked the spirit of mass production (stamping it out) and repetition (the assembly line). Eventually, however, the Streamline replaced the Zigzag. In the early 1930s, when Streamline was displacing Art Deco, the two occasionally got blended, although the union was usually less than successful. Generally speaking, the geometry in Streamline Moderne is more abstract and less representational than that found in Art Deco.

Both Art Deco and Streamline Moderne are essential aspects of twentieth-century modernism. Art Deco might cling to the concept of art as decorative, and Streamline Moderne can represent the functional and the efficient, stripped of all artifice, but each style moved from high art into the everyday world of commercialism. With sales dwindling in the 1930s because of the depressed economy, manufacturers turned to industrial designers to make their products more attractive and more saleable. They realized they were creating products for mass consumption, not works of art for display in a museum. But both manufacturers and designers were simultaneously playing to consumerism, fashioning "objects of desire," not necessarily essential things.

For instance, mass-produced streamlined salt and pepper shakers, finished in shiny chrome or stainless steel, pay homage to an elite tradition, that of the silversmith working expensively by hand. At the same time, they acknowledge the popularization of that tradition by their very numbers and resultant low price. Architects and designers frequently rejected one-of-a-kind crafts and specialized works of art, and aimed at larger markets. The thirties therefore witnessed the rise of a machine aesthetic, an acceptance of the machine itself as art and desirable in that way. The use of such mass-produced items in a traditional, or period, house (i.e., non-modern, such as Queen Anne, Colonial, Georgian, etc.) simply reinforces how popular culture cuts across all lines of tradition and class.

ARCHITECTURE

The Skyscraper

During the period 1929–1931, New Yorkers gawked while a most unusual architectural competition took place. Several Modernistic skyscrapers were racing to completion, often at the rate of more than a story a day. Collectively, they would epitomize the last of the Roaring Twenties and, at the same time, the onset of a new decade.

Leading the contest was the Chrysler Building (1930; William Van Alen), a magnificent Art Deco tower clad in stainless steel and decorated with details symbolizing the giant automotive manufacturer. But a few blocks away stood the emerging skeleton of the Empire State Building (1931; Shreve, Lamb & Harmon); its sleek, vertical Art Deco styling was similarly reaching for the sky. At stake was the claim to being "the world's tallest building." The stately Woolworth Building, farther downtown, had held that distinction since 1913.

As the curious craned their necks ever upward, the Chrysler Building opened its doors first, but its 77 stories and 1046-foot height were temporary claimants to the title. In 1931, the Empire State Building, at 102 stories and 1,250 feet, took the skyscraper honors; it would retain first place for the next 42 years. To accomplish the feat, it proudly boasted a mooring mast for dirigibles. No lighter-than-air craft ever attached there, but the towering mast was altered and became the city's primary television antenna in 1951.[1]

Ironically, the completion of these two towers coincided with the onset of the Great Depression. They both opened to empty offices and "space available" signs. In fact, wags pronounced the Empire State Building "the Empty State Building" as the promises of the 1920s gave way to the realities of the 1930s. The last word in modernity, the skyscrapers also sounded the death knell for Art Deco as an architectural expression. Iconic as they are, both buildings are relics, Art Deco masterpieces erected in a period that was in the process of rejecting that very style. To gain a sense of how hard the Crash hit the architectural and building professions, the following statistics are useful: between 1929 and 1933, employment in the building trades fell 63 percent; in New York City alone, 85 percent of all architects were unemployed during this period. Major construction initiatives like these two structures virtually disappeared in the economic woes of the Depression, but new currents in design were nonetheless being felt across the land.[2]

The crown of the Chrysler Building (1930). One of America's greatest skyscrapers, the Chrysler Building reflected the optimism of the 1920s, not the realities of the 1930s; it opened with the onset of the Depression, but it still enthralled onlookers. (Photograph courtesy of the Library of Congress.)

The International Style

For larger commercial and public buildings, it had only been a few years since the Neoclassical Revival had been the rage in the U.S. Architect John Russell Pope could be commissioned to design the Jefferson Memorial in 1934 and the National Gallery of Art in 1937 in Washington, D.C., and most people would find his traditional, classical designs entirely appropriate. At the same time, many American architects began to sense that they were lagging behind ongoing trends. The impacts of both industrialization and politics were challenging the insularity of the profession in the United States.

The steady emigration of architects from troubled Europe helped introduce fresh, modern tenets, and gradually their American counterparts realized they would have to adapt to a new, more austere, linear approach to design. The Modernism of the 1930s was a marriage of art and industrial design. In 1932, historian Henry-Russell Hitchcock and architect Philip Johnson had mounted an important show at New York's Museum of Modern Art titled "Modern Architecture." The exhibition displayed the work of a number of contemporary architects, most of them European, and employed the phrase "International Style" to describe their work. It later traveled for almost two years and visited many American cities. Hitchcock and Johnson also wrote *The International Style: Architecture Since 1922* (1932), a seminal book that introduced many to these new design trends.

For the general public, the International Style could be summarized as buildings done in an austere, very rectilinear manner. Wide expanses of plain walls, usually finished in white, were a hallmark. The structures themselves were often done in concrete, with the upper stories sometimes cantilevered out over the basic foundations. Doors and windows lacked any trim, and the effect was one of smoothness, a rejection of the traditional textures of stone, brick, and wood. Hitchcock and Johnson in their exhibition and book, argued that a building should be "honest"; that is, it should be a reflection of itself and its underlying construction. It should not be disguised to fit an arbitrary style. By repudiating most decorative elements, the International Style opened the way for the unadorned glass-and-steel skyscrapers that would characterize so much American commercial architecture for the remainder of the twentieth century. The hubcaps and hood ornaments of the Art Deco Chrysler Building, so beloved by generations of onlookers, were declared passé even as the building was rising. The 1930s would prove to be a transitional decade.

One of the first major structures to reflect such changes was the Philadelphia Savings Fund Society (PSFS) building, erected in 1932. Located in the heart of downtown Philadelphia, its lower portion, with stainless steel cladding and rounded corners, is a sharp break from any earlier building. Jointly designed by the American George Howe and a Swiss émigré, William Lescaze, the PSFS building shed existing traditions and boldly proclaimed itself in the International Style. It was the first American office structure clearly inspired by European Modernism.

Not everyone embraced the International Style. Art Deco still had some important adherents who particularly admired its use of freely applied ornamentation. In addition, the world of industrial design was opening up new vistas with flowing, streamlined shapes that were being called Moderne. Thus the stark austerity of the International Style had only limited appeal.

But change would not be denied. Certainly the largest example of the new trend, and one of the most popular with the public, is New York's Rockefeller Center (1933; Reinhard & Hofmeister; Corbett, Harrison & MacMurray; Hood & Fouilhoux). By the end of the 1930s, the vast complex consisted of fourteen buildings and served as an example of civic planning on a grand scale—and it was still growing. Part of the layout includes Radio City Music Hall, a huge theater that has endeared itself to generations of filmgoers, and one of the last truly grand movie palaces in the United States.

A reason Rockefeller Center has proved so popular with the public is its judicious use of open areas. Ice-skating at the sunken plaza in the shadow of the looming RCA Building (1933) is a New York tradition; the huge gilded bronze sculpture of Prometheus (Paul Manship, 1934) looks benignly down on skaters and diners. Throughout the complex are easily accessed displays of art and sculpture, and the center even boasts its own private street, Rockefeller Plaza, a space open to the public. In all, Rockefeller Center displays an enlightened attitude about the role of huge buildings and the ongoing street life below them.

Unfortunately, the economic doldrums of the 1930s and the exigencies of World War II prevented much of this skyscraper revolution from taking place until later. Nevertheless, the new and daring buildings erected during the 1930s probably had more impact on how Americans perceived Modernism than any paintings or sculptures created at the same time.[3]

Frank Lloyd Wright

During all this tumult, Frank Lloyd Wright (1867–1959), the dean of American architects, was uncharacteristically quiet. In the public's eye, his career had floundered somewhat during the later 1920s, and he had been relegated to "grand old man" status. He was sixty-five when the PSFS building went up in 1932, and no one expected any new statements to be coming from him. True to form, he surprised everyone.

Between 1935 and 1937, Wright was responsible for one of the finest private homes ever designed in the United States. In a daring series of cantilevered reinforced concrete slabs projecting through and over a mountain creek in the forested mountains east of Pittsburgh, Wright took the "less is more" credo of the Internationalists and erected the Kaufmann House at Bear Run, Pennsylvania, more popularly known as "Fallingwater." Although Wright was unusually outspoken in his criticism

Frank Lloyd Wright's "Fallingwater" (1937). One of
Wright's greatest works, and a splendid example
of the uses of reinforced concrete and
cantilevering, building techniques often
associated with the International Style.
(Photograph by author.)

of the European Modernists and their effects on design during the twenties and thirties, Fallingwater is in many respects a tip of the hat to their influence. He had the gray concrete painted white, the favorite hue of the day for "modern houses." Further, he employed contemporary technology as easily as any Modernist architect, and he eschewed applied decoration. But Wright married Fallingwater to its precipitous terrain; in much architecture of the 1930s, the natural environment was ignored, even leveled. For too many, the machine—technology—overcame nature; for Wright, ever the iconoclast and lover of the natural world, the site was one with the house. He neither altered nor ignored anything.

Fallingwater, a building that demonstrates the potential of modern architecture, has become one of Wright's best-known and best-loved works. It is not cold and academic, as are too many "modern" efforts. Although it can be seen as a linked series of abstract forms, the effect it has on viewers is one of warmth and human scale.

Back in the limelight with Fallingwater, Wright moved on to other achievements during the period. In the Johnson Wax offices (1936–1939) at Racine, Wisconsin, he took the latest trends in streamlining and made them the focus of his plan. Borrowing from the popular industrial designers of the day, Wright created tubular metal furniture on the main floor that echoed the circles of light and concrete directly above the heads of the workers. Instead of being threatening, it is bright and airy, a most pleasant working environment. For the modern world, Wright attempted to equate the workplace with a spiritual experience, just as the cathedral did in the past.

Responding to a 1938 challenge from *Life* magazine to design a small, inexpensive residence, Wright closed out the decade working on his concept of the Usonian house. The word "Usonian" was his creation, taking the abbreviation of "*United States*" and meaning a kind of broad agrarianism for urban people. Like his earlier Prairie Houses, these buildings are rectilinear in design. All unnecessary elements are eliminated through technological innovation and standardized materials. Although only a few were built, the Usonian homes presaged the enormously popular ranch houses of the 1950s. It could fairly be said that one of Wright's major accomplishments was not imitating the Modernists, but taking their concepts and motifs and making them uniquely his own.

Mass Housing

Most of the discussions about the International Style, pro or con, tend to ignore everyday housing. The needs of average people for shelter may have been low on the professional agenda, but housing was an important component of New Deal policies. As a result, the Roosevelt administration put time and effort into planning the financial aspects of housing, whereas the architectural side was given less priority.

New Deal planners envisioned a series of "subsistence homesteads" and "greenbelt towns" in an effort to provide better housing for people of moderate means. They also worked to create, through the Public Works Administration (PWA), over forty housing projects for low-income families. Idealistic in intent, but flawed in execution, this last effort has unfortunately made the term "projects" a charged one, and the meaning is usually negative. Architecturally, none of these worthy attempts displays much distinction; the profession itself tended to ignore such schemes, which may partially account for their lack of excellence.

In truth, little truly Modernistic housing was erected during the Depression years, and most of that went unseen by the general public. The 1933 Chicago World's Fair, or "Century of Progress," did display two futuristic homes, both designed by George Fred Keck. His "House of Tomorrow" and "Crystal House" elicited some public enthusiasm, but it was mainly limited to the exposition. His designs demonstrated the potential of mass-producing homes just like any other machine-made product, but neither consumers nor the housing industry seemed particularly interested in exploring the subject. Where their residences were concerned, Americans continued to vote for tradition, in both design and construction.

On the other hand, the lack of innovation was only part of a larger Depression problem. In the early '30s, housing starts of all kinds declined by 90 percent. Nationally, that translates as 937,000 new units in 1925, and only 84,000 in 1933. In addition, in 1933 over 1.5 million homes were in default or in the process of foreclosure. The residential landscape therefore consisted of older homes, not new ones.[4]

Most middle-class Americans continued living in traditional houses throughout the decade. The money they had invested in their dwellings was at some risk, but the Federal Home Loan Bank Act of 1932 stabilized many of the tottering savings and loan associations that held mortgages. Two years later, the Federal Housing Act gave active support to the housing industry. It issued twenty-year mortgages that featured low down payments. But chronic unemployment and decreased wages made it impossible for many Americans to build or buy, and a housing shortage grew throughout the depression. By the end of the decade, only 41 percent of Americans were homeowners.[5]

Some good things did however emerge from the depressed building market. In an attempt to keep construction prices as low as possible, manufacturers came up with products like prefabricated door and window units, exterior-grade (i.e., weather-resistant) plywood, improved drywall, and better glues and caulking. Wall paneling was also introduced, and Knotty Pine became something of a best seller for those who could afford it and wanted a Colonial look in their decor.

Period Revivals

The term "Early American" had achieved some status in the 1920s. It signaled a return to the past in residential architecture and decoration, a fashion that continued into the 1930s. In 1931, the American Institute of Interior Decorators (now the American Society of Interior Decorators) was formed, reflecting the growing interest in applied design. But this group, and others like it, also was concerned with historical accuracy in the many revival movements gaining interest in the country. Colonial Williamsburg had opened to the public in 1932, providing added impetus to the group's aim of accurate preservation. Specialty magazines with titles like *The Decorator's Digest* (1932) and *The Interior Decorator* (1934) found a ready public, and a small fad for the authentic "early American" look ensued. An open fireplace, a replica spinning wheel, and the cobbler's bench as coffee table became the style.

The number of professional interior decorators swelled in the United States during the 1920s and 1930s. Many were women, often from upper-class backgrounds. Mainstream women's magazines, such as *House and Garden* and *Better Homes and Gardens*, began to feature their work and ideas, bringing them to a mass audience. Not to be outdone, large, influential department stores like Wanamaker's, Marshall Field, Macy's, Lord & Taylor, and B. Altman included the latest in interior decorating trends in their furniture and accessory displays.

This popular movement toward a usable past remained in vogue throughout the thirties. It dominated American domestic architecture, and the resultant styles were called "period revivals." By and large, the favorites were Colonial (especially the New England farmhouse look), Tudor (or anything vaguely medieval), and Spanish Revival (or the hacienda look). Two distinctive traits of the era were quaintness and eclecticism, regardless of the actual style. People desired something cozy, something harking back to a simpler, more secure, past. In 1933, Walt Disney had released a cartoon entitled *The Three Little Pigs*. An enduring image from that movie is the sturdy house that one of the pigs constructed. It seemed that many Americans wished for the same image of security in their period homes; they wanted to be able to sing "Who's Afraid of the Big Bad Wolf?" and keep the Depression from their door, just as the three pigs did in that prophetic cartoon.

"Antiquing" became a major pursuit, and Sunday drives were often dedicated to finding bits of Americana in out-of-the-way places. Factory reproductions of old things—spinning wheels, deacon's benches, highboys, wagon wheels, and such—sold well, particularly if they were done in "Colonial Maple," genuine or not. This was a far cry from the plain functionalism of the International Style.

Movies and Architecture

Millions of Americans went to the movies each and every week, and they were aware of the emphasis film directors placed on having sets that reflected the very latest in architecture and interior decoration. Exposure to this kind of visual imagery, however, had remarkably little impact on the homes of most middle-class Americans. More likely, such designs would be found in a swank cocktail lounge in a large city. The end of Prohibition meant that nightclubs were open again, and alcohol could be consumed in public. A white lacquered piano, its traditional curves replaced by a more modern sinuousness, might be the center-piece, and the bar could be polished plastic, maybe Bakelite with chrome highlights. Perhaps even the crystal stemware was executed in the most avant-garde design. This was Modernism, and it had its place in fantasy and glittering nightclubs, but one's home remained a bastion of tradition.

Swing Time (1936) stands as perhaps the ultimate Hollywood nightclub movie. A vehicle for Fred Astaire and Ginger Rogers, much of it takes place in a set designer's vision of a sophisticated nightspot. No real club could afford as much floor space as is shown on the screen. The place is cavernous but opulent, with three separate penthouse areas, each spec-tacular in its own right. These were dream clubs, with no real-life equiv-alents. The addition of a jazzy soundtrack makes them even fancier, with visible orchestras and lots of loud dance music.

Materials like chromed tubular steel, Bakelite, glass curtain walls, Vi-triolite, reinforced concrete, and Vitaglass created architectonic sets that would seldom find expression in an ordinary home. The bathrooms in 1930s movies are particularly astonishing. Given Hollywood's Hays Code restrictions, they always lack visible toilets, but are otherwise sumptuous pleasure palaces, a far cry from the cramped, utilitarian spaces that served the same purposes in most homes.

Interior Decoration

In the 1930s, a typical middle-class dwelling would be a mix of the old and the new, with an occasional sprinkling of Art Deco/Moderne furnishings. Popular colors were maroon, cream, mauve, tan, and de-pression green (a medium gray-green found particularly in kitchens). Most rooms had flowered draperies and wallpapers, along with pat-terned linoleum or rugs. Mirrors with shiny accents and in colors like blue and peach were popular. An end table constructed of chromed tub-ing and black lacquered surfaces, a style taken directly from the movies, might be found in an occasional residence.

Upholstered sofa-and-chair sets, often in a popular maroon or rose velour, dominated living rooms, along with another, larger, easy chair. This latter piece was sometimes called a "Bumstead," an item favored by Dagwood Bumstead, the main character in Chic Young's comic strip *Blondie*. Together, these three pieces constituted a typical suite of furni-ture for the middle-class home, and could be purchased for as little as $70 or $80, with time payments usually available. As an economy meas-ure, these pieces were slipcovered, frequently in bold flower prints.

Knickknacks like mantel clocks, decorative lamps, and smoking accessories were common items, and allowed for some innovation in design. The room itself might be traditional, but the added touches could incorporate a few Art Deco and Moderne motifs. Stylized nude figurines, along with tropical fish and jungle birds, greyhounds and whippets, and cocktail sets in chrome and Bakelite could show just how modern a family really was.

For the kitchen, both General Electric and Sears, Roebuck were offering streamlined refrigerators by the mid-1930s. Enameled steel items, such as a combined hutch and work area and a similar eating table were seen everywhere. Often these pieces were decorated with decals, their subjects ranging from flowers to the latest Disney cartoon characters. In addition, a big cookie jar became a design item in the American kitchen during the 1930s. Their shapes could range from replicas of Aunt Jemima to stylized clowns and penguins; no matter what the subject or shape, the cookie jar was deemed important for the well-furnished kitchen.

So-called "Depression Glass," also called "tank glass," desirable among collectors since the 1930s, was cheap, mass-produced glass kitchenware carried by every dime store in the country at the time. An entire service of four place settings could then be had for about two dollars, and extra tumblers cost just pennies. It came in many colors, with pink, burgundy, amber, and several distinctive greens being best-sellers. Because it was so cheap, the dinnerware was frequently offered as a premium at various businesses. "Dish Night" at a movie theater meant Depression Glass would be the prize.

Fiesta Ware was another popular line of table settings. First produced in 1936, it came in five colors designed to be mixed or matched. It was sold in good department stores, but the company also made cheaper versions for variety stores.

Gas Stations

The period revivals were not limited to homes. Even a business as ordinary and commonplace as a gas station reflected the trend. The favorite design for a new station during much of the 1920s and 1930s was a modification of a standard house or cottage plan. Most were boxlike structures, not unlike a foursquare house, often with a canopy extending out over the pump(s). Two oil companies, Pure and Phillips, introduced imitations of traditional, steeply pitched English cottages for their stations during the 1920s. They proved popular among consumers, and almost 7000 of these period structures were sprinkled about, mainly in the Midwest, by the early 1930s. Their success led to Colonial, Georgian, Mission, and even oriental-style stations. The thirties also witnessed a proliferation of vernacular structures—lighthouses, giant oilcans, icebergs, tepees, coffeepots, windmills—that competed for highway attention.

Walter Dorwin Teague, a respected modern designer, was hired by Texaco to create a generic station in 1937. The result was the classic International version, complete with white porcelained enamel steel tiles. No "Early American" wood or stucco tried to give it an anachronistic identity. In a similar vein, several other designers worked with the lowly gas station during the Depression. Raymond Loewy produced plans for both Shell and Union Oil prototypes, as did Norman Bel Geddes for Mobilgas. Although all the designs were quite modern, none of them survived beyond the drawing board. In retrospect, they were simply ahead of their time.[6]

Fairs and Expositions

One way of tracking the changes in architectural preferences for the 1930s is to look at what was featured in two huge fairs held during the decade. The first was the Chicago World's Fair of 1933–1934; the second was the New York World's Fair of 1939–1940. They were wondrous expositions, and were markedly different from one another architecturally.

Along with the rest of the nation, Chicago was mired in what seemed a never-ending depression. But the Windy City is also the "City of the Big Shoulders . . . Building, breaking, rebuilding"—or so said the poet Carl Sandburg—and thus the city fathers had for some time planned for "The Century of Progress." Over 400 acres of marshes along Lake Michigan just south of the Loop were cleared, and there arose a fantasy metropolis not unlike Hollywood's Emerald City in the later *Wizard of Oz* (1939). It was a testament to the impacts of Art Deco on American architectural design, and its theme was "Advancement Through Technology." If nothing else, the fair personified optimism in the face of economic troubles.

Chicago's exposition opened in May 1933. It was supposed to run only one year, but was held over for a second record-breaking season, finally closing in the late summer of 1934. Unlike most ventures of this kind, it made a profit. A $37 million display of modernity, the fair had sparkling promenades that dazzled the eye. It was the largest show of its kind up until then, and it served as the perfect antidote to the dreariness of the Depression. People from everywhere, over 20 million of them, flocked to its opulence and its tawdriness.

Special trains were run to Chicago from across the continent, and they served to introduce the public to the first streamliners. Eventually, the sleek cars and engines of the Union Pacific's *City of Salina* and the Burlington Line's *Pioneer Zephyr* became parts of the displays. The *Pioneer Zephyr* even established a speed record, reaching Chicago from Denver—

Art Deco at Chicago's Century of
Progress. The 1933 exposition featured
many buildings executed in the still-
popular Art Deco tradition, as in this
poster showing the Federal grouping.
(Photograph courtesy of the Library
of Congress.)

a distance of just over 1000 miles—in thirteen hours, traveling at 77.6
mph. This feat attempted to demonstrate that the fledgling airlines had
nothing on the speedy railroads. In addition, Greyhound had a fleet of
sixty modern buses to transport visitors around the fair. They could carry
ninety people (fifty sitting, forty standing), and were called "World's Fair
Greyhounds." (See also Chapter 11, "Travel and Recreation.")[7]

Just being immersed in so much that was so contemporary had to have an impact on the average fairgoer. The towering Hall of Science reinforced the idea that here, truly, was the future. Its working models of new technological devices were fascinating, and an aerial tour via the Sky Ride took the daring above the fairgrounds in a 1930s version of a monorail. The comic-strip world of the popular Buck Rogers was not so unbelievable, after all.

For insurance, the fair also had a mile-long midway and all manner of amusement park rides. Possibly the biggest hit of the extravaganza was fan dancer Sally Rand. Inside her midway tent, Miss Rand danced, apparently nude, behind giant fans and, as a finale, behind a huge translucent bubble. It wowed the audience and was an unexpected success.

The Chicago Century of Progress, however, was not an isolated event. Fairs and expositions flourished in the 1930s despite the Depression; they were a way of rejuvenating sluggish local economies. In 1935, San Diego hosted the California-Pacific International Exposition. The fair was organized to stimulate economic recovery in southern California, and it was drenched in a kind of baroque Spanish Colonial architecture. The buildings may not have been entirely authentic, but they ushered in a small construction boom for more Spanish-influenced designs.

Cleveland, Ohio, was the site of the Great Lakes Exposition in 1936. That same year saw the Texas Centennial Exposition in Dallas. Finally, San Francisco had the bad luck to select February 1939 as the opening for the San Francisco–Golden Gate International Exposition. Its purpose was to celebrate the earlier completion of both the Golden Gate and the San Francisco–Oakland Bay bridges, two magnificent structures that displayed the latest in engineering skills. Although all three fairs drew crowds, their overall architectural impacts were slight. And San Francisco's bad luck was that, a continent away, New York's Flushing Meadow was playing host to what would be the biggest exposition of them all.

Commencing in the spring of 1939 and running until the fall of 1940, the New York World's Fair overshadowed everything; it was the spectacle of the decade. Not even the German invasion of Poland in September of 1939 could cause it to close. Sited on over 1200 reclaimed acres, the entire extravaganza was laid out in "zones," an idea much in vogue at the time. The Long Island Rail Road delivered fairgoers to an ultramodern terminal where Greyhound buses, designed by the renowned Raymond Loewy, would ferry them to various zones. Exposition Greyhound Lines was formed, and Loewy devised huge coaches to carry 160 passengers. All in all, there were over sixty-five miles of paved streets and footpaths. The entire event was bathed in the cool white glow of fluorescent tubes, the first large-scale public demonstration of that form of lighting.

Some of the most distinguished designers and architects of the day were represented at the fair, and their work was, without exception, underwritten by the corporate might of the country. In many ways, the New York World's Fair signified the marriage between industry and the arts. In fact, a stated goal of the extravaganza was to bring together architecture and commerce, to show that modernity, industrial design, and popular culture could coexist. As a result, virtually nothing in the fair escaped commercialization. It is said that there was more souvenir merchandising for this event than any exposition, before or since. Over 25,000 different items bore the official imprint of the fair, ranging from a dainty Heinz pickle to a pin proclaiming "Time for Saraka," a popular laxative that somehow got space at the exposition. There was even an "official" song of the fair, "Dawn of a New Day," penned by the illustrious George and Ira Gershwin and recorded by several of the era's leading bands. More important than baubles and trinkets, however, the New York fair was one of those seminal events that profoundly influenced the course of architecture and design.[8]

The Fair also boasted a good, old-fashioned midway with animal freaks and lots more hokum for those less spiritually inclined. After all, the Century of Progress in Chicago had Sally Rand and her fans, so New Yorkers deserved at least as much. There was showman Billy Rose's *Aquacade*, a showgirl-filled extravaganza that featured champion swimmer Johnny Weissmuller, famous by this time for his Tarzan movies, plunging into a pool daily. One of the most popular attractions at the fair, however, was the Parachute Jump, a 250-foot tower in the amusement area. Some 2 million visitors paid forty cents apiece to ascend the steel frame and then float to earth in colored parachutes.

In many ways it was a celebration of the American automobile. General Motors, Ford, and Chrysler had enormous exhibits. "Futurama," General Motors' vast network of miniature buildings, highways, and motor vehicles, enthralled over 10 million visitors, and proved to be the most popular attraction. Created by architect Albert Kahn and designer Norman Bel Geddes, "Futurama" proposed to show a technological landscape circa 1960. It included half a million model buildings and 50,000 cars, some 10,000 of which actually moved. The utopia it displayed was one in which the automobile dominated, a rather accurate prognostication.

If an automotive culture was a major element of the fair, streamlining certainly was the motif. It translated as leaving the roughhewn past behind, progressing into the sleek, smooth future. Streamlining therefore became an economic metaphor. A "sticky" economy gave way to a "frictionless" one, and urbanity replaced rusticity. With the aid of "consumer engineering," science and technology could bring an end to underconsumption. People would flock to carefully designed products that looked

Trylon and Perisphere at the 1939 New York World's Fair in a poster depicting the sleek, streamlined celebration of modernity. Note the admonition in the lower right, "Travel by Train." (Photograph courtesy of the Library of Congress.)

ahead and symbolized an end to drudgery. The future was a materialistic one, filled with new appliances and the blessings of industry.

Overlooking the fair were the Trylon and Perisphere, the official symbols of the event. The Trylon, a 728-foot needle-like pyramid, gained its name because it was derived from a *tri*angle and a *pylon*. The Perisphere was a 180-foot-diameter hollow sphere set beside the Trylon. Inside was "Democracity," a vast model of the utopian city of tomorrow. Conceived and designed by Henry Dreyfuss, "Democracity" gave visitors a glimpse of an ordered, prosperous future, one that might frighten a viewer today with its marching workers and their automaton-like precision. But in a nation still reeling from a depression and with the clouds of World War II getting darker by the minute, a picture of a strong, albeit militarized, America was probably reassuring.

During its two-year run, the fair displayed everything American. It did have a number of foreign exhibits, but its emphasis was the American mastery of the machine. The many futuristic pavilions celebrated American corporate might; their symbolism presented American technocracy as the savior of the world. And with that world falling hopelessly and helplessly toward World War II, the message was one audiences very much wanted to hear. America's strengths were clearly the focus, and the fair suggested that the Depression was a thing of the past; no current events could challenge the optimism generated by the exhibits.

DESIGN

Background

The 1920s and the 1930s presented a problem for American design, both interior and architectural. The bold ideas of Art Deco were fresh and new in the 1920s, but they were beginning to seem passé in the 1930s. How an item looked was as important as how well it functioned: enter industrial design. The smooth, machine-like Streamline Moderne was supplanting Art Deco, and the flood of European designers and architects to the United States in the years preceding World War II meant the International Style was also gaining new adherents. The Depression decade was therefore one of change in the decorative arts, a period when a number of products were destined to become icons in American consumer culture.

Norman Bel Geddes

Norman Bel Geddes (1893–1958), who first made a name for himself in stage design, moved from the theater to commercial and industrial art. In 1932, Geddes published *Horizons*, a visionary book that applied streamlining to transportation, housing, and everyday products. He prophesied that streamlined shapes would eventually be applied to radios, furniture, cars, and other everyday objects, and would change the way the average person viewed the material world. Geddes' drawings reveal ships with torpedo shapes and airplanes that resemble flying wings with teardrop pontoons, ideas that were echoed in Chrysler's 1934

Airflow, an automobile that was way ahead of its time. *Horizons* and the Airflow made Geddes the popular spokesman for what the future held.

Thanks to an almost unlimited advertising budget, wide brand recognition, a far-flung chain of dealerships, and—most important—a relatively low sticker price, the Chrysler Airflow line generated a lot of interest, although by no stretch of the imagination could the Airflows be considered great commercial successes. After an initial flurry of interest and sales, the public looked elsewhere. Chrysler was nonetheless preparing consumers for the direction automotive design would take for the remainder of the decade. The Airflow's headlights appeared to blend in smoothly with the flow of the chassis. A roundly sloping hood and a swept-back windshield, along with some chrome detailing, completed the emphasis on streamlined design. Beneath the sheet metal, however, was merely a 1934 Chrysler, a rather staid automobile that had undergone few real changes.

This aesthetic brought about a new approach to automotive marketing. Instead of being perceived as utilitarian vehicles, American cars increasingly became design statements. This change in conceptual thinking was not limited to expensive brands, or to small manufacturers offering only two or three custom models; it permeated the industry, and Detroit was frequently the leader, not the follower.

Since streamlining was all the vogue in design during the 1930s, it was only natural that the automobile industry would become part of this movement. Art Deco, so important in the twenties and early thirties, was not well suited to industrial design, especially transportation. Its emphasis on angularity and verticality was ideal for architecture, but worked poorly when translated to airplanes, trains, ocean liners, and cars. Thus the gradual shift to Streamline Moderne and its stress on the imagery of speed played well with automobile manufacturers. A sleek, forward-looking car suggested much more to a receptive public than a traditional boxy auto ever could.

Unfortunately, the recession that struck the country in 1937 doomed the pioneering Airflow. With sales lagging, Chrysler faced financial difficulties and withdrew its precedent-setting cars in 1937, to focus on more traditional models. Ironically, the last years of the decade saw many other auto manufacturers incorporate streamline qualities into their products, so the demise of the Airflows should not belittle their ultimate impact. New design treatments became the rule throughout the industry. Streamlined buses, trucks, and automobiles were becoming commonplace by the late 1930s, and they underwent subtle changes with each model year.

These innovative designers brought acceptance of the concept of "planned obsolescence." In each successive model of a product, "improvements" were loudly proclaimed. Although such changes usually signified little more than cosmetic additions, the growing consumer market responded by eagerly buying the newest models, convinced that this year's was somehow better than last year's. More often than not, the changes consisted of altering the exterior housing of the interior workings, a strategy that continues to the present day.

Henry Dreyfuss

One of Norman Bel Geddes' students in stage design was Henry Dreyfuss (1904–1972). Like his mentor, Dreyfuss worked with a number of theatrical productions until 1935. At that time, he went to work for AT&T. The cradle telephone of 1937 stands as one of his most memorable and widely used creations; the basic black dial model remained the standard until 1950, when it was replaced by yet another Dreyfuss design.

His crowning achievement was, however, the *20th Century Limited*, the great streamlined train of 1938. So thorough was Dreyfuss, he even designed the tableware and matchbook covers used in the passenger cars. Its sleek, torpedo shape suggested to any and all that here was a *fast* train. Gone were the protruding stack, the ungainly cowcatcher, and all the other accoutrements usually associated with a steam locomotive. Even the coal tender immediately behind the engine was encased in a smooth metal skin.[9]

Not to be outdone, the Pennsylvania Railroad contracted the equally esteemed Raymond Loewy to design an all-new *Broadway Limited*. He undertook the project with zest, creating a streamlined vision of chrome, plastics, Formica, and coordinated colors. The Pullman Company, famous for generations of railroad cars, built both trains, and mass magazines devoted pages and pictures to each. These trains represented an engineered future of speed and luxury, not one of delays and canceled runs.

The concept of smooth, controlled power was a popular one for an audience still mired in the Depression. Streamlining suggested that the dynamics of American industry could overcome any restraints, that modern engineering and design would lead to a better world.

Cedric Gibbons

In Hollywood, Cedric Gibbons of Metro-Goldwyn-Mayer was one of the great proponents of Modernist design. He created luxurious sets that incorporated all the motifs of both Art Deco and the Moderne movement: shiny floors, tubular chrome furniture, mirrors, and polished black surfaces. He certainly was one of the most visible designers, since millions saw his sets on the screen in movie after movie. Gibbons was also responsible for one of the most enduring icons of Hollywood: the famous Academy Award statuette, the "Oscar."

Raymond Loewy

Raymond Loewy (1893–1986) came to the United States from France in 1919. He started as a fashion illustrator with the magazine *Vogue* in New York, and then quickly established his own office. From 1929 to 1931 he worked for Westinghouse, designing radio cabinets. His accomplishments were many. In addition to the above mentioned *Broadway Limited*, in 1930 he modernized the exterior casing of a duplicator; in 1936 he drew the plans for the *Princess Anne*, a streamlined ferry plying the waters of Chesapeake Bay. Loewy also created a well-known logo at the end of the decade. Working with the Brown & Williamson Tobacco Company, he devised the famous Lucky Strike package with its series of concentric colored circles.

In 1935, Loewy's studio designed the Coldspot refrigerator for Sears, Roebuck and Company. This sleek refrigerator is a perfect example of Modernism translated into utilitarian terms. In fact, Sears advertised it as having "automotive styling," acknowledging the impact the lines of contemporary cars were having on products of all kinds. Between its introduction and 1940, the trend-setting appliance sold some 275,000 units

Walter Dorwin Teague

Walter Dorwin Teague (1883–1960) began his career as an illustrator, then moved on to advertising. He eventually joined Eastman Kodak, and was responsible for the famous Baby Brownie camera casing. Working closely with management, he epitomized the designer as businessman. His greatest popular recognition came when he was appointed to the "Fair of the Future" committee, a group directly responsible for coordinating the design of the numerous exhibits at the New York World's Fair. He emerged as the primary design theoretician of the fair, and his own work could be found throughout the vast Flushing Meadow site.[10]

Russel Wright

Ohio-born Russel Wright (1904–1906) was more an artist-craftsman than a designer per se. No relation to architect Frank Lloyd Wright, he gravitated toward the commonplace, particularly household objects. Although he was less interested in industrial design than some of his contemporaries, he was a pioneer in bringing stylish plastic and aluminum serving accessories into the American kitchen. Wright recognized the evolving servantless society, and designed objects to accompany such informality. His creations were meant to go directly from the stove to the table.

A versatile man, Wright was happy creating anything from flatware to furniture. In the latter area, he is credited with inventing the sectional sofa. His 1935 Modern Living line became quite popular, especially in blonde woods. The manufacturer linked Wright's name to the furniture in advertisements, making him well known to the public during the 1930s. He followed the Modern Living pieces with his American Modern Dinnerware, a line of ceramics that came in a variety of stylish colors, such as Seafoam Blue, Granite Grey, Chartreuse Curry, and Bean Brown, and it could be mixed or matched, another first.[11] American Modern was introduced at the New York World's Fair.

SUMMARY

Novelty, modernity, and constant change were the traits associated with the 1930s. For example, the skyscraper motif became very popular, with bookends, furniture, radios, and even mundane appliances echoing such building details as setbacks and crowns in their designs. But the industrial designers of the 1930s went beyond simple interior decoration and skyscraper symbolism; they took on the challenge of transforming an array of products into Streamline motifs. This approach can clearly be seen—at first, gingerly—in automobiles, trains, ocean liners, and especially in modern passenger airplanes. Contemporary aircraft suggested speed and unlimited horizons. In fact, people would drive out to their local airports just to watch planes take off and land; it was an optimistic experience. Streamlining on such large-scale efforts suggested a technological future in which all components would work together smoothly.

Roosevelt and the New Deal represented the future. The WPA supported the arts, including new, experimental ones. If the New Deal represented tomorrow, the industrial designers represented planned obsolescence. Streamlining simply covered over a functioning machine; if that machine could be improved, made safer, restyled, then people would have to replace it with a new model. Thus aspects of streamlining might be seen as political.

However it is viewed, the Streamlined look was gradually overtaken by the more angular International Style, but it was not immediate. The Moderne vogue lasted through World War II, albeit in gradual decline. Some designers and architects worked in several camps at once. They might employ new materials (Moderne), follow traditional designs (Art Deco), and still reflect some of the European ideas that were gaining increased attention (International Style). Given the restraints imposed by the Depression, only those materials which could be manufactured economically and on a mass scale by average craftsmen were employed. The economic problems of the day demanded simple solutions to complex design problems. It was a period where the industrial designer rose to a position of cultural and artistic importance.

5

Fashion

BACKGROUND

In order to talk about the fashions of the 1930s, it is necessary to know what came before. It could be said that the stylish woman of the period 1900–1920—the Art Nouveau woman might be a proper description—was liquid, or languid, in her dress. Clothes draped over her voluminously in a manner suggestive of Art Nouveau design. At the same time, she remained very much a part of the Victorian era, which meant she was encumbered with layers and layers of material.

With the end of World War I in 1918 and the onset of the Roaring Twenties, radical changes occurred, at least for those who thought of themselves as being at the forefront of style. An appropriate designation might be the Art Deco woman, a woman whose clothing echoed in many ways the innovations in art and design of the era. Her clothes made her appear boyish; instead of the flowing lines of a few years earlier, the look became angular and sinewy. Women found themselves freed up from many of the restraints of the recent past. Revolutionary changes occurred during the 1920s, because the slim, hoydenish figure dictated a minimum of underlying lingerie. Skirts went up—often to the knee—and multiple layers of clothing were shed for what seemed to many to be a shocking brevity of attire. The whimsical drawings and cartoons of John Held, Jr., capture the 1920s flapper perfectly, all knees and elbows, a lanky, adolescent caricature.

WOMEN'S FASHIONS

The Crash of 1929 destroyed much of the youthful exuberance of the decade; the 1930s would prove to be a cooler, quieter time for fashion. It was time to grow up and be more adult. Probably the most noticeable change in dress emerged with the rediscovery of curves. The waist and bust, both seemingly lost in the 1920s, reappeared, and in fact became objects of attention. With improvements in undergarments, the feminine bosom was emphasized, and waists were cinched by belts. In addition, the back—once hidden, now often revealed—became another focal point. The knees, however, disappeared as skirts got progressively longer, at least for most of the 1930s. In the final years of the decade, however, hemlines once again crept upward.

Youthful slimness remained the ideal—to be curvaceous and slender simultaneously. In addition, the clinging clothes of the fashionable demanded that no unwanted lumps or bulges disturb the smooth lines of the fabric. A slim, well-dressed woman radiated success and smartness; she was chic. Enter the Moderne woman, older and more sophisticated, a woman of the world. The popularity of various diets during the decade testifies to this need to be slender. That a depression was going on and people might need food seldom entered the picture.

Women in the 1930s, especially younger women, looked to the movies, the big department stores, mail-order catalogs, and magazines to learn what was current and stylish. If Sears, Roebuck used some Schiaparelli designs in its new spring line, that was fine. The important thing, however, was that Sears (or Ward's, or Macy's, or the local department store) had items in stock that resembled what Joan Crawford wore in her latest film, or what *Vogue* insisted was the look for the season. Paris continued as the fashion capital of the world, a situation that would not change until after World War II. But what the *couturiers* (fashion designers) of France were dictating and what the women of America were wearing did not necessarily match. Popular dress is not the same as *haute couture* (high fashion), and during the Depression, this distinction was especially apparent.

For most American women, ready-to-wear ruled the day. That a dress had been mass-produced and was available in stores across the country only increased its popularity. The development of assembly-line technology for the clothing industry allowed the greatest range of styles and prices ever seen. The idea of custom-tailored, one-of-a-kind outfits was foreign to the vast majority of shoppers. And if a dress was on sale, so much the better. American fashion by and large was very democratic in its appeal.

In order to hold down costs, some manufacturers offered garments that could be finished at home. A woman would pick out a dress by traditional size, knowing that all the difficult sewing had been completed. Collars, cuffs, and other finish work on shoulders and sleeves were done by professional tailors; the buyer simply stitched up the seams and hem. This particular mode of selling appears, however, to have had limited popularity.[1]

More appealing, apparently, was a move to update or create one's own wardrobe. Pattern books by publishers like McCall's and Butterick abounded, and piece-goods shops offered a wide variety of fabrics and materials. Big merchandisers like Sears encouraged the trend, by featuring sewing, knitting, and crocheting supplies in both their stores and catalogs.

As the decade progressed, the popularity of prints, patterned fabrics with designs imprinted directly on them, grew significantly. These quickly replaced the costly embroidery of the past, and they had another practical side: spots or stains are less likely to show up on prints than on solids, keeping cleaning costs to a minimum. The simple print dress, manufactured from synthetic materials like rayon, and cut to fit average figures, came to be an overwhelming favorite of women during the 1930s. Complete in and of itself, the style required few accessories. Sears, Roebuck probably carried the use of prints to its extreme in the early 1930s with its "Hooverettes," simple wraparound dresses that tied at the side and could fit anyone. They were reversible, so when one side got soiled, the whole dress could be flipped around to expose clean material. First called "Sears-Ettes," they came to be humorously associated with President Hoover and the nation's economic woes; they sold at an attractive Depression price: two for 98 cents.[2]

Among the primary trendsetters for the period were films and fan magazines. The escapist, fantasy images projected on the silver screen percolated through all groups, and were reinforced by photo spreads in the hugely popular movie magazines available during the decade. Eager audiences could copy what they saw and heard, especially Hollywood fashions and hairstyles. Newsstand fan magazines like *Hollywood, Modern Screen, Movie Mirror, Photoplay, Screenland,* and *Silver Screen* made sure to include extensive layouts on which star was wearing what at any given time or in a particular film. In earlier times, actors were responsible for their own clothes, but by the 1930s the leading performers were meticulously outfitted by the studios both on and off the screen. The major studios also had their own fashion designers on staff, and they carefully prepared the costumes for upcoming features. Retailers read the fan magazines and studied what the designers had created, and soon after a film's release, copies of the fashions appeared on their racks. As a result, women were no longer imitating high society styles as they had in the past; they were mimicking what they saw in the movies and making celluloid dreams come a little bit true.[3]

Hollywood celebrated its impact on fashion by releasing *Fashions of 1934*, a spectacle of models, showgirls, and even a bit of plot. Directed by Busby Berkeley, famous for his musicals, the picture stars William Powell and Bette Davis, but they are secondary to the lavish sets and unending parade of beauties displaying the latest styles.

Often the stars—Loretta Young, Fay Wray, Claudette Colbert, Ann Sothern, and even little Shirley Temple—modeled fashions in the larger catalogs, making the Hollywood–consumer connection that much stronger. The star's signature might even be stitched into the label. What these clothes offered the buyer was a mix of sophistication and casualness. The studios also featured their own stars whenever they could. It might be Jean Harlow on a Columbia Pictures set in a clinging gown that left little to the imagination, or it might be Katharine Hepburn in slacks and a shirt, riding a bicycle at Warner Brothers. Blue jeans began to appear in Westerns, and actresses like Barbara Stanwyck were photographed wearing denim. Never before had popular media so influenced the fashion choices of a generation of consumers.[4]

The rebellion against the insouciant twenties began at the feet and worked its way upward. By 1930, the lower hemline was a fact; by the depths of the Depression, it had descended to midcalf and even lower. At the same time, more and more material was being cut on the bias, which meant the fabric hugged the figure, displaying the natural lines of the wearer, and giving a fluid drape to the article of clothing. In an appropriate response to hard economic times, manufacturers used cheaper materials. Instead of silk, cotton and linen, along with rayon, would have to do, and unnecessary details were eliminated.

Belts, along with fitted skirts, brought back feminine waists and hips; the shapeless shift of the 1920s was now a museum piece. With an accompanying reluctance to return to the corsets and stays of an earlier era, the brassiere became an important part of a woman's total wardrobe. Led by companies like Maidenform and Warners, the constricting bandeaux of the 1920s gave way in the 1930s to bras that actually came in sizes. This innovation greatly improved both the fit and the comfort of the wearer, as well as enhancing her figure. Another improvement came with the development of Lastex by the United States Rubber Company in 1931. This miracle fiber, which could be woven with just about any fabric, provided both strength and stretch. Thus the heavy girdles of the past could be replaced by lighter, better-fitting models.

In another concession to the Depression, women could buy cheap undergarments devoid of any lace or trim. Needlework magazines provided handy transfers and instructions so the consumer could embroider her new purchases. Silk lingerie became available only to the well-off;

Dupont's rayon emerged as the fabric of choice for everyone else. Nylon stockings, long promised and thought to be indestructible, finally made their appearance in 1939 and were a runaway success. Until then, women wore silk or rayon hose, and cotton weaves, such as lisle.

Women's shoulders were enhanced as the padded look grew in popularity. At the same time, sleeves became more puffy, creating a new silhouette for the upper body that diminished the waist. The total look emphasized slender but natural lines, rising to an obvious bust and squared-off shoulders. Topping it all off was a hat, an essential item that the well-dressed woman had to have throughout the decade.

The helmet-like cloche of the twenties was replaced by a smaller hat, one that frequently perched jauntily at an angle. These smaller hats came in an incredible variety. The so-called Empress Eugenie, a soft felt item, often with a feather for decoration, gained distinction when Greta Garbo wore one in *Romance* (1930). Another favorite was the pillbox, a round design, flat on top, that also gained impetus from Garbo in *As You Desire Me* (1932). Several variants on Tyrolean models sold well, perhaps because they resembled a man's fedora. Tams, turbans, babushkas, berets, sailor hats—obviously, fashion in the 1930s still demanded that women cover their heads.

In 1933, the composer Irving Berlin wrote the music and lyrics for a song titled "Easter Parade." It was but one number in his very topical Broadway musical *As Thousands Cheer*. It begins with a reference to an "Easter bonnet," certainly a clear reference to the importance hats continued to play in a woman's wardrobe. The hats might not be "bonnets" anymore, but they were nonetheless worn. That same song, incidentally, has another topical reference that perplexes some modern listeners. It has nothing to do with fashion, but does suggest how times change. In the course of "Easter Parade," the singer mentions the "*rotogravure*." Today, the rotogravure would be the glossy magazine section of a contemporary Sunday newspaper. The term refers both to the printing process that allowed for pictures to be reproduced clearly and to the name formerly given to the Sunday magazine itself.

SPORTSWEAR

At the same time that suits and dresses were becoming more formal and adult, sports attire was doing much the opposite. For instance, many women no longer wore heavy stockings when playing tennis. They appeared on the courts bare-legged and donned socks to accompany their footwear, thereby shedding corsets, garters, hose, and several pounds of unneeded garments. By 1933, conservative shorts or culottes might occasionally be seen on the courts. Not only that, but women were choos-

Some beach fashions for the 1930s. This whimsical ice cream stand was apparently wheeled down to the beach each day so swimmers could get their favorite flavors. As can be seen, there was little difference between men's and women's bathing costumes. (Photograph courtesy of the Library of Congress.)

ing to wear slacks for golf, bicycling, and other sports. Sometimes these slack outfits were called "pajamas" because of their loose fit, but they were definitely sportswear and not for sleeping. By the middle of the decade, following the pluck of the tennis crowd, many younger women were being seen in public clad in shorts instead of slacks.[5]

In a similar, revealing way, the bathing suit lost much of its extraneous bulk, becoming more form-fitting and streamlined in the process. Prior to the 1930s, most women's "bathing costumes," as they were discreetly called, were made of dark, heavy wool, hardly conducive to sunning or swimming. With the onset of the 1930s, new, lighter materials found favor for swimming attire, and two-piece suits had become popular by mid-decade. Lastex, with its ability to stretch, became not just the miracle stuff of girdles and other undergarments, but important in the swimsuit industry also. In order to keep their permanents dry, women who took their swimming seriously usually wore rubber bathing caps that covered most or all of their hair. These came in a variety of colors and could be coordinated with bathing suits. The styles of the 1920s may have died out, but the continuing quest for comfort and ease in dress lived on.

One of the side effects of the enthusiasm for outdoor activities was that women acquired suntans. Until the 1930s, a proper woman avoided the sun. A tan was a cultural taboo; only the poorest working farmer's wife had sunburned neck and arms, whereas a society lady carried a parasol, wore a wide-brimmed hat or bonnet, and kept her skin unblemished. Now all that changed. The leisure class reveled in deep tans acquired on luxury vacations, and the working class soaked up the sun's rays on any occasion in order to replicate the look. The stigma was gone. General Electric manufactured ultraviolet lamps for inexpensive home tanning sessions, and Coppertone made a fortune selling its lotions.

ACCESSORIES

For their makeup, women started putting on dark nail polish, matching it to a lipstick. Following the lead of numerous stars, powder, rouge, and mascara received widespread use. Names like Max Factor, Elizabeth Arden, Revlon, and Maybelline could be found behind the mirror of even the most humble medicine chest. This was the era of the pencil-line eyebrow, an effect achieved by plucking out natural eyebrows and then penciling in sharply arched ones. The fan magazines frequently published features showing a popular actress in the process of applying her makeup and giving advice about techniques. It is doubtful that anyone thought of herself as being a painted lady if she followed these moves, although she might have been branded as such just a few years earlier.

Not many women could afford expensive jewelry, let alone real jewels, and so costume jewelry became fashionable. Hatpins and clips were an essential part of a basic wardrobe, along with a variety of earrings. Bangle bracelets were also in vogue. An effective method for dressing up a dated outfit consisted of using bold, unusual buttons. It was a cheap way to create something new from something old. Much of the period's costume jewelry featured Art Deco motifs. The zigzags, chevrons, and other geometric shapes that characterize Art Deco architecture were reproduced freely in enameled pieces, as well as in stamped metal and molded plastic. The closing years of the decade, however, witnessed a return to traditional jewelry, especially Victorian designs.

One breed of dog was immortalized in innumerable pieces of costume adornment: the terrier. President Roosevelt had Fala, his adorable little Scottish terrier, and William Powell and Myrna Loy had Asta, a wire-haired fox terrier, an irrepressible pooch that stole many a scene from them in the *Thin Man* movies of the time. The public loved both pets, and pins, brooches, and other baubles poured into department and jewelry stores, making terriers the dog of choice for millions.

A typical permanent in 1934. Tightly curled and
sculpted hair was the height of fashion for women
during the 1930s. (Photograph courtesy of the Library
of Congress.)

HAIR FASHIONS

The short hair and casual bobs of the 1920s were superseded by longer
tresses. But technology was also present in fashion as marcelled waves
and permanents grew in popularity. Improved electric curling irons and
permanent-wave machines allowed women to enjoy longer hair and
curls that would stay in place for extended periods of time. This fashion
spurred a small subindustry of suppliers who created gadgets of every
description to form and hold the waves. The sculpted look took firm

hold and, despite the Depression, beauty shops prospered with the new hairstyles.

In the early 1930s, Jean Harlow, "the Blonde Bombshell," introduced platinum blonde hair. The color promptly caught the public fancy, in large part because of the success of Harlow's movies and the enthusiasm of her fans. Not everyone could be a platinum bombshell, but dyes, henna rinses, and bleaches enjoyed a vogue as women tried to improve on nature.

John Breck, a New England manufacturer of shampoos, had a stroke of marketing genius in the early thirties. Until then, all commercial shampoos came in only one variety, a kind of generic mix that washed most normal hair. In 1933, Breck began to package his product in three types: dry, normal, and oily. They proved a sensation, and soon Breck's Shampoo was available nationally. Sales continued to climb, and for a while his three varieties dominated the market.[6]

Washed hair had to be dried, of course. Although the electric hair dryer had been around since the 1920s, during the 1930s such refinements as variable temperature settings and multiple speeds entered the growing market for hair products. Big and bulky by today's standards, these dryers were nevertheless a quantum jump ahead of towels and the primitive electric models of a few years earlier.

MEN'S FASHIONS

As always, any fashion shifts for men were more evolutionary than revolutionary. The lounge suit, less formal than the traditional business suit, made its appearance. This meant that single-breasted jackets became as acceptable as the more traditional double-breasted models. For warm-weather wear, the seersucker suit allowed men something lighter than wool and gabardines, and the so-called Palm Beach cotton and mohair suits were big sellers.

Padded shoulders signaled perhaps the biggest style change in men's clothing. Much like women's fashions, the waist was taken in, and the shoulders became broader and broader as the decade passed. The wide trouser, popularized in the 1920s as the Oxford Bag, remained, although at first somewhat slimmed down from its widths of a few years earlier. By the mid-thirties, however, young men's styles displayed high, exaggerated waistbands and a return to extremely wide cuffed bottoms (twenty-two inches was thought stylish). After about 1935, pants again were slimmer and straighter. Older and more conservative males tended to avoid these trends by staying with the tried and true. Young and old, however, did agree on one thing: the zipper fly, standard on most men's pants by the mid-decade, was a marked improvement over old-fashioned buttons. With that exception, for the average man a suit purchased in 1939 closely resembled one bought in 1930.

Men's bathing apparel was as conservative as their business suits. In the early 1930s, dark, heavy, knit wool trunks and similar sleeveless shirts were pretty much the rule at public beaches. Thus a daring variation on acceptable swimwear occurred when men—not all, but a few—started going topless at New York beaches. This controversial new custom immediately caught on with young men around the nation, and Sears, Roebuck was selling trunks with no tops by 1934. Two-piece male bathing attire fought a long retreat for the remainder of the decade, but the one-piece suit and the bare chest were the clear victors.[7]

Johnny Weissmuller, the Olympic swimming champion and later the star of a number of *Tarzan* films, had no hesitation in modeling swimsuits for BVD. By 1939 he was featured in ads wearing a one-piece topless suit that contained Lastex for a smoother, better fit. His trunks still had the white belt that had been a part of men's bathing attire since the 1920s, but they were considerably more abbreviated than earlier models. It may have been daring for some, but the outfit was not nearly so brief as the loincloth he sported in *Tarzan, the Ape Man* (1932). Life might be imitating art, but with reservations.

Lastex, so important to both women's undergarments and men's swimsuits, also helped modify male fashions in another way. Until the stretch qualities of Lastex were utilized in men's hosiery, gentlemen had to rely on awkward garters to hold up their socks. With the elasticized sock reinforced with Lastex, garters became an accessory that men could discard.

Men's underwear also changed. Jockey introduced its now-famous brief in 1934. Until that time, underclothing for men tended to be bulky and generally uncomfortable. "Long johns" and "union suits" (i.e., long underwear that covered arms, legs, and torso) were still worn by numerous old-fashioned males, as were various cuts in coarse lisle or muslin, and even scratchy wool undergarments had their adherents. The acceptance of the soft cotton Jockey briefs demonstrated a final rejection of all the clothing restrictions placed on men by the repressive Victorian era, a period that had lingered in American culture in countless subtle ways.

In the wildly successful movie *It Happened One Night* (1934), Clark Gable removes his outer shirt and reveals he is not wearing an undershirt. Popular mythology has it that the sales of undershirts plummeted after the film's release, although any hard figures to support this bit of trivia are nonexistent. In the same movie, Claudette Colbert dons Gable's pajama top because she has no sleepwear with her. As a result, it is said, millions of women demanded man-styled pajamas of their own. These two stories, embedded as they are in American popular culture, illustrate how people were influenced by what they saw on the screen (see Chapter 10, "Performing Arts," for more on this film).

In footwear, the Bass Shoe Company began to produce its famous Bass Weejuns (the odd name comes from the final two syllables of "Norwegian," the shoes' place of ancestry) in 1936. Comfortable, slip-on moccasins, Weejuns became an instant hit among men, particularly college students. They epitomized a more casual mode of dress, and helped popularize the term "loafer" for footwear. A custom among many men who wore loafers was to insert a shiny penny in the piece of leather that went across the instep, giving birth to the "penny loafer."[8]

PERSONAL GROOMING

Although their clothing styles may not have changed radically, some men's personal grooming habits underwent a shift. Most important was the introduction of dry shaving. Instead of using a razor and soap, in the 1930s men could be well groomed without all the bother. The Schick Corporation introduced the first electric razor in 1931, after much experimentation with developing a small electric motor. It was an instant success. By the end of the decade, the numerous companies in the electric shaver business were selling 1.5 million models a year, with no end in sight. The shavers were not cheap—anywhere from $15 to $25 each— but the high cost did not adversely affect sales.

So popular did electric shaving become that hotels had to be sure an outlet was provided in the bathroom. Ocean liners, trains, and passenger airplanes catered to their patrons by likewise installing convenient power sources. By the end of the decade, electric shavers were being manufactured for women, gaining quick acceptance by those tired of old-fashioned waxes and depilatory creams.

Until the 1930s, antiperspirants and deodorants were marketed almost exclusively for women. It was not considered "manly" to use such products. But that all changed when advertisers, rather timidly at first, began to target men. The introduction by Lifebuoy Soap of the term "B.O." (for Body Odor—and usually spoken in a foghorn-like voice in endless radio commercials) made a previously unspoken topic shed some of its taboo status.

Most American men still combed their hair in the pompadour style, which meant hair creams or greases for the "slicked down" look. Once again, the movies had a significant impact on appearance. As more and more Hollywood actors were seen with their hair natural and tousled by the breeze, the pomaded look gave way. By the end of the decade, lotions and the like were still widely used, but only to maintain a part and some slight control. Many men relied on nothing more than a comb and plain water.

Hats and caps for men still ruled fashion. They were no longer quite so formal, and a much wider variety of headgear could be seen, but a hat of some kind was worn by the vast majority of males. Among the most popular were soft felt snap-brims and Panamas, the latter a lightweight, unlined woven hat. It was a favorite in warm weather. Not until after World War II did the bareheaded look begin its slow ascendancy.

CHILDREN'S FASHIONS

The vagaries of fashion did not omit children, especially little girls. During the 1930s, two influences determined the directions their styles would take: first, the outfits worn by Princesses Elizabeth and Margaret, the two fabulously popular members of the English royal family; second, anything worn by the child star Shirley Temple. These were the days when girls dressed as children and did not wear miniaturized adult clothes. Saque dresses (simple little dresses worn with bloomers beneath), pinafores, sunsuits, and playsuits were the rule. Cheap to buy or to make, these styles dominated the thirties.

Little boys, on the other hand, often wore scaled-down versions of men's suits, although the pants tended to be shorts. Sailor suits were another favorite, complete with scarves, insignia, and bell-bottoms. For boys ages eight to about twelve, knickers (pants that ended just below the knee and were tucked into high argyle socks) continued to be popular. Like the older males around them, most boys owned several hats. One was the traditional white canvas sailor's cap. Another big seller was the aviator's helmet, a strapped leather item that covered the head, including the ears, and often had cheap goggles attached. Charles Lindbergh wore one when he flew across the Atlantic, and popular pilots like Wiley Post and Roscoe Turner sported them. (See Chapter 11, "Travel and Recreation.")

By adolescence, both girls and boys moved on to adult clothing. Boys shed their shorts for "longies" (long pants), and girls graduated to more conventional dresses. As teenagers, they were of course exposed to most momentary clothing fads. The severity of the Depression, however, kept many teens from indulging in such passing fashions, and most crazes were rather brief and of little long-term impact.

SUMMARY

In retrospect, the 1930s were a time of conservative fashion. Although changes did occur, nothing of a truly radical nature revolutionized what people wore. Sportswear became briefer and freer, and dress clothes in some ways reflected the streamlined shapes of the built environment.

Certainly the attenuated evening dresses of the day echoed the verticality of the skyscrapers going up in the larger cities. More important was the shift in influence. Instead of looking to elitist fashion magazines for hints on dress, people turned to movies, magazines, and advertising as the arbiters of taste. High society and the old-line fashion houses found their authority vastly diminished, a situation that would not change in the years to come.

6

Food and Drink

BACKGROUND

President Franklin Roosevelt could say, in his second inaugural address on January 20, 1937, "I see one-third of the nation ill-housed, ill-clad, ill-nourished," but a trip to a new supermarket would never reveal the despair felt by some of the population. The food sections of the leading magazines and newspapers seldom acknowledged the reality of economic conditions. Only occasionally did they run a feature on cost-saving meals that cut corners or omitted expensive ingredients. The government provided information on cheap, nutritious foods and how to substitute them for high-priced varieties, but the program lacked impact.

Food processors were reluctant to participate and did little to change their advertising or their educational messages. Many reports came from local, state, and federal agencies citing malnutrition among the unemployed. A few cases of actual starvation turned up, but they were limited to large cities or chronically poor groups, such as Appalachian miners. The very presence of bread lines testified to the hunger experienced by some. But, although hunger existed, food processors continued to advertise their regular products. Since prices were already low, the industry apparently felt it could do little to alleviate conditions. Because a disproportionate part of the cost of food products came from processing, distribution, and packaging—not the food itself—no one wished to call attention to these hidden charges.

Appearance and reality clashed. For someone dressed in a suit and a tie, the cost of a sandwich or a snack might be prohibitive, so ingenuity ruled the day. A nickel cup of coffee could be stretched at a lunchroom with the addition of a cup of hot water. If the counterman did not object—or if no one was looking—ketchup could be added to the hotwater. The result, maybe with a dash of salt, was a passable tomato soup. And if the place also provided saltines, a good part of a day's eating could be accomplished for five cents.

When discussing what people ate and drank during the Depression years, it is important to realize that what Americans consumed in the 1930s was not very different from preceding decades. Any shifts in food or drink preferences are usually incremental, even though changes in other areas of life may be rapidly occurring at the same time. The Great Depression brought about massive governmental transformations, employment patterns went through significant alterations, and dreams of financial security were shattered, but the average American noticed only slight changes in his or her accustomed diet.

If any revolution had taken place, it was during the period 1880–1930, fifty years that saw a rejection of earlier, less healthy diets and an acceptance of more nutritional fare. From the end of the nineteenth century onward, Americans embraced concepts that led to lower consumption of meats, fats, and starches. In their place, fruits and vegetables came to greater prominence, along with changes in attitudes about what one should eat. In general, there was a marked shift to lighter, less elaborate meals.

During the 1930s, nutritionists—both real and self-proclaimed—stressed the importance of vitamins in a person's diet. In addition, declining economic conditions increased worries about malnutrition. As a result, many people began taking vitamin supplements. Food processors immediately saw an opportunity for increased sales; they began adding vitamins to their products and advertised them accordingly. By the end of the decade, vitamins stood second only to laxatives in direct drugstore purchases, and foods of all kinds boasted how they were "vitamin enriched."[1]

Fashion also entered the nutritional picture. Although the reed-thin flapper of the 1920s was no longer stylish, slimness—especially for women—continued to be the criterion for attractiveness. As a result, a wave of diets appeared in the popular press. They ranged from the silly *How to Always Be Well*, by Dr. William Hay, which advocated either daily enemas or strong laxatives, to such self-serving efforts as "The Hollywood Eighteen-Day Diet," sponsored by California citrus growers, which consisted, not surprisingly, of various citrus fruits. In an ironic turnabout, some Americans rummaged in garbage for edible scraps while others industriously tried to limit their intake of food.

Meanwhile, the production of foodstuffs moved from small producers to large corporations. National brands like Post, Heinz, Kellogg, and

Campbell's were soon recognized by everyone, and these companies spent huge amounts on mass media advertising campaigns. By keeping their myriad products in the forefront of public consciousness, they guaranteed themselves increasing profits and wide distribution.

FOOD

The American Diet

The emphasis on promoting widely known brands and foods led to a general acceptance of an "American diet." The products that sold the most widely became the standards. Exotic, regional, and ethnic foods fell by the wayside, replaced by a national menu. About the only exception to this shift was Italian cooking, which gained a tenuous foothold in a nation rapidly simplifying its tastes in food. Dishes like spaghetti and meatballs cooked in a mild tomato sauce continued to enjoy a wide base of popularity.[2]

Along with increasingly bland choices, culinary standards dropped some: canned peas may not be as tasty as fresh ones, but they (and canned corn, tomatoes, carrots, beans, asparagus, and so on) are much more convenient, possibly cheaper, and may even be seen as more reliable as far as consistency goes. People generally accepted this kind of dilution of quality; if any revolution in food did occur, it was in the arena of efficiency and economy.

Despite the general blandness that was being touted in national publications and broadcasts, a few areas of originality managed to survive into the 1930s. County fairs, regional festivals, and church bazaars still served the distinctive foods of ethnic groups and specific locales. In the South, pork barbeque continued to be a community favorite, whereas in the West it was beef. Cajun cooking had its fans in Louisiana, just as Scandinavian dishes were eagerly devoured in the north central states. Mexican dishes persisted in the Southwest, and hardy New Englanders still celebrated the boiled dinner. Thus pockets of distinctive foodways held on, despite the relentless popularization of the "all-American menu."

By the beginning of the 1930s, Americans were reasonably educated about what and what not to consume, so the decade witnessed few changes in dietary habits. Instead, it was a period of consolidation; the lessons about nutrition learned during the 1910s and 1920s were already in place. What distinguishes the 1930s is not so much *what* people ate, but more *how* food was distributed and marketed, and *what* were the evolving technologies for preserving and preparing food.

A rural grocery store in 1939. Although the more modern supermarket was appearing in larger cities, many people still had to stand in front of a counter and ask for each item they desired. (Photograph courtesy of the Library of Congress.)

Traditional Grocery Stores

The opening of the 1930s saw a nationwide system of small grocery stores serving both urban neighborhoods and rural areas. In the cities, the housewife—perception and reality were very close at this time; women were assumed and expected to do the bulk of grocery purchases—walked to her friendly grocer to pick up a few days' essentials. Except for people who lived in the country or far-flung suburbs, the idea of getting into an automobile and driving to buy groceries would have been unthinkable. In many cases, separate trips to a butcher, a bakery, and maybe a produce dealer had to be undertaken, since many grocery stores of the era carried little in the way of meats, baked goods, dairy products, or fruits and vegetables. Their primary line consisted of staples, such as canned goods and prepackaged products. The full-service supermarket was only emerging in the 1930s.

In urban areas, dairy products usually were delivered directly to one's residence. The milkman made his rounds before dawn, leaving milk, eggs, and butter according to the wishes of the homemaker. His delivery wagon was often just that: a horse-drawn vehicle laden with glass containers. Empty bottles, always returnable in those days, were put out on the stoop (an all-purpose term meaning the front door, the back porch, a side entrance, or wherever it was agreed such items would be placed) with notes for the next delivery. Often these items rested in a milk box, a small, insulated container for safely holding perishables; it was about the right size for several quart bottles, along with a few other items. It was an efficient service that worked well, but suburbs and supermarkets spelled its doom.

In more remote rural areas, huckster wagons were sent out into the countryside by enterprising village grocers. The word "huckster" did not have the negative connotations of cheap and flashy salesmanship that it possesses today; in earlier years, it merely signified a dealer in varied small items. Typically, these wagons contained staples, canned goods, and prepared foods, which could be traded for fresh dairy products, eggs, meats, and poultry. Pushcarts were a common urban sight in the 1930s; they generally displayed an array of fresh fruits and vegetables. For the most part, grocery outlets of all kinds remained small, mom-and-pop enterprises with a decidedly local clientele.[3]

Chain Stores & Supermarkets

Some of these little stores would be part of larger chains: A&P (The Great Atlantic and Pacific Tea Company), IGA (Independent Grocers' Alliance), Grand Union, and several others laid the groundwork for today's one-stop shopping. Piggly Wiggly, a chain based in the Memphis, Tennessee, area, boasted self-service as early as 1916, but the idea caught on slowly. Even in 1930, most chain outlets were still neighborhood groceries; they usually lacked self-service; they seldom had meat counters, instead carrying canned meats rather than fresh cuts; and they featured only a few fruits and vegetables. Their connection to a larger chain entitled them to feature the company's label on various goods and perhaps allowed them to charge a slightly lower price on those products.

The first supermarket pioneers began to appear in the thirties. The King Kullen Market opened in Jamaica, New York in 1930. Called the "World's Greatest Price Wrecker," it was possibly the first real supermarket in the United States. By 1931, the Safeway chain was closing many of its small stores and converting them into larger operations. The following year, the Big Bear Super Market—"Big Bear, the Price Crusher"—opened in Elizabeth, New Jersey, advertising "cut-rate" prices. The Cincinnati-based Albers group began calling itself Albers Super Mkts., Inc., in 1933, the first corporate use of the term "supermarket." That same year, the Kroger chain opened a store in Indianapolis that was freestanding and boasted a surrounding parking lot. Perhaps the title of "first" should go to Kroger because of the parking feature. What may or may not have been foreseen in this last innovation was the gradual end of "walking to the store" and the beginning of a reliance on the automobile for shopping needs.[4]

The phenomenon of the supermarket was, however, predicated primarily on low prices, not convenience. In fact, an early term for them was "cheapies." The first ones tended to be bare-bones operations, often located in abandoned warehouses, with unfinished wooden shelves and tables holding the merchandise. Although the small grocery stores against which they competed were seldom much nicer aesthetically, their limited inventories and cozier neighborhood ambience perhaps made them seem more pleasant.

By contemporary standards, these early supermarkets hardly qualified as "super." They might be more spacious than their predecessors, but they still had crowded, narrow aisles, and their inventory would look absolutely puny when compared to the enormous stock carried by a modern market. When shopping in these primitive stores, housewives relied on cloth bags, paper sacks, cardboard boxes, or baskets to carry their purchases; not until 1937 was the wheeled shopping cart devised.

Shoppers quickly learned the tricks of navigating through the maze of aisles, display stands, and shelves of the evolving grocery store. Smart patrons knew how to read the array of goods, just as astute motorists could discern what they wanted through the forest of signs and gimmicks that lined the roadside. The 1930s witnessed an explosion of consumer choices for Americans, but it was coupled with a growing sophistication among customers. On the road or in a supermarket, people had come to realize that knowing how to interpret the package, from a storefront to the label on a can of vegetables, was an essential new skill.

What the supermarkets could offer, and did, was lower prices. Buying in bulk and selling in quantity was their secret, and it attracted customers, particularly during an economic depression. A media-driven campaign to create the image of the thrifty housewife, a woman skilled in shopping and economical food preparation, had changed attitudes about buying patterns. The new markets, by offering lower prices, encouraged consumers to save money at every turn, and played into the idea that women had a responsibility to stretch scarce food dollars as best they could. This picture of the smart shopper emerged as a dominant motif during the Depression.[5]

Self-Service

Perhaps the most significant shopping innovation of the 1930s was self-service. Until then, most stores, with the exception of the Piggly

Wiggly markets (Kroger also claimed some self-service innovations in several of its early stores), consisted of shelves along the walls holding the goods, and a counter strategically placed so the customer was blocked from reaching the groceries. Instead, the grocer took the shopper's order, and assistants gathered the desired items and they placed them on the counter. They were bagged, the bill was totaled, money changed hands or credit was arranged (if a customer was known, weekly or monthly tallies were commonplace), and the transaction was complete. There were few opportunities to read labels, compare packaging, or do all the other little things that self-service allows. Small wonder it caught on so completely during the thirties; it was a boon for shoppers.

A few amenities were lost in the shift to self-service. Home delivery of groceries, once a practice of many grocers, became a rarity. The delivery boy did not disappear entirely, however. In order to speed up the process, a special bicycle was available for that purpose. Called a "cycle truck," its front wheel was much smaller than the rear; this allowed an oversized wire basket capable of holding several bulging sacks of purchases to be attached ahead of the handlebars. A common sight in American cities throughout the first half of the century, these "trucks" were utilized to carry mail, ferry parts within a large factory, and do general hauling. During the 1930s, such bicycles emphasized the familiarity between grocer and consumer.

The practice of using the telephone to call in an order to a favorite grocer also fell off. The size and anonymity of the larger stores precluded this kind of close relationship, just as most of them refused to grant credit to shoppers. The custom of holding or reserving special items for special customers also was growing less common.

On the positive side, a bigger store meant a larger inventory. Instead of one brand of canned peas, a supermarket might feature two or three. The careful shopper could save a few precious cents by being rigorous in her comparison buying. Since she was free to wander the aisles, the consumer might become aware of new products or new brands she otherwise would miss. The big food manufacturers were supportive of self-service, and they worked hard to gain prominent placement in the new stores. And, if they were willing to admit it, many old-time grocers also welcomed the idea. Self-service reduced their labor costs, and that in turn increased their profitability. By 1937, supermarkets accounted for about one-third of the grocery business.

New Products

In 1939, A&P introduced the self-service meat department. They had their own line of prepackaged meats, allowing the customer to choose cuts and sizes without a clerk. Frozen foods were equally late in arriving at markets. Until the late 1930s, perhaps a few boxes of frozen vegetables might be seen inside a large, glass-fronted white freezer cabinet. The shopper had no access to this cabinet, so an assistant on the other side would have to retrieve whatever choices the buyer made. Probably, all the boxes bore the red, white, and blue Birds Eye label. The official introduction of commercial, packaged frozen, or "frosted," food took place in 1930, thanks to the efforts of Clarence Birdseye, the scientist who perfected a method of flash-freezing perishables and lent his name (as two separate words) to the industry leader.

Actually, frozen foods were not new; growers had packed berries and fruits in a mix of ice and salt since early in the century, but it was done for later wholesale distribution. Birdseye, on the other hand, solved the dual problem of freezing small quantities of produce quickly in order to preserve texture and flavor and putting it up in consumer-sized packages. Ever inventive, the Birds Eye people developed a modern, less expensive, freezer case around 1934 and leased it to grocers for next to nothing. In time, and with such incentives, both the grocers' and the consumers' reluctance was overcome, and frozen food became a standard item in stores. Birds Eye also helped its cause by printing and distributing small, pamphlet-like cookbooks (e.g., *20 Minute Meals*, 1932) that detailed how to use this new discovery.

A variety of other grocery products were introduced in the 1930s. For example, Americans have always had an enormous sweet tooth, a taste that grew throughout the decade. Among commodities, sugar was extremely cheap during the period. It became even more of a cooking staple in the home, and was also used freely in many commercial products. In fact, more sugar was consumed per capita during the Depression than before or since.

Prepackaged Food

In 1931, Hostess Twinkies made their first appearance. Here was a quick, cheap, simple snack or even a dessert. Easy to put into a lunch pail or pick up on the run, Twinkies were an immediate hit both with those who ate them and with housewives who found relief from one more baking chore. Twinkies could epitomize the move toward food requiring little or no preparation—the forerunner of all manner of prepackaged products.

Many of the prepared foods that proliferated during the decade were rather ordinary dishes that benefited from the addition of flavorings and sugar. These inclusions made things tastier, but did little to increase their nutritional value. In fact, in 1933 Arthur Kallet and F. J. Schlink wrote a book entitled *100,000,000 Guinea Pigs*, an indictment of the food industry. A surprise best-seller, the work eventually ran through thirty printings.

Their revelations about adulterated and impure foods and drugs enraged the public, and helped lead the way to a revision of the 1906 Pure Food and Drugs Act. The new law was enacted in 1938, but relentless pressure from the mammoth food and drug conglomerates significantly weakened it. Nevertheless, public awareness about what canned peaches or mayonnaise actually contained had been significantly heightened.

Candy

The move toward prepackaged foodstuffs continued unabated throughout the 1930s, and candy bars certainly qualify as such an item. Since sugar was cheap, candy manufacturers could keep their prices low. The strong sales that candy bars maintained in the face of an economic depression convinced manufacturers to bring out a plethora of new names and new, sweet concoctions. In 1931, Mars, Inc., introduced its Snickers bar, a mix of nougat and chocolate, and Welch's pushed its Sugar Daddy sucker. A year later Mars promoted the novel 3 Musketeers, a blend of one part chocolate nougat, one part vanilla, and one part strawberry. The toffee-flavored Heath Bar came along in 1932, as did Pay Day. Other varieties began to tantalize American palates: Kraft Caramels made their debut in 1933; in 1934 the Zero Bar appeared. Mars Bars and 5th Avenue adorned the shelves of markets and sweet shoppes in 1936. The NECCO Sky Bar came out the following year, and 1938 welcomed Nestlé's Crunch and Hershey's Krackel. There was even an Amos 'n' Andy candy bar; it flourished along with the radio series of the same name. (See chapter 10, "Performing Arts.") When the popularity of the show began to wane during the 1940s, the bar soon disappeared. Of course, these newcomers had to fight for precious shelf space, but the national craving for candy seemed insatiable. Grocers gladly rearranged their displays to accommodate just about any and all new brands.[6]

Food Preparation

Not all the food introductions involved sweets. In good times or bad, people have to eat, and so the thirties saw many other new items make their debuts. The trend focused on products that involved little or no tedious preparation. For many reasons, the live-in cook had become a thing of the past by the 1920s. With the decline of servants, a serious reexamination of the housewife's role in the modern kitchen took place.

It was apparent that paid domestic help, so taken for granted in earlier years, might not be realistic for a housewife trying to manage budget, family, house, and chores. Of course, technology altered the traditional rhythms of American life by introducing many new appliances, but women nonetheless faced chores that in earlier times a maid would have done. So the question of time and the housewife must enter the picture. Middle-class American women discovered that expectations about what they should do were being raised, not lowered. They were supposed to be volunteers, join clubs, participate in new leisure activities, have hours and energy remaining for their children, and spend more time with their husbands. It was an impossible expectation.

As a result, the ritual of dining went through significant change in the first third of the twentieth century. Expectations about food, about dining, were lowered. Meals became simpler, with fewer courses, less complex, time-consuming menus, and not as many dishes to wash. When the Campbell's people figured out in the 1890s how to condense their soup (eliminate the water; the consumer would replace it when preparing the soup), they hit upon what would be the major trend in processed food thereafter: package the product in the simplest way possible and keep any preparation to a minimum. Frozen foods were but one more step in this ongoing change. The big food processors and manufacturers enthusiastically participated in this conversion. For them, it meant the opportunity to introduce a host of new products and to advertise and promote them in terms of "ease," "speed," "simplicity," and "efficiency."

A good example of such a product is Bisquick, which made its first appearance in grocery stores in 1931. It promised to lighten the housewife's workload, and it did. A mix of flour and baking soda, Bisquick allowed baking, especially biscuits ("quick biscuits"), in one easy step. Although it was a boon to cooks around the country, it added to the woes of bakeries. Already reeling from the Depression, fully one-third of all American baking establishments went out of business during the period 1930–1933. Sales of baked goods plummeted, and millions of households turned (or returned) to home baking as a means of cutting costs. Of course, much of this drop was accounted for by fewer sales of commercial desserts like pies, cakes, and fancy pastries; these expensive items were among the first things to be cut from a tight budget.

Another example is Spam. Introduced by Hormel at the beginning of 1937, Spam was truly something new: It came in a small, rectangular can that could be opened by a key that unrolled a metal strip. It was vacuum-sealed, and a little whoosh of air could be detected when the key was first turned. The strip was then removed, the top came off, a knife was run around the insides, urging out the meat, and Spam was ready to serve. A mix of pork products, it kept in the pantry until needed. Spam required no heating, although it could be fried, broiled, or chopped up and served with other dishes—its uses were only limited by one's imagination, a fact that Hormel has capitalized on over the years. Best of all, Spam was cheap.

Spam quickly established itself in America's kitchens. Although rival

Armour a few years later brought out Treet, a virtually identical lunch-eon meat, there was never much of a contest. Spam entered the national diet almost instantly, and typified the urge for effortless cooking.

Ragú spaghetti sauce (1937) and Kraft macaroni and cheese dinners (also 1937) illustrate the quest for kitchen simplicity. Neither product required much preparation other than serving; culinary purists might grimace at the thought, but the average housewife obviously felt other-wise. Within minutes, a traditional hot meal could be put on the table, and cleanup was minimized. Sales soared, and the old idea of laboring over a hot stove took another blow.

Fritos Corn Chips (1932), Nabisco's Ritz Crackers (1934), and Lay's potato chips (1939) provided easy snacks and additions to meals. A pop-ular recipe in the 1930s was to take some crackers, butter them, and toast them in the oven. A variation had the consumer dipping the cracker in water and then heating it so it would puff up. These new approaches to an old commodity were promptly embraced by the public, with Ritz Crackers rivaling Spam for the varied ways they could be fixed and served.

Not all the pre-prepared, precooked food of the 1930s went solely to adults. The Fremont Canning Company, based in Michigan, began ex-perimenting with strained foods in the late 1920s. During the 1930s, Fre-mont was recognized for its Gerber Baby Foods, and they dominated a relatively new niche in groceries. Until that time, food for infants was a specialty product, usually found in drugstores. Gerber, however, mar-keted its jars of strained foods to the public as an "everyday item" in grocery stores, and succeeded beyond anyone's expectations. On all their jars was a drawing of a cute baby, done by artist Dorothy Hope Smith in 1928. It became their trademark and contributed mightily to their suc-cess. By the early 1930s the Gerber sketch had become "America's best-known baby." Within a few years, the product line had undergone expansion, and American mothers considered the new baby foods an essential part of any grocery list.[7]

Refrigeration

For much of the decade, most average Americans still owned iceboxes, the forerunners of the modern refrigerator. Usually built with a wooden exterior that enclosed some form of insulated interior, iceboxes ranged from a very basic one-compartment unit to more sophisticated models that had several doors and different interior arrangements. What they had in common was a reliance on ice as the refrigerant. No matter how fancy, the icebox still required a block (or blocks) of ice to cool it. The degree of insulation reflected the quality of the box, but inevitably the ice would melt and have to be replaced. That meant the iceman would

A 1930s refrigerator. The freezing compartment, such as it was, is located in the small box at the upper right side of the interior. (Photograph courtesy of the Library of Congress.)

have to stop by, usually with a horse-drawn wagon, although trucks began to appear more and more by the late 1930s. He carried large blocks of ice, and his job was to chip off a chunk that would fit neatly into the home icebox.

By modern standards, iceboxes were messy and inefficient. Most of them had very limited storage capacities, the ice melted rather rapidly, and the storage box soon held water, not ice. Despite drains and other devices, the housewife always had to contend with diminishing cold, along with drips and puddles. Finally, iceboxes did not hold very much food, given their refrigerating limitations. This disadvantage necessitated frequent visits to the market to restock on perishables.

Help, in the form of more efficient ways of keeping foods, arrived in force during the decade. In 1925, the General Electric Company (GE) introduced what came to be called their Monitor Top refrigerator. The compressor motor was housed in a cylinder (the "monitor") atop the actual refrigerator. By 1929, GE had sold some 50,000 of these, and the modern kitchen was becoming a reality. Despite the Depression, the company's sales passed 1 million units in 1931 and continued to climb.

With the success of their refrigerator assured, and with the profits rolling in, General Electric had the lion's share of the market. Their Monitor Top had started at an expensive $525 in the 1920s, but it came down to a more reasonable $290 in the early 1930s. That $290, however, is in 1930s dollars; adjusting for inflation, the cost today would be equivalent to paying over $3,500 for a refrigerator, so major kitchen appliances of the time cannot be considered cheap. In an effort to keep sales strong in a depressed economy, GE got Hollywood to produce a one-hour documentary called *Three Women* (1935). Starring, among others, the gossip columnist Hedda Hopper and the cowboy actor Johnny Mack Brown, it celebrates the "complete electric kitchen." Incidentally, *Three Women* was the first Technicolor commercial documentary.[8]

It was not just GE's Monitor Top that changed public attitudes. In 1935 the merchandising giant Sears, Roebuck hired the noted designer Raymond Loewy to create a streamlined refrigerator for their Coldspot brand. That particular unit, far more contemporary than the rather pedestrian Monitor Top, has come to be a design classic. At the same time, rivals Kelvinator and Frigidaire were selling large numbers of their own models. Thus the 1930s saw the decline of the old-fashioned icebox and the rise of the modern refrigerator. By 1941, well over 3 million electric refrigerators could be found in American kitchens. Technology, not just food itself, would change the way Americans ate.

In a last desperate attempt to stimulate lagging sales, many icebox manufacturers dropped the word "ice" and began to refer to their products as "refrigerators." They spoke glowingly of the reliability of ice, the economies to be gained with ice, and generally tried to play on the innate conservatism of families suspicious of anything too new or different. But it was a losing battle from the start, and the traditional icebox disappeared within a few years.

For the Depression-era housewife, her electric refrigerator was a real joy, but it did have limitations. Freezer space was virtually nonexistent. A minuscule interior box held a couple of small trays of ice cubes—ice cubes themselves were a big advance over chipping off pieces of ice from a block—and the unit had a shallow "meat tray" directly underneath. Frost collected throughout the freezing compartment of the refrigerator, forcing the owner to "defrost" it periodically. This chore meant removing everything from the interior of the unit and getting rid of the accumulated ice and frost. Though messy and time-consuming, it was a cheap price to pay for the convenience of keeping ice and selected foods frozen until they were consumed.

With the advent of frozen foods, the tiny box inside the refrigerator was not nearly large enough. Most frozen foods and ice cream had to be consumed when purchased, and meat could not be bought in any quantity. Manufacturers addressed this issue as the decade progressed, and by the end of the 1930s the latest models had considerably larger freezing compartments. Both the food companies and the appliance makers published pamphlets that did two things: they showed the housewife how to use the new electric devices, and they gave hints and recipes that would aid in the actual cooking processes involved. GE had *The Silent Hostess Treasure Book* (1930), Westinghouse printed *The Refrigerator Book* (1933), *Famous Dishes from Every State* came from Frigidaire in 1936, and many similar titles poured forth from other manufacturers and food processors. Technology might change the way Americans ate, but it also had to adjust to the needs, both traditional and created, of the consumer.[9]

Other Appliances

The revolution in the kitchen was not limited only to refrigerators. From the 1920s on, appliance manufacturers were promoting their products as both useful and visually pleasing. Efficiency and beauty were subtly linked. The kitchen sink, once an enameled slab of cast iron that stood on legs with all its plumbing exposed, evolved into a built-in part of modern kitchen cabinetry during the 1930s. Doors replaced the unsightly legs, the plumbing was concealed, and additional storage space was gained in the process. By 1937, GE was advertising the Electric Sink. A combination of electric dishwasher and disposer in one smoothly designed enameled steel unit, the Electric Sink promised relief from the drudgery of washing and drying dishes by hand. The garbage disposer (or Disposall, as it was eventually trade named) allowed the busy homemaker to dump table scraps down the drain into the waiting machine, which then ground and pulverized them into a mush that could be carried away with wastewater. Household technology had clearly become a burgeoning field, led by "efficiency experts" who wanted to make the most of limited space but also desired to add an aesthetic dimension to the previously overlooked kitchen.

The 1920s had witnessed the replacement of the coal or wood stove by electric and gas models, a shift that continued throughout the 1930s. Smaller appliances also became widely available; the lowly electric can opener made its debut in 1931. The coffeepot had been electrified in the

1920s, and many new, improved electric percolators, such as Silex and Sunbeam, came along in the 1930s. Coffee was the beverage of choice for many Americans, and the ability to keep it hot and ready to serve was a popular feature. In 1937, KitchenAid introduced an electric coffee grinder for home use so those who favored fresh-ground beans could have their coffee just the way they wanted it.

In 1930 the Proctor Company (later Proctor-Silex) brought out a pop-up toaster that improved on previous designs. This led to many new toasters, sandwich grills, waffle irons, and similar appliances during the decade. In keeping with the Streamline Moderne vogue, many of these models were sleek, rounded, and chromed, a far cry from the dull, utilitarian designs of the 1920s. They could be brought directly to the table, instead of kept in the kitchen, further modifying dining and entertaining habits. The housewife was now able to join her family, in keeping with the attitude that a woman's place extended beyond the confines of the kitchen.

A popular pastime in the 1930s consisted of inviting friends or neighbors over for an informal supper. Often these gatherings were potluck, with each guest providing a dish. Since informality ruled, cooking at the table—using, for example, an electric grill or an electric waffle iron—was a cozy way of being sociable. No one thought it improper to prepare food so publicly with shiny new appliances, plus it cut costs. With everyone contributing, individual expenses were kept to a minimum, an important consideration during a depression.

In 1930, the Sunbeam Corporation introduced their Mixmaster, destined to become a staple in American kitchens. Priced low for volume sales, it allowed the cook to "stir, cream, fold, and blend." It also further simplified cooking, reinforcing the idea that the preparation of food should be quick and easy. Despite the Depression, the Mixmaster sold briskly, and emboldened Sunbeam to come out with a whole line of accessories, from juice extractors to choppers to shredders. With its success, the word "Mixmaster" entered the language to denote any home mixer, just like "nylons" for hosiery and "Xerox" for copiers.

In the early years of the century, the Hamilton Beach Company had designed a high-speed electric mixer for restaurant and drugstore soda fountains. They, along with their competitors, kept improving on what was in essence a simple gadget. One rival that gained precious publicity was the Waring Blendor—always spelled with an "o"—which capitalized on the popularity of bandleader Fred Waring. In reality, he had nothing to do with the invention; he just lent his name to the 1930s' venture, and the association has carried down to the present. Maestro Waring was introduced to the device in 1936; he immediately saw it as a way to make frothy, iced drinks, principally daiquiris, his favorite. The

machine's inventor had been pushing it for milkshakes, but with Waring's backing, the Blendor quickly became identified as a bar accessory.[10]

EATING OUT

Of course, it should not be thought that everyone sat down and dined
exclusively at home. The United States has always had numerous Au-
tomats, beaneries, cafeterias, coffee shops, delicatessens, diners, greasy
spoons, hamburger stands, inns, lodges, lounges, lunch counters, lunch-
eonettes, restaurants, taverns, tearooms, and other public and private
eateries too numerous to mention. True, the overwhelming majority of
people ate most of their meals in their homes, with the one possible
exception being lunch. Avoiding restaurants saved money, an important
consideration at the time. Nevertheless, many individuals frequented
commercial establishments, such as those who chose not to cook, or those
who were on the road and unable to do so.[11]

Diners

A familiar urban sight in the thirties was the diner, an outgrowth of
the old-fashioned food stand and lunch wagon. The diners of the 1930s
had evolved into distinctive architectural entities. Once a place for work-
ingmen to grab a bite near a factory, later models were shiny, streamlined little eateries that catered to anyone, rich or poor, blue-collar or
professional, wanting a meal.

Diners were always cheap, a step up from a hot dog stand but a step
or two removed from "real" restaurants. They usually stayed open
twenty-four hours, seven days a week. Their menus were endless, and
they served "breakfast all day long." By the end of the decade, over 6,000
diners dotted the downtowns and roadsides of American cities. Numerous companies came into being whose sole product was a stainless steel
structure that resembled nothing so much as a railroad dining car. They
could be mass-produced, trucked to a site, and erected in a matter of
hours. In fact, many people mistakenly thought they were a dining car
moved from the railroad tracks and placed on a concrete slab. The resultant design—a long, narrow room with a shiny, plastic-topped
counter running its length, complete with chrome stools and booths upholstered in plastic—became a standardized part of the American scene.

Restaurants

Enough people "ate out" that the entire restaurant industry grew significantly during the 1920s and 1930s, to about 100,000 units. Along with

the idea of the motor inn, there came the growth of establishments linked through chain ownership and franchises. By the end of the 1920s, some 2400 chain restaurants existed in the United States; even with the Depression, their number grew to about 3000 by 1939. The overwhelming majority of eating establishments were still individually owned and operated. Howard Johnson's, usually associated with multiple flavors of ice cream, pioneered in the concept of franchising. Instead of owning his restaurants outright, Johnson sold the privilege of running them to agents, or "franchisees." These investors were allowed to replicate the firm's distinctive Colonial building with the bright orange roof and cupola; they could use the same menu and offer the twenty-odd ice cream flavors; they could take a percentage of the profits—but ultimate control still remained with Howard Johnson's. By 1940, Johnson could boast more than 125 sites, with only a third of them owned directly by his company; the rest were franchised.

The relative success of the urban chain restaurants led to imitation and variation. Names like Toddle House, Krystal, and White Castle (along with its virtual twin, White Tower) became familiar sights on busy street corners throughout the country. These were not truly family-oriented restaurants. As a rule, they catered to busy working people during the day and to individuals and small groups at night. On the other hand, organizations like A&W Root Beer, Dairy Queen, and Hot Shoppes aimed more for the suburban market, particularly people with cars.

These roadside stands were not drive-ins—the latter, although initiated in the 1930s, did not flourish until after World War II. The stands usually located their operations in the less densely populated suburban neighborhoods, often adjacent to the popular auto camps and tourist cabins outside the city centers. This kind of careful attention to siting led them to attract a more family-oriented clientele, especially travelers. They also hinted at the growing reliance on the automobile that occurred during the 1930s. By employing standardized designs, building materials— and certainly standard menus—the chains were the precursors of the "fast food" restaurants of today. Their standardization kept costs down and made them attractive eating places for millions of Americans looking for quick, cheap food on the go.

One entrepreneur who closely observed the growth of both chain and independent dining was Duncan Hines. Over the years, he had compiled a list of his likes and dislikes in American restaurants. In lieu of Christmas cards, he shared this listing with friends. Finally, in 1936 he was induced to publish it as *Adventures in Good Eating*. It was a wise move. *Adventures in Good Eating* went through innumerable editions and had sold a remarkable 450,000 copies by the end of the decade.

In his little book Hines stressed cleanliness, neatness, decor (too much decoration probably hid dirt, in his estimation), good coffee (he recom-

A streamlined hamburger stand from the late 1930s. Fast food, in the form of diners and stands like the one above, was increasingly part of the culinary landscape throughout the decade. (Photograph courtesy of the Library of Congress.)

mended using a percolator), and the serving of hearty portions of solid American food—"meat and potatoes," and maybe an occasional seafood item. He eschewed sauces and anything faintly "ethnic." Hines did as much as nutritionists, home economists, and the big food processors to nationalize the American diet, at least on the road. Many a restaurateur proudly displayed his little "Recommended by Duncan Hines" sign next to the entrance.

Tearooms

The diner was not the first choice of everyone when it came to eating out. "Tearooms" gained in popularity by capitalizing on the concept of a quiet, intimate restaurant that served nothing stronger than tea or coffee. They seemed the very antithesis of saloons, they were not so bright and mechanical as a diner, and they had the advantage of appealing to both women and families. Many tearooms were housed in historic buildings or quaint, refurbished houses, thus reinforcing their "safe" image and attracting patrons in search of a fanciful or picturesque setting.

With the Depression and fewer people eating out, many of the tea-rooms failed. In addition, the attempts by tearoom owners to make the surroundings charming and cozy ran into opposition from men who desired a more "meat and potatoes" approach to dining. Supporters of the overall tearoom concept—no alcohol, an emphasis on salads and other wholesome food—suggested that perhaps a new name was in or-der if such places expected to stay in business. What emerged in the later 1930s was the "motor inn." Such a term still conjured up a rural, folksy setting, but it also included the more masculine automobile in its nu-ances. This new connotation led to the increasing acceptance of the family-oriented restaurant, making it a permanent part of the highway landscape.

DRINK

Alcoholic Beverages

The period 1920–1933 marked a bizarre episode in American life. Dur-ing those thirteen years, the nation struggled to enforce, through the Eighteenth Amendment, or Volstead Act, the prohibition of the sale or purchase of alcoholic beverages. Doomed to failure before its passage, Prohibition took a terrific toll among brewers, distillers, and all those places that served alcohol. The Twenty-first Amendment, or Repeal, was passed in 1933, and people were again free to enjoy their alcoholic bev-erages of choice, and restaurants were free to serve them. The grocery business, along with liquor and wine stores, welcomed Repeal as well, since they could once more sell bottled alcoholic beverages. The only ones unhappy with Repeal were the Drys, those opposed to the con-sumption of alcohol under any circumstances. For the overwhelming ma-jority of Americans, however, Repeal was a return to a more rational approach to "Demon Rum."

During the years of Prohibition, restaurateurs were forced to watch profits shrink, often to the point of bankruptcy. Cocktails, mixed drinks, wine, and beer have always been moneymakers in the restaurant trade; when they could no longer be served legally, the business suffered, un-less drinks were served illegally—as they were in many restaurants. Part of the folklore of the period, of course, is the rise of the speakeasies, those fabled establishments where one knocked, gave a password, and was entitled to enter a secret world of glitter, fun, and drinks. The very illegality of liquor made it expensive but attractive. Smugglers, bootleg-gers, and occasional gangsters had to be paid off, often along with co-operative police officers. Being able to drink was a mark of conspicuous consumption and rebellion; it meant a person had the cash necessary to indulge a habit not sanctioned by the government. It appealed to that old American streak of individuality, the chance to thumb one's nose at authority. As a result, although Prohibition lasted only through the first years of the 1930s, it still played a major part in the popular culture of the period.[12]

The gangster films of Edward G. Robinson (e.g., *Little Caesar*, 1930, and many others) and James Cagney (e.g., *Public Enemy*, 1931, and many others) chronicle the crime waves of the late 1920s and early thirties. Their images of tough guys and loose women, along with silver flasks and freely flowing liquor, influenced public attitudes toward law and order. The idea of a club that somehow existed beyond the law held appeal, as did the recurring picture of booze being easily obtained and consumed. In fact, it was stylish to laugh at any drinking restrictions; they were in place for others, not for a smart guy. Or smart woman: one particularly strong image at this time was of men and women drinking together, a big change from earlier years, when drinking was primarily a male prerogative.

The sophisticated dramas and comedies of the era showed similar pictures of public alcohol consumption. In her first talking movie role (*Anna Christie*, 1930), Greta Garbo whispered "viskey with ginger ale," and audiences loved it. Or Jean Harlow, clad in a slinky gown, sipped a cocktail in *Platinum Blonde* (1931), and the image became fixed. Clearly, fashionable people consumed alcohol and made no secret of it. Repeal was almost predestined; no one had to convince the public that drinking existed as a part of American life.

One product that survived Prohibition was "near beer." The Volstead Act defined illegal beverages as anything containing more than .5 percent alcohol. A concoction that had been around since the early 1900s, near beer boasted a minuscule .4 percent alcohol. Many breweries happily supplied yeast and malt for the production of this beverage; it helped them stay in business. A variation on near beer was "needle beer," regular near beer spiked with spirits. Needless to say, this latter variant was illegal, but its consumption flourished both in homes and speakeasies.

Beer, wine, spirits—all returned with the end of Prohibition. Not that they had ever been gone; the illegal consumption of alcohol continually rose throughout those troubled years. And, because of alcohol's high cost, most of the Prohibition drinkers tended to be middle class or above; the old imagery of alcohol being the curse of the poor and downtrodden no longer held true. Thus, when Repeal came along, a new class of consumers was in place. Of course, Repeal broadened the base, but drinking in the 1930s had lost most of the stigma it had held prior to Prohibition.

Until Repeal, the alcohol that Americans consumed was inferior or adulterated, a risk that a large proportion of citizens seemed willing to take. It also suggested that most Americans were no longer drinking for the taste of alcohol or to be sociable; they were drinking for the effect of alcohol. When evidence increasingly supported this supposition, the pressure for repeal grew. The exact number of people blinded or crippled by adulterated alcohol will never be known, but popular culture paid these grim facts little mind; it continued to deluge the public with images that put drinking in a favorable light.

Even with Repeal, over one-third of the states, mainly in the South, imposed their own prohibition laws. Three continued to ban the sale of all alcohol other than "3.2 beer," a weak beer with a 3.2 percent alcohol content; most commercial beers contain a higher percentage. Fifteen states, again mostly in the South, proscribed any sales "by the drink," effectively blocking taverns, cocktail lounges, and the like from selling alcohol. The public may have welcomed Repeal, but the states (or often, counties and cities) remained deeply divided about the issue.

The end of Prohibition brought numerous advertising campaigns by distilleries, breweries, and wine makers. When it had been illegal, drinking was done on the sly. Public consumption of alcohol was too risky, and this led many to associate drinking with secrecy and isolation. The advertisements therefore sought to inform people that responsible social drinking could be considered appropriate behavior. They stressed that no one should feel embarrassed about purchasing or consuming alcohol in public, provided it was done in moderation.

The lingering attitudes fostered by thirteen years of Prohibition, coupled with the economic woes of the Depression, caused many Americans to retain the drinking patterns of the twenties and early thirties. The exception occurred among women; after Repeal, a smaller percentage of American women drank, either publicly or privately. Apparently the permissive attitudes of the 1920s, at least for women, did not endure after the end of Prohibition. Most people thought men could drink, but that same majority thought women should not. In 1939, a poll estimated that 70 percent of American males, but only 45 percent of the women, drank alcohol.

Because of the negative connotations associated with the words "saloon" and "bar," euphemistic terms like "lounge" or the more explicit "cocktail lounge" became popular. With Repeal, these new establishments flourished in most larger cities. But private dinners and cocktail parties at home also continued to be in vogue, a carryover of Prohibition practices. By 1933, the idea of drinking as a private activity was well ingrained, and continued throughout the decade. The Adolph Coors Brewing Company capitalized on the desire of many Americans to consume alcohol at home. In 1935 they introduced beer in cans; previously it had been available only in returnable bottles or on tap. The disposable can proved a real boon to the industry (the nonreturnable bottle did not come along until the 1950s), allowing the consumer even greater freedom—and privacy—in his or her drinking habits. For many Americans, however, public consumption of alcohol in bars and restaurants has remained a subject of contentious debate.

Soft Drinks

Even more important than coffee and tea was the burgeoning soft drink industry. Since its birth in the late nineteenth century, this distinctive part of American popular culture has grown steadily. Each year, the consumption of soda, pop, soft drinks, colas, or whatever one wishes to call them, has risen. Certainly, the Depression did not dampen this national appetite for sweet, sugary drinks. Sugar was cheap, as were the other ingredients, primarily carbonated water and flavoring, so the bottlers could keep their prices low.

Probably the first American soft drink that comes to most minds is Coca-Cola. Ever since its invention in 1886, "Coke" has been the industry leader. The distinctive green bottles with the "hour-glass figure," the flowing script, the bright red advertising color—all contribute to instantaneous product recognition. For obvious reasons, Coca-Cola was not enthusiastic about Repeal, and ran a series of "Back to Normal" advertisements in 1933. The "normal" is a veiled reference to the return of legal consumption of alcoholic beverages. The ads depict tired, frowning people who are quickly refreshed by imbibing a Coke. Their fatigued visages fall away, they are invigorated and alert. But their alertness is also a subtle reminder about alcohol and its negative effects. Better a Coke and its mix of sugar and caffeine than, say, a beer.

In 1930, Coca-Cola began to distribute coin-operated coolers to businesses around the country, another industry first. Drop in a nickel and get an ice-cold Coke in return. Three years later they had created a fountain machine that instantly mixed syrup and carbonated water, replacing the previous manual procedure, which was time-consuming and occasionally inaccurate. With that kind of efficiency, a majority of soda fountains could be relied on to offer Coca-Cola to thirsty patrons.

Coca-Cola's primary competitor has long been Pepsi-Cola, a derivative cola drink first made in 1898. In its never-ending attempts to overtake its archrival, Pepsi utilized commercial radio with considerable effectiveness during the late 1930s. The company's advertising department came up with a memorable ditty that anyone within range of a radio came to know by heart. In it, a male chorus extols the good taste of Pepsi, and then adds what a great bargain it is for the consumer. The jingle was a direct jab at Coca-Cola; Pepsi had taken to bottling their soda in twelve-ounce bottles but continued to charge the same amount, five cents. Coke, on the other hand, was continuing to use its ubiquitous 6.5-ounce bottle, then the industry standard. Such was Coca-Cola's commanding sales lead at the time that they pretty much ignored Pepsi's challenge. Those extra 5½ ounces in a Pepsi cost the bottler little more. In the soft drink industry, the beverage itself is extremely cheap, and a few ounces one way or the other make virtually no difference. In addition, a twelve-ounce container costs about the same as a smaller one; like so much in advertising, perception is often far more important than reality.[13]

Of course, other sodas occupied the grocer's shelves besides Coca-Cola and Pepsi-Cola. Dozens of cola drinks had come onto the market with derivative names like "Coke-Ola," "Cola-Coke," "Coak," "Koko Kola," and so on. Some of these imitators were moderately successful, but most are lost to history. Two brands that did manage to hang on during the Depression were Moxie (first brewed in 1876, but not marketed as a soft drink until 1884) and Dr Pepper (1885). Neither of these would-be contenders ever achieved the sales of Coke and Pepsi, but each had its loyal following.

Although it never became a true national best-seller, Moxie did challenge Coca-Cola and Pepsi-Cola in some markets. More important, the trade name "Moxie" entered American speech: it means vigor, nerve (courage), or skill. To have "moxie" therefore came to signify admirable traits, a fortunate connection between the product and the language.

Dr Pepper was marketed in its early years as a tonic that promoted "Vim, Vitality, and Vigor." Its most memorable campaign, however, was a product of the Depression. Consumers were urged to "Drink a bite to eat at 10-2 & 4 o'clock." The 10-2-4 caught on, and for many years thereafter, Dr Pepper was the third-ranked soft drink, right behind Coke and Pepsi.

Various ginger ales, flavored sodas, natural blends like root beer and birch beer (with no alcohol), and citrus-based products like 7-Up and lemon-lime soda also had their adherents. Originally sold as an antacid, 7-Up boasted it contained "lithiated lemon" and used "Takes the 'Ouch' out of Grouch" as its slogan in the 1930s.[14]

Coffee and Tea

Other beverages existed throughout the stormy days of Prohibition. Fully one-third of all adult Americans abstained from alcohol, and the remaining two-thirds consumed many beverages in addition to alcoholic ones. Coffee and tea remained favorites throughout the Depression. General Foods, which already owned best-selling Maxwell House coffee, acquired rights to sell a German product, Sanka decaffeinated coffee, in 1932. The name Sanka is an advertiser's way of saying *sans caffeine* (without caffeine). With this acquisition, General Foods had a strong hold on both portions of the coffee market. Teas also sold well, although some gender bias existed. Many thought that tea was for women, whereas coffee was a more manly beverage, a perception that continued through-out the 1930s.

SUMMARY

For popular culture, the marketing of food and all the items connected with the preparation and storage of food provided many memorable images. From the Monitor Top refrigerator to a Coca-Cola cooler, from Hostess Twinkies to fresh-frozen berries, the American penchant for mer-chandising rose to the occasion. Grim-faced citizens waiting in line for a handout was not the stuff of good copy. The land of plenty, complete with an overflowing cornucopia, was the prevailing image of the time.

7

Leisure Activities

BACKGROUND

Since its Puritan beginnings, American culture has always stressed the value and importance of work: "Work is its own reward"; "Idle hands do the devil's work." To be out of work, to be unemployed, to be idle, therefore carries a certain shame. At the same time, Americans have been taught to treasure leisure, provided that leisure came about because of hard work. Vacations, holidays, a day off—these are the rewards for a job well done.

The onset of the Great Depression presented Americans with a paradoxical situation: increasing layoffs and swelling unemployment gave millions increased leisure time, but it was an imposed leisure, it was idleness. The challenge became how to fill empty hours with activities that were meaningful and would not diminish one's self-esteem. In addition, the choices were limited by a lack of funds. For instance, in cities throughout the nation, departments of parks and recreation found their budgets slashed, just as they discovered that more people than ever were attempting to use their facilities.

During the early days of the economic crisis, the average workweek began to decline, going from forty-eight to forty hours, or what was called "the five-day week." In addition, the National Recovery Administration (NRA) was instituting work codes and fair practices. Together, these further reduced hours at the job, especially overtime. By 1935, two-thirds of the American employees covered by these codes were working fewer than forty hours a week.

People sought activities to fill their increased free time: cities and towns, along with schools and local businesses, sponsored hobby clubs of all kinds, and local YMCAs and YWCAs became important resources for communities. Their indoor tracks, swimming pools, gyms, and game rooms saw significant use during the 1930s. Despite all the efforts to accommodate participatory activities, many people were not taking advantage of the organizations and facilities. They were instead at home, reading the newspaper, listening to the radio, or, it might be inferred, simply staring out a window. A marked rise in sedentary, solitary behaviors did in fact occur during the grimmest days of the Depression. Games like solitaire and pursuits like knitting and putting together jigsaw puzzles occupied an increasing amount of people's time. In all, the 1930s witnessed a variety of leisure activities, some active and some passive, some individual and some family- or group-oriented, as Americans learned to cope with unemployment, reduced resources, and too much empty time.

FADS

The standard definition of "fad" revolves around the concept of a large group of people enthusiastically supporting some temporary fashion or notion. The Depression era was no stranger to fads; in fact, the 1930s saw as much silly behavior as any period in American history. As a rule, the fads were cheap and they consumed time. They were public and escapist, and they attracted both adults and children. Sometimes the subject was food—prodigious quantities of virtually anything edible were consumed. People flocked to pie-eating and egg-eating contests, along with clam-shucking, gum-chewing, hot-dog munching, and coffee-drinking challenges.

Many of the fads focused on endurance. For instance, tree sitters joined with the flagpole sitters of the 1920s, as people climbed to the highest branches of a tree or to the top of a pole and then attempted to remain aloft for days and weeks on end. Generally, some convenient means of collecting money was available on the ground for any contributions, although most of the sitters went to their perches only after arranging a fee. Once up in the air, they stayed for remarkable lengths of time. The good ones whiled away weeks or even months, depending on the deals they had made. For the gawkers down below, the longer the better; it was silly, but it was something to do.[1]

Inspired by the endurance of the aerialists, hundreds of contestants entered six-day bicycle races, 4000-mile roller derbies, and even seesaw-riding contests. There were talking marathons, walking marathons, nonstop piano playing, and kissathons, the last involving staying lip-to-lip for hours—and then days—at a time. Perhaps the silliest of all were the rock-a-thons. Participants continuously rocked in an old-fashioned rocking chair, attempting to stay in motion, and awake, longer than anyone else.

Six-day bike races did not involve a picturesque ride around the countryside. They took place on little makeshift wooden tracks, and two-person teams, usually a man and a woman, circled the track for six entire days, taking turns and fighting exhaustion. Movie stars, especially women, were seen on bicycles in publicity shots, and sales of women's bikes soared. Joe E. Brown, a rubber-faced comedian, hopped on the cycling craze with *6 Day Bike Rider* (1934), an innocuous little movie that emphasizes the popularity this particular fad had for a time.

Likewise, roller-skating briefly became all the rage. Again, it was cheap entertainment; abandoned warehouses and other indoor spaces became skating rinks almost overnight. Variations on simple skating promptly appeared. The Roller Derby was modeled after the six-day bicycle races. A team—once more, a man and a woman—skated round and round a track for 4000 miles. The event began each day in the early afternoon and continued until about midnight, assuring the maximum number of paying spectators. For thirty-five days the teams skated, interspersing regular skating with "jams" and "sprints." A jam involved getting a number of racers simultaneously on the track, thus assuring collisions and general mayhem; a sprint simply meant skating very fast for a brief period of time and adding a bit more visual spectacle for onlookers.

Dance marathons found a new lease on life in the Depression. They had originated in 1928 and had seemingly run their course by 1930. But in the early, dark days of the economic collapse, the dance marathon was rediscovered. The rules were simple: a couple had to dance, or at least keep moving, for an hour. At the end of sixty minutes, they got fifteen minutes off, and then it was back on the floor for another hour. If one fell asleep while on the floor, the other was responsible for keeping him or her upright and mobile. The two could make $20 to $30 a week just holding each other up and shuffling their feet, plus they got eight free meals a day. Dancing all day and long into the night consumed an enormous number of calories, so the meals were rich and filling.

June Hovick, later a Hollywood star under the name June Havoc (and the sister of Louise Hovick, later a famous stripper who called herself Gypsy Rose Lee) holds the dance marathon record: 3,600 hours of continuous dancing. She and her partner, Elmer Dupree, accomplished their dubious feat in 1934; they were upright and moving for over twenty-one weeks, or about five months. For their efforts, the pair shared a prize of $40. In 1938, Horace McCoy wrote a novel entitled *They Shoot Horses, Don't They?* It worked its way up the best-seller lists, and its title says it all: the dance marathons were not fun, and entrants suffered mightily for the meager prizes and free food.

Two exhausted marathon dancers. The marathon
dance craze, grueling as it was, provided a way for
teams to make a few dollars and get some free meals.
(Photograph courtesy of the Library of Congress.)

The bike races and dance marathons were but aspects of the multifaceted 1930s. In the spring of 1935, a fad emerged that swept the country:
the chain letter. So logical, so promising was the premise, that the same
craze has resurfaced every few years, although none of its later incar-
nations have ever equaled the frenzy generated by its first appearance.
A person receives a letter with five or six names and addresses listed at
the bottom. The recipient scratches the first name, and replaces it with
his or her name at the bottom of the list. But there's a catch: the recipient
must send a dime to the person whose name was scratched out. Also,
he or she must make five copies of the letter and send them to five

additional people. In five progressions—and assuming the chain remains unbroken—the sender's name rises to the top and he or she makes a small fortune in dimes. Seldom, however, does the chain remain intact, and even less frequently did anyone make any money.

It began in Denver, swamping the local post offices; even the White House got letters, as did celebrities of all kinds. After about three months of virtual hysteria, the atmosphere calmed, and by July the fad had passed. For a brief moment, however, the nation was seized with a get-rich-quick madness that overshadowed all other activities.

President Herbert Hoover, the nation's much-maligned leader at the start of the Depression, found his surname the butt of many a neologism. "Hoovercart" (and "Hooverwagon") rodeos got their beginnings in 1933. First appearing in North Carolina, but soon all the rage across the country, the events involved the back halves of Model T Fords and teams of mules. The mules were hitched to the car remnants and then raced over an obstacle course. If the whole contraption fell apart, so much the better for the merriment of the audience. Wasn't the economy doing the same thing?

The rodeos were but the first way of ridiculing the president. A "Hooverville" was a collection of tents, cardboard boxes, tarpaper shacks, and the like that sufficed as housing for the homeless and unemployed. Most larger cities had their Hoovervilles, which were usually located close to the railroad tracks. Men and women, wandering the rails in search of work, gathered at these sites, and the temporary structures served as shelter.

In a similar vein, "Hoover Blankets" were the accumulated newspapers under which the jobless and homeless would sleep. "Hoover Flags" referred to empty pockets. When people turned their pockets inside out to show they were broke, the white linings somewhat resembled flags. "Hoover Hogs" was the euphemism given rabbits that were consumed for food. Rundown shoes, usually with visible holes in the soles, became "Hoover Shoes," and "Hoover Leather" meant the cardboard used to resole them. In all fairness, not all the associations were totally negative. A "Hoovercrat" was someone who still had faith in the beleaguered president, although that usage may be damning with faint praise.

If language could make fun of the times, what better way than jokes? In the 1930s, this meant the rise of the "knock-knock joke." It goes like this:

[Set Up]: Knock. Knock.

[Response]: Who's there?

[Teaser]: Hugo

[Response]: Hugo who?

[Punch line]: Hugo your way and I'll go mine.

This fad first reached its peak in 1936. Like chain letters, knock-knock jokes have cropped up perennially ever since. There was even a minor hit by the Vincent Lopez Orchestra titled "The Knock-Knock Song." In the course of the melody, the band members would cry out, "Knock, knock!" A vocalist would respond with "Who's there?" And so it would go through yet another corny punchline, but listeners seemed to love it.

GAMES

Card games, especially bridge, rapidly rose in popularity, along with a concomitant rise in gambling. Much of the time, it was innocent enough. A company picnic might stage contests with small cash prizes. Slot machines, pinball machines, and punchboards were among the devices favored by Americans to win money effortlessly. Even churches got into the act by staging bingo in their parish halls. Some of the gambling was legal, but much of it was not. In the midst of an economic depression, however, anything that promised easy money drew an audience. A 1939 poll found that one-third of the population admitted to occasionally betting a nickel or so on a game of chance.[2]

Bingo, for instance, is the commercial name of a game that had been played at carnivals and fairs for many years before the Depression. Variations of it, called Lotto and Beano, were probably the primary inspirations for what is today called Bingo. Whatever the name, the goal was the same: as a pitchman called out numbers, players tried to line up markers (such as beans) on a prepaid and preprinted card. A completed row—diagonal, horizontal, or vertical—constituted a win and entitled the cardholder to a prize, either goods or cash.

It took Edwin S. Lowe, a man with a talent for seeing opportunity, to capitalize on the popularity of such games. He never got trademark protection for his new game, and soon competitors had their versions of Bingo, to the point that the word entered the language, both as a noun identifying the game and as an exclamation, "Bingo!" meaning that a line had been successfully filled or that something had happened. Lowe nonetheless went on to make a fortune by selling the cards and markers to churches and other charitable organizations. He created thousands of cards with nonrepeating numbers that he sold in the millions; he even published pamphlets that described how to use Bingo in fund-raising activities. By the mid-1930s, thousands of sanctioned Bingo parties were held almost every night of the week across the country. Some grumbled that it was a form of legalized gambling, and sporadic efforts were made to ban the games, but public support won out, much to the relief of small churches and fraternal lodges.[3]

Another idea that blossomed in the 1930s was the punchboard, a small

Three women playing bingo in Louisiana. This well-known game of chance gained great popularity during the Depression. (Photograph courtesy of the Library of Congress.)

block of cardboard containing 1000 holes. Each hole had a slip of paper, or "ticket," inserted in it. Only one of the tickets was a winner. For a nickel, a person could punch out a ticket and see if it was the lucky one. If it was, the fortunate soul received the grandiose sum of $2.50. Obviously, with 1000 holes, a nickel each hole, and only one $2.50 winner, punchboards were enormously profitable (1000 × .05 = $50.00 per board)—only to the house, not to those who gambled on them. By 1939, it was estimated that some 15,000 punchboards were being manufactured each and every day.

The Irish Sweepstakes (actually the Irish Hospital Sweepstakes) was another diversion popular during the thirties. It was organized in 1930 in Ireland, and legalized by the Irish government as a means of raising money for hospitals. Millions of tickets were sold worldwide each year, and only a handful of the winners were Americans, so the odds were not unlike today's lotteries. But the sweepstakes became a mania, to the point that untold numbers of counterfeit tickets were foisted on the unsuspecting.

"Poor man's billiards" was the popular name given bagatelle, a simple game that involved a board with holes at one end. In the early years of the twentieth century, all that bagatelle required was a cue and small ball. Places that had the game usually charged five cents for ten shots. If the player managed to sink all or most of the shots, prizes were given. With time and technology, bagatelle quickly grew in complexity during the 1920s and 1930s. At first, pins were arranged so as to block direct shots to a hole, and these obstacles brought about a shift in the name, to "pin games." Finally, the cue stick was eliminated, and pin games evolved into "pinball." The first pin machine, called the "Whoopie Game," came out in 1930. The shooter had to employ a mechanical plunger to propel the ball through an increasingly complex course. As before, prizes were awarded for high scores. Establishments with pinball successfully evaded the gambling laws for many years by claiming they were "games of skill," not "games of chance." By 1933, sixty-two different pinball games were available, and some 250,000 of them were sold annually.

Ping-pong, another favorite in the 1930s, had been introduced in the 1880s. Cyclical in popularity, it became a minor fad in the 1920s when Parker Brothers trademarked their sets as "Ping-Pong," taking for their own a name that had existed from the beginning of the game. "Ping-Pong" was supposed to suggest the sound of the ball hitting the paddle, and was preferred over "table tennis." In 1931, the American Ping-Pong Association was formed. This group sponsored tournaments where only Parker Brothers equipment was allowed. To compete, the New York Table Tennis Association came into being, and it had no loyalties to Parker Brothers. Sensing that they were working at cross-purposes, the two organizations finally merged as the U.S. Table Tennis Association and began to compete internationally. The 1930s saw over 10 million ping-pong players in the United States alone, and some 5 million tables in private homes.[4]

Pick-Up Sticks was introduced in 1936. The game was based on Jack Straws, an earlier American version, and Marokko, a Hungarian import. In its original form, the "jackstraw," a strip of wood with a hooked end, was used to dislodge specific numbered sticks. Trying to remove a single stick without disturbing the surrounding ones may seem a silly pastime, but it endured. In less than a year, the new version had sold 3 million sets.

For many adults, contract bridge became the rage in the 1930s. Ely Culbertson, a master at traditional bridge, popularized this form of the card game. In contract bridge, partners have to collaborate by "bidding" their hands, an attempt to inform one another of the value of individual cards. The winning team establishes a "contract" of how many tricks it anticipates taking. If this sounds confusing, it should. Bridge is not a

A game of bridge in Oklahoma. Contract bridge became a fad in the 1930s, complete with best-selling books and avidly followed tournaments. (Photograph courtesy of the Library of Congress.)

simple game, and being consistently victorious requires a mastery of the rules, along with intense concentration.

Despite the complexities of contract bridge, tournaments were soon being arranged that involved several teams and many contracts. Elaborate scoring rules, complete with extra points and penalties, were worked out and made part of the game. The more arcane the rules and scoring became, the better people seemed to like it. Even in the worst of the Depression, the sales of playing cards actually rose; some 50 million decks a year were sold during the darkest years. By 1931, over 500,000 people had signed up to take bridge lessons at YMCAs, parks, and anywhere else that offered them. It was conservatively estimated that 20 million people played the game.

Bridge tournaments had the unique distinction of being broadcast, hand-by-hand, over the radio, and experts explained rules and strategies, along with the actual play, to eager, unseen audiences. Culbertson soon found himself on the best-seller lists with a series of how-to books that eager players quickly snatched up. His first two were *Culbertson's Sum-*

mary and *The Contract Bridge Blue Book*, both initially published in 1930. The books sold steadily for years, and the second even enjoyed annual updates. He also ran a daily column in hundreds of newspapers showing how to play sample hands. At the end of the decade, Charles Goren rose to become another recognized expert on the game, and his authority rivaled Culbertson's.

Contract bridge was not the only sit-down game that had its adherents in the thirties. Board games also increased in popularity. Monopoly, the undisputed champion, made its debut in 1935. The origins of Monopoly probably date back to 1904 and something called The Landlord's Game, a little-known diversion that used real estate transactions as part of its strategy. Almost thirty years later, a gentleman named Charles Darrow borrowed from both The Landlord's Game and another real estate contest called the Atlantic City Game. This latter influence helps explain the Atlantic City addresses on the properties that players buy in Monopoly. Darrow copyrighted his mix in 1933 and sold several thousand home-made versions through the mail before attempting to get Parker Brothers, a major toy and game manufacturer, to market his creation.

In one of those classic examples of corporate shortsightedness, Parker Brothers ignored him. Monopoly was "too dull, too complex, and took too long to play," so Darrow privately printed up some sets and in 1934 got Wanamaker's Department Store in Philadelphia and F.A.O. Schwarz in New York to stock them. They were immediately successful, and Parker Brothers took a second look. Darrow and Parker Brothers finally reached an agreement in 1935, and Monopoly grew to be the most successful board game in history.[5]

It was once believed that the capitalistic focus of the game, plus the chance at great wealth, made Monopoly a favorite during the Depression. That theory has never been entirely discredited, but Monopoly's continuing popularity in strong economic times would suggest that it is popular simply because it is a good game. For kids and grown-ups alike, nothing quite equals building a hotel on Boardwalk—and then having an opponent land on it.

TOYS

The toy industry suffered during the Depression. Sales plummeted, and many companies went out of business. But, as factories closed down or slowed production, the survivors had first choice for materials. The result was a rise in the overall quality of American-made toys.

An example of a well-constructed toy is the American Flyer wagon. In 1923, the Liberty Coaster Company was founded in Chicago. By using the metal-stamping technology of the automobile industry, the firm could mass-produce sturdy wagons in great numbers. With an eye to marketing and current fads, the company changed its name to Radio Steel and Manufacturing in 1930. Despite the Depression, the business managed to produce 1500 distinctive red wagons a day—which were now called Radio Flyers. The firm mounted a mammoth display at Chicago's Century of Progress exposition featuring "Coaster Boy" astride his Radio Flyer. It stood over four stories tall, and alerted crowds to the popular product.

Toward the middle of the 1930s, Radio Steel brought out the Streak-O-Lite, a sleek wagon based on the lines of the great streamlined locomotives then setting speed records on railroads everywhere. That model was soon followed by Zep, short for Zephyr, which claimed to be influenced by the Chrysler Airflow, the nation's first mass-market streamlined car. But sales continued to be dominated by the trusty red wagon with the wooden sides beloved by generations of American children.

While the Radio Flyer epitomized quality, a flood of cheap, often shoddy toys from foreign manufacturers also came on the market. Many were made of celluloid, a highly flammable substance best known as the primary component of older motion picture film and shirt collars. Since it could be molded into virtually any shape, celluloid was widely used for inexpensive toys—baby rattles, ping-pong balls, and figurines. Japan became the world's leading exporter of celluloid products during the 1920s and 1930s, endlessly replicating much of American popular culture. Comic-strip characters, sports heroes, movie stars, and other celebrities poured forth, some done very skillfully and accurately, while others were crude caricatures. These cheap toys were associated with low quality and the mark, "Made in Japan," became a term of scorn for many Americans, although sales remained strong throughout the Depression.

Today, of course, Japanese-made products are equated with quality and the term has long since lost its pejorative meaning. Another toy originating in the Far East was the yo-yo, a simple amusement with a long history that happened to peak in the Depression. In 1929, a factory was opened in Chicago that incorporated all the most modern technical improvements, including a slipstring that allowed more tricks to be performed. Because yo-yos have a heritage in the Philippines—the name comes from a word in the Tagalog language, meaning "comeback"—a number of skilled Filipinos were hired to go to school yards and other places where children might hang out to demonstrate the new models and the latest tricks. It was a successful marketing ploy, and the yo-yo caught on. Celebrities were seen with them, Bing Crosby crooned about them, and millions bought them.

One important source for toys during the Depression originated with a cartoon character. Mickey Mouse, the animated creation of the Walt

Disney Studios, first appeared on film in 1928's *Steamboat Willie*. After that, there was no stopping Disney, his talented staff, and his equally talented business partners. By 1930 stuffed dolls modeled after Mickey were in production and the marketing of Disney products was in its initial stages. Over fifteen different Mickey Mouse toys came out in 1931 alone. In short order, the entire Disney menagerie—Mickey and Minnie, along with Donald Duck, Pluto, Goofy, the Three Little Pigs, and the Big Bad Wolf—was being packaged. The studio's cartoons of the 1930s captured a huge audience, but the paraphernalia associated with Mickey, ranging from watches, costume jewelry, and clocks to clothing, soap, and dolls, was an industry of its own.

For example, the Lionel Corporation, best known for its detailed model trains, produced a Mickey and Minnie Mouse handcar in 1934, a time when the company's sales were down. This novelty item did extremely well, and was a factor in keeping the train maker in business. Before the 1930s was over, the Walt Disney Company had established itself as one of the most successful promoters of toys and trinkets in history.

Some of the more popular toys of the 1930s were not just fun; they were also merchandised as being educational. For example, the Playskool Manufacturing Company was founded in 1928. Its catalog featured the classic hammer, nail, and peg table, a basic toy for toddlers designed to teach hand-eye coordination. Similarly, Holgate began in 1930, and made its fame with quality building blocks loved by generations of children. Countless American youngsters have happily pounded away at the sturdy pegs and built endless fortresses, little realizing that they were also learning in the process.

Miniature tin and lead soldiers, items marketed more to boys than to girls, enjoyed substantial sales. Expensive hand-painted soldiers have always had a certain fascination among serious collectors, but the cheap, mass-produced variety sold in enormous numbers for just pennies. Most were crude and not terribly realistic, but that did not seem to deter boys intent on staging backyard battles against their friends' collections. Perhaps it was the threat of a new world war that spurred the popularity of infantrymen, tanks, cannons, and other martial miniatures.

Many children could not afford store-bought toys during the Depression, but they did not lack for playthings. Many popular games and toys emerged during the 1930s that were handmade. Some were truly one-of-a-kind originals; others were taken from plans in magazines, or based on passed-on ideas, or modeled on commercial products. Supplies were abundant: tin cans, orange crates, rope and twine, discarded tires, odd screws and nails, and half-empty cans of paint. It just depended on the diligence of the seeker to locate them.

Rubber-band guns were perfect for shooting desperadoes. The "pistol" was a piece of scrap wood, and the "ammunition" consisted of bands taken from old inner tubes. Nothing could beat a thrilling ride on a homemade scooter on a long downhill city street. Music could be made with all manner of whistles crafted from willow or cane, and the really ambitious might construct a working banjo from a cigar box and some odd pieces of wood. The "strings" were stretched rubber bands. Modern communication could be accomplished with a tin can telephone, a simple affair consisting of two empty cans and a long piece of string. With the string held taut, voices could be carried for two backyards or so. Stilts, noisemakers, miniature boats, kites, slingshots, hoops, and on and on— these makeshift substitutes probably never threatened toy manufacturers' sales, but for millions of kids during the Depression years, they rivaled any commercial versions.[6]

HOBBIES

With high unemployment and reduced working hours, hobbies of every description boomed during the bust. Some were enriching, others were time killers and nothing more. For instance, radio can be seen as a valuable source of information or entertainment, but simply listening to the radio is one way to spend a day, and many people did just that. The same could be said for going to the movies or window shopping. These activities may not qualify as traditional hobbies, but they were the activities of many short on cash and long on time.

More rewarding pursuits also flourished during this troubling decade, and the hobby industry expanded while other businesses were closing their doors. In addition, municipalities sponsored hobby clubs, how-to classes, and the like. By having regular activities in a structured setting, the work ethic was reinforced even for the unemployed. New job skills, like woodworking or auto mechanics, could be learned in a relaxed, no-risk atmosphere, and leisure was turned into a kind of substitute work. A concerted effort was made by commentators and politicians to define the hobbyist as someone who actively participated in an avocation and, in so doing, learned from it and was productive.[7]

In response, innumerable city dwellers took up gardening. It was a good way to save on food bills, the start-up costs were minimal, and the work was healthy. Community plots could be found in most cities, with neighbors dividing up both chores and space. Garden clubs, once the domains of well-to-do ladies of leisure, welcomed a much more diverse membership, and the exchange and expansion of gardening lore became their primary focus.

Hobbies magazine debuted in 1931, followed by hobby columns in many newspapers and magazines. "Hobby Lobby" was a radio show broadcast by over 150 stations in the mid-1930s; it made listeners aware of new activities, particularly those that helped others in some way. Special interest clubs of every sort strove to get their ideas on the show, and the voluntarism espoused by "Hobby Lobby" led to the formation of still more clubs. By the end of the decade, the "new leisure" was highly organized and publicized.

Despite all the emphasis on being productive and learning new skills, many of the most popular hobbies of the 1930s were not productive and taught no new skills. For example, proponents of hobbies as a form of work would argue for cutting the intricate pieces of a jigsaw puzzle by hand and then selling the finished product. But others, looking for a momentary diversion with no particular gain in mind other than whiling away some hours pleasurably, preferred simply to assemble the puzzle. Its creation held no interest. Either way, jigsaw puzzles were one of the most popular time killers of the Depression. At first, they tended to be intricately cut from wood and rather expensive, so their market was limited. But 1934 saw the introduction of die-cut cardboard puzzles. These were so cheap that they could be given away as premiums. Jigsaw puzzles were available everywhere, from newsstands to book stores, from upscale department stores to Woolworth's.

At the beginning of 1932, over 2 million puzzles were sold weekly. Stores featured "puzzles of the week" and "weekly jigs." By late 1932 and early 1933, their peak years, jigsaw puzzles were selling at the rate of 10 million a week. Puzzle clubs sprang up, and members swapped favorites with friends, thereby keeping costs down. Stores rented puzzles, just like lending libraries. The craze cooled down with the inauguration of Franklin Roosevelt, although sales remained high throughout the decade. With the introduction of the New Deal, a major "puzzle" had been solved—or so it was hoped—and perhaps the country no longer felt such a pressing need for the die-cut picture variety.

Another hobby that involved lots of small pieces was stamp collecting. Although the saving of postage stamps dates back to the nineteenth century, it really gained publicity during the 1930s. President Roosevelt was an ardent collector, and his enthusiasm led others to the hobby. In addition, the decade saw countless new American commemorative stamps printed, and that in itself piqued public interest. Of course, it did not hurt that Roosevelt's postmaster general was James A. Farley, a close friend who delighted in supporting his boss's passion by constantly ordering up new issues. The president himself, enjoying one of the perquisites of high office, actually designed a number of American commemorative stamps and was probably the envy of collectors around the nation.[8]

During the decade, stamps honored everything under the sun, from current and historic events (1932 Olympics; Chicago's Century of Progress, 1933), holidays (Arbor Day, 1932; Mother's Day, 1934), famous people (George Washington bicentennial, 1932; Admiral Richard E. Byrd, 1933) to the land itself (national parks, 1934; U.S. territories, 1937). By and large, the U.S. stamps of the 1930s are especially handsome, produced from exquisitely detailed engravings. It was a wonderful time for philatelists, and the sales of albums and related paraphernalia reflect the ever-increasing numbers of people taking up the hobby. Schools and churches encouraged philately, and there was even a radio program for collectors.

Woodworking, ceramics, model airplanes, collectibles, coins, railroad layouts, watercolors and oils, hiking and camping, photography—the list of hobbies pursued during the 1930s is endless. Their most important contribution during the Depression years was a capacity to impart a sense of self-worth to the hobbyist. Jobs might be scarce, but working hard at a hobby fulfilled the need for self-esteem—that what a person was doing had value—and the hobby itself took attention away from the economic difficulties of the day.

SPORTS

The 1930s increasingly saw the mixing of business and entertainment with sports. The spectacular rise of radio as a mass medium meant that athletics of any kind could now be brought into the home. The sports broadcaster, or "sportscaster," took on an important role at stations and networks. Colleges and universities, realizing that there was money to be made from athletics, hired sports information directors whose job it was to promote whatever sport was being played. This professionalization of athletics meant that winning became all-important. With only a few exceptions, the gentleman amateur, such an important figure in earlier sports history, became a relic of the past. The decade instead saw the rise of the player who also earned a paycheck.

Television, still in its developmental stage, was not a factor in any of these important shifts. But change was in the air; the 1930s were but a prelude. The year 1939 saw the first telecast of a major league baseball game—the Brooklyn Dodgers against the Cincinnati Reds. It was not the first sporting event ever presented on the new medium, but its success promised it would not be the last. American sports would never be the same again.

Baseball

The Depression had a serious, negative impact on professional baseball. Attendance plummeted throughout the decade, and did not recover until after 1945. One explanation for this drop in spectators was that people could no longer afford to attend ball games. But, like most simplistic approaches, that is only part of the answer.

American baseball is clothed in layers of imagery and myth. Lights and night play form a case in point. For traditionalists, baseball had always been a "daylight game," and 3 P.M. was the proper starting time. The owners tended to oppose any modernization, any new technology. As always, a deep-seated profit motive underlay most of their objections. Economics, however, also brought about some changes of heart. In 1935, the Cincinnati Reds, despite objections, installed lights so they could play night games, and their attendance soared. Other teams either quickly followed suit or were planning for the change. In another move to boost attendance, 1933 saw the first major-league All-Star Game played. It was done in conjunction with Chicago's Century of Progress Exposition, but quickly became an annual event.[9]

The biggest star in major league ball at the beginning of the decade was Babe Ruth. Others—Lou Gehrig, Dizzy Dean, Joe Dimaggio—attracted fans, but none was so towering as Ruth. In 1930, he made $80,000 as a Yankee—more than any other player, and more than President Hoover. Quipped Ruth, "I had a better year." He epitomized the Horatio Alger story, going from rags to riches and achieving power. He was raised in an orphanage, was always in trouble, but his talent overshadowed everything. For the fans, he was "The Sultan of Swat," "The Great Bambino." But Ruth, great as he was, also epitomized something else: in many ways he was the product of publicity, a figure created by mass media and zealous press agents.

Traditionally, baseball was covered by newspapers or specialized journals. *The Sporting News*, founded in 1886, was the premier sports magazine of the 1930s. By the Depression the *News* devoted most of its reporting to baseball, and enjoyed a high level of respect among fans. Newspapers emulated *The Sporting News*, thereby popularizing complete box scores and all the endless statistics and in-depth articles about players that have come to characterize baseball reporting. Starting in the 1920s, and continuing throughout the 1930s, newspapers sent their best sportswriters on the road, accompanying the home team as it played away games. Reporters like Daniel M. Daniel, Marshall Hunt, Red Smith, Paul Gallico, Ring Lardner, and Grantland Rice became celebrated in their own right as they followed the game.

Radio, it was discovered, was an effective way to relate the events of a game—as it was being played. A knowledgeable commentator could make the game live in people's homes. At first, the owners and leagues opposed broadcasting games, arguing that it would keep away the crowds, and newspapers and *The Sporting News* likewise tended to deride the practice. In a makeshift agreement, two stations per community were usually allowed to broadcast games, but that modest figure soon grew.

By 1938, 260 stations were carrying baseball, and there would be no turning back.

As a rule, much radio baseball in the 1930s was not actually "live." It just seemed that way. The broadcast was a re-created game, a narrative done in a studio, not at the ballpark. Because of technical limitations, the sportscaster frequently was isolated behind a microphone in a studio, relying on telephones to bring him details of the unfolding contest. His real job entailed filling empty airtime, creating the illusion of constant action. "Chatter" was his skill, and millions faithfully listened to descriptions of a runner sliding home or a "long, pop fly to center field . . . he's under it . . . ," and so on for nine innings.

By the early 1930s, sports ranked second only to music in terms of airtime, and a new generation of electronic reporters came to the fore. Tom Manning, Jack Graney, Bill Dyer, Ted Husing, Arch McDonald, Fred Hoey, and Harry Caray became household names as they breathlessly broadcast the play-by-play over the family Philco radio. A young man named "Dutch" Reagan did Chicago Cubs games for an Iowa station. He later became an actor, and finally the fortieth president of the United States.[10]

Together, the sportswriters and sportscasters tended to create images of athletes that often exceeded their actual feats. Thus the era was witness to the rise of the sports celebrity and sports hero or idol. The rigorous training and endless practice were forgotten, replaced by images of instant success and adulation for the lucky few. This attitude was carried over into several baseball films, but nothing of great merit. Comedian Joe E. Brown starred in *Elmer the Great* (1933) and *Alibi Ike* (1935), and Rita Hayworth had a bit part in *Girls Can Play* (1937), but baseball proved difficult for the silver screen during the 1930s.

Softball

The game of softball originated in 1887 as a form of "indoor baseball." With its larger, softer ball, it was suited for play in gymnasiums and other indoor facilities. It was not until 1926, however, that the game got its present name and began working seriously toward standardized rules. With the onset of the Depression, softball bloomed, as factories and offices, schools, churches, unions, and even neighborhoods put nine players on the field.

Various championships attracted sizable numbers of spectators by 1932, and more national attention was being focused on the game. The Chicago World's Fair of 1933 sponsored a softball tournament with designated slow- and fast-pitch categories. These events garnered considerable publicity, and it is estimated that over a million Americans played softball in some capacity by 1936. Both the CBS and NBC radio networks covered national championships, and the numbers of players kept growing; by the end of the decade, 5 million Americans participated, and almost a quarter of them were women. Millions more came to the games as avid fans, and attempts were being made to create professional softball teams.[11]

As part of the national recovery effort, the government built thousands of parks and recreational areas around the country; not surprisingly, many were constructed with the official dimensions of a softball diamond clearly in mind. The National Youth Administration (NYA) also assisted in building fields on private property, allowing churches and fraternal organizations to have proper playing areas. The Federal Rural Electrification Program introduced night lighting to hundreds of such fields long before the major baseball leagues enjoyed night play. So widespread was softball that many sporting equipment manufacturers saw an upturn in business despite the economic hard times. It did not hurt that President Roosevelt himself sponsored a team, the White House Purgers. In many ways, softball was the true national pastime. It was open to virtually anyone, regardless of social or economic status.

Football

In contrast to today, football was not nearly so publicized during the 1930s. For the average spectator, professional games were virtually invisible, being played before small crowds on open fields or in small stadiums. About the only version of football that had much of a following was the college variety. Colleges and universities therefore worked hard at stirring popular interest in the game. In 1935 the Orange Bowl was created, followed in 1936 by the Sun Bowl, and in 1937 by the Sugar Bowl and the Cotton Bowl.

Schools also instituted rule changes that quickened the play of football and cut down on injuries. In 1932, a clause was introduced into collegiate rules that stated the ball became dead when any part of the player (except feet and hands) touched the ground. Padding became a requirement, and in 1939 helmets were mandated for collegiate players. The size of the ball was reduced so it was easier to grasp. This led to more passing and a more visual game. Quarterback Sammy Baugh, who graduated from Texas Christian University in 1937 and joined the Washington Redskins, displayed superlative passing abilities that earned him the name "Slingin' Sammy" (he actually threw in a sidearm style). He became a football star in the late 1930s.

Because football is a visual game and can be fast-moving and violent, there were more movies about it during the 1930s than about any other sport. In 1931 alone, theaters were showing *Mickey's Stampede* and *The Spirit of Notre Dame* (the latter dedicated, of course, to Knute Rockne, the fabled Notre Dame coach), plus two documentaries, *Football Thrills* and *Pro Football*, the latter a Pete Smith "Oddity." Smith built a career around humorous films that purported to "tell all" about numerous sports.

The following year, *70,000 Witnesses*, *Hold 'em Jail*, *That's My Boy*, *All American*, and *Rackety Rax* were entertaining audiences. Even the Marx Brothers got into the action with *Horse Feathers*, a spoof on college football. Groucho plays the president of a small college who is determined to win the big game, and the result is riotous nonsense. After a pause, three more titles joined the cinematic football ranks in 1936: *Pigskin Parade*, *Rose Bowl*, and *The Big Game*; the last includes a host of real collegiate stars. *Pigskin Parade* is interesting because it offered a young Judy Garland her first major role. *Two Minutes to Play* and *Life Begins in College*, the latter featuring the Ritz Brothers, a brother act similar to the Marx Brothers, were on marquees in 1937, as was *Pigskin Skill*, another Pete Smith "Specialty." The forgettable *Cowboy Quarterback* closed out the decade in 1939.

Basketball

Like football, basketball was primarily a collegiate sport. For professional basketball, there were two groups, the American Basketball League (ABL), established in 1933, and the National Basketball League (NBL), created in 1937. The two leagues merged to form the National Basketball Association (NBA) in 1949. Despite the attempts at organization, American basketball during the 1930s consisted largely of individual teams and colleges. Only a few stars emerged, and the sport had to struggle to survive.

At the beginning of the decade, basketball was a slow, low-scoring sport. Scores of 18–14 or 21–15 were not uncommon for an entire game. Defense ruled the game, not offense. In an attempt to speed things up, the leagues adopted the ten-second rule in 1932, meaning that a team must shoot the ball at the basket within ten seconds. Each time a basket was made, the ball was returned to center court and the players had to reassemble for a new tip-off. That cumbersome rule was abolished in the 1937–1938 season. The first big college tournament was held in 1934 at Madison Square Garden. It attracted enough fans that it was continued, and by 1938 it had become the National Invitational Tournament (NIT).

Hank Luisetti of Stanford University was probably the first real basketball star. He scored 1500 points between 1936 and 1939, and he perfected the one-handed jump shot. Until then, virtually all shots were two-handed. His popularity earned him top billing in a 1938 movie called *Campus Confessions*. Hardly a lurid tale, despite its title, it was billed as "a peppy college romance [with] a real basketball game!"

Elite Sports: Horse Racing, Tennis, and Golf

Three sports in the United States have traditionally been viewed as the pursuits of the wealthy: horse racing, tennis, and golf. During the Depression era they were particularly suspect. Yet, for brief periods during the decade, each enjoyed wide public attention and emerged as front-page news.

In racing, a horse named Gallant Fox captivated millions. This steed galloped to victories in the Preakness, the Belmont Stakes, and the Kentucky Derby during the 1930 season. The accomplishment meant that Gallant Fox had won the Triple Crown, racing's highest honor. Keeping it all in the family, Gallant Fox's son Omaha repeated the feat in 1935. And, War Admiral managed it yet again in 1937, thus maintaining a high level of interest in the "sport of kings" throughout the decade.

A visual competition, horse racing got the Hollywood treatment in *Sporting Blood* (1931; an early Clark Gable effort), *David Harum* (1934; with Will Rogers), *Kentucky Blue Streak* (1935), *Wine, Women and Horses* (1937), and *The Day the Bookies Wept* (1939; with a rising Betty Grable). Probably the best-known racing movie of the decade, however, is the Marx Brothers' *A Day at the Races* (1937). The zany trio pretty much takes away any mystique the sport might possess. The Ritz Brothers once again tried to compete with *Straight, Place and Show*, an anemic offering that came out in 1938.

Like horse racing, tennis also suffered from the problem of perception. Although it was estimated that some 11 million Americans played the game during the 1930s, many people saw it as an activity for a wealthy, leisured class.

"Big Bill" Tilden, the leading player of the later 1920s, gave up his amateur standing in 1931 and turned professional. In those days, professional players were virtually invisible, as far as the public was concerned. They played at private clubs and were ineligible for the major tournaments. With his departure, the game was relegated to the back pages of the sports section. Not until 1938 was any real interest in tennis revived. That was the year Don Budge achieved the Grand Slam of tennis: he won the Australian, French, English (Wimbledon), and the U.S. Open tournaments, all amateur events. The first player ever to do it, he was rewarded with a torrent of publicity. Ever so briefly, tennis reappeared on the front pages. But Budge turned pro shortly thereafter and, like Tilden before him, disappeared.

Golf also was perceived as a "rich man's sport," and did not come into its own until after the end of World War II. The 1930s fueled this point of view, especially with a depression going on, but golf nevertheless captured the public imagination for a moment. What stirred Americans was a young amateur from Georgia named Bobby Jones. Unlike tennis, both professionals and amateurs could play in "open" tournaments. Jones achieved in golf what many thought was unattainable: the "Grand Slam." In 1930 he won the British Amateur and the British Open. When he returned to America, he received a ticker-tape parade in New York City. But that was just the start. He followed those victories by winning both the U.S. Open and the U.S. Amateur championships, giving him all four major championships. This feat allowed Jones to bask in reams of media-generated celebrity.

In the popular mind, Bobby Jones was the little guy beating the pros. The public took him to its heart, and golf had its first real superstar. He soon retired from the game, but remained in the limelight throughout the decade. He had a weekly radio show that re-created highlights of his illustrious career, he made several golf instruction films for Warner Brothers, he lent his name to Spalding for a new line of clubs, and he was instrumental in designing and setting up a new course in Augusta, Georgia, that became home to the Master's Golf Tournament.

The Depression did have one beneficial side effect for everyday golfers. As memberships fell off in once-exclusive country clubs and private courses, the directors had to open them to public play. In addition, many municipal courses were built during the Depression years, doubling the number a decade earlier.

Miniature Golf

Although traditional golf had its followers, another form of the game completely eclipsed it: miniature golf. The fad swept the country in 1930. It was estimated that 4 million Americans played miniature golf on any given day at 40,000 different courses. It had first appeared at a place called Fairyland, a tourist attraction on Lookout Mountain, Tennessee, and was devised by Garnet Carter. He quickly sensed great potential in the sport and adopted an artificial turf composed of cottonseed hulls that provided a good putting surface. Once his creation began catching on, Carter could not control it, and innumerable competitors entered the picture. In response, he organized a National Tom Thumb Open Championship at Fairyland in 1930. The event attracted many players, but by this time miniature golf was a true fad and had spread across the country. Carter's tournament was but one of many competitive events.

Courses appeared on empty lots, rooftops, roadsides, and anywhere else there was a level surface. It took little capital to establish a barebones layout, although the more elaborate constructions could cost tens of thousands of dollars. In the meantime, the obstacles grew in size and imagination, and skill became secondary to complexity and challenge. There seemed no end in sight for the game, and then the bubble sud-

A home-built miniature golf course in Chicago. Miniature golf swept the nation in 1930, and courses—some fancy, some not—sprang up everywhere. By 1931, however, the fad had died out. (Photograph courtesy of the Library of Congress.)

denly burst. By 1931, the fad was over, and empty miniature golf courses littered the landscape.[12]

Boxing

A pole apart from any other sport was—and is—boxing, a bruising, bloody contest. In its marketing, it would seem that the audience for this spectacle consists primarily of red-faced men with cigars and derbies; clearly, it was not for women. Americans have always been of two minds about professional prizefighting: supporters see the sport as a demonstration of the "manly art of self defense," a choreographed dance between two opponents employing both science and brawn. The opposition reads no poetics into it, but views it as legalized mayhem, even slaughter. Both sides found support for their arguments during the 1930s, when professional boxing made news headlines almost constantly. For most Americans, "boxing" translates as heavyweight boxing. The other divisions—featherweight, lightweight, welterweight, et al.—mean little, and therefore receive only cursory attention. And, in a kind of musical chairs, the heavyweight crown rested uneasily on a series of heads until 1937.

The rotation began in 1930, when the German boxer Max Schmeling gained the heavyweight title by defeating the reigning champion, the American Jack Sharkey. Schmeling lost to Sharkey in a fifteen-round rematch in 1932. Next, Primo Carnera of Italy knocked out Sharkey for the title in 1933. Carnera was in turn kayoed by Max Baer in 1934. In the next shuffling, Jim Braddock defeated Baer in 1935. More important, perhaps, was a 1936 nontitle bout involving former champion Schmeling and a rising young American boxer named Joe Louis. Schmeling floored Louis and seemed in line to regain the title. But Schmeling was denied the bout, and Louis instead faced Braddock in 1937. Louis won the fight and was proclaimed the world's heavyweight champion.

Joe Louis reigned, undefeated, from 1937 until 1949 and his retirement. He defended his title twenty-five times—his opponents were dubbed "Bum of the Month"—and proved an immensely popular champion. But of all his victories, none was sweeter than his defeat of Schmeling in a much-ballyhooed 1938 championship fight, a match that incidentally established the power of radio. More than half the radio owners in the United States—over 22 million people—listened in as Louis pummeled his hapless opponent. It was, simply, the "good" Louis versus the "bad" Schmeling. For both fighters, tremendous national pride was at stake. Schmeling's handlers talked of him as the "hope of the Aryan race," and the Nazi propaganda machine spewed out reams of racist hate in the days before the fight. The quiet Louis—"The Brown Bomber"—typified much that was good about America in an era of segregation in most sports, and hopes ran high. Once in the ring, Schmeling was down and out in the first round, and the nation breathed a collective sigh of relief. Louis's decisive victory salvaged American honor, and it silenced many racists and Nazi sympathizers.

Although few Americans ever attended a prizefight, there was nevertheless much public interest in the so-called sport. Hollywood found staging and filming a match an easy thing to do, and a number of fight movies were made during the 1930s. The opening of the decade saw *The Big Fight*, starring "that shufflin' laugh-maker, Stepin Fetchit," a popular black comedian who unfortunately was forced to take on many stereotypical roles. Joe E. Brown lent his comedic talents to *Hold Everything* (1930), and Wallace Beery and Jackie Cooper made the justly famous *The Champ* in 1931. James Cagney continued his action films with 1932's *Winner Take All*. An emerging Spencer Tracy has a bit part in *Society Girl* (1932). *Police Call* (1933) is actually a "B" boxing epic, as are *Kelly the Second* (1936) and *The Kid Comes Back* (1937). Better by far is *Cain and Mabel* (1936), a big-budget pugilistic comedy with Clark Gable and Marion Davies. Ham Fisher's popular comic strip character Joe Palooka is featured in *For the Love of Pete* (1936) and *Taking the Count* (1937). Two boxing features with primarily black casts are *Spirit of Youth* (1937; starring Joe Louis as himself) and *Keep Punching* (1939; featuring light heavyweight Henry Armstrong). Finally, *They Made Me a Criminal* (1939, with John Garfield) and a screen adaptation of Clifford Odets' *Golden Boy* (1939; featuring William Holden in a star-making role) take a more serious look at the fight business. Boxing may have not been universally liked, but during the 1930s it was certainly part and parcel of American popular culture.

Skiing

Until 1932 and the Winter Olympics at Lake Placid, New York, most Americans had never attempted skiing. Unless a person lived near some mountains, the opportunity simply had not presented itself; it needed more promotion. In 1931, the first Ski Train was organized. It consisted of a passenger train that took members of a Boston ski club to the New England slopes. By the time of Lake Placid, Northeastern railroads were running a number of special trains to nearby ski resorts.

In those simpler days, skiing required little: wooden poles, hickory skis, and leather bindings were sufficient. The first tow, a simple rope affair, came in 1932, and the lodges tended to be rustic and cheap. All the fanciness and expense associated with the activity came later, although a glimpse of the future came in 1936 when the Union Pacific Railroad opened Sun Valley in Idaho. This extensive resort attracted many to winter sports.

Hollywood was late in recognizing the potential in skiing, but finally cranked out *Winter Carnival* in 1939, one of the first of many such movies. In the meantime, the public got ahead of the movies; by 1940, over 2 million Americans skied regularly.

Ice-Skating

Sonja Henie, a native Norwegian, emerged in the 1930s as an ice-skating star, and she went far in gaining popularity for the sport. She earned gold medals for figure skating in the 1928, 1932, and 1936 Olympics, as well as numerous other titles and championships. Henie retired from competition in 1936, joined a professional skating revue, and then tried the movies. She was an instant hit. Her films were usually set in some kind of winter wonderland that allowed her to display her expertise on ice. Pictures like *One in a Million* (1936), *Thin Ice* (1937), *Happy Landing* (1938), and *Second Fiddle* (1939) delighted audiences and convinced millions of people to go out and buy a pair of skates. During Henie's years of stardom, the number of skating rinks in the United

States increased dramatically, and how many would-be Olympians were trying jumps and twirls on frozen ponds and lakes will never be known.

Swimming

Clarence "Buster" Crabbe and Johnny Weissmuller parlayed Olympic exploits into profitable movie careers. Both had swum during the 1920s and attracted some public attention. In 1932 Weissmuller starred in *Tarzan, the Ape Man*, becoming, in the process, the definitive Tarzan for many. Then in 1933 Crabbe did a serial, *Tarzan the Fearless*, and a Tarzan look-alike film entitled *King of the Jungle*. Weissmuller came right back in 1934 with *Tarzan and His Mate*. He went on to make ten more Tarzan films, whereas Crabbe shifted to science fiction, playing both Buck Rogers and Flash Gordon in several popular serials. By this time swimming had become secondary for both actors, although many of their films allowed them to plunge into water and demonstrate their expertise. Finally, they both got to don bathing suits for the New York World's Fair. They were featured in Billy Rose's Aquacade, a water spectacle that attracted large crowds and further helped popularize swimming.

Auto Racing

By the Depression, American racing cars had gotten larger, the speeds were higher, and the major domestic automakers displayed an interest in the sport. Public attention mounted as Buick, Chrysler, Ford, Hudson, Packard, and Studebaker all developed custom speedsters, and the Indianapolis 500 served as a kind of proving ground for automotive innovation. By 1936, the first Daytona 250 had been held, utilizing the beach, dunes, and track. The winning speed was just slightly over 70 mph.

Hollywood reacted by churning out a spate of racetrack films: James Cagney in *The Crowd Roars* (1932), Wallace Reid in *The Racing Strain* (1933), Paul Kelly in *Speed Devils* (1935), Ann Sheridan and Pat O'Brien in *Indianapolis Speedway* (1939), and even a Buck Jones Western, *Ride 'Em Cowboy!* (1936), a mix of horses and horsepower. The audience was limited, but it was enthusiastic.

Bowling

Bowling got significant media coverage in the 1930s. Newspapers in particular devoted considerable space to detailed averages and scores. Bowling alleys flourished and, unlike today's totally automated complexes, boys set the pins by hand, hoping no stray balls would come

Jesse Owens accepting a gold medal for the broad jump at the 1936 Summer Olympics. Owens's achievements in track and field were particularly noteworthy and countered much racist Nazi propaganda of the era. (Photograph courtesy of the Library of Congress.)

crashing into them. Churches, schools, offices, and industries all sponsored leagues.

Metro-Goldwyn-Mayer produced an unusual short film—MGM labeled it an "Oddity"—entitled *Strikes and Spares* in 1934. Put together and narrated by Pete Smith, the creator of a number of such movies about various sports, it consists of tricks and stunts performed by professional bowler Andy Varipupa.

OLYMPICS

In the summer of 1936, the Olympics were held in Berlin, Germany. By this time, Adolf Hitler had risen to become that nation's leader, and he was determined to make the Olympics a showplace for his National Socialist, or Nazi, party and its ideologies. Americans were vaguely aware of Nazism and its racist politics, but the truth became more widely known during the Summer Games. Hitler banned all German Jews from participating, a move that led to calls urging other nations to boycott the games, but to no avail. In fact, two American Jewish athletes were prevented by their coach, not German authorities, from running in the 400-meter relay in order to avoid controversy.

During the games, Jesse Owens, a black track star from Ohio State University, distinguished himself and brought honor to the United States by winning four gold medals: the 100- and 200-meter dashes, the broad jump, and as a member of the 400-meter relay team mentioned above. Hitler was appalled, since Owens victories challenged the Nazi view of Aryan superiority. He refused to award the medals personally (German officials had also attempted to handicap Owens), and the resultant storm of publicity awakened many Americans to the true nature of Nazi-run Germany.

It may have been a time of economic crisis, but Americans responded by actively participating in a variety of sports. And when they were not actually playing, they were lively spectators.

8

Literature

BACKGROUND

The Great Depression put millions of Americans out of work. Through-out the decade, unemployment was a problem that would not go away; despite the efforts of government and industry, it hovered over the coun-try, a dilemma that resisted even the best-intentioned solutions. If any advantage accrues from being jobless, it is the gift of time. For many, however, time was an onerous burden, emphasizing their loss of work. But for others, it allowed the freedom to read. The print media enjoyed large audiences throughout the 1930s; books continued to be published in quantity, new magazines appeared, and newspaper readership re-mained strong.

BOOKS

Best-sellers

There are a few surprises about what people read during the 1930s. Some of the so-called "classics" of the period—at least in current critical estimates—appealed to only a few, or to specific segments of the audi-ence. In the publishing world, many works sell slowly but steadily, and therefore remain in print. They are seldom ranked as best-sellers, but over the years may gain huge sales and readership. On the other hand, a substantial number of the era's most popular titles—based on sales alone—are today forgotten. Often, it takes hindsight to recognize quality, just as it is easy to get swept up in enthusiasm for something more ephemeral.

In the 1930s, to be considered a true best-seller, a book had to sell over 1 million copies in a short period of time, usually a year or less. Many succeeded, despite the economic downturn. In those days, virtually all books were available only in hardbound editions. Cheaper paperback reprints did not become a major force in American publishing until 1939 and the founding of Pocket Books. At the time of their introduction, softcover books were an immediate success, and other publishers quickly began releasing their own imprints. With the advent of the inexpensive paperback, many genres of literature, such as westerns, mysteries, adventure tales, and science fiction, went almost exclusively to a paperback format, with only a few thousand copies being released in hardcover.

An overriding theme of escapism runs through a large percentage of the popular books of the decade. Almost half of the best-selling novels of the period 1930–1939 are detective stories. Works with exotic locales and historical settings were also strong contenders, with about a quarter of the titles fitting that broad category. Erskine Caldwell (1903–1987), a writer of earthy tales about the South, practically carved out a genre for himself with three big sellers (*Tobacco Road*, 1932; *God's Little Acre*, 1933; and *Journeyman*, 1935), but he pales in comparison to a pair of detective novelists, Ellery Queen and Erle Stanley Gardner.

"Ellery Queen" was actually the pen name of two cousins, Frederic Dannay (1905–1982) and Manfred B. Lee (1905–1971). The duo began their joint career in the 1920s, and became consistent writers of best-sellers in the 1930s and 1940s with titles like *The Dutch Shoe Mystery* (1931), *The Egyptian Cross Mystery* (1932), and *The Chinese Orange Mystery* (1934). Their stories are tales of detection, with little violence beyond the mandatory murder that sets the case in motion.

Even more impressive is the accomplishment of Erle Stanley Gardner (1889–1970). This prolific writer who had penned over eighty mysteries by the time of his death will always be remembered for creating the character of Perry Mason, a resourceful lawyer/detective who never lost a case, no matter what the odds. The first Perry Mason, *The Case of the Velvet Claws*, appeared in 1933. From then on, there was no stopping Gardner. In the 1930s alone he wrote twenty-four detective novels under his own name, and one under the pseudonym A.A. Fair. In sheer sales, Gardner was far and away the best-selling writer of the period, if not the entire twentieth century. Perry Mason entered the popular pantheon of heroes, a character known to virtually everyone, whether from the novels themselves or from six feature films cranked out by Hollywood during the decade: *The Case of the Howling Dog*, 1934; *The Case of the Curious Bride*, 1935; *The Case of the Lucky Legs*, 1935; *The Case of the Velvet*

Claws, 1936; *The Case of the Black Cat*, 1936; and *The Case of the Stuttering Bishop*, 1937.[1]

Not everything written in the Depression era dealt with detectives. Four of the top-selling novels of the 1930s focused on history and a sense of place and continuity. In each the land provides roots and belonging. *God's Little Acre* (Erskine Caldwell, 1933), *Gone with the Wind* (Margaret Mitchell, 1936), *The Good Earth* (Pearl S. Buck, 1931), and *The Grapes of Wrath* (John Steinbeck, 1939) told huge audiences that it was of utmost importance to establish this kind of connection to the soil, to the land. It was destructive to be a wanderer, to be out of touch with one's heritage.

Of the four, nobody told that story better than Margaret Mitchell (1900–1949). A reporter for the Atlanta *Journal*, Mitchell began writing *Gone with the Wind* in 1926, ostensibly for her own amusement, if the mountains of publicity for the novel and its author are to be believed. The story of Scarlett O'Hara, Rhett Butler, and Tara (Scarlett's family home) has become part of the national memory. By the end of the decade, the book had gone through innumerable reprintings, was available in a variety of translations, and continued to sell briskly. In 1939, three years after the book's initial publication, the movie version electrified audiences, becoming one of the greatest films Hollywood ever turned out, yet remaining a faithful adaptation of the novel.[2]

The remarkable acceptance of *Gone with the Wind* perplexed—and angered—a number of critics who charged that it was little more than a Southern soap opera. Their complaints, however, fell on deaf ears. Success does not automatically equate with mediocrity, although serious, thoughtful commentary on the novel was long in coming. Here was the perfect Depression-era story, a tale of people beset with every conceivable calamity and how they overcame disaster. The closing words of the novel, spoken by the indomitable Scarlett, seemed to many a prescription for all the problems of the time: "I'll think of it all tomorrow. . . . After all, tomorrow is another day."[3]

Margaret Mitchell joined a group of popular historians who took events, wrapped them in fiction, and produced some of the most entertaining and well-received novels ever written. Writers like Pearl S. Buck (*The Good Earth*, 1931), Charles Nordhoff and James Norman Hall (*Mutiny on the Bounty*, 1932), and Hervey Allen (*Anthony Adverse*, 1933) had already achieved success in this area. Walter D. Edmonds (*Drums Along the Mohawk*, 1936) and Kenneth Roberts (*Northwest Passage*, 1937) continued with romantic narratives about the American past, a topic that grew in popularity throughout the troubled decade. Hollywood, always alert to any trends, made big-budget movies of all these novels, capitalizing on their enormous renown at the time.

Some writers attempted to speak more directly to the Depression, but they could never gain the readership of those who clothed their novels

Author Margaret Mitchell and her best-selling novel,
Gone with the Wind (1936). The 1939 movie version of
this popular book served to heighten its appeal.
(Photograph courtesy of the Library of Congress.)

in historical wraps. James T. Farrell (1904–1979) took a decidedly anti-capitalist view in his naturalistic *Studs Lonigan* trilogy (1932–1935), and John Dos Passos (1896–1970) was openly Marxist in his trilogy *USA* (1930–1936). Both novelists had many loyal readers, and certainly their work has come down to the present as significant contributions to American literature, but they were hardly best-sellers in their own time. Even John Steinbeck (1902–1968) trod proletarian ground in *In Dubious Battle* (1936), then returned to some of those themes in 1939 with his hugely successful *The Grapes of Wrath*. In fact, *The Grapes of Wrath* stands as one of the few books critical of the American political and economic system ever to achieve widespread popular success.

Nonfiction

In nonfiction, relatively little that was written about the Depression, the New Deal, or the impending war sold well. These events were present in people's thoughts, but apparently they did not wish to read about them in books. Self-help, biographies, memoirs, travels books, and cookbooks seemed to rule the day, suggesting that Americans were more concerned about personal improvement, exotic places, and eating well.

The United States has always had a certain fascination with self-help. Back in Ben Franklin's day, readers were inspired by wise sayings from his popular *Poor Richard's Almanac* ("Early to bed, early to rise, makes a man healthy, wealthy, and wise," and so on). Perhaps by the 1930s people were beyond simple homilies, but that did not stop Walter B. Pitkin from publishing *Life Begins at Forty* in 1932, the depths of the Depression. The book's message was elementary: people at midlife were the luckiest generation ever, if they would just seize the moment and live each day to the fullest.

Four years later, Dale Carnegie (1888–1955) brought out *How to Win Friends and Influence People*, a book that outlined easy steps for achieving the title's promise. Carnegie's work was condensed in *Reader's Digest* the same year. With that fortunate tie-in, the book remained in print throughout most of the remainder of the century, achieving sales in excess of 10 million copies, a stupendous total for a nonfiction title.

Book Clubs

For fiction and nonfiction alike, there were book clubs, led by the Book-of-the-Month Club (organized in 1926) and the Literary Guild (founded in 1927), both of which flourished during the 1930s. With large membership lists, these organizations fostered the success of best-sellers, causing many books that otherwise might have languished to achieve that status. Both clubs were attacked by literary snobs for lowering tastes and moving toward homogenization in literature; "standardization" became a negative rallying cry for those opposed to any broadening of the readership base. Standardization or not, the huge print runs for book-club editions could be more than 75,000 copies for titles by their most popular authors. They may have been playing to the mass audience, but the clubs often were the difference between success and disappointing sales for writers.

Federal Writers Project

Not every author could have a book-club contract, and many found the Depression a difficult time. Fortunately, the government organized the Federal Writers Project (FWP) in 1935 as a method of providing meaningful work for otherwise unemployed authors. During its peak year, 1936, the FWP employed some 6500 writers. They ranged from second-string reporters to prominent, published authors down on their luck. In fact, only about 10 percent—650 people—qualified as working, professional writers when they were enlisted into the program.

From the beginning, Henry Alsberg, who oversaw the program, decreed that fiction was to be avoided. It was simply too controversial, too open to criticism and misinterpretation, to be underwritten by the government. Taking the safe road, the group began the task of creating a series of guidebooks to the nation, an effort that culminated with the *American Guide* series, a set of fifty-three volumes that described all the states and regions of the country.

The *American Guides* were comprehensive and exhaustive in their coverage. Little escaped the attention of their researchers. From folklore to ecology, the guides provided polished commentaries on the true "state of the union" during the late 1930s. Since most of the writers remained anonymous, appropriate credit for well-crafted writing cannot be assigned accurately, but the consistent quality of the undertaking demonstrated that professionals, not hastily assembled amateurs, were doing the work. By salvaging crumbling documents and locating long-lost records, the project helped to preserve elements of American history that might otherwise have been lost, and gave the FWP a high level of credibility, as well as providing gainful employment for a lot of good writers.[4]

MAGAZINES

General Magazines

There were over 3000 periodicals during the 1930s, but only a handful could be called "popular" or mass-circulation magazines. Fewer than 100 titles reached a large, diverse audience. Instead, an overwhelming percentage of magazines were directed at small, selected audiences. They went to professionals in various businesses, they appealed to specialized occupations, and they attracted tiny niche groups. Thus, when discussing popular culture and magazines, the sample is of necessity a very limited one.

When the Depression decade began, national magazine circulation stood at approximately 80 million; by 1940, it was close to 100 million. People continued to read and subscribe to magazines despite the crisis, and the industry was led by a handful of older magazines that appealed to a representative cross section of readers. Ironically, although most of these periodicals managed to struggle through the economic turmoil, a few have since fallen by the wayside. In general, popular, or mass, magazines depend on continuing reader loyalty and advertising revenues for their survival. When either falls off sharply, the demise of the magazine usually follows. During the 1930s, the *Saturday Evening Post* (founded 1821; ceased weekly publication in 1969), *Ladies' Home Journal* (1883), *Good Housekeeping* (1885), *Cosmopolitan* (1886), *Collier's* (1888; ceased publication in 1957), *Vogue* (1892), *House Beautiful* (1896), *Redbook* (1902), *Better Homes & Gardens* (1922), *Reader's Digest* (1922), and *Time* (1923) were among the survivors, enjoying both numerous readers and substantial advertising volume.

On the other hand, some notable American magazines, often old friends in thousands of homes, disappeared. Sentiment could not carry them. Thus *Scribner's* (later called *The Century*; 1870–1930), *The Smart Set* (1900–1930), *Vanity Fair* (1913–1936), *Literary Digest* (1890–1938), and the oldest of them all, *The North American Review* (1815–1939), were among the many journals that saw their last issues go out during the 1930s.

But hope springs eternal, even in the magazine business, and many new titles came into being during these turbulent years. Such well-known periodicals as *Advertising Age* (1930), *Fortune* (1930), *Broadcasting* (1931), *Family Circle* (1932), *Esquire* (1933), *Newsweek* (1933), *U.S. News & World Report* (1933), *Bride's Magazine* (1934), *Mademoiselle* (1935), *Yankee* (1935), *Consumer Reports* (1936), *Life* (1936; ceased weekly publication in 1972), *Look* (1937; ceased publication in 1971), *Popular Photography* (1937), *Woman's Day* (1937), *U.S. Camera* (1938), and *Glamour* (1939) were founded at this time. More important, all survived the decade.

Saturday Evening Post

The giant among popular American magazines of the 1930s was the *Saturday Evening Post*. In each issue, this large-format weekly offered a surefire mix of fact and fiction, lots of photographs and illustrations, many features, more often than not a cover by the renowned artist Norman Rockwell, and pages and pages of advertising—the lifeblood of the magazine. From 1930 until 1939, the *Post* averaged a remarkable 100 or so ads an issue (more in good economic times, fewer in bad; see Chapter 3, "Advertising," for more on this topic). In the area of fiction, the *Saturday Evening Post* was the premier story magazine of the period, running over 200 short stories a year. It should be noted, however, that the 1930s were boom times for the genre: unlike today, many magazines ran stories during the period, and the industry as a whole published some 1000 fictional pieces annually.

Steering the *Post* with a sure hand was the astute George Horace Lorimer (1867–1937), the magazine's editor for many years. He had joined the *Post* in 1898, became acting editor in 1899, and assumed full command shortly thereafter. He guided the magazine's fortunes until his death in 1937, when Wesley W. Stout took over and did little to change the successful format established by his predecessor.

Lorimer, a genius at discerning American tastes, delivered his interpretation into millions of homes, making believers of countless readers. By the Great Crash of 1929, the *Saturday Evening Post* was the unchallenged carrier of an American vision of opportunity and prosperity. The stock market debacle did little to change that view—at least from the perspective of the *Post*—and Lorimer and his associates worked hard at presenting an endless, uplifting variety of historical romances, sports yarns, Westerns, and urban tales with businessman heroes, along with nonfiction success stories that would have made Horatio Alger proud.

The magazine's huge subscription list suggests that many readers wanted a continuation of that success-oriented vision; in 1929 the *Post* was circulating almost 3 million copies a week, a figure that dropped only slightly during the decade, making it the undisputed leader in the field. Lorimer was steadfastly opposed to President Roosevelt and his policies, but that opposition obviously had little impact on subscribers. In an apparent contradiction of reality, *Post* readers bought the magazine and simultaneously voted for Roosevelt and the New Deal. As long as the magazine painted a nostalgic picture of an America that possibly never was, they were satisfied.[5]

Advertisers eyed the subscription numbers happily; here was a true mass audience. Since the magazine had national distribution, it served as a marketplace for products available everywhere. The *Post* pioneered in standardizing consumer wants, and most of its ad copy reflects this unification of the buying public. Even in the depths of the Depression, nationally known products were boldly displayed on the pages of the *Saturday Evening Post*, a tacit rejection of any economic collapse.

Reader's Digest

Another magazine that flourished during the 1930s was the *Reader's Digest*. Founded in 1922 by DeWitt and Lila Wallace (1889–1981; 1889–1984), this familiar, purse-sized anthology of condensed articles was circulating about 250,000 copies a month in 1930; by the end of the decade it had swelled to 4 million. Such extraordinary success grew out of the content of the monthly: like the *Saturday Evening Post*, the *Digest* celebrated the American way of life, a robustly conservative and insular view that argued for hard work, family, and common sense—exactly the things so ardently espoused by George Horace Lorimer.

People liked the *Digest's* message; that the magazine also boiled books and articles down to their basic content added to the appeal. Plus, the *Digest* did something the *Post* almost never did: it titillated its readers with endless slightly suggestive jokes and articles that included sex in their focus. Never off-color, the *Reader's Digest* nonetheless kept the subject of sex before its growing audience, and no one seemed in the least offended.

In order to find articles appropriate to the magazine's ideology, editors at the *Digest* actually culled a rather narrow range of publications. Not surprisingly, the *Saturday Evening Post* was one of them, as were such lesser-known (but equally conservative) journals as the *North American Review*, *McClure's*, and *Forum*. Often, the articles excerpted for publication in the *Digest* were "plants": pieces placed by the editors in other publications for later inclusion in the *Digest*. In this way, the *Reader's Digest* fostered the illusion that it was being selective, choosing only "the best" from a range of magazines.

By 1931, the *Digest* had introduced unsigned, original articles in its contents. This new feature was so successful that signed authorship was allowed by 1933. During the mid-1930s, fully half the magazine was comprised of such materials. Even though these commissioned pieces tended to reinforce the philosophy of the Wallaces, the public received them enthusiastically. The chatty, upbeat writing, along with the jokes, features ("My Most Unforgettable Character," "Life in These United States," et al.), and tidbits of folk wisdom kept attracting more and more readers to the *Digest*. Despite its success, the *Digest* was very much a bare-bones magazine. Not until 1939 did simple line illustrations begin to appear. And it was 1955 before advertising was introduced; prior to that time, the *Digest* had relied on subscriptions and newsstand sales alone, working on the theory that any advertisements might somehow compromise the content of the magazine and its relationship with both readers and contributors.[6]

Life

A major figure in American journalistic history is Henry R. Luce (1898–1967). In 1923 he created *Time* magazine, the first modern newsweekly. In 1930, he brought forth *Fortune*, a thick, slick periodical devoted to business. It was a spin-off of *Time's* "Business" section, and despite the gloomy state of the economy, it quickly snared an enthusiastic and large audience.

One of Luce's proudest accomplishments came about in 1936 with the beginning of *Life* magazine. The title comes from an older *Life*, a humor magazine founded in 1883. It had fallen on hard times in the 1930s and was put up for sale. Luce happened to be toying with the name *Look*, but a bargain price for the humor magazine changed his mind. He bought the struggling *Life* to acquire the name for his own publication, a journal that would prove to be a bold new venture into photojournalism.

On November 23, 1936, a slim first issue of *Life* magazine appeared on newsstands. It cost a dime and offered more photographs than text. The premier issue was an instant hit, selling out wherever it was available. Subsequent issues also sold well, making it one of the most successful magazine start-ups ever. Within four months, it was selling over a million copies a week on newsstands. In fact, the immediate success of *Life* almost did it in. Luce actually lost $6 million with those first issues. He had estimated the new magazine would sell 250,000 copies per week in its first months; the upstart, however, almost doubled that figure. Since ad rates were based on the lower circulation, Luce had to make up the per-copy costs out of his own corporate pockets (see Chapter 3, "Advertising," for more on advertising in *Life*).

The success of *Life* did not go unnoticed. Gardner Cowles, Jr., was a friend of Luce's, and he, too, knew something about the publishing business. In 1933, he began syndicating the popular picture section of his family's newspaper, the *Des Moines Register and Tribune*, to twenty-six different papers. That move did not satisfy demand, and so he decided to launch his own photojournalism magazine in 1937. He borrowed some start-up money from Luce, and the title he chose was *Look*, the same one his friend had toyed with earlier.

Until its demise in 1971 (it was briefly resurrected in the mid-1970s, but was finally laid to rest in 1979), *Look* survived in the shadow of *Life*. *Look* was seen by many as a cheaper imitator, a magazine that focused too much on personalities and glamour. *Life*, on the other hand, was perceived by many as going after the meatier, more important stories. The distinctions between the two publications might be a bit exaggerated, but they nevertheless persisted throughout the life of both magazines.[7]

Life began with a singular emphasis on celebrity. Debutantes, high society, and wealth were certain circulation-getters, and the magazine regularly ran glossy photo essays on the doings of the upper classes. In addition, gore and grisliness got plenty of space, along with humorous pictures of cute animals and children. *Life* might be perceived as serious and thought-provoking, but it was also capable of playing to the lowest common denominator. Neither advertisers nor readers seemed to object to the mix, however; its circulation continued to rise throughout the decade, and when the clouds of World War II began to build in Asia and Europe, it was *Life* staffers, cameras in hand, who recorded the descent into the conflict.

Liberty

After Lorimer, the Wallaces, and Luce, there remains but one other name to be added to the list of those who influenced the direction of American magazine publishing: Bernarr Macfadden (1868–1955). A colorful, self-proclaimed "physical culturist," Macfadden had burst upon the magazine scene in 1899 with *Physical Culture*, a journal promising long life and good health through diet and exercise. *Physical Culture* was wildly successful, and an emboldened Macfadden in 1919 introduced *True Story*, the first of an extensive line of confessional magazines he would publish. It, too, did extremely well, and so in 1931 he purchased a struggling weekly called *Liberty*.

Liberty had first appeared on newsstands in 1924, the shared child of the Chicago *Tribune* and the *New York Daily News*. The magazine featured some of the tabloid sensationalism of its parent *Daily News*, but it could never develop a solid advertising base. It consistently lost money—even as it was building circulation—and was finally sold to Macfadden, a multimillionaire from his other publishing adventures.[8]

Throughout the 1930s, only three weekly general-interest magazines could boast a steady circulation of over 1 million or more: *Saturday Evening Post*, *Collier's* (a weekly very much in the *Post* mold), and *Liberty*. All three of these magazines paid little heed to the Depression. They filled their pages with fiction, a few facts, and lots of entertainment that provided a kind of spiritual uplift for troubled times. Yet, even with that impressive circulation, *Liberty* lacked significant advertising and was in financial difficulty.

Certainly *Liberty* was different from most other general magazines. It featured a "Reading Time" note with each article, a small block in which it was guaranteed that a particular piece would take no more than "9 minutes, 40 seconds" (or whatever figures were provided) to read. The articles tended toward the tawdry and sensational, with breathless prose on Al Capone, Huey Long, and other questionable celebrities. Macfadden did, however, use *Liberty* as his personal soapbox to urge the re-election of Roosevelt in 1936, a stand that placed him and his magazine poles apart from the more conservative *Saturday Evening Post* and *Reader's Digest*.

Under Macfadden's guidance, *Liberty* continued to gain readers, but it suffered from the reputation of being directed at the working class, not the more affluent middle class. Rightly or wrongly, many advertisers stayed away, their ad dollars going to other publications. For instance, the new *Esquire* (introduced in 1933) was one of the first American magazines to employ target marketing. It identified its audience, and then sold potential advertisers on readership profiles created for just this purpose. *Fortune* (1930) did likewise, becoming one of the most advertising-heavy monthly magazines in the country, and at a time when the nation was mired in the depression. *Time* followed suit, especially in light of the challenges laid down by two 1933 upstarts, *Newsweek* and *U.S. News & World Report*. Finally, *Life* is the true success story of target marketing. Its immediate acceptance by middle-class readers convinced advertisers that this was the place to be; by 1939 it charged more for ad space than any of its competitors, and would-be advertisers lined up to place their copy.

In reality, advertising expenditures in magazines rose very little in the 1930s—from $150 million in 1931 to $156 million in 1940—but advertisers grew much more selective about where they placed their dollars. It was the beginning of the end for the old-fashioned general magazine. Even with his marketing genius, Macfadden could not attract substantially increased advertising, and so *Liberty* struggled on into the 1940s, was sold, and died quietly in 1951. With its demise, the nation lost one of the most popular magazines of the 1930s. Its appeal was broad, and it made no pretensions about being elitist or intellectual. Even its covers were a kind of simplified version of the nostalgia created by Norman Rockwell for the *Post*. They were competent, but they were not the equal of the competition.

It was not with *Liberty*, however, that Macfadden marked his place in American publishing history. It was with the confessional magazine that he created something unique, a product unlike anything seen before or since. The success of his *True Story* helped Macfadden spawn *True Detective Mysteries, True Experiences, True Ghost Stories, True Lovers, True Romances*, and *Master Detective*, along with *Click, Hollywood, Modern Marriage, Modern Screen, Motion Picture, Movie Classic, Photoplay, Screenland, Screen Romances*, and *Silver Screen*. In 1933, he even brought out *Babies, Just Babies*, a short-lived journal that boasted Eleanor Roosevelt as one of its editors.

As if the many magazines were not enough, Macfadden also owned ten newspapers, among them the notorious *New York Evening Graphic*—the "PornoGraphic," as it was known to those who detested its sensationalism. The tabloid journal gained a reputation for tampering with photographs to capture certain effects—what the editors called a "composograph." Readers eventually tired of its diet of sex and scandal, and the *Evening Graphic* died in 1932. That setback was only temporary, however; in 1935 the monthly circulation of all the Macfadden magazines totaled over 7 million copies.[9]

Given the push of success by the Macfadden publishing empire, confessional magazines reached their peak in the 1930s. Their appeal was pure escapism, and a "their problems are worse than mine" attitude had to strike a resonant chord with Depression-era readers. For instance, a popular 1932 film, *I Am a Fugitive from a Chain Gang*, first appeared as a feature in *True Detective Mysteries* in 1931. The public response to the article was such that Hollywood quickly bought the rights and rushed the movie into production. Personal problem-solving had become a staple, spreading even to the more "genteel" magazines of the period.

PULP MAGAZINES

Close cousins to the confessional journals were the pulp magazines. So called because they usually were printed on thick, cheap pulpwood paper, they were somewhat akin to comic strips in their simplicity. Hardly a new product of the 1930s, pulps had been around since the nineteenth century and the heyday of the dime novel. With best-sellers drawing large audiences and the comic strips a daily reading experience for millions, the pulps occupied a curious middle ground between the two. Because their format was print, in content they stood closer to short stories than they did to the much more visual comic strips of the day. But their content—action, adventure, detectives, cowboys, romance, love, and sex—was more often in the spirit of an adventure comic strip than of the subtleties of a novel. They almost always featured a lurid cover, an irresistible invitation to see what lay inside, a tradition that the comic books of the late 1930s enthusiastically adopted.

However the pulps might be classified, millions of them sold each month. They were shunned by critics and librarians, but their fans cared not a whit. As long as the next issue of *Argosy Weekly, The Bat, Black Mask Magazine, Nick Carter, The Spider*, or *Thrilling Detective* could be found at the neighborhood newsstand, they were happy. Pulps were the perfect distraction for people with time on their hands and a desire to escape from the harsh realities around them.[10]

These magazines also brought about a surge of interest in science fiction and fantasy. Magazines like *Amazing Stories, Astounding Stories*, and *Wonder Stories* collectively sold more than 1.5 million issues a year at the height of their popularity in the mid-1930s. These futuristic compilations effectively recorded the aspirations of the present, both visually and in their texts, and the future became but an extension of the present.

For the writers involved with the pulp industry, it was not an easy way to get on the road to riches. Magazine short stories abounded during the 1930s, and "big name" periodicals like *Redbook* and the *Saturday Evening Post* often paid over $1000 for a piece by a well-known author. Virtually all the major popular writers of the decade eventually wrote for magazine publication. Some, like Rex Beach, Corey Ford, MacKinlay Kantor, Kathleen Norris, Mary Roberts Rinehart, Damon Runyon, Raphael Sabatini, and P.G. Wodehouse, made their real incomes from magazines, not from books. But for those souls who ground out fiction for the pulps, the going rate was a strict, quantitative one: three or four cents a word. A 3000-word story might fetch $120, and rarely did writers retain rights to their work. But such hard-nosed economics were in keeping with the genre, from the cheap printing and paper to the garish illustrations and melodramatic stories.

Summary

All told, magazines, even the pulps, did well during the Depression decade. By 1938, there were over 1200 weeklies and some 2000 monthlies vying for the public's attention. Estimates place their combined weekly and monthly circulation at around 150 million, a figure greater than the total population of the country at the time. Most women's magazines climbed in circulation, and several supermarket "giveaways" evolved into profitable publications. For instance, the "A&P Menu Sheet" had grown into *Woman's Day* by 1937. Similarly, *Bride's Magazine* went from a free handout to a full-fledged periodical in 1934. In all, the decade saw popular magazines maintain or even improve their circulations, and a number of new publications successfully entered the field.

NEWSPAPERS

Background

Unlike most other nations, the United States has never had a true national newspaper. Whereas most books and magazines enjoy distribution across the country, the vast majority of newspapers have at best a limited regional audience. Just about everyone looked at newspapers, but what someone in Omaha was reading was different from the choices in Phoenix or Boston. The front-page stories might be the same, but state and local news differed, as did local ads and features. Although the newspaper per se is classified as a mass medium, the individual messages received by the audience might well go through changes both obvious and subtle.

In many ways, the newspaper business changed significantly during the Depression. The flush times of the 1920s had imbued American newspapers with a sense of never-ending prosperity, a feeling that readership and advertising volume would continue to rise with each passing year. In reality, American newspapers had been in decline throughout the first third of the twentieth century, going from 2200 separate dailies in 1900 to 1942 dailies in 1930, and to 1888 dailies at the end of the decade. Most of this loss took place because of a movement toward consolidation.[11]

During the first third of the twentieth century, papers tended to be-

Ohio newsboys ready to sell their papers. The primary form of newspaper distribution, aside from newsstands, was young boys who either hawked the papers on street corners or delivered them directly to homes. (Photograph courtesy of the Library of Congress.)

come more general and less partisan in their content. The "political rag" was seen as an anachronism, which meant that larger cities tended to have too many competing newspapers. Businesses correctly sensed that this situation led to less effective advertising. They preferred one or two dominant papers in which to present their copy, rather than a cluster of overlapping ones that individually reached fewer people. The newspaper publishers, attempting to save money, began to combine morning and evening editions into a single issue, a procedure that allowed for changing editions and more efficient use of their facilities. Finally, as the century progressed, manufacturing and delivery costs rose markedly, eliminating borderline operations. As the industry consolidated, a number of papers went out of business. The towns and cities supporting two or more competing newspapers declined steadily after 1900.

Chain Ownership

Coupled with consolidation was chain ownership. A chain consists of several papers under a single ownership. It allows for savings in materials and labor, and can even mean shared staff and facilities. In 1900, eight chains existed, and they controlled 27 papers; by the mid-1930s, over sixty chains controlled over 328 papers, publications that accounted for 40 percent of total newspaper circulation. Most of these linked papers were larger urban ones, as Scripps-Howard, Gannett, Hearst, and Cox moved into chain ownership. The days of the independent daily, bravely charting its own course, were numbered.

Between 1930 and 1940, almost half of the independent papers in the country ceased to exist—they either went out of business or became parts of chains. Rural and small-town weeklies stopped trying to compete with their city counterparts, and began to focus almost exclusively on local events to retain readers. In the meantime, competition continued to decline. In 1930, eight major cities of over 100,000 had only one paper; by 1940, the number had swelled to twenty-five. Even New York City, that most competitive of newspaper towns and home to so many famous newspapers, felt the change. Early in the century, it had boasted some twenty dailies. It began the 1930s with nine daily papers, but by 1940 the number was reduced to seven.

Newspaper Decline

As the country fell more deeply into the Depression, the effects of the calamity quickly became apparent in the nation's newspapers: advertising space plummeted. In 1929, newspapers displayed a record-setting $860 million in advertising. By 1933, that figure had shrunk to $470 million. A slow comeback began in the mid-1930s, but the recession of 1938 stalled it. By 1939, advertising expenditures of $552 million had risen only to 1920 levels, figures nowhere close to those of 1929. As is usually the case, smaller papers suffered most from the decline in advertising.

Nevertheless, $552 million is not to be scoffed at. The sums spent on newspaper ads constituted well over a third of what American firms spent for advertising of all kinds in the 1930s. These large numbers need to be put into perspective: in 1930, newspapers took about 48 cents of the national advertising dollar. By 1940 their share had fallen to 36 cents, but that was still more than one-third of the total. During the same period, magazines consistently averaged 34 cents out of the ad dollar. What caused the decline for newspapers was the relatively new electronic medium of radio. In 1930, radio could claim only about 3 cents of the advertising dollar; by 1940 its share had soared to 20 cents, and most of that came at the expense of newspapers.

Advertising may have fallen off, but a great many people still read a newspaper regularly. Circulation rose from 40 to 41 million throughout the decade (newsstand purchases and home delivery). In 1930, the U.S.

population was 122 million persons; that means about a third of the population purchased a daily paper. If two to three people read each issue, over half the nation looked at a newspaper on a regular basis. Truly, here was a mass medium.

An additional set of figures must, however, come into play: In 1940 the population had risen to 132 million, an increase of 10 million (about 8 percent). The circulation increase from 40 to 41 million readers is less than 3 percent. Taking circulation and population together, the general population rose at a faster rate than newspaper readership. Despite their modest gains in circulation, newspapers were in reality going through a slow but steady decline.

In 1930, 1942 dailies were published; the number fell to 1878 in 1940—a net loss of 64 papers. For comparison's sake, there are approximately 1500 dailies today, or a loss of 378 newspapers since 1940. The decline that began in 1900 simply accelerated throughout the twentieth century and is continuing into the twenty-first.[12]

Radio probably did more damage to the newspaper business and readership than did the Depression. Newspapers might be the average American's first choice for news, but radios were becoming omnipresent, a ready source for late-breaking stories. Also, radio took an increasing portion of ad revenue, carried news, gave instantaneous updates, provided live sporting events, consistently entertained—and it came into homes for free. Radio's popularity zoomed upward during the 1930s, going from 14 million home receivers in 1930 to over 44 million by 1940. Unfortunately for the newspaper industry, there was no commensurate gain in circulation or advertising. In fact, one way many newspapers stayed profitable was to acquire radio stations. Publishers saw radio as a surefire moneymaker, and invested in stations accordingly. In 1930, newspaper interests owned about 90 stations; by 1940, 250 stations were affiliated with newspaper publishing companies.

Another way papers sought to lure readers and maintain profits was to become more visual. Wirephotos (photographs electronically carried by wire directly to a newspaper office) were introduced in the early 1920s. The photographer's life, as well as that of the subjects, became easier when electric flashbulbs replaced the annoying and dangerous explosive-powder lights in 1931. The Associated Press initiated a wirephoto service in 1935, allowing its subscribers fast access to innumerable photographs of news events. Competing news syndicates quickly followed suit. By 1938, about a third of a big metropolitan daily's content consisted of pictures. Technology kept marching on, and by 1939, color telephotos were a reality, and were almost immediately incorporated into the Sunday magazine sections of many papers.

Syndication

Bowing to the success of *Time, Life,* and other newsmagazines, newspapers increasingly compartmentalized their stories in the 1930s. There were pages on national news, world news, business, the arts, society, and so on. And, despite drops in their revenue, most big-city papers expanded their operations. With all the furor in Washington about Roosevelt and the New Deal, newspaper bureaus in the nation's capital experienced rapid growth. The president, no stranger to publicity, cooperated by inaugurating regular press conferences, as well as his fabulously successful "Fireside Chats" on radio. As war in Europe became more and more likely, overseas coverage saw a similar expansion.

Given the excitement in Washington and foreign countries, smaller papers were at a disadvantage. They could ill afford to staff bureaus in cities far from their home base. Thus news syndicates like the Associated Press (A.P.) and United Press (U.P.) experienced tremendous growth. They could provide the reporters and the stories—for a fee, of course— that an individual newspaper could not hope to provide. Although both the A.P. and the U.P. go back to the late nineteenth century, it was in the 1930s that they came into their own. As news became less regional and more national and international, only the far-flung syndicates could file regular stories to their growing lists of subscribers.

With widespread syndication there came a certain amount of standardization. The syndicated features found in one paper might just as easily be found in another. In this way, the insularity of a small-town daily lessened, and it came more into the mainstream of American life. This standardization occurred not just with news stories; the comics, the horoscopes, the bridge columns, the latest Hollywood gossip, the box scores, the advice columnists, the financial pages—all of these graced the paper because they were syndicated. In fact, the comics gained the enviable reputation of being the single most popular feature in American dailies during the 1930s (see Chapter 12, "Visual Arts," for more on comic strips).

Columnists

The success of syndicated materials led to the appropriately named "syndicated columnists." These were writers who spurned objectivity in favor of lively, colorful, opinionated styles, and their pieces usually appeared on the editorial page. In the early 1930s, most of them tended to be anti-New Deal, but had little effect on legislation or voters. As proof of this contention, in 1932, 60 percent of American daily newspapers opposed Roosevelt, yet he won in a landslide. In 1936, 63 percent opposed his candidacy, but he again won overwhelmingly. By 1940, and

Roosevelt's quest for an unprecedented third term, 75 percent of the dailies voiced opposition, but the president was re-elected once again.

Of course, not all syndicated columnists wrote political pieces and not all appeared on the editorial page. Many commented on the passing scene. One of the most widely syndicated writers in the 1930s was O.O. McIntyre whose column was titled "New York Day by Day." His unpretentious columns seemed to appeal most to those outside big cities, although the title might suggest otherwise. Franklin P. Adams (who used the initials F.P.A.) wrote sophisticated trivia in his "The Conning Tower." It, too, was widely syndicated and quoted.

Some columnists relied on gossip and celebrity-watching for their appeal. Chief among them was Walter Winchell (1897–1972), whose "On Broadway" was carried by over 1000 papers, most of them a considerable distance from the Great White Way. His "Winchellisms" occasionally entered the language for a brief vogue, such as "middle-aisle," a verb form that meant to wed. "Renovate," on the other hand, signified a divorce (from Reno, Nevada, where divorce was easily accomplished). Such was Winchell's popularity that he had a long-running radio news show that began with a staccato telegraph sound, and then his imperious "Good evening, Mr. and Mrs. North America and all the ships at sea . . . let's go to press! FLASH!" The fifteen-minute show ran from 1930 until 1949 as *The Jergens Journal*. It was consistently one of the nation's top-rated radio programs.

Capitalizing on Winchell's fame, the Metro-Goldwyn-Mayer film studio released *Broadway Melody of 1936* (it is actually the second of four *Broadway Melodies* over the period 1929–1940). In this movie, radio star Jack Benny plays a Winchell-like columnist hungry for a story. The plot is trivial; the music by Nacio Herb Brown and Arthur Freed is wonderful, and includes "You Are My Lucky Star," a song destined to become a standard.

Close on Winchell's heels, at least in popularity during the 1930s, were Hedda Hopper (1890–1966) and Louella Parsons (1881–1972). Both women wrote widely syndicated newspaper columns that focused almost exclusively on Hollywood and the stars. Their success helped spawn a number of movie magazines, ranging from the purely gossipy *Screen Romances* to the slightly serious *Silver Screen*. Parsons parlayed her fame and influence into a popular radio show, *Hollywood Hotel* (1934–1938), which she hosted. Not to be outdone, Hopper gained a program of her own in 1939, *The Hedda Hopper Show*, a fifteen-minute mix of chatter and celebrities that ran until 1951.

Other columnists mixed gossip and political rumors, such as Drew Pearson (1897–1969) and Robert S. Allen with their "Washington Merry-Go-Round." This widely circulated column grew out of a book by the same name that they anonymously published in 1932. The success of the book, a collection of articles rejected by their respective newspapers, led to their quick syndication by United Features, and even some radio time for the two men. From 1935 to 1940 they were on the Mutual Network with their investigative reports.[13]

Warm, humorous writers also enjoyed wide syndication. For example, Eleanor Roosevelt, the First Lady, had a long-running column entitled "My Day." It began in 1935 and chronicled her thoughts and activities for many appreciative readers. The folksy Will Rogers (1879–1935), "the cowboy philosopher," wrote a daily paragraph on some current topic. Similarly, poet Edgar Guest (1881–1959) began contributing verse to his syndicate at the turn of the century. Over the next sixty years, he composed over 11,000 poems. By the 1930s, he was appearing in hundreds of papers. The poetry, usually lightly humorous and sentimental ("It takes a heap o'livin' in a house t'make it home") became beloved by several generations of newspaper readers. It might be doggerel and damned by critics, but the audience seemed not to notice. Guest's immense readership was a testament to the roles simplicity and sentiment often play in popular culture.

Finally, among all the syndicated writers, mention needs to be made of those who monitored the nation's manners and mores. Emily Post (1872–1960) provided the last word on etiquette; her 1930s column was syndicated in over 200 papers and she even had a radio show that premiered in 1931. Dorothy Dix (Elizabeth M. Gilmer [1870–1951]) and Beatrice Fairfax (Marie Manning [1873–1945]) wrote advice-to-the-lovelorn columns. Dix had the distinction of being the highest-paid woman columnist of the 1930s, and Fairfax was memorialized in song. In 1930, George and Ira Gershwin penned "But Not for Me." In the number, lyricist Ira Gershwin has the words, "Beatrice Fairfax, don't you dare," probably the only mention of such a columnist in the annals of American popular music. All three women became unofficial arbiters of taste and behavior, their words anxiously read by millions who wanted to know about proper dining and dating.

Reporting

The surprising success of so many columnists led to a rise in interpretive stories by regular (i.e., nonsyndicated) reporters in the 1930s, a trend that has carried down to the present. In traditional newsgathering, the "4 Ws" were predominant: Who? What? When? Where? The 1930s, however, found a fifth W often a significant part of the story: Why? Certainly the era was one of confusion, and it reassured people to have events explained in easily understood terms. As a result, reporters delved more and more into the details behind a story, interpreting the facts as they were presented. It may have challenged traditional tenets about objectivity, but it became part of American journalism.[14]

For the average reader, however, the popular image of the newspaper reporter was not molded by adherence to journalistic standards or by writing ability. Throughout the decade, Hollywood released a string of movies—some good, some bad—about newspapers and reporters. These films shaped public awareness of the profession, and created the stereotype of the fast-talking, wisecracking reporter who always gets the story. Starting in 1931 with *The Front Page*, a film version of the Ben Hecht-Charles MacArthur play of the same name, the image of the busy newsroom, the harried editor, the race to make a deadline, and the constant chatter of all involved became the standard. *Platinum Blonde* (1931) features the most noted platinum blonde of the era, Jean Harlow, in a comedic romance with an ambitious reporter. Over a dozen other newspaper/reporter pictures came tumbling out of the movie studios during the decade: *Shriek in the Night* (1933), *Libeled Lady* (1936, with Jean Harlow again), *Nothing Sacred* (1937), *The Thirteenth Man* (1937), *Too Hot to Handle* (1938), *Everything Happens at Night* (1939, an excuse to allow skater Sonja Henie to perform on the ice), and *His Girl Friday* (1940). The final film, *His Girl Friday*, brought the list full circle because it was a remake of 1931's *The Front Page*. Clearly, the newspaper reporter made a convenient hero, and audiences obviously responded to the characterization.

SUMMARY

No evidence exists that would suggest Americans lessened their reading during the thirties. On the contrary, the sales and circulation of books, magazines, and newspapers remained strong throughout the decade. Both novels and nonfiction flourished, often with an emphasis on American history. In adversity, the nation sought reassurance in its roots. General interest magazines like the *Saturday Evening Post* and *Collier's* enjoyed a widespread audience. *Time*, *Newsweek*, and *U.S. News & World Report* (the last two both founded in 1933) indicated continuing interest in analytical news reporting, and *Life* and *Look* (founded in 1936 and 1937, respectively) explored the world of photojournalism. Many newspapers consolidated their operations for the sake of economy, but the average American continued to read a daily paper. Advertising in both newspapers and magazines declined during the Depression, and certainly publishers felt the sting of falling revenues, but readership remained high.

9

Music

BACKGROUND

In 1932, Duke Ellington penned a little ditty called "It Don't Mean a Thing (If It Ain't Got That Swing)." Hardly his greatest composition, its title nevertheless sums up the music scene for much of the 1930s. Swing was king, and all other music had to follow in its footsteps. In no period, before or since, has one musical form so captured the popular fancy.

The 1920s had been labeled "the Jazz Age," and jazz contributed an important component of the music played during those years. But there were many other choices available for listeners and dancers; "jazz" named the decade more because of its associations with gangsters, drinking, sex, and general disregard for gentility.

Swing, on the other hand, is more encompassing. A trip to the dictionary will reveal a long list of definitions after the entry *swing*. It can be a noun—"The band played swing"; an adjective—"It was a swing band"; an adverb—"The band played swingingly"; or a verb—"The band swung the music." Four parts of speech, but still no real definition of the word itself. The pianist Fats Waller was reputed to have said, after being asked to explain "swing," "If you have to ask, you'll never understand it."

Perhaps the best way to describe the swing phenomenon is to say that it involves a contagious rhythmic feeling, a desire to snap the fingers, tap the toes, and get up and dance. That definition of course transcends time and focuses on the physical side of swing. Historically, swing—by itself—usually refers to the emergence of innumerable large bands during the 1930s that played primarily for dancers. This is not to say that small groups or vocalists could not also "swing"; they could, and many did. Orchestras and sextets and quartets and trios and singers have "swung" at different times, but when talking about "The Swing Era," the 1930s is the period and the big dance bands are the main attraction.

JAZZ AND SWING

Although jazz played a significant role in the swing phenomenon, jazz itself has never been a major component of popular culture. Instead, it survives by blending many disparate musical forms. Thus, its appeal is directed at innumerable subgroups, avid followers of particular forms who often disdain others. The swing of the 1930s certainly grew out of jazz, but those who embraced swing might genuinely profess an ignorance about jazz. Swing was a facet of popular culture that grew on its own, not because of its links to jazz. Inflections taken from jazz were certainly there, but swing was part of a much larger cultural, historical, and musical movement that swept aside virtually everything before it. It really didn't mean a thing if it didn't swing, at least for a while; by the mid-1940s, however, the craze had run its course.

In the 1920s, the Jazz Age, the bandleader Paul Whiteman had crowned himself "The King of Jazz." Uneasy lies the head that wears the crown; within a few years, an entirely new musical royalty was enthroned: Count Basie, Duke Ellington, and the King of Swing, Benny Goodman. But before the usurpers—along with all their many followers—could begin their reigns, a revolution had to be fought over the type of music being played.

The Crash of 1929 hit the music business hard. Two-thirds of the nation's unionized musicians were out of work in 1933. Paul Whiteman, now king of a shaky realm, had to release ten members of his thirty-piece band. The solution to the problem was out there, but it took several years for struggling bands, record companies, and radio producers to discover it.

BLACK MUSICIANS

There were a number of trailblazing black orchestras during the 1920s and early 1930s that eagerly experimented with new directions in music. Recording executives thought an insufficient audience existed for these bands, and tended to ignore most of their efforts. A few of the more daring companies, looking to niche audiences, did issue what they called "race records." These were recordings of blues and jazz, almost always by black performers and aimed at black consumers. It was finally discovered—particularly when sales were down—that a growing number of white listeners also displayed a strong interest in this music.

The dawn of the 1930s saw a significant audience already familiar with many different bands, both black and white. Unfortunately, the bulk of black musicians labored under the tyranny of segregation. Those known to a white public were usually heard on recordings, since most clubs and other outlets observed strict segregation, and the majority of radio stations refused to play black artists. The opportunities to perform before white audiences were therefore limited, and integrated bands were virtually unheard of until the later 1930s.

For example, the Fletcher Henderson orchestra was probably the hottest band in the land at the beginning of the 1930s, but the ban on black musicians kept his genius concealed from a potentially huge audience. Although Henderson finally recorded for Victor in 1932, a lack of effective promotion and distribution kept his music from spreading. It was not until 1935, when Henderson began selling arrangments to Benny Goodman, that recognition came, and then it arrived through a successful white band.

The Big Bands

One black entertainer who had gained recognition among white audiences was trumpeter Louis Armstrong (1901–1971). A native of New Orleans, Armstrong had early on established considerable fame playing jazz with a variety of groups. He was widely recorded, especially as an accompanist to blues singers, and by 1930 his throaty vocals were becoming as popular as his trumpet playing. Several successful European tours added luster to his name, and by 1936 he even had a part in *Pennies from Heaven*, a movie musical with Bing Crosby. Armstrong made the transition from musician to entertainer during the late 1930s, although he continued to be one of the best trumpeters in the business. He joined an elite minority of black personalities who had access to the white-dominated worlds of stage, screen, and radio.

Despite the setbacks and segregation, the word spread in musical circles about a new dance music, and this word filtered down to a growing public. Sometimes it was gotten out by bands playing in large cities at clubs or dance halls; more often it was delivered by groups large and small that crisscrossed the country, playing wherever and whenever they could. Orchestras that traveled a lot and did not consistently play the big cities were called territory bands. Hundreds of them dotted the landscape, setting up for endless one-night stands, packing up, and moving on to the next town.[1]

As bands began to proliferate, they were divided into two categories: swing or sweet. A swing orchestra played many up-tempo numbers,

Trumpeter Louis Armstrong and his orchestra in 1937. Armstrong was
an important and popular performer throughout the decade.
(Photograph courtesy of the Library of Congress.)

emphasizing rhythm and hard-driving arrangements that revealed the
jazz roots anchoring the music. They encouraged listeners to get up and
dance; these are the bands—Benny Goodman, Harry James, Count Basie,
Duke Ellington, Jimmy Lunceford, Fletcher Henderson, Chick Webb,
Charlie Barnet, Artie Shaw—that are recalled from the period and given
critical attention. What they played was a synthesis of popular dance
numbers and jazz.

A sweet orchestra, on the other hand, continued the tradition of "country club music," a more sedate and restrained approach to performance.
Its innocuous, bouncy rhythms never got in the way of conversation and
dinner. At the time, the sweet bands—Guy Lombardo and His Royal
Canadians, Hal Kemp, Eddie Duchin, Wayne King ("The Waltz King"),
Fred Waring and His Pennsylvanians, Sammy Kaye ("Swing and Sway
with Sammy Kaye"), Shep Fields and His Rippling Rhythm, Larry Clinton, and Frankie Carle, to name just a few—drew equally large crowds
and sold almost as many recordings.

One of the most popular groups of the later 1930s, the Glenn Miller Orchestra, illustrates both the differences and the similarities between the sweet and swing categories. Miller was capable of playing slow, syrupy ballads, often sung by a vocalist who made no attempt to "swing" the lyric. But he could also perform jazz-tinged arrangements of up-tempo tunes that any swing band could envy. Miller straddled both camps, and he pleased both.

RECORDINGS AND SHEET MUSIC

The entertainment industry watched how the public seemed to be growing more attuned to the swing phenomenon. At the time, Americans usually learned about new trends in music through sheet music, phonograph recordings, and their radios. Sheet music dates back to colonial times, and sales remained impressive throughout the 1920s. A popular hit could sell 500,000 copies or more. By the 1930s and the Depression, however, the bottom fell out of the sheet music market. A song that boasted sales over 200,000 copies was considered a real success. Woolworth's, once a primary carrier, closed its sheet music departments, leaving Kresge's as the main outlet. Never again would sheet music be an important component of popular music.[2]

Mass production of recordings had begun in the 1890s; by 1910, records were the primary means of producing music in homes. The Columbia, Victor, and Edison labels dominated the business in the early twentieth century, but Brunswick, Gennett, Okeh, Paramount, Perfect, HMV, and Vocalion emerged as strong competitors, introducing many Americans to popular dance music. With the onset of the Depression, recording sales and income plunged from $46 million in 1930 to $5 million in 1933. In the late 1920s, the sale of over 350,000 records qualified a song as a hit. By 1931, that figure had declined to 40,000 records, and showed no signs of rising. The combination of sound pictures and radio struck the industry hard; in desperation, the leading recording companies slashed prices to an average of 35 to 75 cents a disc. But even that drastic measure failed to boost sales appreciably.[3]

In 1932, Victor introduced a new product, the Duo. This gadget consisted of a 78-rpm turntable and not much else; it had no tubes or speakers. The Duo jacked into a radio, sold for a rock-bottom $16.50, and was an immediate success. However, it served only as a stopgap; it could not prevent record sales from continuing their decline. The music business needed a tonic, not another record player, but it was not until 1934 that record sales again began to climb to their former levels. The tonic proved to be swing music.

BENNY GOODMAN (1909–1986)

Radio figured prominently in the popularization of swing, since this was the means by which most Americans received music in the 1930s. In 1932, Glen Gray and the Casa Loma Orchestra were offered the opportunity of a lifetime. They were to be the featured band on *The Camel Caravan*, a network radio show that showcased dance music. More in the style of Paul Whiteman than Fletcher Henderson, Gray and his Casa Lomans nonetheless played some tightly arranged, up-tempo numbers that got people listening to new trends in popular music. More important, from late 1934 until May 1935, a young clarinetist named Benny Goodman participated in a three-hour Saturday night broadcast on NBC. He and his orchestra split airtime with Xavier Cugat, a Latin bandleader, and Ken Murray, maestro for a decidedly sweet group. The coast-to-coast show was called *Let's Dance*, a name shared with Goodman's theme song. The program originated in New York City, and ran from 10:30 P.M. to 1:30 A.M. Goodman's slot was the final hour, which meant he was heard on the West Coast much earlier, thereby ensuring a larger audience and greater exposure.

Goodman parted company with the radio show in 1935, and embarked on a nationwide east-to-west road tour with his band. For much of the journey, the group did not do well. Audiences wanted current hits or old standards. Frustrated, the band pulled into the Palomar Ballroom in Los Angeles in August of 1935. But the Angelenos were ready; they had been listening to *Let's Dance* and wanted more of the same. The concert was a rousing success, and Goodman went on to become the "King of Swing."

Heading back east, the band played to a warm welcome in Chicago; the Windy City labeled the new music "swing." The name stuck, and the Swing Era was officially under way. In June 1936, *Saturday Night Swing Session* debuted on CBS, another coast-to-coast hookup. In March 1937, Goodman played the Paramount Theater on Times Square in New York City. As the band performed, the audience, mostly young people, got up and danced in the aisles. Goodman made a return visit to the Paramount in 1938, and the same thing occurred. For the first time, mainly working-class adolescents were taking an event and turning it into a national fad. This was popular culture at the grassroots level.

On January 16, 1938, Benny Goodman and His Orchestra stormed one of the citadels of high culture, Carnegie Hall. That evening he played what was called a "Jazz Concert," although "Swing Concert" would probably be a more accurate description. Either way, swing became the talk of the land. Reportedly, no one danced in the aisles, but the black-tie audience tapped its feet and enjoyed the exposure to this new phenomenon.

The Carnegie Hall venture even included some black musicians—Teddy Wilson, Count Basie, Lionel Hampton, among others—performing side by side with their white counterparts. In a segregated society, swing acted as a bridge, bringing blacks and whites together. Not only that, it assimilated popular and high culture in ways seldom attempted before. Any resistance was soon worn down as its popularity swept across the country. Thanks largely to concerts and radio, but also to records, jukeboxes, and the movies, swing had the largest audience any musical form had ever enjoyed.

THE TRIUMPH OF SWING

In the summer of 1938, a Swing Festival on Randall's Island in New York City drew 24,000 people. The event featured twenty-five bands and lasted some six hours. In December of that same year, critic John Hammond presented "From Spirituals to Swing," with staid Carnegie Hall again providing the stage. So successful was the undertaking that Hammond brought forth a second edition of the concert in 1939.

Keeping pace with all the live performances were record sales. They reached $26 million in 1938, selling at the rate of 700,000 discs a month, and virtually all of them were swing recordings. In 1939, Columbia Records, a perennial third behind Decca and RCA Victor, introduced a new, laminated disc that they advertised as having much better sound quality and longer life than the shellac records of the competition. It sold for 50 cents, but no one seemed to mind. By that time, eager buyers were snatching up 140 million recordings a year. Said Duke Ellington, "Jazz is music; swing is *business*."[4]

Two national magazines closely followed the swing phenomenon, chronicling its meteoric rise and eventual fall. Chicago-based *Downbeat* (founded 1934) and New York-based *Metronome* (founded 1932; an outgrowth of two previous publications of the same name that dated back to the 1880s) quickly established large circulations, and their readerships showed no hesitancy about voicing opinions. Both journals were fiercely combative about jazz and swing, taking to task anyone who voiced opposition to either. In addition, each had annual popularity polls that significantly influenced record sales.

MUSIC AND THE DEPRESSION

Since the nation was enduring an economic depression in this era of musical innovation, it could reasonably be expected that at least some of the period's music would reflect the crisis. And a large number of songs about those difficult times were written, though few of them were heard by a mass audience. There were union songs, and protest songs, along with songs about miners and farmers and migrants, but there were no big hit topical songs.

Part of this obliviousness came about because the focus of American popular music was narrowing. The music and lyrics might grow in sophistication, but the subject increasingly became that of romantic love. Very little music that reached large audiences addressed the issues of the day; instead, it talked of romance and relationships. The Depression was seemingly on the minds of everyone but songwriters.

"Brother, Can You Spare a Dime?" (Jay Gormey/E.Y. Harburg, 1932) is the great exception. Other attempts, like "There's No Depression in Love" (Dan Dougherty/Jack Yellen, 1931) and "Are You Makin' Any Money?" (Herman Hupfield, 1933), went nowhere, suggesting that the public really did not want musical reminders about the negative aspects of the crisis.

In 1929, lyricist Jack Yellen and composer Milton Ager had written the score for an early MGM sound musical, *Chasing Rainbows*. The film is forgotten today, but out of it one song emerged that was destined to be associated with the 1930s, the Depression, and President Roosevelt and the Democratic Party. The number is "Happy Days Are Here Again." Even today, loyal Democrats haul out the number and play it for their conventions and gatherings.

Another song that spoke to the era is "Life Is Just a Bowl of Cherries" (Ray Henderson/Lew Brown), which first appeared in the *George White Scandals of 1931*, a yearly Broadway revue. The popular Ethel Merman sang it, and its infectious lyric (life *will* get better) struck a responsive chord. If "Life Is Just a Bowl of Cherries" gives a bright side to the Depression, "Brother, Can You Spare a Dime?" presents a grimmer picture. The number debuted in *New Americana*, another musical, and was performed by Rex Weber. The overwhelming majority of people did not hear the song on Broadway, however; they listened to the recording by Bing Crosby, a crooner more associated with love lyrics than with anything having even a vaguely social content.

Balladeer Woody Guthrie, a major voice in the left-wing movements of the 1930s, attracted a following, albeit a limited one. His song "So Long, It's Been Good to Know Ya" (1935) became what is called a "Dust Bowl ballad." It reflects the hard times of the Depression, especially for rural people. Ironically, the song gained its greatest popularity in 1951, when a folk group called the Weavers recorded it.

Earl Robinson wrote socially significant songs, such as "Joe Hill" and "Abe Lincoln" (both 1938); they had a cult following, but failed to attract a big, diversified audience. Probably his most popular composition was

"Ballad for Americans" (1939), a frankly pro-American song that was a hit at the New York World's Fair. Everyone knew World War II was in the offing; it became a question of when. Owing to public demand, the song was featured three times a day at the RCA Pavilion.[5]

The foregoing were the exceptions, however, not the rule. In any popularity sweepstakes, love and romance completely overshadowed social consciousness. Especially attractive were male vocalists who sang close to the microphone in a soft voice, "crooning" their music. Actually, crooning came about because of radio, the leading purveyor of popular music in the country. A vocalist had to sing softly into the microphone in order to keep electronic distortion to a minimum, and so a number of artists had acquired this skill. Gradually, radio technology went through significant improvements and such singing was no longer necessary. But the style had established itself, listeners were used to it, and it became a trademark for many vocalists both during the Swing Era and later. Rudy Vallee, Bing Crosby, Russ Columbo, and a host of others became favorites in the early 1930s, and crooning culminated with Frank Sinatra as the star of trumpeter Harry James's orchestra at the end of the decade.[6]

DANCING

While millions were purchasing swing recordings, an equally impressive number were taking to the dance floor. Swing was melodic; it could be hummed, whistled, sung, and, for a whole generation of devotees, danced to. The 1920s may have had the Charleston, but the 1930s had the Shag, the Lindy Hop, the Suzy Q, the Big Apple, the Little Peach, Truckin'—a collection of dances summed up in one word: jitterbug. It was fast and furious, improvised or practiced. The Swing Era's attitude toward dancing can be found in the title of a hit tune associated with the Jimmy Lunceford band: "Tain't Wha'cha Do (It's the Way That You Do It)," penned in 1939 by Sy Oliver and Trummy Young.

Harlem's Savoy Ballroom, "The Home of Happy Feet," became the mecca for devoted jitterbugs. In fact, throughout the swinging 1930s the Savoy's management had to replace the club's hardwood dance floor every three years. An anthem of the era was "Stompin' at the Savoy" (1936; Goodman, Sampson, and Webb), an up-tempo dance classic that shares its lineage with both Benny Goodman's orchestra and Chick Webb's Savoy house band.

YOUTH AND SWING

In any study of the 1930s and music, the importance of youth culture must be addressed. The 1920s may have had its bright and showy "flaming youth," but the 1930s had young music connoisseurs, particularly in the area of swing. Their knowledge of the musical changes occurring during the decade was unique. These swing experts effectively challenged the elitist authoritarianism that had traditionally dictated taste in the arts; for their part, they brought about a refreshing openness to music. They also bought millions of records, giving them the all-important commercial clout to accompany their aesthetic preferences. The old wisdom that "experts" dictated standards for art, literature, and music came tumbling down in the Depression. The decade saw a democratization of the arts, and much of it was propelled by those young people who emerged as the new cognoscenti. Their victory over entrenched interests revolutionized the industry, opening once-closed doors to musicians and leading to the ascendancy of rhythm 'n' blues and rock in the 1940s and 1950s. As popular as they were, both jazz and swing practiced a kind of exclusivity: you had to be a fan, know the bands and sidemen, and collect the records.

SONGWRITING

Although the 1930s are associated with swing and the many dance bands, the decade was also the golden age of American songwriting. During these turbulent years, composers and lyricists including Harold Arlen, Irving Berlin, Hoagy Carmichael, Duke Ellington, Dorothy Fields, George and Ira Gershwin, Jerome Kern, Jimmy McHugh, Cole Porter, Leo Robin, Richard Rodgers and Lorenz Hart, Harry Warren, and Alec Wilder collectively defined American popular music. And that is just the short list; many other distinguished names also deserve a spot on any such compilation. They took the thirty-two-bar popular music format and turned it into art at the same time the big bands were making dance classics with similar materials.[7]

Almost weekly, it would seem, new songs by these consummately talented people appeared. They were destined to become standards— songs known by a large audience that remain popular for generations. In 1930, to choose a year at random, the Gershwins penned "Embraceable You," Hoagy Carmichael had "Georgia on My Mind," Rodgers and Hart were putting the finishing touches on "Ten Cents a Dance," and Cole Porter was completing "What Is This Thing Called Love?" Such a list is just the tip of the proverbial iceberg. Very quickly, the number of American popular standards grew to remarkable proportions. For whatever reasons, the 1930s produced some of the finest and most enduring music in the history of the idiom.

American popular music has been remarkably consistent throughout the years. The inroads of jazz, swing, and, later, rhythm 'n' blues and rock 'n' roll, cannot be denied, but for sheer longevity and uniformity, the pop song remains recognizably the same. It is almost always written in a verse-chorus form, in which the verse poses a situation and then the chorus (the melodic part that most people know best) brings about some kind of resolution. During the 1930s, this format was especially dominant; jazz and swing, for all their appeal, had to adapt more to the pop format than it to them. In many ways, the 1930s marked the high point of the popular song in American musical culture.

AUDIENCE FRAGMENTATION

If the traditional popular song reached its peak in the 1930s, another significant event was simultaneously diminishing its impact. This paradox came about through a combination of forces, technology and variety chief among them. On the technological side, music lovers had hundreds of recordings from which to choose, varied radio programs and stations, and a changing marquee at the local movie theater where sound movies now enticed them. What was happening in music—along with other areas of popular culture—has come to be called the demassification, or fragmentation, of the medium. The traditional popular song now had competition from every side: jazz, swing, country, hillbilly, novelty, semiclassical, and on and on.

Like the music, the audience underwent some shifts. Listeners began to divide along the lines of race, gender, age, education, location, and many other variables that sociologists delight in employing when explaining change. Young people preferred up-tempo swing to syrupy ballads. Women liked crooners better than blues belters. The more educated wanted sophisticated lyrics, not raw emotion, and rural folks leaned more toward country singers. These sweeping generalizations were all correct and all open to debate. On one thing people did agree: the 1930s clearly pointed to the future. American musical choices and tastes had splintered, and no one "style" or "type" would ever again define the music or the audience.

Even with the dominance of swing as the most popular format, other music also attracted large audiences. With radios in practically every home, and with recordings of all kinds readily available, virtually any taste could be satisfied. What this breakdown meant was that a group like Bob Wills and His Texas Playboys could introduce something called "Country Swing" (also known as "Texas Swing" and "western swing") in the Southwest. Throughout the 1930s, his band filled dance halls every night they were on the road, yet they had no real following outside Texas and some neighboring states. Within their territory, however, they capitalized on radio broadcasts and record purchases to create a hybrid that utilized both country music and swing.

Sound movies similarly influenced who listened to what. For example, Westerns have long been a popular genre in film. A number of cowboy actors were elevated to stardom when they sang in their own pictures. A pioneer was Ken Maynard in the early 1930s, but Gene Autry soon surpassed him to become one of the most successful of the "Singing Cowboys." In fact, he had a minor hit with "That Silver-Haired Daddy of Mine" (1934). Small wonder he sang it in eight separate episodes of *The Phantom Empire* (1935), a twelve-part serial. Had it not been for the movies, "That Silver-Haired Daddy of Mine" might have passed unnoticed.

CLASSICAL MUSIC

In the broad area of classical music, little attracted the public during the 1930s. George Gershwin continued his forays into "serious music," often returning to earlier works in new settings. He played his justly famous *Rhapsody in Blue* (composed in 1924) in a number of theaters, usually to large crowds. Early 1932 saw the Boston Symphony premiering his *Second Rhapsody*, a composition that furthered his investigations into the marriage of blues, jazz, and traditional composing. Gershwin's *Cuban Overture* (1932) and *Variations on I Got Rhythm* (1934) were also performed at this time. His folk opera *Porgy and Bess* (1935; libretto by Ira Gershwin, with DuBose and Dorothy Heyward) includes many short, popular songs that have stood on their own for decades as standards: e.g., "Summertime," "I Got Plenty of Nothin'," and "It Ain't Necessarily So."

In 1935 the conductor André Kostelanetz assembled a sixty-five-piece orchestra for radio's *Chesterfield Time*. The show brought lush arrangements of standards and the semiclassics to the masses. It had a following and was consistently ranked number one by critics and listeners alike. Composer/conductor Morton Gould similarly explored light classics with his *Cresta Blanca Carnival*. The Longines Symphonette and *The Voice of Firestone*, given generous commercial support, also hopped on the semiclassical bandwagon.

Richard Rodgers likewise explored the extended, not-quite-classical format with a ballet, *Slaughter on Tenth Avenue*, written for the play *On Your Toes* (1936). Much beloved by symphony and pops orchestras, it has entered the repertoire of many such organizations, and is a perennial crowd pleaser.

Two more academic composers of the period who attracted some public attention were Ferde Grofé and Aaron Copland. Grofé began his career in the 1920s by writing arrangements for Paul Whiteman's orchestra, an activity which gave him exposure to the concept of symphonic jazz, particularly George Gershwin's *Rhapsody in Blue*. Its success led Grofé to compose *The Grand Canyon Suite* (1931), a musical exposition on a natural wonder of America. One part of the suite, "On the Trail," became quite popular. Philip Morris cigarettes took this piece and made it their signature on radio; the clop-clop of mules' hooves as they descend the canyon trail immediately identified the orchestration as Grofé's and—more important—the tobacco company's theme. The composer's work could also be heard at the New York World's Fair, where several compositions were performed on Novachords, electronic organs that simulated various orchestral sounds and served as precursors of the modern synthesizer.

Aaron Copland also experimented with jazz in the 1920s. Like Ferde Grofé, he reached out for more accessible music, and he began to achieve a larger audience during the 1930s. His *El Salon Mexico* (1936), *Music for Radio (Prairie Journal*; 1937), and *Billy the Kid* (1938), along with two film scores, *The City* (1939; shown continuously at the New York World's Fair) and *Of Mice and Men* (1939), were all favorably received. By and large, however, most serious music had a limited following during the Depression; the big dance bands and the nation's fascination with swing simply overpowered it.

The Federal Music Project (FMP), one of many New Deal agencies, put at least 15,000 unemployed or underemployed musicians to work. Nikolai Sokoloff, former conductor of the Cleveland Symphony, headed up the program, and it is estimated that the FMP underwrote a quarter-million public concerts for some 150 million people. The FMP emphasized performance more than it did composing, although it singled out many American composers. Instruction in music and music appreciation were also stressed, allowing some 500,000 students to take lessons under government auspices. The FMP sponsored research on American blues and folk music, accumulating a priceless collection that was eventually housed in the Library of Congress. The project stands as one of the few examples of government interest in the arts and its enthusiastic support of them.[8]

THE DISC JOCKEY AND THE JUKEBOX

Broadway shows, once a primary provider of pop songs, suffered mightily during the Depression. In 1930, thirty-two musicals opened; in 1934, only ten—and all ten were financial failures. But Americans had no shortage of new music; the movies were doing well, and radio was booming. And there to play the records sat the "radio jockey." Sometime in the late 1930s he—there were virtually no women spinning records then—was dubbed a "disc jockey," and the name stuck. The first well-known DJ was Al Jarvis, broadcasting from Los Angeles in "The World's Largest Make-Believe Ballroom." Jarvis's show began in 1932; in 1935

Martin Block had his own "Make-Believe Ballroom" in New York City, a show that eventually could be heard nationally. One of Block's features was "Saturday Night in Harlem," which gave precious exposure to black bands and singers, then a rarity on radio. Others across the land picked up on his successful format—chatter, records, chatter, commercials—and the disc jockey soon occupied a major portion of the broadcast day.[9]

In 1933, Prohibition was rejected; people could legally consume alcohol once again. Repeal was strongly embraced by the music business at all levels. The reopening of lounges, bars, and nightclubs meant they had to have music, either live or recorded. The jukebox became a standard fixture in these establishments, its neon and flashing lights serving as a kind of summation of 1930s design. It was architecture, a skyscraper in miniature. More important, it was a moneymaker. By 1939, over 225,000 jukeboxes could be found scattered across the nation, and they played almost half of all records sold. Their popularity even spurred a novelty song, "The Music Goes 'Round and 'Round" (1935; Hodgson/Farley & Riley), a reference to the visibility of the spinning records within the machine.

Another form of mechanical music also emerged in the 1930s. In 1934, Muzak, a service that went directly to restaurants, dance halls, factories, and offices, was made available. It piped in soothing background music with no attempt made to provide the latest hits or dance numbers. This was packaged music just below the level of consciousness, a kind of subliminal sound massage.

When dealing with pop music and what is good and what is mediocre, people instantly see themselves as experts. Any attempt to list "the best" becomes a subjective exercise and will not be to the liking of all. But that did not stop a group of radio producers in April of 1935. On that date *Your Lucky Strike Hit Parade* premiered on the NBC network. "We don't pick 'em, we just play 'em," was the slogan, and the show became an immediate hit. By surveying record and sheet music sales, the promoters promised a scientific estimate of the nation's popular preferences. Once a week, the show would breathlessly work its way up from Number Ten to Number One, the ten top-selling songs in America at that time. Accurate or not, audiences loved the suspense, and of course they got to hear their favorites performed each week. It was a winning formula; *Your Hit Parade* stayed on the air until 1959. It was also on television from 1950 to 1959 (a 1974 revival flopped), but eventually fell out of favor.

SUMMARY

For musicians and music lovers alike, the 1930s brought significant changes in the music business, covering sheet music, recordings, radio, sound movies, and—at the very end of the decade—the promise of television. The 1930s witnessed the dramatic rise of recordings at the expense of sheet music, the interdependency of recordings and radio, and the impact swing had on all facets of the music business.

THE 1930S

10

Performing Arts

BACKGROUND

When considering the performing arts—movies, radio, television, theater, and dance—and the popular culture of the 1930s, it must be kept in
mind that the two pre-eminent areas in this large category were movies
and radio. In any given week, on any given day, far more people listened
to their radios or attended movies than went to plays, saw dancers perform, or watched that new medium, television. A comparison of numbers is, however, grossly unfair; movie attendance and radio listenership
were calculated in the tens of millions, whereas the figures for the others
were, at best, in the thousands. Television came about so late in the
decade that people had little time to experience it. Theater and dance,
also part of the performing arts picture, served more as complements to
movies and radio, instead of being direct competitors.

MOVIES

There may have been an economic depression, there may have been
widespread unemployment, but Americans of every stripe still flocked
to the movies. Somehow, sitting in a darkened theater with a flickering
image up on the screen took people away from their problems. The addition of sound made the experience that much better, and by the early
1930s, virtually all theaters were wired for this latest technological innovation. From comedy to tragedy, movies seemed a good antidote to
the myriad woes lurking outside the theater's doors. Attendance, like the
stock market, had fallen, but films still proved irresistible.

At the beginning of the decade, admission prices tended to range from about 25 cents to 50 cents—more for highly publicized films with big-name stars at the grand movie palaces. The lower figure was for small neighborhood theaters showing only second-run features, movies previously exhibited at larger, fancier houses. At the first-run theaters, there were lower prices for matinees and children, usually something on the order of 25 cents until 2 P.M., 35 cents until 6 P.M., and 50 cents thereafter. As economic conditions worsened, fewer patrons attended the movies; they were feeling the pinch of declining income, and "entertainment" seemed a reasonable place to trim budgets. Theater owners, all too aware of a falloff in admissions, employed the obvious first solution of cutting prices. In 1930, ticket prices started dropping, and by 1933 they had declined an average of 20 cents, meaning that the neighborhood houses often charged only a dime, and the bigger palaces maybe a quarter.

Next, most theaters switched to a new format: the double feature—two complete movies. One was usually a "quality" picture; it had recognizable stars and more costly production values, such as special effects, location shooting, top screenwriters, a lush musical score, and heavier advertising. The second feature, however, was what came to be called a "B" movie. It was short, maybe just over an hour, and cut budgetary corners wherever it could—a canned score, repetitive plots, crude effects, and few, if any, big stars.

As if two full-length features were not enough, patrons also got a cartoon, a newsreel, maybe a short humorous piece or a documentary, and, on occasion, an episode of a weekly serial. Many theaters added a "dish night," an evening when cheap crockery was given away to lucky ticketholders. Other popular gimmicks included "bank night" and Bingo, both of which allowed a fortunate few in the audience to leave with some extra cash in their pockets. "Two for one" passes were tried; on certain days or at designated hours, two people could attend a performance for the price of one. And, with an eye on both their patrons' comfort and the cash register, the theaters added "iced air." No more sweltering in a room barely refreshed by oscillating electric fans; now it was "70 degrees cool inside."

Despite these efforts to lure audiences, by 1933 one-third of all American movie theaters had been forced to close. That year, however, was the nadir. Along with the 1934 economy, the retail end of the film business began to show some signs of revival. But many of the changes initiated during the previous three challenging years remained in place. The double feature became a part of the American audience's expectations and experience. The Bank Nights might disappear, but no one rushed to turn off the iced air. And, although many theaters were shuttered, even in 1933 over 75 million people went to the movies every week.

These millions witnessed the most diverse collection of films in the history of American cinema. From Edward G. Robinson's snarl in *Little Caesar* (1930) to the zaniness of the Marx Brothers in *A Night at the Opera* (1935) to Scarlett and Rhett in *Gone with the Wind* (1939), the 1930s encompassed a dizzying array of pictures that kept the patrons coming, so that by the end of the decade movie attendance had climbed back up to around 100 million a week.

To regain that lost audience, Hollywood itself had to change. The studio system, well established by the 1920s, became more and more a partnership between business and craft. The business sector provided cash, especially in the difficult early years of the Depression, and those already in motion pictures supplied the expertise. It may sound like a deal with the devil, but it kept Metro-Goldwyn-Mayer, Universal, Warner Brothers, Columbia Pictures, Paramount, United Artists, and all the other studios solvent and functioning. Although this marriage resulted in more attention being paid to making profits than to creating art, the industry was still capable of pleasing its legions of fans. One way involved offering the latest technology.

Technical Changes

Sound pictures had become a fact of movie life by the late 1920s. Seemingly overnight, the approximately 19,000 movie houses around the country had to accommodate this momentous event, and they did. In a remarkable display of catering to their public, most theaters successfully made the switch from old equipment to new. The studios also complied: "100% talking" had become the norm for Hollywood productions by 1930.

In addition to embracing sound, the industry earnestly experimented with color during the 1930s. For instance, *Paramount on Parade* (1930) was an all-star musical revue that featured several dance numbers in an early two-color Technicolor process. But the resultant hues were far from true, and audiences came away disappointed. Not until 1935 and *Becky Sharp* was a satisfactory three-color process made available for feature films. Technicolor was expensive, and so the majority of movies continued to be shot in trusty, economical black and white. Over the decade, inferior imitations of Technicolor abounded; some used sepia tones and tried to pass themselves off as authentic. Others, such as Anscocolor, Cinecolor, Magnacolor, Multicolor, and Trucolor, employed processes that washed out any vibrant hues and resulted in a diluted image. It took a long time for color of any kind to establish dominance; not until the late 1960s did the balance shift to color films. In the 1930s, color proved to be the exception, not the rule.

For the most part, the Depression went unacknowledged. And those rare films that did face contemporary problems seldom fared well at the box office. But, by their very avoidance (or seeming avoidance) of issues, the movies were speaking loudly and clearly to their devoted fans.

Gangster Films

One of the first movie crazes of the 1930s was a rash of gangster films. Public taste tends to be cyclical, and embraces first one kind of film, then another, and then another after that. Those movies fortunate enough to be both produced in, and reflective of, any particular cycle usually do well. Those that fall outside the cycle are as a rule doomed to oblivion, at least as far as the fickle public goes.[1]

Most gangster films follow a predictable pattern: a small-time mobster (juvenile delinquent, sociopath, thief, etc.) rises in his "profession." He enjoys wealth and power, often for much of the movie, but then he must pay. Usually his downfall is abrupt, whereas his success has been lengthy and celebrated. In the eyes of many, the gangster remained a glamorous figure. During a time of economic and social disorder, life on the wrong side of the law had its appeal. Films like the aforementioned *Little Caesar* (1930), *Public Enemy* (1931), with Jimmy Cagney creating his version of a criminal, and *Scarface* (1932) gave the public a distorted view of the American myth of success. In these films, education is downgraded, a waste of time for the man of action. Those who do acquire formal learning are portrayed as weak and powerless.

In American popular entertainment, anti-intellectualism has always been an important theme. The teacher, the scholar, and the man of learning have long borne the jokes aimed at their accomplishments. Ironically, the early 1930s was a time both of considerable lawlessness and of public concern about education. A host of criminals, with such romanticized names as "Legs" Diamond, "Baby Face" Nelson, "Machine Gun" Kelly, "Pretty Boy" Floyd, "Ma" Barker, and Bonnie and Clyde, had captured the nation's imagination, their actions heightened by the frenzied news coverage they were afforded. With law enforcement often seen as inept and corrupt, the success of these latter-day outlaws, both real and on screen, fed into a national resentment toward authority and its failures. Small wonder, then, that crime films found a receptive audience—even as the younger members of that same audience were remaining in school and gaining educations in the face of declining job opportunities.

Censorship

Gangster movies constituted but one selection on an ever-widening menu of choices Hollywood provided its voracious fans. Nonetheless, much was made of such films, to the extent that the movie industry had to consider self-censorship—or face the probability that outsiders would take on the job. In 1933, a group of Catholic bishops established the Legion of Decency. Their aim was to cleanse films of elements they thought harmful to the public, especially youth. The prelates threatened boycotts of both studios and individual movies if they did not meet and maintain certain standards. In response, in 1934 a beleaguered Hollywood created the Production Code Administration, familiarly known as "The Breen Office" for its leader, Joseph I. Breen. It was designed to supplant the Motion Picture Producers and Distributors of America, or "Hays Office," an industry association led by Will Hays, that attempted to monitor content. The Breen Office had the dubious responsibility of enforcing "the Code," a lengthy, detailed listing of what should be avoided in American movies. No swearing, no sex, no drugs, no explicit violence, no nudity, no this, and no that—the Code had evolved since its initial 1922 appearance, but it had not been strictly enforced. Breen, caving in to much outside pressure, especially from the Legion of Decency, began to apply the Code restrictions without appeal. Producers and directors had to cease making their gangster sagas, at least in the manner of the early thirties.

Altogether different from the usual run of gangster movies is *I Am a Fugitive from a Chain Gang* (1932). Directed by Mervyn LeRoy, its plot involves the true story of a man caught in an unjust prison system. The main character is a victim of the cruelties of the Southern chain gangs, a very real blot on the penal system of the period. He escapes and moves back into legitimate society. There he achieves success and all goes well, but he is found out and returned to prison. After that, things fall apart—not unlike the social fabric at the time—and he becomes a hunted man, outside the system that taunted him. As bleak as anything that came out during the Depression, *I Am a Fugitive from a Chain Gang* provides no easy solutions in its dark closing frames. Many in the audience could no doubt see certain parallels in their lives and those being enacted on screen. No lifelines were being tossed out in 1932, and individuals found themselves up against seemingly uncaring, insurmountable forces.

Similarly, William Wellman's *Heroes for Sale* (1933) depicts a veteran, Tom Holmes, enduring one calamity after another. A resilient character, Holmes represents a kind of symbol for the country itself. No matter how discouraging things become, he muddles through. His experiences with unemployment and a confusing capitalistic ethic can be seen as passing; things will eventually get better. Nonetheless, the imagery of *Heroes for Sale* is dark and threatening, an approach that puts the film outside the usual run of Hollywood features.

The Police and G-Men

I Am a Fugitive from a Chain Gang and *Heroes for Sale* were exceptions. They did not portend any new trends for Depression movies. "Crime Does Not Pay!—Except at the Box Office" instead became the watchword. Edward G. Robinson might still colorfully portray a racketeer, but he would have to suffer mightily for it. The new heroes were the once-maligned federal law enforcement officers, or G-men, as they were popularly called. A renewed respect for law and order began to manifest itself in films of the mid-1930s, reflecting a public desire for authority figures. Villains remained plentiful, but they acted out their roles on screen to be hissed at, not admired. Oily lawyers, crooked politicians, dealers, and manipulators—these were convenient targets, and federal agents, along with honest public servants and brash reporters, rooted them out and exposed their malfeasance. *"G" Men* (1935) features former bad guy Jimmy Cagney in the FBI, and *Bullets or Ballots* (1936) has the versatile Edward G. Robinson as a lawman who goes undercover, thus allowing him to be both hero and gangster in the same film.

On a totally different note, Warner Oland began a remarkable series of films as Charlie Chan, the fictional Chinese detective of many an Earl Derr Biggers potboiler. Between 1931 and his death in 1938, Oland made sixteen Charlie Chan films; Sidney Toler took over the role in 1938 and churned out twenty-two more before his demise in 1947. These cheaply made whodunits delighted audiences throughout the thirties, and fans apparently did not find it incongruous that the Swedish-born Oland would portray an Asian character. These movies helped to reinforce the Code edicts against crime and corruption, they managed to supply a healthy dose of thrills, and the box office receipts were substantial.

Hollywood also found audiences receptive to images that affirmed basic, traditional views of American culture. The gangster may have been a somewhat romantic figure, but his bravado, his derring-do, could also be put forth by more traditional types. Thus Westerns, historical epics, war adventures, and love stories of every description continued to pour forth. No one type of film completely dominated the industry.

Westerns

Often ignored in any discussion of Hollywood and the early 1930s is the Western. No genre of film better exemplifies good triumphing over evil—the white hats defeating the black hats—and there was no shortage of cowboy movies during the period. The contrast between a gangster and a cowboy is immediate: one disdains the law, the other venerates it. In order to be successful—at least in American terms—both good guy and villain have to climb the ladder of success. The difference is that the gangster will have to fall off eventually, whereas the "good" cowboy usually gets the girl, the ranch, the horse, and achieves happiness.[2]

The majority of Westerns from the era are extremely low-budget productions, which means they were shot on the back lots of small Hollywood studios and served as the quintessential "B" pictures. Formula writers like Zane Grey provided endless plots for these "oaters." Grey alone contributed *The Border Legion* (1930), *Fighting Caravans* (1931, with a young Gary Cooper), *Riders of the Purple Sage* (1931), and *Robber's Roost* (1932) in the space of three years. A roster of reliable actors including Hoot Gibson, Buck Jones, Jack Holt, Tim McCoy, Tex Ritter, Bob Steele, Ken Maynard, and William Boyd (better known as Hopalong Cassidy) dutifully mounted their steeds and rode into the California sunset in one picture or serial after another.

The mythic qualities of the Western—wide-open spaces, rugged independence, clear-cut moral decisions—have appealed to audiences since the beginnings of the film industry and the first attempts at articulating this distinctive part of Americana. Edwin S. Porter's pioneering *The Great Train Robbery* (1903) practically wrote the script for all subsequent Westerns, and John Ford's epic *Stagecoach* (1939) is considered a model for bringing most of the symbolic connotations together. *Stagecoach*, however, is not a back-lot, shot-on-the-cheap production; it stars John Wayne, Claire Trevor, and Thomas Mitchell, and was photographed in Ford's favorite locale, Monument Valley, Arizona. It was a breakthrough film for Wayne, putting him in the select company of actors like Gary Cooper (*The Plainsman*, 1936), Henry Fonda (*The Trail of the Lonesome Pine*, 1936), Joel McCrea (*Wells Fargo*, 1937), Tyrone Power (*Jesse James*, 1939), and Errol Flynn (*Dodge City*, 1939).

Most of the 1930s "B" Westerns have been mercifully forgotten, but the values they represented live on in the American psyche. And a few of those performers—Tom Mix (with over 400 low-budget Westerns in a career that spanned almost thirty years), Gene Autry, and Roy Rogers—rose to a kind of quasi-star status in the industry. Mix was the real thing, a former marshal and a marvelous rider, thanks in no small part to his "wonder horse" Tony, whereas Autry and Rogers were "Singing Cowboys," vocalizing and strumming their guitars, often while astride their own prize horses, Champion and Trigger. There was even "The World's Only Singing Cowgirl" in the person of Dorothy Page, who starred in, among others, *The Singing Cowgirl* (1939) and *Water Rustlers* (1939). Collectively, the violence was low and the humor was corny, but for several generations of moviegoers, Mix, Autry, and Rogers epitomized the straight-talkin', fair-dealin', sharp-shootin' cowboy.

Musicals

Two other types of Depression-era films meriting attention are musicals and comedies, in particular the so-called "screwball comedies." The jump from musical to comedy is not a great one, since many film comedies utilized music as part of their plots. In fact, the term "musical comedy" effectively bridges any gap between the two genres. Given the cyclical nature of cinema, musicals were not much in favor at the box office until 1933.[3]

In that year, an almost bankrupt Warner Brothers released *42nd Street*. Categorized a "backstage musical" because it supposedly gives the audience an insider's view of the doings of the cast, it helped create the myth of the gutsy chorus girl. In the plot, Ruby Keeler, who later tapped her feet to fame and many more major roles as a result of this movie, takes over at the last minute for the ailing star, played by Bebe Daniels. Featuring a memorable score by Harry Warren and Al Dubin, *42nd Street* signaled the rebirth of the type, and it allows for some social commentary not often found in popular films.

Nineteen thirty-three was probably the bleakest year of the Depression; unemployment had reached its peak, affecting some 25 percent of the labor force. The worsening crisis had shaken the country's faith in hard work and deferred gratification, a situation that allowed directors and screenwriters an unusual forum. Movies like *42nd Street* affirm the old mythology of labor and its resultant rewards; dancing your heart out would bring about good things.

Flush with success, Warner Brothers released *Gold Diggers of 1933*, and the point was reinforced. Ginger Rogers, emerging as a star in her own right, sings the Warren/Dubin "We're in the Money." She voices some of them in pig Latin—for what reason, no one knows—and the audience can actually believe that it is also "in the money." *Gold Diggers of 1933* ends, however, on something of a somber note. Joan Blondell, usually a wisecracking comedian, gets to sing "Remember My Forgotten Man," a haunting number which features images of hollow-faced men, mostly forgotten veterans, marching in hopeless circles. It served as a grim, realistic reminder of the Depression lurking just outside the doors of the theater.

The studio completed its 1933 trilogy of feisty musicals with *Footlight Parade*, and cast none other than Jimmy Cagney as a hardworking producer who is broke, but not down and out. In all three pictures, Ruby Keeler and Dick Powell get to sing and dance, creating a partnership that endured for much of the decade. The two personify youthful earnestness and innocence. Their appearances, both together and in separate pictures, also captivated audiences. Powell could croon (passably) to Joan Blondell in *Broadway Gondolier*, a piece of fluff from 1935; Keeler could dance (quite well) on a giant human typewriter in *Ready, Willing, and Able*, a forgettable musical from 1937.

Busby Berkeley

42nd Street, Gold Diggers of 1933, and *Footlight Parade* boast remarkable choreography by Busby Berkeley, who created a visual cinematic style that is bold and imaginative. Almost alone, Berkeley defined 1930s dance. He had come to Hollywood from Broadway, and he went to work creating film sequences of massed dancers that continue to amaze viewers. With military precision, his performers blossom into lush flowers, become complex geometric forms, shrink and expand—all in time to a jazzy musical score. Audiences were enthralled, their perspective often the "Berkeley top shot," an overhead camera that looks directly down on the dancers, allowing all the surreal shapes and patterns to evolve. Moviegoers also got treated to much feminine pulchritude, despite the Code and all its restrictions. Perhaps the Breen Office hesitated to censor what was ostensibly being presented as "art." Art or cheesecake, the Berkeley sequences are firmly grounded in Depression America. He makes it clear that his dancers are members of the chorus, sweating and straining for minimal pay. They are not elitist members of a ballet troupe, and the working-class plots address the very real issues of unemployment and "getting by" as best as one can.

The sets on which Berkeley works his magic are also significant. The Depression musicals allow Art Deco or, as it came to be known later in the 1930s, Streamline Moderne, to dominate the background throughout both the dance numbers and the narrative. (See Chapter 4, "Architecture & Design.") These are hard, shiny, glossy sets, stripped down to a basic black and white with chromium accents. They establish a milieu that is urban and upscale; it reflects the characters' aspirations and, presumably, those of the audience. These movies promise an escape from unpleasantness, and both Art Deco and Streamline Moderne provide the perfect settings.

Fred Astaire and Ginger Rogers

Busby Berkeley was superb, but he was not the only choreographer/designer to have an impact on the audience's visual expectations. As the Depression wore down, the slick imagery of Fred Astaire and Ginger Rogers began to replace the earnestness, the sense of responsibility, which characterized so many of the movie musicals of the early 1930s. Fred and Ginger also dance—just the two of them—but it is carefree and fun, not regimented and geometric. Beginning with *Flying Down to Rio* (1933), nominally a Delores Del Rio vehicle, the Astaire/Rogers team steals the show with "The Carioca." Their grace, flawless timing, and pure sense of style made them stars overnight. Astaire insisted on doing his own choreography, and he brought a level of sophistication to the movies never before seen. Instant hits with audiences everywhere, the duo starred in eight more films during the thirties: *The Gay Divorcee* (1934), *Roberta* (1935), *Top Hat* (1935), *Follow the Fleet* (1936), *Swingtime* (1936), *Shall We Dance?* (1937), *Carefree* (1938), and *The Story of Vernon and Irene Castle* (1939). Each movie typifies elegance and poise.

Every detail in the Astaire/Rogers movies is a cinematic vision of fashion. Often the work of designer Van Nest Polglase, a man who saw to it that the two danced in Hollywood's singular interpretation of the big-city nightclub, their stark modernity and polished surfaces effectively display Astaire's tuxedos and Rogers' gowns. Here is escapism at its best: these sequences satisfied an audience hungry for images of good fortune, and not necessarily the plucky chorus-girl-makes-good films shown earlier. Because of the popular success of the Astaire/Rogers films, screen musicals achieved a remarkable urbanity in the later years of the decade.[4]

Other Musicals

Many other acting pairs gained fame via the musical route. Although the operetta form has never been terribly popular in the United States, for a few years Jeanette MacDonald and Nelson Eddy made it their personal property. After a surprisingly successful adaptation of Victor Herbert's *Naughty Marietta* (1935), the two teamed up again for a Hollywood version of Rudolph Friml's *Rose Marie* (1936). Possibly their most successful pairing, the film includes "Indian Love Song," the number usually associated with the "singing sweethearts." *Maytime* (1937; music by Sigmund Romberg) and *Sweethearts* (1938; music by Victor Herbert) concluded their efforts during the decade, and the magic was admittedly wearing thin. MacDonald is much the stronger of the two, whereas Eddy, an adequate singer, is wooden as an actor. Nevertheless, the fanciful costuming and romantic sets, coupled with fairy-tale plots and the duo's exuberant vocalizing, won a place in the hearts of many 1930s' moviegoers.

Numerous other singers and dancers rose to brief or continuing movie fame during the Depression years. Bing Crosby, a star of radio and recordings, churned out numerous mediocre films that capitalize on his easygoing crooning style. Only the most die-hard Crosby fans can recall *Too Much Harmony* (1933) and *Here Is My Heart* (1934), two typical products of his popularity. Sustained by wafer-thin plots, the movies give Crosby ample opportunity to sing such ditties as "The Day You Came Along" and "Love Is Just Around the Corner." The pictures did reasonably well, and demonstrated how different media—radio, recording, and film—can interconnect.

Although Bing Crosby will always be thought of as a crooner and not a movie star, his sometime partner Bob Hope will be best remembered as a film comedian. But in the 1930s, Hope made several movies that allowed him to show off his admittedly limited vocal skills. His signature theme song, "Thanks for the Memory" (Leo Robin and Ralph Grainger), was introduced in the film *The Big Broadcast of 1938*. Hope, along with Shirley Ross, sings the frequently topical lyrics on screen, and made the number an instant hit. Others were impressed also; "Thanks for the Memory" garnered "Best Song" at the 1938 Academy Awards.

The Big Broadcast of 1938 was Hope's first feature, but hardly his last. Ross and Hope shortly shared the screen again in the appropriately titled *Thanks for the Memory* (1938). The device of using the name of a hit song as a movie title was nothing new or original. People obviously enjoyed the pairing, because Ross and Hope were reunited a third time with *Some Like It Hot* (1939), an innocuous comedy that should not be confused with the hugely successful film of the same title that came out in 1959.

W.C. Fields and Mae West

Comedians W.C. Fields and Mae West brought both physical humor and a way with words to the movies of the 1930s. Both had come from a theatrical background, and Fields had enjoyed some success in silent films. Then, in the 1930s, he appeared in a number of classic short features, among them *The Dentist* (1932) and *Tillie and Gus* (1933). His familiar diction and gestures created a array of memorable characters he used over and over. In *The Old-Fashioned Way* (1934), Fields hits his stride as a movie comedian. He demonstrates his apparently genuine dislike of children with Baby Leroy, a popular child star of the time with whom Fields supposedly had a real-life feud. In addition, he plays a cheat, a fraud, and various other irreverent roles with which he would always be associated. Then, in an ingenious play-within-the-movie, the old melodrama *The Drunkard* is presented, and Fields gets to do a tippler, a favorite guise. Not only does he have the opportunity to do multiple parts that are all contained in one character, a Fields trademark, but he also gets to comment trenchantly on American manners and mores as he saw them. With his film persona well established, Fields marched on to a succession of popular comedies such as *It's a Gift* (1934) and *You Can't Cheat an Honest Man* (1939).

Mae West, on the other hand, had made her reputation on stage as the unchallenged queen of suggestiveness. With looks, double-entendres, and a sinuous walk, she was considered "too hot" for the movies in the 1920s. As receipts dropped with the Depression, the studios relaxed their strictures and welcomed West to the film capital. In her debut picture, *Night After Night* (1932), she infatuates the usually unflappable George Raft with her sex appeal. The new Hollywood Code had not yet come into effect, and West takes advantage of the fact. The innuendos fly and her notoriety was immediate. Quickly following up on that fame, West wrote and starred in *She Done Him Wrong* (1933), a re-creation of her stage role as Diamond Lil. This risqué comedy, which also features Cary Grant, helped push him to fame and star status while further burnishing Mae West's colorful image. Several more adult comedies followed, although nervous censors at the new Breen Office tried—albeit not always successfully—to make her tone down some of the more outrageous dialogue and situations. Her success was such that in 1936 she reported an income of $480,833, making her one of the highest-paid individuals in the nation, regardless of profession.

For the decade, the output of W.C. Fields and Mae West is unique. Much of their work challenges traditional American values and beliefs, and attempts, through comedy, to undermine them. Not that they are revolutionary—far from it. But if the essence of comedy is an assault on customs and "proper" behavior, then these two artists did it as well as anyone in Hollywood.

The Marx Brothers

Anarchy in the movies was not limited to W.C. Fields and Mae West. Throughout the 1930s a madcap trio of brothers diligently undermined just about every convention they encountered. The siblings were the Marx Brothers—Groucho, the "brains" and wiseacre of the trio; Chico, the piano-playing caricature of an Italian immigrant; and Harpo, the lecherous but harmless mime. Actually, there were five Marx brothers, all of whom performed from childhood on. Gummo, the middle son, left the group early, preferring the private sector to the uncertainties of vaudeville. Zeppo, the youngest of the quintet, had the distinction of being the "unfunny Marx brother." He played a hapless straight man, and likewise pulled out after appearing in their first five movies.

The Depression years were ripe for a comedy team like the Marx Brothers, and they instantly rose to popularity. Their movies also introduced the incomparable Margaret Dumont, a veteran stage actress who became something of a repertory player with the Marxes, appearing in many of their best pictures. Her role is always the same: to be the target of Groucho's endless insults and a victim of his schemes. It may have seemed an unenviable task, but she performs it brilliantly. Rich, haughty, and always befuddled as to what is actually happening, she emerges as a major player in her own right.

Nothing was sacred to the trio, and they ridiculed everything. At a time when some of the nation's most solid institutions appeared to be built on flimsy foundations, the Marx Brothers were merciless. They mocked the government, politics, education, industry, wealth, society, family—any group was fair game.

In six 1930s' films—*Animal Crackers* (1930), *Monkey Business* (1931), *Horse Feathers* (1932), *Duck Soup* (1933), *A Night at the Opera* (1935), and *A Day at the Races* (1937)—the brothers created a skewed universe of their own, one far distant from the realities of the day. They provided a wacky antidote to a disordered world, but it was a nihilistic one. Groucho grins and leers, joking constantly; Chico does a takeoff on Italian stereotypes; and Harpo silently reduces all that he encounters to a shambles. For the troubled 1930s, the Marx Brothers' brand of anarchistic comedy played surprisingly well. After the mid-thirties and stricter Code enforcement, the comedians reined in some of their zaniness. Their movies lose a good bit of irreverent swagger and become much more tame. Groucho's double-entendres and topicality are no longer quite so wicked, Chico's hustling for quick dollars lacks some of its previous zest, and Harpo is less of a lecher. Censorship achieved its goal, but the price was the dilution of a level of absurdity never again attained in the movies.

As far as audiences were concerned, the Marx Brothers' most successful venture was *A Night at the Opera*. Classical music and opera are always safe targets for comedy. It is the old story of low culture taking on high art. As usual, buffoonery wins out over elitism. In a series of skits in settings that range from the elegant staterooms of an ocean liner to a grand opera hall, the Marxes demolish anything that hints at being "cultural." And, of course, the long-suffering Margaret Dumont, this time a *grande dame* in opera circles, is there to bear the brunt of their actions. For a nation still in the throes of a seemingly never-ending depression, *A Night at the Opera* provided just the kind of rude comeuppance that Americans so enjoy. For once the have-nots are victorious over the haves.[5]

The Screwball Comedy

Looniness, absurdity, wackiness—those qualities did not disappear from American films with the decline of the Marx Brothers. Instead, they were transferred to a type of comedy entirely new to the screen. Aptly named "screwball comedies," these popular pictures set up ridiculous plot situations that were resolved in equally ridiculous ways. One of the first to begin to articulate the genre, and still a favorite, is *It Happened One Night* (1934), a laugh-filled story that defies reason, but reason has little to do with screwball comedies. Directed by Frank Capra, *It Happened One Night* stars Clark Gable and Claudette Colbert, both of whom were established in their film careers. Gable was typecast as an action hero, a ladies' man with muscles. Colbert had just played Cleopatra in a Cecil B. De Mille costume epic of the same name (1934), and the studios perceived her as a very feminine romantic lead. Neither actor was thought of as a comedian.

In *It Happened One Night*, the two enthusiastically trade wisecracks, revealing themselves to be skillful comic artists. The movie revolves around a simple question: when will the two antagonists realize they are in love? Director Capra keeps the waters roiled as the two would-be lovers work their way up the East Coast by bus, by car, and, in a classic bit of visual comedy, by hitchhiking. Of course, love wins out in the hilarious closing frames, but not before lots of misunderstanding, bad timing, and turmoil have their time on screen. It hardly sounds funny, but funny it is, and the fast-moving script and tight direction keep it that way. Hollywood seemed to agree: in an unheard-of sweep, *It Happened One Night* took Best Picture, Best Actor, Best Actress, Best Director, and Best Screenplay at the 1934 Academy Awards, a feat not equaled until 1975.

Screwball comedies mark a shift in movie content. Although they rely on stereotypes to a degree, they do so by turning them around. For example, *It Happened One Night* does not concern itself with sophisticated lovers living in a luxurious Art Deco world; its milieu is very much 1930s Depression America. Crowded buses full of working-class passengers, decrepit autocamps run by suspicious proprietors, and the grim reality of being broke form the background for this picture. The theme of the picture, however, is a traditional one of reconciliation, of letting love conquer all. The success of this and other screwball comedies signaled a return to a more positive kind of movie; the grim, negative images of the early 1930s were to be replaced by a more affirming vision.[6] (For more on this film, see Chapter 5, "Fashion," and Chapter 11, "Travel and Recreation.")

In a similar vein, *Mr. Deeds Goes to Town* (1936, directed by Frank Capra), *My Man Godfrey* (1936), *Easy Living* (1937), *The Awful Truth* (1937), *Joy of Living* (1938), *Bringing Up Baby* and *Holiday* (both 1938, and both starring Cary Grant and Katharine Hepburn), *You Can't Take It with You* (1938; Frank Capra, this time garnering Best Picture and Best Director Academy Awards), and *Mr. Smith Goes to Washington* (1939; Capra making his third appearance) demonstrate how American beliefs can be sustained. Without exception, these are warm, optimistic films. Themes range from a once-wealthy man reduced to being a butler, and teaching his rich employers that money cannot buy happiness (*My Man Godfrey*), to that of a multimillionaire who wants to give his fortune away to needy people (*Mr. Deeds Goes to Town*). Whatever the plot devices, the screwball comedies live up to their name: they portray the nation becoming a better place, either through love or through simple, generous humanity. They are a far cry from the hard-boiled pictures of the early 1930s, and their wacky casts of characters give them a broad, humorous appeal.

Fantasy, Horror, and Science Fiction

Fantasy and horror presented another cinematic way of escaping the harsh realities of the Depression. The period 1931–1936 was especially rich with both types of films. Perhaps because these marked the grimmest years economically, the escapism provided by such movies struck a needed chord with gloomy audiences tired of constant bad news. Just as with the gangster films of the period, it is tempting to make all kinds of sociological associations with fantasy and horror movies, but to draw any sweeping conclusions about their being direct responses to economic chaos, or to say that they depict situations that parallel reality, is to tread on dangerous critical ground. These movies were but components of a cycle—fantasy and horror are part of cinema history, and in Hollywood, success begets imitation. Perhaps audiences were ready for escapism, given the times, and the studios were certainly prepared to crank out fantasy and horror as long as they would sell. The associations best stop there.

In 1931, Universal Studios released director Tod Browning's *Dracula*. Dark and shadowy, it introduced American moviegoers to an entirely new type of picture, and they loved it. Bela Lugosi, an unknown Hungarian actor with a bizarre accent, plays the evil Count, a role that catapulted him to instant fame. This is Hollywood fantasy at its best. A colorful advertising campaign—"this ruthless, strange, exciting drama of the 'undead' " cried the theater placards—simply furthered public curiosity. An accurate count of how many subsequent Dracula films have been inspired by that stylish original is probably nonexistent.

The success of *Dracula* led producers to look for other subjects likely to frighten moviegoers. A new cycle commenced, and the studios wanted to get in on the excitement before interest waned. Universal again moved ahead of the competition, releasing *Frankenstein* that same year. Once more, they had a hit on their hands, one even bigger than *Dracula*. The venerable Mary Shelley tale of science run amok had been brought to the movies a number of times before, and director James Whale was doubtless influenced by these sources. He cast Boris Karloff, a veteran English actor, as the vilified monster. It was a brilliant move; overnight Karloff became the definitive Frankenstein—or, more properly—Frankensteinian monster. Most people today know that Dr. Frankenstein and the creature are not one and the same; the doctor's name has become, incorrectly, the name of the monster. In reality, Karloff's character lacks a name. No subsequent "creature," however, has been able to escape the nuances that Boris Karloff gave the role. He "is" Frankenstein, just as Bela Lugosi came to be associated with his interpretation of Dracula.

Setting the film in a bleak, fantastic land not unlike the Transylvania of *Dracula*, Whale builds suspense, refusing to let the audience see what Dr. Frankenstein has wrought, until suddenly he reveals the creature. And what the audience sees is the lumbering gait, the wires and pins, the deep-set eyes, and the strained, pathetic attempt to speak—coupled with the realization that "It's alive!"—to quote a famous line from one of the many sequels to this much-imitated series. It was horror, it was escapism, and it was Depression-era Hollywood at its most imaginative.

With Dracula and Frankenstein up and running, only the briefest period of time passed before they were joined by *The Mummy* (1932, Boris Karloff), *The White Zombie* (1932, Bela Lugosi), *The Ghoul* (1934, Boris Karloff), *The Black Cat* (1934, Bela Lugosi and Boris Karloff together), *The Bride of Frankenstein* (1935; James Whale once more directing, and Karloff reprising his character), *Dracula's Daughter* (1936, Lugosi doing likewise), and various and sundry bats, lost souls, freaks, invisible men, monsters, and mutants. This abbreviated list attests to the remarkable popularity enjoyed by these exercises in horror.

A considerable part of the success achieved by such movies lay in their use of special effects, but characterization and the establishment of mood and setting are also important elements. The effectiveness of the makeup for the creature in *Frankenstein* cannot be denied, but the plot focuses on Dr. Frankenstein and his creation, not on greasepaint. In the rash of fantasy films released during the early 1930s, plot and character too often become subordinated to technical bravura; the grotesqueries begin to emerge as more important than the stories unfolding on screen.

In many ways, *King Kong* (1933) is the definitive 1930s fantasy film. Its story of a mythic "king of the apes" has remained a popular favorite for years. Over time, however, what one remembers about the film is the special effects. Kong, truly a king and larger than life, grasping a tiny Fay Wray in a furry paw atop the Empire State Building—the scene is memorable because of all the technical wizardry employed in constructing the sequence. Acting and character are virtually absent; any emotions stirred by the episode are thanks to editing, miniatures, and a host of other devices.

Audiences at the time did not know that Kong is a composite of models, both full-scale (the massive head, in particular) and miniature (most of the action scenes). Studio craftsmen manipulated tiny arms and legs, process photographers captured them on film, editors arranged the frames sequentially into coherent sequences, and Fay Wray added her unique capacity for screaming to the sound track.

The overwhelming success of the film led RKO to rush out *Son of Kong* later that same year. The sequel proves that a movie needs more than

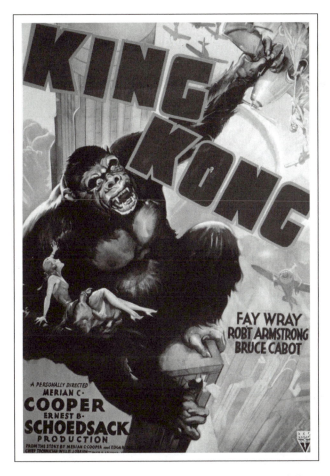

A theater poster for *King Kong* (1933). One of the
great fantasy films of all time, *King Kong* typified
the escapist movies that Hollywood produced
during the 1930s. (Photograph courtesy of the
Library of Congress.)

special effects to sustain it. "Baby Kong" has none of the nobility of his
illustrious father. The mystery and the grandeur are gone, and *Son of
Kong* soon languished at the box office. Nevertheless, other producers
were not oblivious to the success of *King Kong*. If supported by a halfway
decent screenplay, special effects-centered movies could make money.

Closely tied to the horror and fantasy films of the 1930s are the science-
fiction features that came out at that time. American audiences had their
first introduction to what the future might hold with *Just Imagine*, a 1930
musical supposedly set in 1980. Largely forgotten today, *Just Imagine* is

memorable for its evocation of the later twentieth century. Not surprisingly, it looks rather like a sleek, polished version of the 1930s, not the 1980s, with strong Art Deco and incipient Streamline Moderne accents abounding. In fact, the film is not unlike the milieu established for many of the Fred Astaire/Ginger Rogers musicals that were released a few years after *Just Imagine*.[7]

Adolescent Features

As if fantasy, horror, and science fiction were not enough, the movies every now and then purported to show "reality" and the pains and pleasures of growing up. The 1930s discovered that teenagers could be a marketable commodity. In the second half of the decade, MGM began to release the Andy Hardy movies, one of the most popular film series of all time. It all began with *A Family Affair* (1937), a lighthearted look at small-town America starring Mickey Rooney as Andy, the typical American teen, and Lionel Barrymore as his father, the wise Judge Hardy. So unexpectedly successful was this first title that the studio quickly followed with *You're Only Young Once, Judge Hardy's Children, Love Finds Andy Hardy*, and *Out West with the Hardys*, all released in 1938. In *You're Only Young Once*, veteran actor Lewis Stone replaces Barrymore, a role he repeated for the next fourteen Andy Hardy stories. In so doing, Stone became one of Hollywood's most beloved Hollywood players, a father who is always there for his son, and a fountain of sage advice. The films portray an America that probably never was, but one that people longed for just the same. The series relentlessly reinforces the mythic "American way of life," and ignores any unsettling contemporary events. Audiences flocked to these simplistic movies that sugarcoat both past and present.

Mickey Rooney, by virtue of his role as Andy Hardy, came to symbolize the American male teenager, or at least the way millions of anxious parents and politicians wanted to perceive him. But Rooney served to fill only part of the picture; if he epitomized the adolescent boy, then Judy Garland, another stock player from the MGM studios, emerged as the model teenage girl. The two made just three films together prior to 1940—*Thoroughbreds Don't Cry* (1937), *Love Finds Andy Hardy* (1938), and *Babes in Arms* (1939)—but the chemistry was such that they were teamed up numerous times in subsequent years. Garland went on to portray Dorothy in the smash *Wizard of Oz* (1939), a role that allowed her to exude a healthy innocence that doubtless reassured the parents of teenage daughters across the land.

With attendance at movies starring adolescent actors soaring, Hollywood quickly brought new releases to the screen with fresh young faces in the leads. Performers like Deanna Durbin (*Three Smart Girls*, 1936;

others), Jackie Cooper (*That Certain Age*, 1938; others), and Jane Withers (*Pack Up Your Troubles*, 1939; others) were cast in films designed to cash in on the success of this newly discovered genre. By the end of the decade, the major studios had stables of promising players who acted out the trials and tribulations of teenage love and romance in one forgettable film after another that nonetheless demonstrated the strength and profitability of the youth market.

Child Actors

Not all of Hollywood's focus was on teenagers, however. Child actors, or those under ten years of age, have always been a part of movies. Children were moneymakers in the silent comedies of the 1920s, and the industry saw no reason to tinker with success. For instance, Jackie Cooper and Jane Withers had had successful careers as child actors in films like *The Champ* (1931, Cooper) and *This Is the Life* (1935, Withers), but they inevitably grew up. They, of course, were not alone in that dilemma, and the industry constantly searched for a new crop of promising child performers. Many hopeful parents groomed their little ones to become movie stars. Despite the Depression, dancing schools flourished as kids tried to master tap and ballroom dancing. By the mid-1930s, the studios faced a glut of unemployed child actors, an ironic situation that mirrored the real world beyond the sound stages. Of the thousands of youngsters who auditioned for parts, only a tiny handful ever got on screen, and even fewer had any long-term success.

Of course, there is always an exception, and in this case it was a truly precocious little girl named Shirley Temple. Without a doubt—and regardless of age—she was the most popular movie star of the era. Between 1934 and 1939, Shirley Temple took top billing in thirteen films. After a couple of unremarkable one- and two-reelers made at age five, she stole the show in *Stand Up and Cheer* (1934), and her spectacular career was under way. In quick succession, she was cast in *Little Miss Marker* (1934) and *Now and Forever* (1934). That was all it took; the boom was on. Within two years, her fan mail was topping 60,000 letters a month, and she was even visited on a film set by Eleanor Roosevelt.[8]

While the child actress was busily churning out films, a huge Shirley Temple industry moved into high gear, mass-producing an array of records, books, playthings, and clothes popularized in her movies. If boys had their toy soldiers, girls had their Shirley Temple dolls. In 1933 alone, merchandisers sold 1.5 million Shirley dolls, the birth of a marketing dream. Just like Barbie dolls today, the Shirley dolls could be had in many varieties and prices. Even the boxes they came in were considered valuable.

Soon her income from endorsing these items exceeded anything the studio paid her. It was said she was photographed more than President Roosevelt; she appeared on the cover of *Time* magazine (the youngest subject ever); she was the top Hollywood box-office attraction from 1935 to 1938; and she had the distinction of achieving true celebrity status at an age when most children were still mastering their ABCs.

The persona Shirley Temple creates in her films was perfect for the Depression years. A combination of self-reliance and innocence, she guides adults through a threatening world while simultaneously needing their love and wisdom. Her character works hard, is honest and fair in all her dealings, radiates wholesomeness, and—most important—is capable of righting a world gone askew. Small wonder she brought reassurance to audiences hungry for some optimistic messages. Whether portraying an orphan or an heiress, her angelic looks and infectious good humor uplifted millions, young and old, throughout the 1930s.

Newsreels and World Events

At the end of the decade, the specter of war crept across the landscape. The nation went from the Depression and all its economic woes to the realization that soon a conflict would break out and the United States, despite the pleas of isolationists, would be involved. Hollywood was of two minds about the impending crisis. The majority of commercial films portray an innocent world where no mention is made about current events, and few directors or screenwriters attempted to allude to the possibility of war. A tiny minority of films, however, addresses current events. *The March of Time*, a monthly newsreel series, premiered in 1934. Underwritten, appropriately enough, by the publishing house responsible for the magazines *Time, Life,* and *Fortune,* these approximately fifteen-minute documentaries had the courage to discuss contemporary issues in frank, unequivocal language and images. Almost from its inception, *The March of Time* dealt with fascism, neutrality, isolationism, and especially Nazism and the rise of Adolf Hitler. But these were quarter-hour newsreels, a small part of the larger theatrical bill; they were not full-length features.

United Artists released *Blockade* in 1938. Marketed as a drama about espionage, it is set in the Spanish Civil War, an event fresh in everyone's minds. Starring Henry Fonda and Madeleine Carroll, *Blockade* quietly sides with the Spanish government through the respected Fonda, and takes a small stand against the rising forces of fascism. Warner Brothers, which had made a number of gritty, common-man films in the early 1930s, brought out *Confessions of a Nazi Spy* early in 1939. This film reflects the popular consensus of who the enemy will be through its provocative title, and even prompted a protest from the German government. Warner Brothers cast their veteran star Edward G. Robinson as a G-man ferreting out a vast Nazi conspiracy within America's borders. *Blockade* may have been muted; *Confessions of a Nazi Spy* is blatant in taking sides.[9]

The German invasion of Poland in September 1939 shook Americans and the film industry out of their complacency, yet both patrons and studios continued to prefer their entertainment to be nontopical. Not until Pearl Harbor in December of 1941 did the sleeping giant called Hollywood awake. Then war movies started to pour out just as fast as the studios could produce them, and the nation was engaged in full-scale conflict.

Moneymakers of 1939

At the end of this tumultuous period, two of the greatest pictures of the 1930s were released, and neither has anything whatsoever to do with World War II. One is a children's fantasy; the other, a sweeping historical drama. The films are *The Wizard of Oz* and *Gone with the Wind*; both came out in 1939, and both were produced by Metro-Goldwyn-Mayer. War clouds might be gathering in Europe and Asia, but Americans would rather—in the words of Scarlett O'Hara in *Gone with the Wind*—"think about it tomorrow."

The Wizard of Oz has enchanted generations of children and adults with its combination of the real and the fantastic. Its deserved success made a star of Judy Garland, and the memorable Harold Arlen/E.Y. Harburg score took two Academy Awards. The ingenious mix of Technicolor and sepia—particularly at the opening of the story—illustrated new uses for color processing, but the success of *The Wizard of Oz* depends not on story, stars, music, or technology. It works because all these elements mesh perfectly. Director Victor Fleming would never again achieve the sustained level of imagination he briefly enjoyed on that film, although he would, in the months following, share in the overall direction of *Gone with the Wind*.

Loosely based on the book by L. Frank Baum, *The Wizard of Oz* contains some elements of the prairie populism that often crops up in the original, but aside from a few glimpses of honorable poverty (Uncle Henry and Auntie Em's farm, for instance), it avoids anything remotely topical. True, the "real" world of Kansas is presented in sepia, whereas the "dream" world of Oz is presented in lush Technicolor, and one is stark and the other is fantastical. It is doubtful, however, that the producers were attempting to make subtle references to the 1930s or agrarianism. The one exception might be the wondrous Edwin B. Willis sets. For the Oz portions of the story, they are pure Streamline Moderne, and the towers of the Emerald City evoke an optimistic view of the future, far more so than the mixes of Art Deco and Modernism attempted earlier in films like *Just Imagine* and the many Warner Brothers musicals. In fact, the New York World's Fair (1939–1940) was up and running at the same time as the movie, and the resemblances between "The World of Tomorrow" and the Emerald City probably are not entirely coincidental. Oz may be "over the rainbow," but Dorothy knows that "if you dream hard enough . . . and follow the yellow brick road. . . ." In this respect, the escapism of *The Wizard of Oz* might apply both to events of the 1930s and to the growing threat of world war. But Dorothy is also sufficiently levelheaded not to go overboard with that kind of thinking. She does not look for things that are not there, and she finally returns to Kansas and good Midwestern sensibility.

Gone with the Wind cloaks itself in a romantic story and stoutly resists any contemporary references. That very denial of the present could be a response to it, but audiences were so taken by Scarlett O'Hara and Rhett Butler that it is doubtful that many saw the film in such terms. Based on Margaret Mitchell's blockbuster 1936 best-seller of the same name, *Gone with the Wind* enjoyed some of the best pre-release press agentry of any movie before or since. A nationwide, two-and-a-half-year contest was conducted to select who would play Scarlett. It was correctly assumed that Clark Gable had the role of Rhett secured. Fan magazines breathlessly reported on anything even remotely associated with the project, and MGM went so far as to replicate the portico of Tara, Scarlett's family home, for a gala opening night at Loew's Grand Theater in Atlanta. All the hoopla paid off: *Gone with the Wind* was an immediate, enduring hit.

The movie did not come about easily. Although very much the project of producer David O. Selznick, it of course required a director. George Cukor started in that role, but after nine weeks of shooting he was replaced by Victor Fleming. Not even Fleming, fresh from his success with *The Wizard of Oz*, could handle such a mammoth production; he collapsed on the set, and MGM finally had to have the help of Sam Wood to bring it to completion. A number of screenwriters wrote and rewrote the script, cameramen came and went, and no one seems absolutely sure who should get credit for what, although the Academy nonetheless awarded the Best Director prize to Fleming, along with seven additional Oscars to others connected with the production.

Variously called "the greatest movie ever made," "a woman's picture," "a potboiler," and "an expensive soap opera," *Gone with the Wind* certainly wraps up the 1930s in grand style. An expensive exercise in historical escapism, it taps into the country's continuing fascination with its own past. Perhaps the story's recurring theme of overcoming adversity, of moving from victim to survivor, is about as "timely" as *Gone with the Wind* ever gets. But for sheer entertainment—the real reason people attend the movies—it stands as the champion of the decade.[10]

Summary

Much has been omitted from this survey of the popular cinema of the 1930s. *The Thin Man* films with William Powell, Myrna Loy, and Asta; the Saturday afternoon serials with Buster Crabbe playing both Flash Gordon and Buck Rogers in one thrilling, cliff-hanging episode after another; *Our Gang*; Laurel and Hardy; Johnny Weissmuller and *Tarzan*; Walt Disney and *Snow White*—but space limits preclude covering all the riches that poured forth from the studios during the decade. The 1930s remain remarkable for the number of films that have come down to the present, still watchable, still enjoyable.

RADIO

Although millions of Americans went to the movies every week, there was still plenty of time left to listen to what had emerged as the most popular, most pervasive mass medium ever: radio. The word itself is somewhat a made-up one, a shortened form of "radiotelephony" and "radiotelegraphy." At the beginning of the 1930s, slightly over 600 AM (amplitude modulation) stations were on the air, broadcasting to some 12 million receiving sets. By 1940, the figures had grown to over 800 stations, and there was a whopping increase to 51 million sets. Radio prospered in the 1930s, despite the Depression, and the receiver established itself as a household necessity.

Many of the larger, floor-model receivers could serve as fine pieces of furniture. Often done in exotic veneers with striking styling, a top-of-the-line radio could cost hundreds of dollars. Since much American family life in the evenings revolved around the living room radio, this significant investment was seldom begrudged. Manufacturers like General Electric, Crosley, Philco, RCA, Magnavox, and Atwater Kent pitched their products as much for their elegance as for their electronic excellence.

As it insinuated itself into the everyday lives of Americans, radio assumed a unique importance: it provided up-to-the-minute news, weather, and sports; it entertained continuously, from music to drama to comedy; and it educated with endless self-help and instructional shows. By 1940, listeners merely had to twist the dial to find just about anything; the broadcast schedule offered something for everyone. Radio leveled regional and social differences and barriers by its very ubiquity. Everyone shared in the same programming, making radio the most national of all popular media.[11]

For most Americans, radio was considered a necessity, along with food and shelter. Even in the worst of the Depression, very few people de-

Everyone enjoyed the radio. By far the most popular
mass medium ever, 1930s' radio informed and
entertained the nation during its worst economic
crisis, and it did so from elaborate cabinets like the
one shown here. (Photograph courtesy of the Library
of Congress.)

faulted on their radio payments. Unlike movies or plays, radio gave the
illusion of being free. Once the receiver was paid for, no other costs were
involved, or so it seemed. Advertisers quickly grasped the importance
listeners placed on radio and were willing to put their dollars into commercials: ad spending went from slightly over $3 million in 1932 to well
over $100 million by 1940.

The commercialization of programming was not the only area of radio to experience rapid growth. Network broadcasting, whereby several stations were linked by telephone cable, had begun in the 1920s. The 1930s saw the National Broadcasting Company (NBC), with two networks, the Blue and the Red; the Columbia Broadcasting System (CBS) arose as a strong competitor; and the Mutual Broadcasting System (MBS), founded in 1934, was rapidly gaining listeners. This kind of growth meant the demise of much local, or independent, programming. Small stations quickly affiliated with the networks, recognizing that this form of broadcasting had greater resources for developing new shows. As the networks grew, costs rose and famous entertainers were signed to binding contracts. If smaller local stations had no network connections, they frequently found they lacked the financial ability to undertake their own programming. In the meantime, countless orchestras, combos, comedians, and other "local talent" lost long-standing jobs as their stations affiliated with the networks.

By 1931, the commercial power behind the networks had begun to assert itself. Most stations dropped out of direct production; they were essentially reduced to being carriers of network programming. In turn, advertising agencies began to develop their own ideas and formats. The agency-run "radio department" emerged as one of the most important divisions at broadcast studios. Although the networks were still given the right to approve programming, the big sponsors had grown so powerful that such approval was more a formality than a privilege. In addition, syndicates began to prepackage all manner of shows for both networks and independent stations. These productions were particularly attractive to smaller stations that could not afford to put together anything on their own that approached the syndicates' caliber of work.

Comedy and Variety Shows

American radio introduced an avid listening public to hundreds of personalities who grew to be household names. Some of these entertainers moved directly to radio from vaudeville, bypassing the movies, while others mixed film and radio careers. Whatever route they took, once they found a niche in broadcasting, they often rose to an unparalleled level of popular fame.

A good example is the career of Rudy Vallee, a modestly talented crooner who achieved great fame and popularity during the 1930s. Vallee left Yale University in 1928 to form a band, The Connecticut Yankees, with himself as vocalist. He was fortunate that several of his club appearances were carried live on radio. These broadcasts introduced listeners to his signature singing style—a weak voice projected by a megaphone. By staying very close to the sensitive radio microphone, he could achieve the same amplification effect.

Vallee made his series radio debut in *The Fleischmann Hour* at the end of the 1920s, opening each segment with his familiar "Heigh-ho, everybody!" The NBC show quickly became a network hit and set a standard for much subsequent musical variety programming. *The Fleischmann Hour* ran until 1936; at that time, it became *The Royal Gelatin Hour*, and continued until well into 1939. The two names given the show suggest some of the balances of power existing during the period. The series came about because of Vallee's popularity, but it was underwritten by corporate interests, in this case yeast and gelatin manufacturers. Vallee was nominally in charge, but his sponsors, along with their advertising agencies, had the right of prior restraint, which gave them de facto control of any content. Seldom did radio entertainers oversee their own productions. Radio might be a creative medium, but other interests held the financial reins of power.

The genial host of the series, Vallee frequently appeared as a star in his own right. His guests were usually fellow performers, although the show broke some new ground by allowing dramatic excerpts to be read by stage and film actors. These passages were written for radio and not the theater, suggesting the growing importance given the medium and its unique characteristics. The success of his series heightened Vallee's popularity in other areas, especially recordings. For much of the 1930s, the crooner enjoyed hit records with titles like "The Whiffenpoof Song," "The Maine Stein Song," and "I'm Just a Vagabond Lover."

Comedian Eddie Cantor likewise took advantage of the crossover opportunities available in popular entertainment. Already established as a star in vaudeville and on Broadway, Cantor made his radio debut on Vallee's Fleischmann show in 1931. Several months later, because of listener response to that program, he began *The Chase and Sanborn Hour*, a comedy-variety program that led to a long and successful radio career.

Facial grimaces, exaggerated gestures, playing to the crowd, or, in Cantor's case, rolling his big, wide eyes, were the visual things that got audiences to respond to entertainers in the days of vaudeville. But this kind of byplay could not be seen by those listening at home, although they could hear the laughter of the studio audience. Laughter by itself was not enough, however; the days of the old-time vaudevillians were numbered. A new generation of performers, trained in nonvisual techniques, quickly replaced them unless they adapted to the medium of radio. Vallee and Cantor were among the survivors. Their engaging personalities, coupled with Vallee's crooning and Cantor's vivacious high spirits, carried over on radio as well as they did on the stage. Throughout the 1930s, the two entertainers were consistently ranked among the top audience favorites.

Amos 'n' Andy

Perhaps the perfect performers for radio were Freeman Gosden and Charles Correll. Those names mean little to most people nowadays, but *Amos 'n' Andy* will evoke a response from just about anyone familiar with the early years of broadcasting. The characters of Amos, Andy, Kingfish, Lightnin', and Sapphire, and the Fresh-Air Taxi Company (where Amos and Andy worked) were created for what has come down as probably the most popular radio show of all time.

Amos 'n' Andy started out as *Sam 'n' Henry* in 1926 in Chicago. The station unwisely gave up the show, and Gosden and Correll changed the name of their property to *Amos 'n' Andy* to avoid any copyright battles. In 1929, NBC picked up their contract, and *Amos 'n' Andy* became a network offering, which brought the show national exposure. It was an immediate hit, and its popularity continued throughout the 1930s.

It is difficult to explain the success of *Amos 'n' Andy*. Theaters would stop their movies and pipe in the nightly broadcasts, rather than lose potential audiences to home radios. Department stores did likewise. In the 1930s, Gosden and Correll basically had only two sponsors: Pepsodent Toothpaste (Procter & Gamble) from 1929 to 1937; Campbell's Soup took over from 1937 onward. During that time, *Amos 'n' Andy* ran fifteen minutes a day, five days a week, and was usually broadcast in the early evening.

After a long, slow decline, the show was canceled in 1960. During its thirty-odd years on the air, *Amos 'n' Andy* attracted one of the largest repeat audiences in the history of radio. Gosden (Amos) and Correll (Andy) were two white male performers of many voices; their characters were blacks, and included both men and women. The series was, in some ways, a radio version of the old-time minstrel show: white performers in blackface doing caricatures of African Americans. In fact, the two actors frequently posed in full makeup for publicity shots, and no attempt was made to hide their identities. Their scripts were written in a stereotypical "Negro dialect"—and delivered exactly as written. Phrases like "I'se regusted," "Hello dere, Sapphire," and "Holy mackerel, Andy!" became part of national speech, and listeners exchanged summaries of the previous night's episode, usually delivering them in some approximation of the characters' patois. What should have been an issue of racial stereotyping seldom entered any superficial discussions of *Amos 'n' Andy*, although several civil rights organizations did protest the show, to little avail.

A facile explanation might be that "times were different then," and it is true that racial insensitivity was much more overt. The movies did not hesitate to caricature African Americans, recordings featuring black artists were openly sold as "race records," and other radio shows had char-

Freeman Gosden (l) and Charles Correll (r) performing as "Amos 'n' Andy." One of the most popular radio shows ever, *Amos 'n' Andy* amused listeners throughout the 1930s. (Photograph courtesy of the Library of Congress.)

acters just as stereotypical as Amos or Andy. The NAACP was particularly vocal in its criticisms of the series, but both the network and the sponsors for many years turned deaf ears to their protests. In the meantime, the show continued to attract a true mass audience that cut across the lines of race, age, and gender. For those directly involved with *Amos 'n' Andy*, there was no arguing with success.

A better explanation would be that the shows were genuinely funny. The scripts presented likable characters, the plots told tight stories, and there was no meanness or violence. Plus, *Amos 'n' Andy* played on radio, an aural medium. In 1930, at the height of their popularity, Gosden and Correll made a movie, *Check and Double Check*; the title comes from an expression used in the series. The film did not do well. Perhaps hearing the show—as opposed to seeing it—tempered the obvious stereotyping. The mind can create whatever images it wants. Of course, it can also erase any hints of racism with relative ease, something that many listeners must have done during the nightly broadcasts.[12]

Other Radio Comedians

While *Amos 'n' Andy* was securing its distinctive niche in programming history, the networks, along with some larger independent stations, busily searched for other categories of entertainment that would likewise draw in listeners. Fortunately, a real-life married couple, George Burns and Gracie Allen, was waiting in the proverbial wings. They were vaudevillians who would make a successful transition to radio and, in the process, create a new, radio-based kind of performing. After doing numerous guest spots in movies and radio in the early 1930s, CBS gave them shared billing with the Guy Lombardo orchestra on *The Robert Burns Panatela Program* in 1932. The fact that a long stogie was a permanent prop for George Burns was either pure serendipity or canny marketing by Robert Burns, a cigar maker. A mix of music and comedy, the show attracted a strong following, and assured Burns and Allen continued radio popularity throughout the decade. In fact, it was soon renamed *The George Burns and Gracie Allen Show*, a title which indicated more clearly what really attracted the audience.

Shows like *Amos 'n' Andy* and *Burns and Allen* demonstrated a new approach to comedy. The routines were clever and quick, relying on verbal humor instead of visual antics. More important, however, was the creation of familiar, evolving characters in those routines. Audiences had expectations about how Amos, Andy, George, and Gracie would act in given situations. Movie actors created screen personas (Gary Cooper as the lean, slow-talking cowboy, Marlene Dietrich as the seductive woman, etc.), and radio comedians discovered they could do likewise. Instead of isolated skits or one-liners with no reference to the deliverer, radio comedy moved more and more in the direction of humor that relied on audience identification of the comedian. Continuing jokes were just as funny as snappy one-liners.

When they were in vaudeville, George Burns was the funny man, and Gracie Allen fed him lines. But the couple discovered that when the roles were reversed, the laughs increased. Thus Burns became the bemused husband of the constantly addled Gracie. He may have seemed the straight man, but he frequently got to deliver the rejoinders, not just the setups. A brilliant comedian in her own right, Gracie had to remain in character throughout the show. Listeners looked forward to her non-sequiturs, her scatterbrained solutions to even the simplest problems, and her dizzy ideas. Week after week, this domestic narrative played out and, given the natural intimacy that defines radio, the team proved ideal for the medium.

Similarly, former vaudevillian Jack Benny developed his own memorable character. Debuting in 1932 on NBC, *The Jack Benny Show* quickly became a listener favorite and endured until 1955. The main figure throughout was, of course, Jack Benny himself, miser, would-be violinist, and a perpetually youthful thirty-nine. Benny had immediately sensed the need for continuity on radio, with the resultant carefully rendered figure and the standing jokes. He bolstered his show with an outstanding cast of regulars—announcer Don Wilson, bandleader Phil Harris, impressionist Mel Blanc, and Eddie Anderson as the put-upon Rochester, Benny's faithful servant—who added to the unity. Each of them had a prescribed role, an identity that was sustained in every broadcast. This kind of consistency created a familiarity that his fans obviously cherished.

Jim and Marian Jordan also moved from vaudeville to successful radio careers. They entered the medium in 1925, but rose to national fame in 1931 in a show entitled *Smackout—The Crossroads of the Air*. A comedy-and-variety mix of skits, *Smackout* (the main character, a grocer, was usually "smack out" of everything) featured two characters, played by the Jordans, Fibber McGee and Molly. By 1935, *Smackout* had become a memory, and *Fibber McGee and Molly* was helping to define situation comedy. Each episode revolved around an event, or "situation," in the fictive couple's life at 79 Wistful Vista, probably the best-known radio address in the nation at that time. The jokes flew back and forth, but a plot was also prominent.

A standing gag was Fibber's absentmindedness. For instance, he might not remember where he put something, and then he would recall: in the closet! Fibber McGee's Closet became, in the 1930s and 1940s, a national joke. He would open the closet door, and for the next few seconds all the audience would hear was the crashing of every conceivable object that might be stored there. The sound effects team had the responsibility for the aural chaos, and they always rose to the occasion. Listeners knew the crash was coming; it was just a question of when. Here, in action, was the imaginative side of radio. No sight gag could ever be as funny as what the sounds suggested for the notorious McGee closet.

Soap Operas

Not all was comedy in 1930s radio. Pathos, along with a healthy dose of bathos, also found a vast audience. Soap operas—so called because most of them were sponsored by soap companies and dealt with emotional stories and characters—became very much a part of the typical radio day. The first soap operas began in the late 1920s and early 1930s, and they were usually broadcast daily on weekday mornings and early afternoons, the assumption being that housewives would tune in for their favorite fifteen-minute dramas. It was further assumed that men would be neither interested nor available, and so the "soaps" became a small but significant area of network radio created by and for women, an unusual situation in what was essentially a male-dominated medium. Their emphases were women—their love lives, their families, and the trials and tribulations of domestic life. It might have been gender stereotyping, but the audience was there and it was an enthusiastic one.

Some of the more popular and enduring 1930s soap operas include *Backstage Wife* (1935–1959, NBC), *Just Plain Bill* (1932–1955, CBS), *Lorenzo Jones* (1937–1955, NBC), *Ma Perkins* (1933–1960, NBC and CBS—this show had the distinction of being on the two major networks simultaneously for a while), *One Man's Family* (1932–1959, NBC—an evening show instead of daytime), *Our Gal Sunday* (1937–1959, CBS), *Pepper Young's Family* (1936–1959, NBC), *The Romance of Helen Trent* (1933–1960, CBS), *Stella Dallas* (1937–1955, NBC), and *When a Girl Marries* (1939–1957, CBS). That is just a partial listing of the dozens that existed during these years. Some lasted for only a few episodes, while others lingered into the 1950s. A few even made the transition to television. Seldom were big-name actors involved; the soap opera world was a tight one, and players would breathlessly rush from stage to stage, studio to studio, in order to perform their roles in multiple dramas.

Two individuals, Anne and Frank Hummert, were probably the most important names in soap opera production during that hectic era. Together, they wrote and oversaw some thirty different daytime serials. The couple, from all accounts, was extremely demanding, but high standards assured quality production values. Advertisers agreed; the Hummerts accounted for over half of the ad revenue generated by soap operas. At times, their agency had as many as eighteen different serials going simultaneously.[13]

For housewives and anyone else—clearly soap opera audiences went beyond the stereotype—the daily serials dished up a bit of escapism. They featured molasses-like pacing, a deliberate touch on the part of writers—if a listener missed an episode or two, little or no catching up was required—and their simple plotting and black-and-white characters required minimal attentiveness. At the same time, just like many movies of the period, soap operas were rituals of affirmation: marriage, family, and friends. Often set in rural locales, the stories took simple folk and cast them into dramatic situations. Good, solid American values would win the day, although it might take a seeming eternity to reach resolution. The characters could then march on to the next problem, reassured about the verities of country life. Even series that used urban settings tended to have their characters return to lessons learned at Mother's knee or, better, have Mother herself appear to remind them of what they should know. Moralistic and conservative, the soap operas served as a kind of guidepost in the 1930s. No problem was too great, no situation too complex, for their simplistic solutions. Of course, the crises were never-ending; listeners could be assured that when the present episode finally met resolution, a new calamity awaited.

Radio Drama

The popularity of soap operas conclusively demonstrated to both advertising and network executives that dramatic productions could prosper on radio. Many "serious" dramatic series were therefore created during the decade, among them *Lux Radio Theatre* (Lux was a popular beauty soap of the time). Hosted from 1936 until 1945 by the celebrated Hollywood director Cecil B. De Mille, *Lux Radio Theatre* presented one-hour adaptations of leading motion pictures, and it often used the same stars who had appeared in the movie. The series illustrated the close connections between film and radio, and served as an ideal way of publicizing motion pictures while at the same time having a top-ranked radio show.

Another dramatic series that enjoyed acclaim in the 1930s was *First Nighter*. Supposedly broadcast from "The Little Theater off Times Square," this show actually originated in Chicago and, later, Hollywood. It attempted a theater-like atmosphere, and each episode had "Mr. First Nighter" being shown to his seat by an usher. Over the years, various actors took a seat on the aisle; it was their job to introduce an hour-long radio version of a stage production or—more likely—an original radio drama. The shows were of uneven quality, but nevertheless captured a good audience share. *First Nighter* ran from 1929 until 1953; during that run, more Americans were introduced to the stage, or at least the radio version of a play, than ever actually attended a theatrical production. Radio was serving its purpose as a mass medium, reaching uncounted multitudes who otherwise would not enjoy such performances.

News and Information

Although soap operas, comedies, dramas, and variety shows occupied a good part of the broadcast day, radio in the 1930s was becoming the primary carrier of news and information. As the Great Depression deepened in the early thirties, a note of desperation crept into public life. President-elect Franklin D. Roosevelt sensed this malaise, and took the unique step of using radio as a weapon against discontent. He had enjoyed a substantial victory over Herbert Hoover in the election of 1932 and, in March 1933, just days after taking office, Roosevelt initiated a remarkable series of broadcasts to the American people called "Fireside Chats."

Originating directly from the White House, these informal conversations were aimed at putting the public more at ease about the ongoing crisis. During the next several years, the president would conduct over forty such "chats," beginning each with a reassuring, "My dear friends." He chose his words carefully, using a simple vocabulary, but never condescended to his audience. As a result, he built a sense of intimacy between his listeners and himself. Critics charged him with unfairly utilizing the airwaves for political purposes, but the president remained undeterred. He had found an effective use for radio, one essentially unexplored up until then, and he exploited it throughout his administration. All reports suggest his chats did indeed have a calming effect on the public, and the power of the medium was therefore reinforced. It is estimated that upwards of a quarter of the nation tuned into the Fireside Chats, or some 30 million listeners. Never before had such a vast audience simultaneously shared in any public speech, making Franklin D. Roosevelt the nation's first media-savvy president.[14]

At the same time that Roosevelt was attempting to calm a concerned populace, a number of radio news reporters rose to prominence. This new breed of journalist was likewise learning about the potential of radio during the 1930s, and helped bring distinction to the networks. Newscasters (a relatively new designation that replaced "reporters") like Elmer Davis, Gabriel Heatter, H.V. Kaltenborn, Raymond Gram Swing, Lowell Thomas, and Walter Winchell were on the air, redefining the traditional image of a reporter. Instead of a straight, objective reading of events, they brought a personal style to their scripts, often adding interpretive commentary to ongoing stories. News on the radio was no longer quite the same as news found in print media. It had color and it had personality.

With war imminent, people relied on their radios for late-breaking bulletins about the deteriorating international situation. Entertainment might remain radio's primary function, but listeners sought information along with escapism. In any discussion of that period, the name of Edward R. Murrow emerges ahead of those of his contemporaries. A member of the CBS news team, Murrow brought an unequalled sincerity and gravity to his reports. In the darkest days before war broke out in Europe, he covered the approaching conflict, a calming voice in the face of disaster.

Dr. John R. Brinkley

As radio increasingly demonstrated its influence in the late 1920s and early 1930s, a few individuals attempted to take advantage of the power—real or perceived—the medium possessed. One of the first was Dr. John R. Brinkley, the "goat-gland doctor." A physician living in Milford, Kansas, Brinkley began in the 1920s to peddle over the air revolutionary "transplants," along with an elixir he had concocted, which "guaranteed" to give men a new level of sexual potency. So convincing were his promotions that in 1930 his Kansas station had the dubious distinction of being the most popular, as well as one of the strongest—in terms of wattage—in the nation. That same year, the Federal Radio Commission denied Brinkley a license renewal. The agency said he was perpetrating fraud. If that were not enough, he also lost his medical license.

He appealed, and a Kansas court upheld the FRC. The commission said that a radio station existed for the public's interest; it did not exist for personal gain. It went on to say that if a station could not demonstrate that it operated in the public interest, it could lose its license. Brinkley then tried using Mexican facilities to regain his influence, but the doctor had lost his base and he faded from the radio scene. Nevertheless, for a brief moment the Kansas doctor served as a radio celebrity, one of the first to use electronic media as a means to questionable ends.[15]

Father Coughlin

At about the time Dr. Brinkley was challenging the FRC, another individual was embarking on a crusade that would also employ radio as its primary messenger. Father Charles E. Coughlin, a priest at the Shrine of the Little Flower in Royal Oak, Michigan, stands as another example of how radio can be abused, but also how the abuses can stay within the narrow confines of the law. Beginning in 1930, Father Coughlin initiated a series of radio sermons that were as political as anything President Roosevelt could have envisioned. His message was a simple one: a cabal of international bankers, consisting of an assortment of Jewish financiers, Wall Street brokers, and Communist sympathizers, threatened the very foundations of democracy. Later, he would add the New Deal to his list. Only a turn to Italian-style fascism would save the Republic. He mixed invective with a mellow delivery that often lulled listeners to his true message. In the depths of the Depression, Father Coughlin held sway over an audience estimated at upwards of 40 million listeners, or more than Roosevelt usually got for his Fireside Chats. They, in turn, inundated his church with at least 80,000 letters a week, most containing a contribution. In no time, the Shrine of the Little Flower was taking in $5 million a year.[16]

The Columbia Broadcasting System, his parent network, became troubled when Coughlin would not allow them access to his scripts prior to delivery. They finally canceled his contract in 1933. Undeterred, Coughlin organized an independent network financed by listener contributions. That move was followed when he, along with the help of several other disaffected politicians, created the Union Party in 1936. By this time, however, Coughlin's appeal had waned. His new party did poorly, despite strong support from his network, and stations began to leave the organization. The Catholic Church finally took a stand against his extreme political positions and by the end of the decade he was unable to afford either a network or radio time. In his heyday, however, Coughlin's voice was a significant one on American radio. He demonstrated that, given the right of free speech, almost anyone with a strong radio personality can take to the airwaves and attract a large audience.

The War of the Worlds

Late in the decade—Halloween 1938, to be exact—another radio innovator demonstrated ways that the strengths of radio might be misused, albeit innocently. On that fateful evening, Orson Welles broadcast a dramatization of H.G. Wells's novel *The War of the Worlds*. It was a part of his series *Mercury Theatre on the Air*. For Halloween, listeners got both a trick and a treat.

Despite repeated statements throughout the broadcast that the show was a dramatization, many in the audience became convinced it was the real thing. Welles had cleverly camouflaged his warnings so that many missed them. For much of the hour, the inattentive worried that Martian invaders were roaming the swamps of New Jersey. It was a perfect demonstration of the imaginative power of radio, along with the potential for mass hysteria brought about by slick production methods.

Since the government controlled the airways, *The War of the Worlds* raised the issue of responsibility. If a gullible public is fooled by a radio show, whose responsibility is it that the public not be fooled again? It was a contest involving free speech and creative programming versus the FCC's mandate to protect the people from media hoaxes and misrepresentations. Because of the furor the broadcast evoked, the FCC came down heavily against productions that might frighten or dupe the public. It was an acknowledgment that radio was a medium of unquestioned power, and one that needed rules so that power would not be abused.[17]

Summary

Space does not permit mentioning all the shows, stars, and technical developments that contributed to the development of radio in the 1930s. Suffice it to say that by the end of the decade, commercial radio had ensconced itself in the homes and automobiles of most Americans. It served as their very first choice for entertainment. With the passage of time, however, a shift away from a steady diet of music and comedy occurred. More drama, more sports, and more news and reporting on special events came to play a larger role in scheduling. Certainly radio carried more of the nation's popular culture than any other medium, and it would continue to do so for another decade.

TELEVISION

The concept of transmitting pictures via the airwaves moved from the fantastic dreaming of science-fiction writers to the pages of popular magazines in the early years of the twentieth century. As wireless communication evolved into radio, it was only a matter of time before images would be added to sound in a way that people could both watch and listen in the comfort of their homes.

Throughout the 1930s, engineers labored mightily to make television a reality for American consumers. Everyone knew the technical problems associated with the medium would eventually be ironed out; it was just a question of when. Leading the attack was David Sarnoff and his team at the Radio Corporation of America labs. As a vice president of the RCA colossus in the 1920s, Sarnoff had distinguished himself by establishing the first radio network, the National Broadcasting Company. A futurist, he popularized the word "television," seeing in it the potential to meld sound and image, and to transmit the result over great distances. Sarnoff wanted RCA to be in the forefront as television evolved into a profit-making industry.

Unfortunately, the 1929 stock market crash and the continuing popularity of radio—along with the huge profits being generated by that medium—dissuaded most sustained efforts at any commercial exploitation of television. The experiments nonetheless continued: in 1930, NBC was granted permission to operate W2XBS (the predecessor of today's WNBC) in New York City; the following year found CBS operating W2XAB (today's WCBS), also out of New York. The two rivals used movie theaters and popular radio and vaudeville personalities as hosts to promote their new technologies, presaging the entertainment function that television would eventually fill so well.

In the summer of 1936, NBC television went on the air. It was a pretty limited affair—space atop the Empire State Building, a handful of bulky receiving sets, and an invitation-only group of about 200 people to witness the first telecast. David Sarnoff appeared on screen, as did some radio personalities, along with a few models and other entertainers. Somehow, despite the limited facilities and meager guest list, the people present sensed the importance of this event.

Another player in the emerging field of television was Allen B. Dumont. He supported the concept of home television reception, as opposed to theatrical presentation. Using facilities constructed in New Jersey, he broadcast signals to specially equipped New York offices and hotel rooms in 1930. Although his efforts drew little attention, in a few years Dumont proved himself a pioneer in developing a market-ready receiver. His company's "The Clifton" went on sale in 1938, making it the first commercially available television set.

A year earlier, NBC had a truck equipped with a mobile television transmitter cruising the streets of New York City. Nineteen thirty-eight saw the live television performance of *Susan and God*, a Broadway play, the same year that Dumont's receivers were going on sale. Nevertheless, this steady expansion of television, while suggestive of things to come, still could not be considered real popular culture. Only a few thousand receivers existed, and most of them were concentrated in metropolitan New York.

Expanding the boundaries of television, NBC telecast a variety show appearing on the stage of the newly built Radio City Music Hall, mobile units covered several baseball games in the New York area, and other sporting events followed in close succession. As if to underline television's versatility and mobility, RCA continued its experimental broadcasts, and crews televised the annual Macy's Thanksgiving Parade for the first time in 1939.

The World's Fair and Television

Prior to the Macy's parade, RCA "went public" at the glossy New York World's Fair in June 1939. One of the most popular exhibits, judging by the long lines and continual crowds, was the RCA display; it introduced television to a mass audience. Throughout each day, RCA featured continuous telecasting by its affiliate, NBC, and banks of receivers with five-, nine-, and twelve-inch screens where people could watch the proceedings. RCA even had sets for sale, at prices ranging from $199.50 (roughly $2500 in today's dollars) to $600 ($7500). During the 1939–1940 run of the fair, it is estimated that slightly over 120 of RCA's model TRK 660 receivers were bought. It may have been a slow start, but most knew that eventually the costs would come down, the picture would improve, and the programming would begin to rival that of radio.

At the dedication of the RCA Pavilion in Flushing Meadow, none other than President Roosevelt was in attendance, and he appeared on television. Roosevelt was the first head of state ever seen on the new medium, but he would be far from the last. A short time later, the king and queen of England also appeared, both in person and on screen. Not only the RCA Pavilion featured TV; so did exhibits sponsored by Ford, Westinghouse, and General Electric. Despite the obvious dominance by RCA and its new receivers, Dumont sets were displayed at the Crosley Appliance building. Wherever a person turned at the World's Fair, he or she was likely to encounter television. By the end of that busy year, the future of television was becoming clear: it would be the next major entertainment medium. Only the onset of World War II prevented the immediate, widespread adoption of the new marvel.[18]

THEATER

Broadway—the very word evokes associations. Glamorous opening nights, with gowned women and tuxedoed men gracefully stepping from limousines; glittering lights and crowds at the box office; the magic of live performances; renowned actors playing their roles in sumptuous theaters—these are some of the pictures that cross the mind when speaking of Broadway. Such sparkling images, based mainly on sentiment, have long been accepted. The facts, however, suggest an entertainment form that enjoys limited exposure, attracts only a small percentage of the potential audience, and experiences infrequent success.

In the 1930s, few people attended theatrical productions, in comparison to the numbers who went to movies, listened to radio, read newspapers, and so on. In addition, theater was primarily an urban entertainment, so rural Americans tended not to be theatergoers. Theater tickets were expensive, especially compared to movie tickets—a dime, maybe a quarter, would buy a double feature and more at a movie house. It took, at a minimum, several dollars to see a stage play, and that was the extent of the purchase—no second play, and certainly no newsreels or cartoons. With that kind of pricing differential, many people for many reasons opted not to attend theatrical productions. As a result, the audience did not represent a cross section of the population. Plus, if a play had any success at all, it was usually adapted to film to capitalize on its fleeting popularity. Moviegoers might even get to see some of the original cast in the motion-picture version. Thus one very popular art form brought a less popular one to a mass audience through a media crossover. The film version could differ markedly from the stage original, but millions of people could honestly say they "saw the movie of the play."

As for the plays themselves, radio productions like *First Nighter* and *Mercury Theater on the Air* purported to bring "drama" to millions, but seldom did they do straight readings of Broadway offerings. Instead, they featured original scripts that better fit the limitations of radio. Many hungry stage actors supplemented their incomes with frequent on-air performances. So, aside from those movies that were based on stage plays, traditional theater had few outlets for mass audiences.

Musicals

The International Ladies Garment Workers' Union (ILGWU) sponsored a musical revue titled *Pins and Needles* in 1937. A completely unanticipated success, it ran until the end of the decade, setting a record for musicals with 1108 performances. No one in the largely unknown cast was paid over $55 a week and it lacked the trappings of a big Broadway musical, but it struck a chord with New York audiences for several years. The play's "big song" was "Sing Me a Song of Social Significance," surely the most socially significant song title of the Depression. But *Pins and Needles* was virtually unheard of by most of the nation, despite its long run. It may have been mass culture for Broadway fans, but for everyone else, it languished in obscurity.[19]

A further review of the decade brings up the titles of many other plays that experienced commercial (i.e., New York) success. Certainly, almost anything that Richard Rodgers and Lorenz Hart, Cole Porter, or George and Ira Gershwin penned stood a better-than-average chance of being "big box office." These gentlemen were composers and lyricists, and their forte was the Broadway musical. Usually musicals are bright and breezy, with a fair number of hummable tunes. Anything that took minds off unemployment and discouraging economic news was favored over something that reinforced glum feelings. The sophisticated songs of these writers easily found a receptive, albeit limited, audience.

With a new production almost yearly, Rodgers and Hart were among the most prolific of the many composers who found favor in the 1930s. Songs like "Ten Cents a Dance" (*Simple Simon*, 1930), "Little Girl Blue" (*Jumbo*, 1935), and "My Funny Valentine" (*Babes in Arms*, 1937) flowed from their collective genius, setting a new standard for the musical theater. Thanks to recordings, radio, and the movies, their music achieved two distinctions: much of it became popular in its own time, and—more importantly—many of their songs have become "standards," melodies and lyrics known by both a variety of performers and the public over a long period of time.

Right behind Rodgers and Hart in terms of sheer productivity is Cole Porter. Porter started out the 1930 Broadway season with *The New Yorkers*. The play is forgettable, but "Love for Sale," a controversial song about a prostitute, has entered the "standard" repertory. Porter was a constant presence in musical theater throughout the decade, contributing some of the more adult—and certainly some of the most sophisticated—lyrics of the period. Like Rodgers and Hart, Porter's view of the world had little to do with the economic crisis or the New Deal, although they might not escape passing mention in his remarkable catalog of songs. Thanks again to movies, radio, and recordings, he became widely known and his music has come down to the present as some of the best of the era.

George and Ira Gershwin were likewise celebrated during the 1930s. Their musicals usually did well, and George enjoyed the added reputation of being a "serious" musician. In 1924, he had premiered *Rhapsody in Blue,* a concert piece that received considerable acclaim. A number of preludes and other compositions followed, solidifying his position as a significant American composer. It is with the brothers' film and theater music that most listeners are familiar, however, and in that area the Gershwins are fully the equals of Rodgers and Hart or Porter.

Girl Crazy, a Gershwin musical penned in 1930, featured Ethel Merman's rendition of "I Got Rhythm." The song, along with her performance, made her one of the all-time stars of the Broadway stage. The play itself went a long way. In 1932, just two years after being on stage, it came out as a Paramount movie comedy. A number of other Gershwin musicals followed—*Strike Up the Band* (1930), *Of Thee I Sing* (1931), and *Let 'Em Eat Cake* (1933). The last two contain numerous Depression-era references in their lyrics, so even musical theater could occasionally be topical. Finally, the Gershwins surprised the theater world with *Porgy and Bess* (1935), one of the few successful American attempts at opera.

Critics have never been able to decide if *Porgy and Bess* is musical theater posing as opera, or opera that contains elements of popular musical theater. The arguments are essentially academic; *Porgy and Bess* is unique in American musical and theatrical history. Its memorable score has made it a favorite of both concertgoers and theatergoers. Recorded innumerable times, in its entirety and most of the songs individually, filmed, and often on tour, this "folk opera" has successfully straddled the difficult line between high art and popular entertainment.

Songwriter Irving Berlin and author Moss Hart (not to be confused with the Lorenz Hart of Rodgers and Hart) teamed up for a unique Depression musical, *As Thousands Cheer* (1933). Designed like a daily newspaper, different sections of the revue are introduced by headlines, such as "Heat Wave Hits New York" and "Lonely-Heart Column." The lyrics are trenchant, and real, living people are the subjects. Hoover, Roosevelt, and John D. Rockefeller are among the butts of satire. *As Thousands Cheer* ran for 400 performances, proving that sophisticated Broadway audiences could laugh at the troubled times, if only for a couple of hours in a theater.

Many other musicals came and went during the 1930s, reinforcing the commonly held belief that musical comedy is the safest route to success on Broadway. For a decade enduring one economic problem after another, that might seem the best course to steer. The advent of sound in the movies further reduced theater attendance and with Hollywood's insatiable appetite for actors who were also good speakers, the pool of available stage talent shrank. By 1933, ticket prices stood at rock bottom—but they still cost more than a movie ticket—and attendance continued to be weak. A number of enterprising playwrights nonetheless attempted to present more traditional dramas on stage, and at times met with modest success.

Drama

Three playwrights who stand out are Maxwell Anderson, Robert E. Sherwood, and Clifford Odets. Each in his own way responded to the times, couching in dramatic terms many of the anxieties that Americans faced on a daily basis. All three shared the good fortune of having sensitive film treatments done of their stage work, allowing them exposure to the popular audience.[20]

Winterset, a 1935 work by Anderson, was the playwright's rumination on the infamous Sacco-Venzetti case of the 1920s. He dramatized the background of the event, and employed blank verse for his dialogue. As a rule, plays in verse do not do well on the American stage, but the producers were willing to take a chance. The gamble paid off; in only a year, RKO had produced a close film adaptation of the drama. The movie introduced audiences to Burgess Meredith, re-creating his stage role. Off-beat as it was, *Winterset* had only modest returns, but it allowed Meredith to embark on a lengthy film career, with only occasional returns to the stage. Not only did Hollywood reach much larger audiences, but it also provided secure and lucrative employment to actors.

Robert Sherwood had his name in lights with the 1936 production of *Idiot's Delight*. Although World War II was still several years away, many people sensed a conflict was inevitable unless attitudes and politics changed. In this play, Sherwood voices a strong message of pacifism, that war truly is an "idiot's delight." He places a group of people in a small hotel in the Italian Alps where they can talk and rediscover old associations. The play ends with the bombs of a new war bursting in the distance. Despite public opposition to American involvement in wars of any kind, it drew critical acclaim. *Idiot's Delight* won a Pulitzer Prize for Best Play, further burnishing the dramatist's image.

Three years later, and with World War II a certainty, Clark Gable and Norma Shearer starred in a strong film adaptation. The pacifist theme of the original took on new meaning in 1939, and the motion picture was rather daring. In an industry not particularly noted for tackling controversial issues, *Idiot's Delight* carried a clear note of antifascism. With the combination of an award-winning play and stars of the caliber of Gable and Shearer, Hollywood apparently felt it was worth the risk. It also offered the unique opportunity to see Clark Gable—his character is an entertainer—do a song-and-dance routine to "Puttin' on the Ritz."

Finally, there is Clifford Odets. In 1935, he had four plays running on Broadway, a remarkable feat: *Awake and Sing!, Waiting for Lefty, Till the Day I Die*, and *Paradise Lost*. Nineteen thirty-seven saw the opening of *Golden Boy*. The next year, *Rocket to the Moon* was on the boards. Yet in all this flurry of creativity, only one of his plays made it to the screen in the 1930s. In 1939, with William Holden making his film debut, *Golden*

Boy was released. Odets was a colorful figure, his plays raised controversy, and they did reasonably well at the theater box office. His themes, however, frightened off the big movie studios, illustrating some fundamental differences between Hollywood and Broadway at that time.

Golden Boy is less propagandistic than much of Odets' work; it focuses more on the human condition than it does on politics. Its theme of a young man trying to choose between prizefighting and music is clearly the stuff of a popular film. The main character lives a bleak working-class life and yearns to break free. The violin is one route, but it is slow and uncertain. Boxing, his other skill, looks faster and more direct. But he breaks his hand in the ring; now he can have neither. Although the movie version is somewhat watered-down from the stage version, neither is a cheerful story of youthful dreams. Occasionally Hollywood took off the rose-colored glasses, and this is one such example.

In other parts of the country, regional and local theater groups struggled to survive. Given the economic realities of the day, the majority of such efforts failed. Funding was all but unavailable, and the rights to the more popular contemporary plays were expensive. Many groups attempted to make do with older plays or with new, original material. Audiences, however, usually stayed away, and so there was no solid financial basis to support local theater.

The Federal Theater Project

Among the more interesting chapters of any history of American drama during the 1930s are those detailing the rise and eventual fall of the Federal Theater Project (FTP). In 1935, the Works Progress Administration (WPA), one of the many "alphabet agencies" founded during the Roosevelt administration, authorized funding for a federally sponsored program to support theater projects across the nation. The Depression had put innumerable people in theater-related jobs out of work. Attendance was down sharply, theaters were closed or operating on a shoestring, and many foresaw play production in the United States coming to an end unless help was not immediately forthcoming.

Hallie Flanagan, a dynamic academic from Vassar College, was appointed head of the new agency. Wasting no time, she plunged into hiring and production. It was decided that a variety of plays would be presented across the country, thus extending employment far beyond the boundaries of New York City. In 1936, the FTP presented a dramatic version of Sinclair Lewis's *It Can't Happen Here* simultaneously in twenty-one cities. The play, which tells of fascism coming to America, was very much an ideological one, and set the tone for the group and its subsequent history.

In 1937, attempting to reach out to as diverse an audience as possible, the group built an outdoor theater on Roanoke Island, off the coast of

North Carolina. In that setting, Paul Green's historical drama, *The Lost Colony*, was staged. A success then, it has continued to play on its island setting.

Under the leadership of playwright Elmer Rice, "The Living Newspaper" was developed. A mix of news and drama, fact and fiction, editorial and satire, "The Living Newspaper" served as one of the FTP's more controversial endeavors. Using contemporary headlines as their starting points, writers and actors combined their talents to comment on such topics as government bureaucracy (*Triple-A Plowed Under*, 1936), monopolies (*Power*, 1937), and the Depression (*One-Third of a Nation*, 1938). *One-Third of a Nation* was an exceptionally busy play, incorporating a cast of 67 actors who portrayed 195 characters—one way to provide employment to many. Sure to raise the hackles of politicians, "The Living Newspaper" got the fledgling organization into trouble with a number of officials. Nevertheless, it is estimated that 12 million people in New York City alone attended one or more of the "Living Newspaper" productions.

The daring of the FTP continued unabated. In 1938, they crossed racial barriers by introducing *The Swing Mikado* in Chicago. A jazzy interpretation of Gilbert and Sullivan featuring an all-black cast, it did well and went to New York in 1939. Broadway professionals were so taken by the FTP production that they mounted *The Hot Mikado* several weeks later. New Yorkers had the unique opportunity to see two versions of the same play, each backed with top swing musicians. Eventually *The Hot Mikado* ended up at the New York World's Fair, where tickets cost under a dollar.[21]

With some momentum behind it through its various productions, the FTP looked to expanding its offerings, but forces were gathering which would ultimately spell the demise of this enterprising group. The House Un-American Activities Committee, an investigative arm of Congress, began to look into the project, attempting to find Communist influences within the group. In 1939, under pressure from several sides, federal funding was withdrawn from this innovative government agency and it had to cease operation. It was a blow to stage productions. At its peak, the FTP had provided employment for about 10,000 persons in 40 states. It also demonstrated the difficulties involved when government attempts to do anything with the arts. For a brief moment, however, American theater had a strong supporter, and certainly reached out to publics that normally were not involved in theatrical activities.

DANCE

In the 1930s, organized dance did not fare well, at least in terms of public acceptance. In fact, few Americans were even aware of any movements in modern dance; it was not well publicized, and their attention was focused elsewhere. With the Depression and declining audiences, dance companies found themselves facing dire times. A few pioneers— Martha Graham, Hanya Holm, Doris Humphrey, Charles Weidman, Ruth Page—worked tirelessly in the 1930s, but with little or no acclaim. Exciting things might be happening, but there was no audience other than a handful of aficionados. To average Americans, serious dance was elitist culture and foreign to their experience or interest.

It might therefore seem that no dancing occurred during the 1930s, but nothing could be further from the truth. While the high art of Terpsichore labored on in near anonymity, the popular art of dancing flourished. Broadway musicals were redefining stage choreography, and Hollywood's "All Talking! All Singing! All Dancing!" extravaganzas presented dancers as they had never been seen before. The movie camera discovered new angles, new shots, and new methods of presenting action. Ruby Keeler might not just tap-dance; now she had dozens—or hundreds—of others exactly synchronized with her, thanks to choreographer Busby Berkeley's gift for positioning and moving dancers in front of the all-seeing camera. Performers like Eleanor Powell (*George White's Scandals of 1935*, debut; many others), Ann Miller (*New Faces of 1937*, debut; many others), Buddy Ebsen (*Broadway Melody of 1936*; many others) and Ray Bolger (*The Great Ziegfeld*, 1936; many others) rose from obscurity to major dancing roles in dozens of Hollywood musicals.

For millions of moviegoers, this *was* dancing. Nothing ambiguous or esoteric here; fifty chorus girls prancing on the wings of an airplane in *Flying Down to Rio* (1933) epitomized film musicals. It was entertainment, nothing more. Throughout the decade, Broadway and Hollywood dancers hoofed to the popular songs of the day, and the customers loved it. Fred Astaire and Ginger Rogers brought debonair ballroom dancing to new heights, and choreographers racked their brains to present their numbers in new and offbeat ways. All of which led set designers to create some of the most remarkable stage illusions ever seen. As far as the musicals of stage and screen were concerned, dancing was in fine health.

Meanwhile, the American people were dancing as never before. Instead of being observers, they were eager participants. The jitterbug, the Lindy, the Camel Walk, the Shorty George, the Susie-Q, the Sabu, the Toddle, even the old Lambeth Walk—along with waltzes, fox-trots, congas, sambas, and rumbas—brought millions onto the floor. In the 1930s, swing was king. The big bands played everywhere, and what they played was dance music. Halls, open-air pavilions, and clubs that allowed dancing flourished.

The 1920s had loosened the strictures against public dancing, especially popular dances like the Charleston. By the 1930s, only a few religious groups and some straitlaced communities still had rules regarding dancing. It was cheap entertainment, and at just the right time. Popular music had moved ever closer to the rhythms of jazz, and mainstream media were picking up on the new songs. And radio had come into its own, including more music shows on its schedules. The sales of recordings—dance recordings—skyrocketed, and radio and the movies mirrored this interest.[22]

One slightly odd form of dance that is immediately associated with the thirties is the dance marathon. Hardly dancing at all, but instead grotesque endurance contests, the press quickly focused on these "pageants of fatigue" and, for a brief period, marathon dancers were avidly followed by the public (more on this fad can be found in Chapter 7, "Leisure Activities").

CIRCUSES

Other performances that the public attended throughout the 1930s were circuses. Although a very traditional form of American entertainment, it reflected little of the ongoing trends of the period. Nevertheless, it qualifies as popular culture and merits mention.

The 1920s had been a prosperous time for traveling circuses. Companies like Ringling Brothers and Barnum & Bailey, Sparks, Christy Brothers, and Sells-Floto crisscrossed the country, bringing the big top to communities large and small. The Depression, however, changed all that. Circuses have always been dependent on the discretionary cash of their patrons, and in the thirties there was little to spend on anything. Smaller circuses went bankrupt as audiences shrank, and the larger ones cut back on shows, schedules, and performers. By 1932, a ticket to a well-known circus could be had for a quarter.

Clyde Beatty, a wild animal trainer, became one of the most popular circus performers of the period. Well established as a top-drawing act by 1930, Beatty was marketed as a symbol of the Depression, a common man overcoming great odds. His trademark consisted of entering a cage filled with varied species of animals and then making them obey his commands. In 1932, when he was bitten while rehearsing for a show in Indiana, his recovery was front-page news. The metaphor was clear: Beatty had overcome fear—just as President Roosevelt had promised in his inaugural speech—and was triumphant. Beatty left Ringling Brothers in 1934; he joined Cole Brothers, and the new group was renamed Cole Brothers-Clyde Beatty Combined Circus.[23]

In 1933, Mickey Rooney starred in a movie titled *The Big Cage*. His youthful character idolizes Clyde Beatty; to no one's surprise, Beatty plays himself in the picture. A forgettable film today, it enthralled audiences weary of a never-ending depression. Such was Beatty's fame that he made the cover of a 1937 issue of *Time* magazine as a fearless American.

In the realm of circus animals, nothing exceeded Gargantua. A gorilla brought from Africa, Gargantua began to appear as a Ringling Brothers attraction in 1938. The ape's face was disfigured into a nasty sneer, the result of an accident some years earlier, and his fierce demeanor made him an instant hit among audiences. Gargantua was immediately likened to King Kong, the legendary ape of the film of the same name. In fact, in 1938 Warner Brothers re-released *King Kong*, the hit movie of 1933. Although there was an instant tie-in between the two, the images seen in the movie endured longer than those seen in real life. Today, Gargantua is forgotten—he died in 1949—but *King Kong* still resonates in people's hearts.

SUMMARY

The 1930s were a rich, exciting period for most of the performing arts. Because of new technologies like radio, popular culture reached even the most isolated people and places. Every town had at least one movie theater, and it was a time of blossoming for the popular arts. While carnivals and fairs were also part of the American popular culture of the 1930s, they were adversely affected by the Depression, and faced failure in many rural areas. The Depression was depressing, but screwball comedies were there to cheer up people, along with George Burns and Gracie Allen and the Marx Brothers. Or folks could escape into fantasy with Frankenstein or follow the yellow brick road to Oz. The choices were so great, the entertainment so geared to wants and needs, that only the most pessimistic could fail to enjoy it all.

THE 1930S

11

Travel and Recreation

BACKGROUND

Americans have always had wanderlust. From the earliest pioneers setting off for the frontier to contemporary nomads taking "extreme vacations" by climbing in the Himalayas or trekking the Kalahari, the urge to get up and go has long been a national characteristic.

Sometimes that wanderlust arose from necessity, not choice, or desperation, not inclination. The worst days of the Depression saw large numbers of the unemployed just drifting. They moved, individuals to groups of a dozen or more, from town to town, always with the faint hope that the next stop might mean a job. While this aimless search hardly qualified as "travel," it nevertheless illustrated the American penchant to move on and find something better. In 1932, about a million such souls roamed the rails and highways of the country, victims of an economy in which they played little part.

The terrible Dust Bowl of the 1930s, when nature joined with poor farming methods and poverty, also put thousands on the road. John Steinbeck's *The Grapes of Wrath* (1939), a classic of American literature, chronicles the exodus of Oklahoma farmers from their devastated land and their journey to California in hopes of a new beginning. Here was travel of a totally different kind, with images of "Okies," their jalopies and wagons piled high with meager possessions, wandering the highways of a nation that seemed to be turning its back on them. In many ways, these people were refugees in their own country.

Many other Americans, however, traveled for recreation. They had the desire—along with the means—to enjoy touring, be it by car, train, plane, or luxurious ocean liner. For all the hobos, "deadheads," and roamers across the face of America in the 1930s, there were far more citizens who still had jobs, some time on their hands, and a few dollars in their pockets; the decade offered them many opportunities to see the countryside, if not the world.

AUTOMOBILE AND BUS TRAVEL

Since Henry Ford's pioneering Model T in 1908, the preferred means of travel for most Americans has been by car. The automobile is possibly the most significant invention in the country's history, influencing every aspect of national behavior. By 1931, American automobile manufacturers had produced over 50 million motor vehicles; by 1939, the total had reached 75 million. The Depression notwithstanding, car ownership had swelled to over 20 million autos by 1935, and continued to rise steadily. Half of American families owned their own vehicles, although most bought the cheapest car they could. By 1935, 95 percent of all the automobiles sold cost under $750 (about $9300 in contemporary dollars). The hard times merely reinforced the inherent strength of the automobile market. Gasoline was one of the few commodities to enjoy steady sales throughout the Depression years. It has long been true that the average American family spends more on transportation than it does on food. In fact, keeping one's car ranked ahead of home ownership or having a telephone, electric lighting, or even a bathtub in a survey conducted during the 1930s.[1]

A popular comic strip of the era was Frank King's *Gasoline Alley*. The title refers to a narrow lane that bisected many residential blocks of the time. People built their garages so they would face this alley and not the street; the front-facing driveway beside a house was still relatively unknown. The content of this gentle, good-natured strip often focused on the activities of the alley: cars, their repairs, their performance, and general automotive lore.

In the 1930s, *Gasoline Alley* found a large, receptive audience in a nation looking for stability. The quiet humor and warmth of the characters was a welcome antidote to the fear and anxiety felt throughout the nation. Nothing much exciting happened in its panels, but the timeless cycle of birth and life, marriage and family, young and old, reassured readers. Here was middle-class America, tinkering with its cars. Readership of the strip stood in the millions, and public expectations were clearly met in the series.[2]

It might therefore come as a surprise to learn how challenging driving a car could be in those days. Many city streets—but by no means all—were paved. That paving, however, could consist of bricks, cobblestones, and other rough surfaces. And once a driver reached the outskirts of town, conditions changed abruptly. No interstate highways existed; a three-lane road was considered quite modern, and few of these could be found. Not until 1938 were four-lane "superhighways" even considered by highway departments. In all, the country had about 500,000 miles of two-lane highways during the 1930s, and only about 350,000 miles (70 percent) of these were paved. Even with all their deficiencies, they served as a network that connected people and places; they were, in their own way, a national mass medium.[3]

As the decade wore on, more and more roads were built, and many existing ones were surfaced. Some of the credit for this must go to the Civilian Conservation Corps (CCC), the Works Progress Administration (WPA), and other federally funded New Deal groups that changed the landscape of the nation. The WPA alone was responsible for over half a million miles of such construction. For the traveler, these improvements were good news.

Such amenities as service stations, rest rooms, lodging, and restaurants tended to be few and far between, so trips and itineraries had to be planned carefully. As traffic increased, however, strip development along the highway followed. Gas stations, eateries, cabins, and souvenir shops multiplied. Astute travelers quickly mastered interpreting the signs along the road, not just what they said—"gas," "food," "lodging"—but also what they signified. Coca-Cola, Sealy mattresses, linoleum flooring, Howard Johnson's foods, and Texaco gasoline meant no surprises; they were comforting reminders of American efficiency and know-how, and the highway served as a popular promenade to display and advertise them.

By the end of the decade, commercial strips had become part of the roadside landscape. In addition, small shopping centers had begun to appear, usually close to a busy highway and with easy access. These forerunners of the malls and megamarts of the postwar years were simple affairs, usually an L-shaped cluster of stores and a large paved parking area. With an increasing volume of traffic, parking emerged as a priority for the motorist. Speed took away the luxury of looking at each little roadside shop, but a substantial lot, edged on one or two sides by businesses, allowed for more leisurely viewing. In the short space of ten years, both drivers and passengers had mastered an entirely new vocabulary of signs and symbols to accommodate their consumer needs. They had learned to "read" the roadside and make quick decisions about what types of goods and services were available.[4]

In 1935, the city fathers of Oklahoma City used traffic woes as a way to raise income. The parking meter, or "Park-O-Meter," came into being. Initially, they cost $58 apiece, and paid for themselves in short order. After that, the income went to the municipality. Other cities lost no time

The 1937 Chrysler Airflow sedan. Photographed here in the lobby of the 1930 Chrysler Building, the Airflow was the first streamlined American automobile and attracted considerable public attention. (Photograph courtesy of the Library of Congress.)

in adopting the device, and the ubiquitous parking meter became a part of the American scene.

Starting in the 1920s, and growing steadily in the 1930s, American families embraced a recreational habit that involved their personal automobiles. This was the "Sunday Drive." Instead of being used just for transportation or errands, the car was now being used for pleasure. Most travelers accepted the dirt, gravel, ruts, rocks, and holes as part of the experience. There was no need to rush, because implicit in the Sunday

Drive was a lack of a set destination. A family wasn't going anywhere, it was just "out for a drive."

Admittedly the cars of the 1930s surpassed those of preceding decades, but they were still no matches for the powerful, option-packed models of today. Automatic transmissions were virtually unknown in lower-priced models, air conditioning was all but unobtainable, and even the best tires tended to be unreliable. No well-equipped driver set forth without a spare or two, as well as a complete kit for repairing and/or changing tires. Gas tanks were small, and gasoline mileage left much to be desired by modern standards: the average vehicle had a cruising range of about fifty miles. If those limitations were not enough, thousands upon thousands of drivers kept their older cars in running condition throughout the Depression. Money was scarce and budgets were tight, so the 1930s witnessed a high proportion of creaky, dilapidated automobiles laboring down the nation's roads.

Frank Capra's hilarious Hollywood film *It Happened One Night* (1934) offers endless examples of the trials and tribulations of road travel in 1930s America. The two stars, Clark Gable and Claudette Colbert, wend their way through the countryside, hitchhiking, riding in buses and taxis and, at times, in decrepit automobiles. In the process, they have to contend with all manner of highway rascals in this classic screwball comedy. Closed gas stations, run-down auto camps (the 1930s term for a crude cross between a motel and a roadside cabin), and predictable mechanical breakdowns compound their woes. Presumably, everything depicted in the movie had at one time or another happened to members of the audience, and so a close sense of identification between fiction and reality was quickly established. (See Chapter 10, "Performing Arts," for more on this film.)

LODGING

For those driving some distance, lodging could prove challenging. A traveler could always stay overnight at a traditional hotel. As a rule, these establishments were located in towns and cities, generally close to the railroad station. Often ornate structures occupying prime business land, their expensive construction costs were reflected in room rates and restaurant charges. Since their primary clientele had been males who traveled alone on business, their facilities were designed accordingly. Rooms tended to be small and unadorned, and most hotels did almost nothing to cater to families; even their restaurants exuded a masculine air, with a smoky bar or lounge as important as tables for diners.

As long as they had the lodging monopoly, hotels could maintain their costly services. The advent of the automobile, however, changed who traveled and the way they did it. Auto camps began to spring up throughout the country with the increase of people on the road. Typically, they offered the weary traveler a gas pump, a small convenience store with some cheap souvenirs and a few groceries, and a choice between a single-room cabin and a place for erecting a tent. The more luxurious provided a bare-bones recreation hall, café, and covered camping facilities.[5]

These roadside auto camps competed among themselves for scarce tourist dollars, forcing them to improve their offerings. Instead of an open field for setting up a tent, they provided raised platforms that kept the tent floor dry during rain. Ramshackle cabins were replaced by more orderly rows of reasonably well-constructed cottages. By the mid-1930s, *Popular Mechanics*, a magazine with a large following among do-it-yourselfers, ran articles explaining how to build tourist cabins that would attract business. Folksy names like "Kozy Kamp," "Para Dice," "Dew Drop Inn," and "Tumble Inn" added to the appeal of these tourist stops. It was apparent that the family was welcome, and parents appreciated the fact.

The auto camps and freestanding cabins continued to evolve. Connecting roofs, or carports, between buildings linked the cottages and protected parked vehicles. This innovation led to the creation and construction of the auto court or, as it came to be known, the motel (motor + hotel). It first appeared in California; by the end of the 1930s, an increasing percentage of new lodging consisted of these efficient units.

Motels appealed to families. They were cheap, and no porters, bell captains, or other personnel stood around expecting a tip. Bags could be transported from auto to room quickly, with no embarrassing parade through a lobby, so there was no need for expensive luggage. Both check-in and checkout were speedy, and parking convenience was assured. Most motels at first tended to be only one story in height, eliminating the chore of lugging bags up flights of stairs. The room itself frequently had a window or two that provided some ventilation; it also had a screen door, and gave a sense of openness. Hotel rooms, on the other hand, were cramped and close; they were frequently up several flights of narrow stairs, and might have only one small window that looked out on an airshaft.

By the mid-1930s, a swimming pool, perhaps along with some playground equipment—all visible from the highway—became standard fixtures for motels wanting to catch motorists' attention, especially those traveling with children. It did not matter whether or not the pool was actually used; it, along with the clustered beach chairs and umbrellas, suggested a higher level of quality than competitors who did not offer such amenities.

Some operators formed chains with such names as Alamo Plaza,

United Motor Courts, Deluxe Motor Courts, and TraveLodge. The number of courts and motels went from slightly over 3000 at the end of the 1920s to well over 13,000 in 1939. At the same time, hotels reported sharp drops in occupancy rates. It was estimated that about 85 percent of all vacationers traveled by car during the period. Tourist facilities of all kinds quadrupled between 1927 and 1935, going from about 5000 establishments to some 20,000.[6]

In true American fashion, gimmicks abounded to attract travelers. A Kentucky entrepreneur opened Wigwam Village in 1933. At first, he peddled just gasoline and food out of a tepee-shaped structure, but frequent requests led him to construct six "sleeping rooms" whose exteriors resembled wigwams. Even a "trading post," a small souvenir shop, was opened. Most of the help was required to dress in Indian garb, reinforcing the escapist motif. From all reports, the site proved popular and attractive to travelers, which led to myriad other theme-related motels across the country, including several Indian spin-offs. Wigwam Village itself became a small motel chain, with its distinctive tepees found at several locations in nearby states. The idea of wigwams, or any other unusual building type, may seem strange, but in the 1930s the motel was in its discovery phase, attempting to find those devices that would ensure success.[7]

Despite the rapid growth of the motel business, some doubt lingered about this economical form of lodging in the minds of many Americans. Motels were casual and they allowed people to travel almost anonymously. Presumably, not everyone stopping at a motel had the most honorable intentions; patrons were not under the eye of authority. In a lurid article written for the popular *American Magazine* at the end of the decade, F.B.I. Director J. Edgar Hoover proclaimed motels, tourist cabins, and anything in between to be immoral and leading to corruption. Hoover was quite a crime-fighting celebrity in his own right, and his words carried considerable weight, even if much of the message consisted of sensationalism.

TRAILERS

Not everyone, however, needed a motel. Some intrepid travelers were pulling their own "cabins" behind their cars. Home craftsmen had been fashioning vehicles to tow behind their automobiles for some years, and so the concept was neither new nor foreign to consumers. In the 1920s and 1930s, the trunk on the average automobile was minuscule by today's cavernous standards. And if anyone wanted to sleep in a car, he or she had to be a contortionist. Seats did not recline, and interior space was cramped. So it was left to Yankee ingenuity to provide for the needs of the automotive traveler.

Trailers on the move in Florida in 1939. The phenomenal popularity of trailers lasted until the end of the decade and the onset of World War II. (Photograph courtesy of the Library of Congress.)

At the end of the 1920s, handyman Arthur Sherman built himself a box on wheels. He fashioned his creation out of Masonite, a cheap hardboard. Acquaintances admired his work, so he had carpenters assemble several more, and sold them. Then a few more, and a few more after that, until, in 1936, he had 1,100 people working for him, putting together "Covered Wagons" at the rate of 1,000 a month. Sherman had captured a mass audience for his creation and it had become part of the popular culture of the 1930s.

The Sherman Covered Wagon was simplicity itself. At just under $400, it was fairly affordable, easy to maintain, available, and could be readily imitated. Soon, in addition to the Covered Wagon brand, Vagabonds, Indians, Kozy Coaches, Silver Domes, Split-Coaches, and a host of others could be identified; at least 700 commercial builders were assembling trailers of one form or another in 1936. Trailer fever had hit the United States.

The manufacturers began to make their vehicles larger, adding more and more amenities like complete kitchenettes, chemical toilets, self-contained water supplies, and increased storage. Clearly they were mov-

ing toward the house trailer, or mobile home. By 1935, thousands of
families were packing up and moving to trailer camps across the nation.
Florida led the rankings, with over 17,000 sites available, most of which
could accommodate about 100 trailers each. Sunny California boasted
some 6000 camps, and Michigan was close behind with over 4500. Every
state in the union had facilities; North Dakota, although it was at the
bottom of the list, had more than 100, a respectable figure. These nomads
had discovered that living in a trailer was generally cheaper than resid-
ing in a conventional home, plus they found themselves among like-
minded individuals. It all tapped into that primordial American
wanderlust.[8]

In the midst of this boom, a man named Wally Byam formed the Airstream Trailer Company. His product had the distinction of being constructed entirely of aluminum, instead of the usual hardboard and wood
framing then in vogue, and his visionary creation was ultrastreamlined,
resembling an airplane or a spaceship more than a conventional trailer.
Byam saw his product as a recreational camper, not as a home on wheels,
and he refused to convert his innovation to this alternative form. What
he and his partners could not foresee was that his Airstream Trailer
would eventually become one of the most popular and enduring travel
trailers of all time.

Widely read magazines of the day, such as *Harper's, Life, Popular Mechanics*, the *Saturday Evening Post*, and *Time*, chronicled the phenomenon,
but the bottom fell out of the trailer market in the recession of 1938, and
the country's mad romance with trailers was over. Before it all collapsed,
however, other areas of popular culture picked up on the success of
trailers. *Ella Cinders*, a nationally syndicated newspaper comic strip, had
a long-running episode that dealt with the subject, and several radio soap
operas had their heroines living the trailer life. Montgomery Ward, the
huge merchandiser, added a furnished trailer to its catalog. There was
even the "Roosevelt Caravan," a string of fifty trailers pulled by new
cars promoting Franklin Roosevelt and his programs as part of the 1936
presidential campaign.

Public Transportation

Whatever their mode of transportation, Americans took to the road by
choice, not by chance. The automobile may have been the undisputed
preference for personal travel by the 1930s, but it was not the only way
to get to a destination; mass transit was a major force in the country's
urban centers. For example, the adventuresome could go from Boston to
New York City by bus and trolley. The journey first involved obtaining
a "Wayfinder," a detailed listing of regional routes and schedules. Once
aboard, there were numerous stops in small New England towns and

the expenditure of an entire day (twenty-plus hours) to do it. But the final fare, at about a nickel each stop, came to approximately $2.40. By using a combination of buses, trolleys, and electric interurban rail transit, even a trip to New York City from Chicago was possible. No doubt other such lengthy jaunts could be undertaken; there certainly was no shortage of commercial transportation.[9]

Because of the slow improvement of state and federal roads through-out the country, bus usage grew rapidly. In 1930, 20 percent of all in-tercity travel was by bus, and that figure continued to increase during the Depression years. Greyhound Bus Lines had coast-to-coast routes in the thirties, and their success led a number of smaller companies to form National Trailways in 1936. The additional lines meant that the United States had an effective intercity and cross-country bus system in place by 1935.

Around 1935, the Greyhound Corporation began running full-page, four-color advertisements in the *Saturday Evening Post* extolling the pleas-ures of a long-distance trip via "a Greyhound." The illustrations show buses that are progressively more streamlined over time, buses that in-creasingly become as sleek as the racing Greyhound logo of the com-pany. Although the ads depict happy families getting on board, most bus passengers were commercial travelers such as salesmen, intent on going from town to town to conduct business. The average American family still drove an automobile when traveling. Nevertheless, the im-pact of increased bus use was felt by the nation's railroads; they saw both the number of passengers and revenues decline, while bus and car miles continued to climb.

Where buses could offer distinctive service was in the area of tours. These were extremely lucrative, and Greyhound in particular set about inaugurating tour packages around the country. These usually included round-trip transportation, hotel accommodations, and visits to selected sites. Niagara Falls, the national parks, big cities, and scenic vistas—all were included at one time or another. So successfully did Greyhound organize tours that the company finally created its own travel agencies; they did well throughout the Depression era.[10]

The aforementioned *It Happened One Night* unabashedly employs a Greyhound bus as part of the story. Other films likewise used "the Hound" as a basis for their plotting. *Cross Country Cruise* (1934) has a murderer traveling by bus, but he is no threat to the other passengers. The man is apprehended, of course, and the idea of bus travel suffers not at all. Greyhound actively supported the picture, lending a bus to selected theaters as a prop. The vehicle was parked outside the movie house, a hint of what could be seen inside.

Fugitive Lovers (1934), a comedy starring Robert Montgomery, was a big box-office draw at the time. He embarks on a picturesque cross-country bus tour with—among others—the Three Stooges as company. The movie marked an early outing for the zany trio, but the fabulous scenery and the comforts of the bus may have been the most lasting impressions audiences carried away from the film.

The following year saw the release of *Thanks a Million*, a breezy musical with Dick Powell and the Paul Whiteman Orchestra. Once again, a Greyhound bus figures prominently in the plot, carrying Powell to his sweetheart, Ann Dvorak. Interspersed with all the music are images of comfortable, convenient bus travel, the same image that the Greyhound Company was studiously trying to create in its advertising. Any assistance that Hollywood might provide was no doubt gratefully accepted.

Most cities boasted at least a couple of taxi companies, although the economic downturn hit cabs hard and many firms went under. During the grimmest years of the crisis, a typical taxi charge might total twenty cents for a one-mile ride, about half of the fare just a few years earlier. The survivors, however, profited in the later 1930s and became a familiar part of the urban scene.

The stereotype of the cabbie as a wisecracking man, someone who has "seen it all," was reinforced in two period films: *Taxi!* (1932) and *The Big City* (1937; also called *Skyscraper Wilderness*). The first picture stars James Cagney, taking on his role in fine, swaggering style; the second features Spencer Tracy in a similar part. Anyone who traveled much in metropolitan traffic could identify with these two little-known movies, especially given the popular leads in each.

Whether by bus, trolley, or even cab, at the end of the decade it was estimated that the average American city dweller used commercial transit 265 times a year, a high level of public utilization.

TRAIN TRAVEL

The railroads were king, or so they thought. In their imperial way, they turned a blind eye to some important warning signals. Air travel was still in its relative infancy, the bus and coach lines appeared to offer little real competition, and auto travel, though growing rapidly, did not figure into their calculations. As a result of such shortsighted thinking, the railroads were slow in adapting to the modern needs of actual or potential passengers.

The 1930s, moreover, witnessed a profound shift in public opinion about travel. No longer was the automobile a horseless carriage; it had evolved into the family locomotive, one that could take people anywhere. Buses, too, had become more popular; in fact, 1935 witnessed a first: more people rode buses than trains. Despite the shifting demographics between highway and rail travel, trains still offered a variety of choices to the consumer. If some Americans were riding the rails in boxcars, others were enjoying a much different level of comfort and service on passenger trains. The country was crisscrossed with railroad tracks, and dozens of companies vied for the precious passenger dollar. Very few towns were not served by a railroad. Great terminals in the nation's cities welcomed passengers into a temple-like atmosphere, a world of bustling porters, clouds of steam, and boards with endless lists of arrivals and departures.

The railroads' miscalculations were based on a history of success. Much of the National Park system in the West had grown because of the impact of passenger rail service. For instance, Yellowstone Park, isolated from any major highways, welcomed 45,000 rail visitors in 1915; only 7,500 came by automobile. By 1930 and an improved road system, a paltry 27,000 took the train to the park; 195,000 drove their cars. For the American traveler, momentous change had occurred, but the still prosperous railroad companies ignored the message.[11]

In spectacular magazine and poster advertisements, the railroads continued to present the romance of steam engines and gorgeous vistas. During the 1930s, it became increasingly clear that the viewers of those magnificent scenes were auto travelers, not train passengers. The enticements of the ads may have convinced some families to visit Glacier or Yosemite, but they had no interest in taking a train to do it.

It would be unfair to say that the railroads ignored passenger service. During the 1930s, every day, at every hour, passenger trains were pulling out of and into stations across the nation. Some of the trains were quite miserable, with old, dilapidated cars, poor service, and erratic schedules. Some were merely adequate, a means of moving people from one place to another. Some were quite good, with dining cars, bar cars, sleepers, and compartments. This last feature offered a variety of choices, ranging from staterooms to an efficiency module called a "roomette," a self-contained unit that was introduced on selected trains in 1937.[12]

Several of the major American railroads spent prodigious amounts to create and maintain a few luxury trains. They had finally become aware that people with money, those able to travel first class, were abandoning traditional train transportation for airlines and highway travel. In response, they cut fares to lure more passengers, and they increased creature comforts for coach travelers, offering such amenities as lounge cars equipped with radios. The addition of receivers to trains was a tacit admission of the ubiquitous role radio was coming to play in Americans' lives. The Baltimore & Ohio air-conditioned its all-parlor train, the New York–Washington *Columbian*, in 1931. This move was an industry first; it proved so popular that by 1936 almost 6000 passenger cars enjoyed this feature.

The change that most people noticed, however, was the move to

Southern Pacific's *Daylight*, a typical streamlined train of the era. The image of fast trains, encased in sleek bodies, was a dominant one for much of the decade. (Photograph courtesy of Library of Congress.)

streamlining. The sleek, forward-looking engines of the Grand Central Rail Road, the Pennsylvania, the Burlington, the Santa Fe, and the Union Pacific have come to be associated with the 1930s and the 1940s, that period before the virtual collapse of passenger rail service in the United States. Names like the *City of Salina* (1934), the *Super Chief* (1936), the *California Zephyr* (1937), the *Hiawatha* (1937), and the *Mercury* (1939) can still conjure up pictures of beautiful people in elegant clothes, sipping cocktails while the sun dips behind snow-capped mountains, beckoning them onward. It is all very romantic, and it is imagery that continues to cast its spell in the popular imagination. These diesel-powered locomotives may not have been much faster than their more traditional steam counterparts, but they *looked* faster, and they also looked modern and fashionable, important qualities when forming opinions.[13]

The movies have always liked trains. They are a controlled environment, with their compartments and rows of seats, and they therefore make for compelling drama. The camera can remain focused on a limited set, and the passing scenery is just background. A film like 1934's very successful *Twentieth Century* is a case in point: adapted from the stage, another entertainment medium that has used trains effectively, the story unrolls during the railroad trip itself. Glamorous actors like Carole Lombard and John Barrymore reinforce the idea that train travel is a sophisticated mode of transportation. During the course of the film, the characters move from modern compartments to a sleek cocktail lounge. Always in the background is the motif of motion, of movement—from one affair to another or from one place to another.

Warner Brothers' *42nd Street* (1933) also features images of train travel. In the novelty tune "Shuffle Off to Buffalo," virtually the entire cast is shown in a cutaway sleeper car, the women in various stages of undress, peek out from their berths. Once again the concept of the passenger train as a place for romance (and perhaps for some improprieties) is presented, albeit in a humorous way.

The Silver Streak (1934; not to be confused with the 1976 comedy *Silver Streak*), set in the West, gives a tightly controlled picture of railroads and speed. A train must race against time in order to save lives. The image of the engine cutting a swath of smoke and steam in the vastness of the desert is well done. Airplanes might be faster, but in the 1930s nostalgia for the thundering locomotive still could stir audiences.

Streamlining, as far as trains are concerned, may have reached its apogee in *Sweet Music* (1935), an innocuous trifle starring crooner Rudy Vallee. Although 1935 is a bit early for depicting Streamline imagery in a popular, mass-market movie, the film nonetheless looks to the future for one of its sets, a passenger train. All shiny curves and bullet shapes, this train suggests it is ready to break any and all speed records.

AIR TRAVEL

Perhaps nothing captured the American travel imagination like the magnificent zeppelins, or dirigibles, that traversed the skies during the early 1930s. Named for Count Ferdinand von Zeppelin (1838–1917), a German scientist and engineer instrumental in the development of lighter-than-air craft, the great airships were poised to become a significant force in aviation.[14]

Hollywood, that reliable reflector of trends and styles, brought out several movies that featured zeppelins. Howard Hughes directed the exciting *Hell's Angels* (1930), a special-effects-filled picture that features dogfights around a German zeppelin in World War I. In 1931 came *Dirigible*, another aerial epic.

Between those two films was *Madam Satan* (1930), a comedy of sorts directed by Cecil B. De Mille. A story about upper-class high jinks, this curious feature is partially set in a dirigible. De Mille, a master of lavish productions, staged some scenes for this melodrama in what has to be the most surreal, Art Deco-drenched passenger compartment ever envisioned for a zeppelin. The special effects staff at Metro-Goldwyn-Mayer had to figure out how to simulate a realistic in-flight disaster that involved lightning and the packed compartment suspended in the air, then parachute the characters back to earth. The movie provided two challenges: first, to be a stylish representation of the latest fads and fashions, and second, to provide the thrill and spectacle of an aerial calamity. Although by modern standards this movie is only moderately successful in either area, *Madam Satan* is nevertheless a bizarre film, and it clearly demonstrates how Hollywood was always on the lookout for new gimmicks, couched in contemporary terms, to lure in the customers.

The U.S. Navy saw dirigibles as an effective extension of the fleet, and lobbied strongly to have such aircraft included in their budget. In the midst of the Depression, the admirals persuaded Congress to approve the construction of the *Akron* (1931) and the *Macon* (1933). The *Akron* generated a lot of good publicity for the navy, flying around the country and engaging in maneuvers. It carried four small biplanes on its huge frame, releasing them while airborne and then "recapturing" them while still aloft. The *Akron* was, however, doomed; in 1933 she went down in a storm with the loss of seventy-three lives, the worst air disaster until that time. The *Macon* likewise plunged into the ocean in 1935. With these two failures, the U.S. government effectively retired from any further airship development until World War II.

On the other hand, the privately owned Goodyear Tire and Rubber Company, long active in dirigible research, continued work with nonrigid airships, or blimps. By 1941 and the outbreak of World War II, Goodyear blimps had transported several hundred thousand passengers and carried countless advertising messages on their exteriors.

Despite the setbacks suffered by the U.S. Navy, Germany strove to perfect these unwieldy craft and was the nation most advanced in overall airship utilization. The pride of their fleet was the *Graf Zeppelin*, a mammoth 775-foot dirigible that circumnavigated the globe, including stops at Lakehurst, New Jersey, and Los Angeles. As a result of these exploits, the United States in 1930 issued a set of three commemorative airmail stamps, each depicting the *Graf Zeppelin* in flight. Now extremely rare and valuable, the stamps were in denominations of 65 cents, $1.30, and

A U.S. Navy dirigible. America's romance with lighter-than-air craft
lasted until 1937 with the disastrous crash of the German *Hindenburg*.
(Photograph courtesy of the Library of Congress.)

$2.60. Three years later, to celebrate Chicago's Century of Progress
Exposition, yet another stamp was printed, this one showing the *Graf
Zeppelin* heading for the towers of Chicago. It came in a 50-cent denom-
ination and is equally sought after by philatelists.

The Graf was a popular airship, known to millions. The *Graf Zeppelin's*
sister ship, the *Hindenburg*, was built in 1936; it was the most luxurious
dirigible in the skies, and great hopes were held out for it to make such
air travel commonplace between America and Europe. The *Hindenburg*
flew without incident from Germany to Lakehurst and back in May 1936,
accomplishing the journey in the record time of just under sixty-five
hours. As a result, public interest in airships was at an all-time high, and
it appeared that regular transatlantic dirigible travel was now a reality.
Nine more flights ensued, usually with a number of celebrities on board.
The passengers raved about the smooth, quiet ride.[15]

In May 1937, as always a crowd turned out at Lakehurst for the *Hindenburg's* arrival; among them was Herb Morrison, a reporter for NBC
Radio News. As it approached the mooring mast, something went terribly wrong and the great airship burst into flames. Morrison, micro-

phone in hand and wits about him, managed to report the disaster live over the airwaves. As he watched and reported—"Oh, the humanity!" he cried, swept into the emotion of the event—thirty-eight people died in the flaming wreckage. The disaster closed a fascinating chapter in aviation history; no one wanted anything more to do with airships. The tragedy, however, did little to diminish a seemingly never-ending public fascination with daredevil airplane stunts and feats. Wing walkers, aerial acrobatics, races, and mock combat could always draw a crowd at fairs and carnivals.

Charles Lindbergh (1902–1974), who had thrilled the country with his solo flight to Paris in 1927, took to the air again during the 1930s. He and his wife, Anne Morrow Lindbergh, envisioning great growth in commercial aviation, made an epochal flight to Asia, and then in 1933 worked to create a North Atlantic route for future airliners. Following these journeys she wrote a pair of best-sellers—*North to the Orient* (1935) and *Listen! The Wind* (1938)—that are lovely evocations of their adventures.

With each passing year in the decade, airplanes were flying higher, faster, and longer. In 1931, the American aviator Wiley Post could keep listeners glued to their radios or readers eagerly awaiting the latest newspaper edition that chronicled his latest exploit. That year, Post raced around the world in his *Winnie Mae,* a single-engine, high-wing monoplane with detachable landing gear that gave it greater speed and distance. Post capitalized on his fame by telegraphing accounts of his journey to a news syndicate which then breathlessly released them to a waiting public. Even with all the ballyhoo, he accomplished something significant: he and his navigator had circled the globe in eight days, fifteen hours, and fifty-one minutes, a new record. Because of all the publicity surrounding the 1931 flight, Post—dashing in a black eye patch and leather gear—took off again in 1933, but this time he was alone. He and the *Winnie Mae* beat their own record by over twenty-one hours, making him both the fastest and the first to do it solo. Distances were shrinking, and the public avidly followed each new accomplishment.[16]

Another of the daredevil pilots was Roscoe Turner. A master of the art of self-promotion, Turner fashioned his own flying suit, a powder blue affair with exaggerated whipcord breeches. He sported a splendid waxed moustache that flared to sharp spikes, and frequently was photographed in a leather helmet with the goggles pushed back at a rakish angle. For a final touch, he traveled most places with a pet lion cub. He even had a custom parachute made for his mascot, and the lion sat with him in the cockpit. Colorful as he was, Turner was also a superb pilot, winning a collection of trophies and setting a number of records during the 1930s.

Turner established much of his fame through aerial racing, a popular

aviation spectacle that flourished in the Depression era. The annual National Air Races involved two events that gripped public attention, the
Thompson Trophy and the Bendix Trophy races. The first was a closed-
course race where small planes buzzed around a set pattern that used
tall pylons as markers. The closer and faster a pilot could shave a pylon,
the better the elapsed time. Pilots competed for cash and recognition,
and their planes pushed the limits of both civilian and military aircraft.
The Thomson Trophy races were dangerous, and a number of daring
fliers crashed and died, but such tragedy only whetted the audience's
appetite for more.

The Bendix Trophy was based on time and distance, usually a coast-
to-coast flight. Initiated in 1931, this race likewise drew the top aviators
of the day. Jimmy Doolittle of the Army Air Corps, Howard Hughes,
Frank ("Meteor Man") Hawks, and Roscoe Turner were some of the pilots who combined distance with speed and endurance. In fact, Hughes
carried these goals far beyond the original boundaries of the event. A
movie director, an inventor, and a millionaire, he climbed into his self-
designed *Hughes Special* in 1935 and reached the almost unbelievable
airspeed of 325 miles per hour. Two years later he sped across the country in under eight hours, and in 1938 he circled the globe in three days,
nineteen hours, and fourteen minutes, more than halving Wiley Post's
1933 record.

The public, never sated, saved some of its adulation for a young aviatrix—as women pilots were then called—named Amelia Earhart. In
1928, she had already earned some fame as the first woman to fly the
Atlantic, but as a passenger. With her boyish good looks, Earhart quickly
became something of a celebrity. In 1932, she made her own solo flight,
across the Atlantic, again the first woman to do so. She flew from Hawaii
to California in 1935, quickly following that exploit with yet another solo
flight from Mexico City to New Jersey. She was the first flier, male or
female, to accomplish either of these feats. It came as no surprise when
she announced plans for a round-the-world flight in 1937.

She and her navigator proposed a 27,000-mile journey that followed
the Equator. Somewhere over the vast reaches of the Pacific, her plane
disappeared. In news stories that rivaled in emotion any event of the
decade, Earhart's lost flight was chronicled. Extensive searches were immediately instituted, but no traces of the ill-fated plane could be found.
The disappearance of Amelia Earhart has entered American popular
folklore; movies have been produced, books have been written, new
searches have been attempted, and conspiracy theories of every kind
have been advanced, but she remains missing, a tantalizing, unsolved
mystery of the 1930s.

The daring of these pilots spread to the newspaper comics. Adventure
series like *Ace Drummond* (1935–1940) competed for space on the

crowded funny pages. Purportedly drawn by Captain Eddie Ricken-backer, a renowned World War I flying ace, the strip was really the work of Clayton Knight. It even included a small panel entitled *Hall of Fame of the Air*, where the exploits of real fliers were celebrated. Frank Miller's *Barney Baxter in the Air* (1935–1950), aimed at the youth market, involves an adolescent boy in all sorts of aerial adventures. With the approach of World War II, Barney pushes hard for military preparedness, making his strip one of the first major series to suggest that war was inevitable and the nation needed to be ready for it.

There were others—*Scorchy Smith* (1930–1961) and *Tailspin Tommy* (1928–1942) also did well—but probably the most popular of all the fly-ing strips was *Smilin' Jack* (1933–1973), a long-lived mix of humor, romance, and adventure. The creation of Zack Mosley, the series could easily remind readers of Wiley Post, Roscoe Turner, and even Amelia Earhart, since a galaxy of women fliers wanders in and out of the stories. Awkwardly drawn at best, the strip enthralled its readers with its me-ticulous attention to mechanical detail. The romance may have come directly from radio soap operas, but the airplanes came from the head-lines.[17]

Every technological advance allowed a few more feet of altitude, a few more miles per hour, a few more minutes in the air. By the mid-1930s, this meant that altitudes above several thousand feet, speeds over 125 miles per hour, and distances exceeding a thousand miles were becoming commonplace. To lure the would-be travelers who had never flown, as well as more seasoned fliers, aeronautical designers worked diligently to make the aircraft of the 1930s suggest speed and efficiency. They had little to go by, but despite the lack of precedent, the designers prevailed, and sleek, streamlined forms began to characterize commercial aircraft—shapes that have continued to dominate flight to the present.[18]

No airplane of the period better summarizes the changeover than the Douglas DC-3. These craft, designed in 1933 as the DC-1 and first man-ufactured as the DC-2, carried their passengers in relative comfort during the day. However, the airlines also wanted to offer customers berths for long-distance night flying. Douglas answered their demands in 1936 with the DC-3, a larger version of the DC-2. By day it seated twenty-one per-sons; at night it offered berths for fourteen in its "Skysleeper," or DST (for Douglas Sleeper Transport). The DC-3 was fast—it could cruise at almost 200 mph, an astonishing speed for any commercial plane at the time—and it was fabulously reliable. Over 11,000 DC-3s were built, mak-ing it the most successful, most profitable airplane of all time. In 1939, the DC-3 carried some three-quarters of all air passengers in the United States.

The 1930s saw the theatrical release of over twenty-five commercial films that were aviation-oriented. The decade opened with two World

The Douglas DC-3. The most popular airliner of all time, this streamlined craft, introduced in 1936, epitomized the future of commercial aviation. (Photograph courtesy of the Library of Congress.)

War I dramas, director Howard Hughes's *Hell's Angels* (1930) and Howard Hawks's *The Dawn Patrol* (1930). This latter picture, starring Richard Barthelmess and Douglas Fairbanks, Jr., was so successful that it was remade in 1938 under the same title. The second version features Errol Flynn, Basil Rathbone, and David Niven, three of the top names in Hollywood at the time. These movies indicated the direction the majority of future aviation pictures would take: war stories with lots of combat footage.

Forgotten titles like *Lucky Devils* (1932), *Sky Devils* (1932), *Airmail* (1932), *Wings in the Dark* (1935), *Devil Dogs of the Air* (1935), and *It's in the Air* (1935) brightened marquees during the early days of the Depression. Mostly potboilers, they did provide an exciting moment or two of flying. But a pair of exceptions also came along: *King Kong* (1933) and *Flying Down to Rio* (1933).

Few might think of *King Kong* as an aviation film, and they would be right. It is a classic mix of horror and fantasy, one of the memorable movies of the 1930s. But the final sequence, with the giant ape perched atop the newly built Empire State Building, brushing off attacking army biplanes as if they were annoying gnats, is one of those cinematic moments that has become an icon. The most advanced aerial weapons of the day are virtually impotent against this primeval force. The planes' flashy acrobatics and speed signify little. Popular culture eagerly embraces technology with one hand, but with the other regularly displays an accompanying undercurrent of distrust of too much reliance on science (for more on this film, see Chapter 10, "Performing Arts").

Flying Down to Rio likewise is hardly a picture about the wonders of flying, but it contains one of the great film flight sequences. In this delightful musical, technology is not ridiculed; instead, it is a vehicle for showcasing the talents of dancers Fred Astaire and Ginger Rogers for the first time. But even Astaire and Rogers take a backseat to a bevy of chorus girls as they kick up their heels in unison while standing on the wings of a large airplane "flying down" to the famous Brazilian city. A triumph of special effects, the scene makes absolutely no social or technological comments, but it does display the wonder and fun only movies can provide.

Exotic locales and hard-boiled action characterize *China Clipper* (1936). Named for the legendary flying boats that were then plying the Pacific, it stars Pat O'Brien and Humphrey Bogart. The film suffers from a formulaic plot, but it certainly heightened public interest in commercial aviation. Its celebration of an ongoing event showed how timely the movies could be, a fact doubtless appreciated by the struggling airlines.

The British produced a landmark film in 1936, entitled *Things to Come*, based on *The Shape of Things to Come* (a 1933 book by H.G. Wells). In fact, Wells himself contributed the screenplay for the movie. Directed by William Cameron Menzies, *Things to Come* received wide U.S. distribution. A cinematic look at different eras of the future, the picture predicts a more regimented style of life, with leaders parading around in what can only kindly be called modish garb. But its images of massed aircraft, all done up in a kind of streamlined style, presage the huge formations of bombers that came to be such an important part of World War II. It is a frightening vision of military aviation and the destruction that it might wreak. Certainly, *Things to Come* approaches flight in a far different way than the razzle-dazzle and heroics usually given flying during the 1930s.

The remainder of the decade returned to more traditional aerial imagery. As the war clouds over Asia and Europe darkened perceptibly, the American screen often emphasized thoughts of preparedness. There were, however, some exceptions. *Fly-Away Baby* (1937) was part of an ongoing Warner Brothers series chronicling the adventures of reporter Torchy Blane, ably portrayed by Glenda Farrell. This particular film has the intrepid newswoman taking to the air in order to catch some killers and get her story. The Torchy Blane movies, based on a pulp magazine series, totaled nine features and ran from 1936 until 1939.

More significant, perhaps, were films like *Test Pilot* (1938), a shared vehicle for Spencer Tracy and Clark Gable. These big box office stars portray a flier (Gable) and a mechanic (Tracy) who put experimental aircraft through their paces. The story includes footage about testing the military's then-new B-17 bomber and the importance attached to military superiority.

In a similar vein, *Wings of the Navy* (1939) extols the training received by young recruits in the armed forces. By the late 1930s, any thoughts of neutrality were in the process of being conveniently forgotten by Hollywood, and the content of many action films reflects this loss of innocence.

Sea Travel

Ocean travel, although the privilege of only a relative few, was played up in the popular press and became a subject of note during the Depression years. Most of the great liners sailed under the flags of foreign nations. Flying the tricolor of the French Line were the *Île de France* and the *Normandie*, the latter perhaps the quintessential ocean liner of the 1930s. Arriving in New York Harbor in 1935 on its maiden voyage, the *Normandie* carried almost 2,000 passengers in unsurpassed comfort. In first class, no two staterooms were alike, and Modernism ruled the day. Individuals who were at the very forefront of the most fashionable styles could be counted among its designers and decorators.[19]

The English, once the rulers of the sea, were not to be outdone by the French. They were well represented by several liners, but the *Queen Mary* served as the flagship of Cunard Lines for much of the decade. The *Queen Mary* was built in 1934 and made a triumphant New York arrival in May 1936. Like the Normandie, the *Queen Mary* epitomized luxurious travel.

The foreign lines pitched their advertisements at United States travelers, and Americans in turn were fascinated by the imagery of both the ads and these grand ships. Curiously, the United States, with its colorful history of sail-powered clipper ships from the nineteenth century, did not participate in this ongoing contest. Despite the absence of liners under the American flag, most of the passengers—perhaps 75 percent of the total—crossing the Atlantic were from the United States. Using the most stylish graphics of the period, the various lines painted a picture of modern luxury at sea. The placement of the ads in magazines, newspapers, travel agencies, posters, and billboards guaranteed that millions would see the alluring vision of a lifestyle associated with the very rich.

This vision was translated into popular images that were much more accessible. The movies, of course, did the best job and reached the largest audience as filmmakers became enamored of the ocean liner. A remarkable string of comedies, mysteries, and musicals came out of Hollywood that were set, either in whole or in part, on sleek, polished liners. First came *Transatlantic* (1931), a minor film that was, nevertheless, a pioneer. It presents Art Deco as a style of contrasting blacks, whites, and geometric forms. These decorative motifs went on to influence a host of imitators and convinced movie patrons that life on the high seas was very good indeed.

Reaching for the Moon (1931) likewise presents an ocean liner that is absolutely the last word in Art Deco stylishness. A likable comedy designed by William Cameron Menzies, *Reaching for the Moon* impressed on the public a sense of Modernism that was probably absent in real life. Art took the lead, and humdrum existence was invited to imitate it. It is doubtful that audiences, after viewing these movies, went home and promptly redecorated their houses with the latest in Art Deco accessories, but it is likely that their views on contemporary design went through subtle shifts. Modernism was no longer so "foreign," so "new." And Hollywood was just gearing up for the onslaught. Ocean liners done in chrome and geometrics were but part of a much larger presentation of nautical images that celebrated modernity.

In 1934, *Chained* brought together Clark Gable and Joan Crawford for some shipboard romance. The ship, of course, presents a backdrop consisting of the most fashionable design trends. In like manner, *Transatlantic Merry-Go-Round* (1934) limps along with its plot, but shines in its re-creation of a sleek liner. The film also tips its hat to radio, once an implacable enemy of the movies. Jack Benny and a host of other radio stars are on board when a crime occurs; the resultant story gives them a chance to perform their specialties against an Art Deco background.

A better movie is *The Princess Comes Across* (1936). A mix of crime and comedy, it stars Carole Lombard and places her on board still another fictive studio-made ship. America might continue to be mired in a depression, but Lombard's acute sense of 1930s high fashion gives no hint of it. Here is movie escapism at its best, clothed in the glossy surfaces that audiences could only take to be de rigeur for the era.

By 1936, Streamline Moderne had begun to displace the more angular Art Deco. Metro-Goldwyn-Mayer's set designers were given what would appear to be a free hand, because they constructed a Moderne battleship for *Born to Dance* (1936). A musical starring Eleanor Powell, the movie is a showpiece for Powell's dancing and the music of Cole Porter. But the huge, stark white battleship and the cast of hundreds overwhelm the senses, imposing a weird sense of Modernistic order on an otherwise chaotic story.

In a similar naval vein, *Follow the Fleet* (1936) has the nonpareil dance team of Fred Astaire and Ginger Rogers cavorting against a Moderne backdrop of ships and sailors. The following year, RKO Pictures had the duo at it again with *Shall We Dance* (1937). As always, the plot is secondary to the dancing. The story, however, does get Astaire and Rogers aboard a white, streamlined liner that echoes the ads of the major steamship companies. By 1937, streamlining came more into play as a part of everyday life, particularly in mechanical devices like refrigerators and household appliances. Both films reinforce what was already fact; art now was imitating the commonplace.

Dodsworth, a 1929 novel by the American writer Sinclair Lewis, was translated to the silver screen in 1936 (and won an Academy Award for set decoration). Part of the story takes place on a transatlantic liner, and the studio designers created a stark white vessel that suggests both modernity and loneliness. The ship is pure design, a mechanism devoid of human touches. The 1930s might celebrate a streamlined entry into the future, but the decade could also take the extreme precision of modernism and make it suggest that there might be cold, technological days to come. Such pessimism, however, was a minority view, and most predictions were for better times.

Possibly the epitome of all the liner-associated pictures is *The Big Broadcast of 1938* (1938). The movie has plenty of stars—W.C. Fields, Bob Hope, Dorothy Lamour, Martha Raye—but it also boasts a streamlined ship created by Norman Bel Geddes, one of the premier theatrical and industrial designers of the day. In a climactic race against another liner, the film's S.S. *Gigantic* resembles nothing so much as a waterborne spaceship. Here are the Buck Rogers/Flash Gordon motifs of the comic strips carried over into 1938 and pointing toward the optimistic world of tomorrow that would shortly be celebrated in the New York World's Fair.

The ocean liner, real or imagined, was an ideal symbol of the Moderne Machine Age, an image Hollywood fostered. It symbolized glamour, luxury, and convenience. With their sparkling white superstructures, polished metal railings, and sumptuous interiors (the first-class dining salon in the very real *Queen Mary* measured 305 feet long), the liners represented all that was modern and stylish. Although most of the audience would never set foot on an ocean liner, streamlined or otherwise, the repetition of such imagery created a popular acceptance of these vessels that carried over into the mundane objects of everyday life.

SUMMARY

There may have been a depression crippling the nation, but it had little visibility on the American road. Car ownership grew, as did automotive tourism. The railroads saw a decline in passengers, although American popular culture refused to acknowledge the fact. The image of the streamlined locomotive spoke to an optimistic faith in technology. Air travel was still in its infancy, but the success of airliners like the DC-3 promised much for the future. Unfortunately, a series of disasters extinguished hopes of making lighter-than-air craft a popular means of aerial transportation. Finally, the glossy sophistication of sea voyages became a significant part of movie imagery, even if few people ever took a cruise.

THE 1930S

12

Visual Arts

BACKGROUND

Formal painting and sculpture have always had a tenuous relationship with Americans. During the eighteenth and nineteenth centuries, despite growing national literacy, the arts were often ignored or viewed with skepticism. Only a few artists enjoyed public acclaim, and people seldom visited museums or galleries. Things changed little in the first decades of the twentieth century, despite the opening of many more museums. Improved technology allowed the mass reproduction of paintings and drawings on a scale unimagined in earlier times, but in the eyes of most Americans, the artistic movements of the 1910s and 1920s were confusing and unintelligible. "Modern art" was characterized as decadent, the work of "foreigners," and resistance to it was seen as proper and patriotic. A few daring museums presented shows that introduced new currents of visual expression, but for the most part exhibitions tended to retreat into the tried and true, using representational art—still lifes, landscapes, portraits—as their foundation.

Even with the insularity of American taste, a few significant works achieved both critical and public acclaim. And, as is usually the case in art, the popular realm began to incorporate some of the suspect elements found in more elite art, with the result that Modernism crept into popular works, albeit slowly and circuitously. But tradition, in the form of representational art that displayed an intense interest in national themes, continued its hold on the popular audience. That many of the "traditionalists" often employed Modernist motifs and techniques in their work was conveniently overlooked at the time, and only in retrospect is this aspect of their achievements acknowledged.

The reader is also directed to Chapter 4, "Architecture and Design." Some Depression-era designs lifted even the most mundane products close to the realm of art, and the many critical theories accompanying Streamline Moderne frequently spilled over into discussions of painting and sculpture as well.

PAINTING AND ALLIED ARTS

Few serious artists prospered during the Depression years. Their works were seen, if at all, by a limited, elitist audience, and the larger mass audience remained ignorant of the many changes occurring in American art at the time. Both collectors and museums lacked the cash for purchases, and many galleries closed during the crisis. Not until the federal government took the unprecedented step of subsidizing the arts did the future brighten for talented painters and other artists.

Regionalism

If any one school of painting rose to national prominence, it was Regionalism. The artists considered Regionalists employed themes of national identity, using the land as a carrier of meaning. Instead of Paris and sidewalk cafés, the Regionalists might paint an American diner and fill it with typical small-town citizens. A conservative movement rather than a radical one, Regionalism celebrates a nostalgia for the past, especially the rural past that was fast disappearing with technology and urban growth. In addition, the Regionalists made no attempt to debunk American institutions and values, as did so many artists in previous decades; they preferred to take American history and mythologize it, elevating the commonplace and giving it heroic status.

Many artists claimed to be Regionalists, but two attracted the most attention, both critical and popular, during the period. They are Grant Wood (1891–1942) and Thomas Hart Benton (1889–1975).[1] Of the two, Wood was the better known, primarily on the basis of one painting, *American Gothic*, a work he first exhibited at the Art Institute of Chicago in 1930. This simple portrait of two people drew instant acclaim. Crowds lined up to view the work, and the Art Institute promptly purchased it for their permanent collection, paying the princely sum of $300. Since then, Wood's picture has become instantly recognizable to millions, both in its original form and as the object of parody. Countless advertisers have employed the image, usually humorously, as the backdrop for every conceivable product, relying on the audience's familiarity with the painting to assist in presenting their message.

Wood went on to create many other notable paintings, but nothing else he did ever approached *American Gothic* in popularity. He had struck a resonant chord with virtually all Americans, and he capitalized on it. Publicity photographs showed Wood attired in overalls, a folksy Iowan who represented the Heartland. He spoke obliquely about his work, changing stories about *American Gothic* to please his public. Many of his subsequent works plainly show an attempt to recapture whatever it was that *American Gothic* possesses, but none succeeds.

American Gothic may be the best-known single painting of the 1930s, but the self-appointed spokesman for the Regionalists was Missouri-born Thomas Hart Benton. Unfortunately, his pleas for recognition too often sank into polemics, a strident voice that lacked diplomacy. He demanded a "manly," representational art, free of the false affectations of Modernism and European influences. This kind of approach might play well to an unsophisticated audience, one unfamiliar with artistic trends since the turn of the century, but it soon grew tiresome. Nevertheless, in December 1934, *Time* magazine chose Benton for its cover in a wide-ranging feature on contemporary American art. Benton took this opportunity to lambaste much of the current artistic community, and claimed that Regionalism superseded any Modernist movements.

Despite his tendency to pontificate and exaggerate, Benton did have considerable popular appeal. He helped to invigorate the long-moribund art of mural painting, contributing a number of outstanding large works that attracted wide audiences. He freely used allegory, along with the folktales and legends of heartland America, as his text. Writhing, elongated figures, with all their serpentine contours, became his trademark, and he formularized it into compositions, all the time saying that his work was a repudiation of Modernism. Among the Regionalists, Benton was clearly the most colorful, and he helped immeasurably to make many people aware of this approach to art.

Urban Realism

The Regionalists weathered the Depression, but the impending war soon overshadowed their efforts. Meanwhile, many other artists were striving for recognition, and most could be grouped as urban and social realists. Cities have inspired American artists since the early nineteenth century and the beginnings of industrialization. The unemployment and despair seen in too many American towns and cities during the Depression brought about a new wave of interest in the urban scene. Many artists, like Edward Hopper (1882–1967) and Charles Sheeler (1883–1965), depicted the American city as essentially cheerless, a drab, ugly place. Whereas earlier interpreters had imbued the city with a syncopated life, many of the urban painters of the 1930s, particularly Hopper and Sheeler, sucked the life out of it. In their work, the city tends to be eerily quiet, and an overriding feeling of loneliness permeates it, as if people cannot connect with each other. There is a sense of detachment—often the viewer is placed at a distance from the subject, and looks across considerable space at the scene. Perhaps in some ways it reflects the economy, frozen and silent, unable to move.[2]

Hopper's cityscapes are painted in such a way that the urban hustle and bustle is absent, as if a kind of inertia has stifled all activity. Sheeler's unsullied factory landscapes, on the other hand, depict the power of industrial America, but no workers run the machines he so lovingly details. The manufacturing potential may be there, but it has not been unleashed. With great factories standing idle in the Depression, Sheeler's paintings provide mute comment on the unrealized power of American industry. Both artists had their followers, and they are certainly significant American painters. But the mass audience, although attracted to their realism, did not grant them celebrity status, and their fame was limited to museums and galleries.

An altogether different view of the city is provided by Reginald Marsh (1898–1954).[3] For him, a city street has nothing in common with an immaculately planted Iowa hillside any more than it does with an empty factory complex. It is a raucous, honkytonk place, full of the gritty details of life. It may not be pretty, but it is alive, and he plunges the viewer into the midst of noisy chaos, a place of bustling visual turbulence. He examines the big, crowded milieu familiar to millions of Americans. Edward Hopper's city scenes make the onlooker ponder, but Marsh's are more celebratory—this is the city, this is the way it is, and there is no need to be moralistic about it.

Thanks to several mural commissions and his own vibrant paintings, Reginald Marsh achieved a modest popular success. Although he enjoyed satirizing the rich in many of his works, his poor and downtrodden manifest a certain dignity, a sense that they are comfortable and belong in this environment. Marsh reflected the growing urbanism of the United States, and his candor in depicting the inherent life of a large American city (almost always New York) appealed to a broad cross section of the population.

Federal Art Project

In 1933, the administration of President Roosevelt created the Public Works of Art Project, a six-month program designed to employ 3750 artists and aid in the creation of over 15,000 works, including 700 public murals. Run by the Treasury Department, it was judged a success, and from it grew a much more ambitious program for all artistic endeavors.[4]

The newly created Works Progress Administration (WPA) was given the mandate to create meaningful jobs for thousands of unemployed citizens. The WPA in turn formed a number of "alphabet agencies," such as the Federal Art Project (FAP). It became a beacon of hope for unemployed artists and teachers of art, just as similar agencies came to the aid of theater, music, and writing. In each instance, many individuals who otherwise would have been without work found rewarding projects within their areas of expertise. At no other time has the government offered such largesse to the arts.

The FAP peaked in 1936, when 5300 artists and artisans were on its rolls. The program survived until 1942, making it one of the longest-running federal projects of that type. In all, the FAP spent over $35 million, and some 12,000 artists received assistance through its generosity. Its output was significant: over 4500 murals, 19,000 sculptures, and more than 450,000 paintings and prints are attributed to this one agency.

With few private patrons anymore, and with galleries going into bankruptcy, artists had to rely increasingly on the generosity of the government. This collaborative effort resulted in hundreds of public murals being executed under the aegis of the agency. The FAP did have one stipulation: works had to depict "American themes," either from the present or from history. Artists looked to the national past for orientation and direction, and this approach helped lead to the fascination with anything and everything "Early American" that boomed throughout the decade.[5]

Many of the FAP murals depict cowboys, farmers, aviators, laborers, mail carriers (a disproportionate number of the murals were done in post offices across the land), and folk heroes. For the most part it was a sanitized view of early America, essentially presenting white male Americans happily working in a chosen land. Americans wanted a meaningful past, and larger-than-life renderings of that past helped give meaning to the chaotic present.

Accompanying this search for a past was a tremendous growth in interest toward the nation's heritage. For example, square dancing flourished during the 1930s, and country music began to be heard on the radio. The Library of Congress went in search of the roots of early American music, compiling a series of records that helped preserve a rapidly disappearing art. In addition, the WPA was responsible for organizing and publishing *The Index of American Design*, a compendium of national arts and skills, and *The Historical American Buildings Survey*, a vast collection of measured drawings of virtually every important architectural site in the nation.

Photography

At the same time that the WPA was collecting documentation about America's past and art, photographers were lugging their cameras into cities and out to the countryside to capture American life on film. Their work was called "social documentary" and "photojournalism," and their photographs of coal miners, sharecroppers, child laborers, immigrants, and the destitute constituted a new level of social awareness. Photographers like Margaret Bourke-White (1906–1971), Walker Evans (1903–1975), Lewis Hine (1874–1940), Dorothea Lange (1895–1965), Carl Mydans (b. 1907), Arthur Rothstein (1915–1985), and Paul Strand (1890–1976) gained a modicum of fame with their hard-hitting black-and-white studies.

Bourke-White's *You Have Seen Their Faces* (1937; written with Erskine Caldwell) can still stir emotions with its portraits of American farm families facing bad economic times; Rothstein's *The Depression Years* (1978) provides a good photographic overview of the country during the crisis and contains a mix of urban and rural images. Photographer Walker Evans joined forces with the writer and critic James Agee to produce *Let Us Now Praise Famous Men* (1939; revised 1941). The two focused on farm families, especially sharecroppers, and their double plight: the Dust Bowl and the economic chaos of the period. The book's combination of lyrical text and searing photographs showed just how unequal the ordinary, daily lives of people were. Collectively, these books helped establish photojournalism as a legitimate literary form.[6]

When *Life* magazine came into being in 1936, its success was due in part to the growing public interest in photojournalism. Eastman-Kodak, the huge film and camera manufacturer, was aware of this interest, and they sensed they were losing a large part of the lucrative home camera market because of a flood of cheap competitors' models. In response, they brought out the Baby Brownie in 1934, a simple point-and-shoot camera that used easily available roll film. Naturally, they recommended Kodak film. The Brownie sold for $1.00, making it as inexpensive as anything in stores at the time, plus it took bigger pictures than most others. Despite the Depression, the Brownie swept the nation, eclipsing its competition.

Other popular developments in amateur photography included Kodak's inexpensive movie camera, the 8mm Cine-Kodak Eight, introduced in 1932. In 1935, RCA pioneered in sound photography by unveiling the Sound-on-Film movie camera, making sound home movies possible for the first time.

Sculpture

A less popular visual art was sculpture. The average citizen equated sculpture with large, public statues of long-dead historical figures that could be seen outside courthouses and in parks. It was traditional and realistic carving. As a result, most American sculpture lagged behind the trend-setting European examples of the 1930s. Unless one lived in New

Gutzon Borglum carving Mount Rushmore in 1938. This spectacle of sculpting huge faces out of a mountainside captured the public imagination during the late 1930s. (Photograph courtesy of the Library of Congress.)

York or Chicago and had access to the leading museums, modern sculpture was unseen, and therefore had no popular impact.

Not so the work of Gutzon Borglum (1867–1941). The public readily accepted his creations as great sculpture. They were large—"mammoth" might be a better word—and were nothing if not representational. Throughout the 1930s, under the watchful eye of photographers and journalists, Borglum hacked away at Mount Rushmore, a mountain located in the Black Hills of South Dakota. First with dynamite and then with pneumatic drills and 400 assistants, he roughed out the faces of four presidents—George Washington, Thomas Jefferson, Abraham Lincoln, and Theodore Roosevelt. Hitched up to a precarious system of scaffolding that allowed him to swing across the face of the mountain, he blasted away at the busts, generating not only sculpture but also lots of publicity. Critics assailed the project as the worst kind of tasteless exhibitionism, but the public loved it. Mount Rushmore became a National Memorial, and millions have journeyed to South Dakota to see the huge likenesses.[7]

Paul Manship (1885–1966) also exemplified American taste in sculpture for the decade. His smooth, stylized works appealed to many, and his monumental figure of Prometheus above Rockefeller Center's skating rink has charmed generations of New Yorkers. Although the piece is quite traditional, it seemed to sum up the average American's view of what public sculpture should be: large and easily identifiable.

In a similar vein, James Earle Fraser (1876–1953) impressed untold thousands with his sixty-foot-tall *George Washington* at the 1939 New York World's Fair. No matter that Fraser had made his mark almost forty years earlier with the moody *End of the Trail* (1894) and the 1913 Buffalo/ Indian Head nickel. For the average fairgoer, the towering statue of the first president symbolized American power and wealth, a far more appropriate use of sculpture than some nonsensical assemblage that no one could understand.

ILLUSTRATION

Although Americans might not be aware of the work being done by many dedicated artists of the period, that does not mean they lacked exposure to significant paintings and drawings. Continuing a trend begun in the nineteenth century, American illustrators were creating a body of work that merits attention. For magazines, books, posters, and advertising, these frankly commercial artists turned out thousands of pictures that ranged from the amateurish to works that could stand beside anything produced by their more "serious" counterparts. The 1930s was a rich decade for American illustration, and it is unfortunate that too many skilled practitioners of the craft have been forgotten or remain anonymous. Much of their output contributed to raising the public consciousness about art in general, and certainly they achieved a level of sophistication in illustration that anyone can admire.

Throughout much of the twentieth century, critics have shunted aside most American illustrators, maintaining that their work is too narrative or too commercial, that it lacks a high seriousness of purpose. But this derisive attitude has been the bane of all popular culture; it is often difficult for elitist critics to accept work aimed at a mass audience. For whatever reasons, the problem seems to worsen if the work is hugely successful and has a large, receptive audience. If so many people like it, can it possibly be good?

N.C. Wyeth

During the 1930s, the dean of American illustrators was N(ewell) C(onvers) Wyeth (1882–1945), who had commenced his career almost thirty years earlier. A prolific artist, Wyeth did over 3000 magazine illustrations, beginning with a cover for the *Saturday Evening Post* in 1903. His signature could also be found on murals, paintings, and advertisements. By the 1930s, would-be clients were lined up, anxious to offer him commissions.[8]

The *Ladies' Home Journal, Woman's Day, Good Housekeeping, McCall's,* and *Redbook* were among the magazines taking his work, and such diverse companies as International Harvester, the American Tobacco Company (Lucky Strikes), General Electric, Frankfort Distilleries (Paul Jones whiskey), and Coca-Cola were among his commercial associations. With all these commissions, he still somehow found time to create murals for banks, schools, hotels, and other institutions, the majority featuring episodes from American history. Financially secure, he enjoyed the luxury of painting for its own sake. In an acknowledgment of his renown and popularity, most of this mature work was purchased by museums, galleries, and individuals; he finally presented his first one-man show in 1939, a fitting capstone to a distinguished career.

Norman Rockwell

If N.C. Wyeth was the dean of American illustrators, then Norman Rockwell (1894–1978) reigned, for the general public at least, as the king. No American illustrator has enjoyed greater popularity. A superb technician and stylist, Rockwell was also endowed with a storyteller's imagination. Most of his thousands of pictures are essentially narrative; they reveal a bit of story that viewers find easy to follow. His greatest successes can be viewed on the covers of the *Saturday Evening Post*, the primary carrier of his work. In all, Norman Rockwell executed 322 cover illustrations for the immensely popular magazine, a span of accomplishment that began in 1916, when he was only twenty-two, and continued until the end of 1963. Because of the magazine's large circulation, each cover was seen, on average, by 4 million people, giving him the largest audience ever enjoyed by an artist before or since.[9]

In reality, Norman Rockwell was a classical painter, working in the established European tradition of bourgeois storytelling. But, even more than N.C. Wyeth, Rockwell focused on the passing American scene. He painted the small towns and their citizens, but despite his penchant for folksy settings, Rockwell is hardly a Regionalist. His canvases are Anywhere, U.S.A., and he is even less a Social Realist. He focuses on the ordinary and the familiar, and casts them in a warm, often humorous, glow. The viewer can identify with a Rockwell narrative and make sense of the story. Because of this approach, and because of his technical skills, he set the standards for American illustration from the 1920s through the 1950s.

The Depression never occurred in a Rockwell painting. He wisely sensed that most Americans preferred not to be reminded of the economic collapse, particularly on the covers of their favorite magazines or in the illustrations accompanying stories or advertisements. Instead, Rockwell reassured the country that the nation's values were sound, that social and political rituals had meaning, and that the family and the individual would ultimately triumph. At the same time, he suggested that a little stubbornness, a little laughter, and maybe even a bit of mischief would lighten everyone's spirits.

With the onset of the 1930s, Rockwell's *Post* covers shifted slightly from his earlier ones. He executed sixty-seven covers during the decade, about seven a year, and there is a marked decline in the presence of children. Adults become his focus, perhaps in recognition that this was a more serious—more "adult"—period in the nation's history. He also allows some contemporary celebrities into his creations: the rugged actor Gary Cooper graces a 1930 cover, allowing himself to be daintily made up by a studio employee; Jean Harlow, the reigning "Blonde Bombshell," wows a group of gaga-eyed reporters in 1936; and two coeds swoon over a photograph of leading man Robert Taylor in 1938. In addition, Rockwell displays a growing appreciation of fashion trends. The slim—but curvaceous—look favored by stylish women is duly depicted. His men, however, remain attired in shapeless suits that could come from almost any decade, a wry comment on the lack of distinctive style for most American men of the period.

Although Norman Rockwell will always be associated with the *Saturday Evening Post*, he was, like N.C. Wyeth, simultaneously doing illustrations for many magazines. His work appeared in *Boys' Life, Judge, Ladies' Home Journal, Leslie's, Liberty, Literary Digest, Popular Science*, and *Woman's Home Companion*. He devoted much energy to the Boy Scouts, illustrating their guidebooks and doing an annual calendar for them from 1925 to 1975.

By the 1930s, Rockwell's fame was assured, and advertising representatives flocked to his Vermont studio in an attempt to get him to draw or paint something extolling their products. As a result, a steady stream of illustrations poured forth lauding Fisk Tires, Overland automobiles, Edison Mazda (now General Electric), Sun-Maid Raisins, Jell-O, Interwoven Socks, Coca-Cola, Orange Crush, the Red Cross—over 150 companies and organizations in all. His carefully lettered signature always appears in his work, even the most mundane advertisements. In this way, the name Rockwell soon became familiar to millions. A simple tactic, but it helped sustain his growing fame and popularity. Plus his signature suggests an unspoken endorsement of the product.

The names of most of those illustrators who followed in Rockwell's footsteps have disappeared—as have those of most of the "serious" artists presumed to be superior to him. But Norman Rockwell survives, as well-known now as during the 1930s. His has been the lasting art, successfully blurring the line between high and low culture by focusing on popular culture. His work appeals to a large, diverse mass of people, and his public acceptance has ensconced him as the most beloved—and possibly the most influential—American artist of all time.

Leslie Thrasher

Another leading illustrator during the 1930s was Leslie Thrasher (1889–1936). Forgotten now, Thrasher sold his first cover to the *Saturday Evening Post* in 1912, four years before Rockwell accomplished the same feat. In 1926, he got a dream assignment: he was to produce one new cover a week for *Liberty* magazine, at $1000 per cover. He went on to do 360 covers for the *Post* rival until his contract ran out in 1932.[10]

Thrasher's work, although not up to Rockwell's standard, is nonetheless good, old-fashioned realism. Narrative in approach, many of his *Liberty* covers depict the life and times of "Lil," a typical middle-class woman—she just happens also to be very attractive—who works as a stenographer, has a boyfriend whom she eventually marries, and ultimately gives birth to a baby boy. The storyline is not unlike that found in the enormously popular comic strip *Blondie* (see below) that ran at the same time. Readers liked Lil, and contributed plot and picture ideas in a long-running contest sponsored by *Liberty*. A forgettable movie, *For the Love o' Lil* (1930), along with a weekly radio show, capitalized on her fame, a good example of how popular culture themes are seldom limited to a single medium.

Haddon Sundblom

Another illustrator needs to be mentioned, simply because one of his creations has been so completely accepted by the public: Haddon Sundblom (1899–1976). He is responsible for the Santa Claus who now dominates Yuletide imagery. The artist did advertising for the Coca-Cola Company, a contract that included creating a yearly Christmas painting featuring Santa holding a Coke as he makes his merry rounds. Beginning in 1931, and continuing for the next thirty years, Sundblom painted Jolly Old Saint Nick enjoying "The Pause That Refreshes." Soon, every other illustrator in the country was imitating the Sundblom model—rotund, ruddy complexion, big smile, twinkling eyes, and all the rest. Prior to 1931, Santa Claus tended to be more of an elfin figure, at times almost a gnome. In addition, earlier Santas were not always so merry; they could at times be rather frightening or mischievous. N.C. Wyeth did several interpretations of Santa Claus, but the man behind the beard seems almost sinister in comparison to Sundblum's merry figure. Norman Rockwell wisely adopted this virtually generic version of Santa in the 1930s, divorcing himself from some of his own Saint Nicks of earlier years.[11]

Summary

The Golden Age of American Illustration fizzled out in the 1940s, replaced by photographs and snazzy graphics, a situation that has accelerated in recent years. Thus the 1930s were the magnificent last gasp of an old tradition. Audiences today have no realization of how important illustration was during the early years of the twentieth century, nor do they know the talents of the vast majority of artists working in the field at that time. Americans might not have been going to museums in great numbers, but they were being exposed, on the pages of books and magazines and other sites, to a significant body of fine art.

CARTOONS

Just about everyone read the daily comics in the 1930s. It was the rare American newspaper that did not have at least a full page of the exploits of *Blondie, Dick Tracy, Flash Gordon, The Gumps, Krazy Kat, Mary Worth*, and innumerable others. Yet it has been only since the 1950s that the artistry of the American comic strip has come to be appreciated as an important visual art form. Today, the 1930s are seen as a high point for cartoon art, and many of the artists of the period have enjoyed museum retrospectives of their work. During the 1930s, however, the comics were usually viewed as little more than daily doses of humor and adventure, a mindless respite from the grim realities of the time. As is the case with so much popular culture, only in hindsight is the worth of an artist or a movement appreciated.

It would require several books to list and describe all the comic strips popular during the decade. According to a *Fortune* poll done in 1937, the ten leading newspaper comics were ranked as follows, beginning with the most popular:

1. *Little Orphan Annie* (created in 1924 by Harold Gray [1894–1968])
2. *Popeye* [correct title: *Thimble Theater*] (created in 1919 by Elzie Segar [1894–1938])
3. *Dick Tracy* (created in 1931 by Chester Gould [1900–1985])
4. *Bringing Up Father* (created in 1913 by George McManus [1884–1954])
5. *The Gumps* (created in 1917 by Sydney Smith [1877–1935]; continued by Gus Edson [1901–1966] after Smith's death in 1935)
6. *Blondie* (created in 1930 by Chic Young [1901–1973])

7. *Moon Mullins* (created in 1923 by Frank Willard [1893–1958])
8. *Joe Palooka* (created in 1930 by Ham Fisher [1901–1955])
9. *Li'l Abner* (created in 1934 by Al Capp [1909–1979])
10. *Tillie the Toiler* (created in 1921 by Russ Westover [1886–1966])

Because a number of these strips had their beginnings some years earlier, readers were familiar with many of them by the onset of the Depression. They doubtless felt comfortable following their favorite characters. In addition, audiences obviously liked to be amused: eight of the ten front-runners are humorous strips. Only *Little Orphan Annie* and *Dick Tracy* are more dramatic in their plots and, with their exaggerated villains and events, most readers knew better than to take them too seriously.[12]

A comic strip is a fictional narrative in visual form. Each day the individual pictures, or frames, that constitute an episode add to the ongoing story and characterizations. In a variety of ways, a comic strip can be compared to a piece of motion-picture film. A movie is also comprised of many individual photographs that take on meaning only when run through a projector at the proper speed. Walking in at the middle and then exiting before the end would hardly be a satisfactory way to watch a film. Similarly, an individual episode of any comic might not be particularly funny or enlightening, but when read on a daily basis, the stories begin to cohere and the characters take on distinctive personalities. Most of the more successful strips of the 1930s did a good job of keeping the audience both entertained and satisfied.

Little Orphan Annie

Little Orphan Annie enjoyed widespread popularity almost from the day of its debut in 1924. Harold Gray lacked any outstanding artistic skills, but he made up for the deficiency with his ability to spin a good yarn. Annie is just that, an orphan. Inexplicably "adopted" by Daddy Warbucks, the plucky redhead with the pupilless eyes spends little time with her guardian. As a rule, she is on the road with her faithful dog, Sandy, getting involved with some of the most complex plotting ever to appear in the comics. The speech balloons above each character are filled to capacity; no American strip has contained so much dialogue, before or since.[13]

During the 1930s, *Annie* boomed; its mix of ultraconservative capitalism and strong nationalism appealed to many during the troubled decade. Gray had little patience with things like child labor laws, poverty, or welfare. Annie always picks up odd jobs, no matter how menial. If a person is poor, he or she probably shares responsibility for the situation.

A strong person (i.e., a good person) finds work; those who do not are bums. Those who live "on the dole" are beneath contempt. With high unemployment and a worsening depression, such messages might seem out of step with the times. As the threat of war grew in the latter part of the decade, Gray went after "foreigners" with an enthusiastic nativism. Faithful readers of the strip apparently accepted his simplistic solutions to the country's ills without question.

Annie's popularity got her into another visual medium in the 1930s, with the release of two feature movies, *Little Orphan Annie* in 1932, and a follow-up in 1939. The National Broadcasting Company, aware of the large audience for the strip, introduced a long-running radio serial in 1931. Annie was a rarity: she was not a male, and she had no particular super powers. But she was tough, and that was a desirable quality in 1931 America. With a colorful cast of characters straight from the newspaper strip, Annie makes her independent way. Her adventures charmed children and adolescents who saw in her the freedom to do almost anything.

Sponsored by Ovaltine, a popular chocolate powder that was mixed with milk, the serial soon offered premiums to listeners. Toys and novelties featuring both Annie and Sandy, along with wristwatches, pop-up books, and cheap jewelry, were available from catalogs and dime stores throughout the 1930s. Regardless of its ideological slant, *Little Orphan Annie* had a devoted following.

Dick Tracy

In a somewhat similar manner, Chester Gould was responding to the headlines and sensationalism that accompanied crime and lawlessness during the period. Because of Prohibition, bootlegging was rampant, and various gangs and factions were literally at war with each other over the lucrative trade. In the early 1930s, the law seemed powerless against figures like Al Capone and John Dillinger, and Hollywood was quick to jump on the crime bandwagon with a deluge of gangster films. Up until that time, however, the comic pages had seen little of criminals. Thus *Dick* (from American slang, meaning a detective) *Tracy* (a pun on "trace," to locate, or apprehend) broke new ground and quickly won a sizable audience in the hotly competitive comics business.[14]

The world of *Dick Tracy* is both visually and morally one of black and white. Gould, like Harold Gray, was at best a mediocre artist, but he made the most of his limited talents. Stark silhouettes, speeding cars, the precise rendering of guns and other mechanical objects, along with some of the most bizarre villains ever drawn, are his trademarks. On the moral side, the law is always right, and if Tracy has to shoot a bad guy, that is the price for a life of crime. If he accomplishes this task with a machine gun and mows down a whole group of thugs in one bullet-filled pass, so much the better. Death is a regular feature of the strip, but it is so staged and apparently painless that few chose to complain.

The popularity of this cartoon police officer was soon carried over into all kinds of Dick Tracy toy guns, games, badges, and the like. The hawk-nosed detective appeared in four movie serials between 1937 and 1941. There was also a radio serial in the late afternoon; it commenced in 1935 and ran until 1948. If America ever had vigilante fantasies, Dick Tracy was there to act them out.

Blondie

Not all the strips espouse a right-wing point of view. Most, in fact, are apolitical. A case in point is *Blondie*, a family strip that premiered in 1930. The creation of Murat "Chic" Young, it began with the whimsical adventures of a flapper named Blondie who wows the boys and has not a care in the world. Her primary beau is Dagwood Bumstead, an earnest college student and heir to millions, who wins her hand in marriage. So far, so good. But then the Depression worsened.[15]

Young realized the Roaring Twenties were over. The story of a "dumb blonde" who is about to become very rich would probably have limited appeal to an audience facing an economic crisis. So he abruptly changed the strip in response to the times. Dagwood is disinherited, Blondie goes from flapper to middle-class housewife, the couple lives in a typical small house, and the focus subtly shifts from Blondie to Dagwood.

Dagwood emerges as the put-upon American husband, a well-meaning bumbler who needs the common sense of Blondie to muddle through, although he can enjoy occasional small victories. He can always savor his inimitable "Dagwood Sandwich," a tasty concoction made from everything in the refrigerator and pantry—and a classic bit of Americana. Young had the challenge of providing a gag a day, yet doing it in such a way that the continuity of the family would not be broken. He more than rose to the occasion. *Blondie* became a portrait of normalcy in chaotic times. The content may not be the stuff of great literature, but the strip endures and readers see themselves and their lives reflected in a comic mirror.

The strip quickly became a national favorite (and even international; *Blondie* has long enjoyed wide foreign distribution). Movie rights were assigned, and Penny Singleton and Arthur Lake achieved minor stardom as the leads in twenty-eight *Blondie* features that ran from 1938 to 1950. Toys, games, and novelties appeared, and by the end of the decade a radio comedy had been produced, starring none other than Penny Singleton. The multiple media tie-ins reinforced the popularity of the characters.

Visually, the comics have assisted readers in their perceptions of the world. The dark, threatening frames of *Little Orphan Annie* and *Dick Tracy* suggest that one cannot be too careful; danger lurks around every corner. But *Blondie* provides a brighter, cheerier vision. Within the family, safe in a home—there lies security. Tracy and Annie seldom enjoyed this kind of security; they had to operate in a cold, uncaring environment, separated from home and family. Clearly, the loner faces more risks in American society.

Science Fiction

Other strips taught additional visual lessons.[16] Science fiction came to the comics in 1929 with *Buck Rogers* (Phil Nowlan [1888–1940] and Dick Calkins [1895–1962]). Because it was new and different, the series enjoyed a certain following, but the images of scientific invention come across as crude and dated even by the standards of the early 1930s. In 1934, however, Alex Raymond's (1909–1956) stylish *Flash Gordon* made its newspaper debut. Here was Streamline Moderne in all its glory. Sleek rocket ships cruise to gleaming, Modernistic cities. No doubt the way generations of Americans would imagine the future was influenced by this beautifully drafted strip.

Hillbilly Funnies

A pole apart from science fiction were the hillbilly funnies that prospered during the decade. Al Capp created *Li'l Abner* in 1934. In the strip he has an event called Sadie Hawkins Day, a day when girls can ask boys to dances and other social affairs. This 1937 bit of inventiveness was soon celebrated by high schools and colleges around the country, and it served as an acknowledgment of the growing importance of teenage culture.

At about the same time, Billy DeBeck (1890–1942) was introducing a character name Snuffy Smith in his popular *Barney Google* strip. Who would have thought that two series about Appalachia, rustic mountain culture, and abject poverty could find an audience during the Great Depression? But they did, and each contributed to the folklore about the region. Although the humor could be biting, it was seldom cruel, and perhaps seeing how these down-and-out characters coped gave a measure of encouragement to readers.

Animal Strips

The use of anthropomorphic animals is as old as cartooning itself. Walt Disney recognized this fact early in his career and built a fortune on

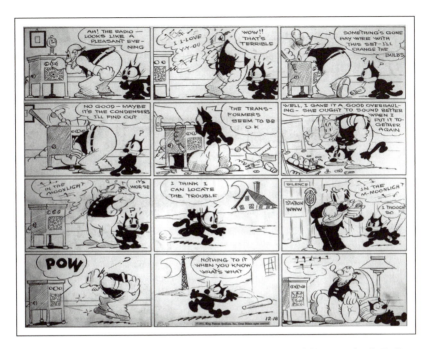

Felix the Cat. In this widely read comic strip of the period, Felix had adventures that sometimes involved other areas of popular culture, such as radio in this example. (Photograph courtesy of the Library of Congress.)

Mickey Mouse, Minnie Mouse, Donald Duck, and all their companions. Other comic strips like *Krazy Kat* (1910–1944) and *Little Orphan Annie* (1924–1979; her dog Sandy cannot speak, but can add his signature "Arf" at opportune moments), right down to the more modern *Peanuts* (1950–2001) and *Garfield* (1978–   ), have long enlivened the comic pages.

During the 1930s, a popular favorite in this genre was *Felix the Cat* (1923–1967). Created by Pat Sullivan in 1917 as an animated cartoon, and debuting as a comic strip in 1923, the feisty Felix was a perfect character for the Depression. He is a survivor; nothing can overcome his spirit, and he battles poverty, hunger, loneliness, and technology with equal aplomb. His ingenuity and endless good spirits made for great daily reading. The strip was taken over by Otto Messmer in the early thirties, but if anything the series became even more lyrical and aesthetically satisfying with this change. *Felix the Cat* continued as one of the leading newspaper comics of the decade, one of those strips that reacted to the uncertainties of the Depression with humorous scorn.

The comics visually reinforced American values and beliefs. They are one of the purest forms of popular culture, and the 1930s marked one of their most expansive and innovative periods. Using the mass medium of newspapers, they are inexpensive, they enjoy wide distribution, millions read them on the same day, and they rely on simple graphics to tell their stories. Abstraction in any academic sense is absent from the frames of a typical newspaper strip. Instead, they aim at the largest mass audience and, through daily repetition, create a familiarity and acceptance rarely found in almost any other medium.

Big Little Books

Another form of visual comic art also came along in the 1930s: the comic book. Some antecedents of comic books also gained a significant measure of popularity during the decade. In 1932, the so-called Pop-Up Books were introduced by Blue Ribbon Books. This series consisted of small booklets that featured characters that popped up from the pages when the volume was laid flat. The enterprising publishers decided to capitalize on the large readership for newspaper comics by using the heroes of the daily strips for the figures so distinctively displayed.

The interest shown in these early Pop-Up Books immediately led to other innovations, the clever Big Little Books in particular. The first offering in this marketing phenomenon was issued in 1932 and involved the adventures of none other than Dick Tracy. The product of the Whitman Publishing Company, the book measured 3⅝ inches wide, 4½ inches tall, and 1½ inches thick, had cardboard covers, and contained 350 pages. The left-hand page contained text, and the right-hand page featured a single frame from the comic strip. With the exception of the garishly colored covers, all was in black and white. The book cost a dime and set the standards that most succeeding volumes followed.[17]

The Big Little Books were an immediate hit. Eventually, Whitman issued over 400 separate titles, and other publishers lost no time in joining them. Dell Publishing (Fast Action Books), Fawcett Publications (Dime Action Books), and Saalfield Publishing Company (Little Big Books) were among the industry leaders. So fierce was the competition that Whitman changed the line's name to Better Little Books and Big Big Books in 1938, an attempt to differentiate themselves from the competition. Print runs for most titles averaged 250,000 to 350,000 copies, and they could usually be obtained in five-and-dimes, as well as chain and variety stores.

Initially, the majority of the Big Little Books were reprints of leading newspaper strips like *Dick Tracy, Flash Gordon, Buck Rogers, Little Orphan Annie, The Gumps, Tarzan*, or various Disney characters. Within a short time, however, they came to include illustrated novels, such as *Moby Dick, Treasure Island, A Midsummer Night's Dream*, and many others, along with radio favorites, like *The Lone Ranger, Gang Busters, The Green Hornet*, and *Jack Armstrong*. Even movie stars like Shirley Temple, Jackie Cooper,

Jane Withers, Will Rogers, and Tom Mix had their own Big Little Books stories. Children and adolescents soon were building "libraries" of these popular, inexpensive volumes.

Comic Books

The combined success of newspaper comic strips and the Big Little Books in the early 1930s hastened the birth of the modern comic book. Attempts had been made back in the 1920s to reprint newspaper comics in some sort of booklet form, but they had not done well. Finally, with *Funnies on Parade*, a 1933 giveaway that featured several popular cartoon characters, the concept started to catch on. This one-shot publication led to other collections of reprints, but they were no longer free: they cost 10 cents, the amount that all comics eventually charged throughout the 1930s. The following year saw the publication of *Famous Funnies*, the periodical generally accepted as the first modern comic book.[18]

As the success of *Famous Funnies* grew, competing publishers began to enter this new market. In 1935, Dell issued *Popular Comics*, another reprint series. At this time, the standard format of sixty-four pages per issue was established. By 1938, titles like *The Funnies, The Comics, Super Comics, King Comics*, and *Tip Top Comics* had joined the fray, and they increasingly featured all-new material. Reprints became a thing of the past. A unique popular art form had been born.

At the mention of comic books, many people immediately think of Superman. The Man of Steel made his debut in 1938, the creation of writer Jerry Siegel (1914–1996) and artist Joe Shuster (1914–1992), in *Action Comics*. Although the industry had been turning more and more toward original (instead of reprint) action adventures, no one was prepared for the success of Superman.

By 1939, a new *Superman* comic of its own was launched, and soon was selling over 1 million copies per issue. In a clever reversal, a newspaper strip based on the comic book came out later that same year, and a radio show was close behind. Almost immediately, other publishers readied their own superheroes. Batman was introduced in 1939, along with a number of other characters who possessed superhuman attributes—most of whom are justly forgotten. But the stage had been set, and soon one superhero after another graced the brightly colored covers of comic books at newsstands across the land.

Editorial Cartoons

Neither a comic strip nor a traditional illustration, the editorial cartoon occupies a niche of its own. Although its history is a long one, the American form of this comic art came into its own in the nineteenth century

"The Spirit of the New Deal!" Not all cartooning involved comic strips;
editorial cartoons were also popular. This C.K. Berryman example in
support of government New Deal programs appeared in 1933.
(Photograph courtesy of the Library of Congress.)

with the drawings of Thomas Nast. Since then, the editorial cartoon has
emerged as a standard part of most daily newspapers, with one or more
such drawings gracing—appropriately enough—the editorial page.
Opinionated, partisan, timely, sarcastic, angry—all voices and all moods
can be expressed in this unique visual format.

The Depression stirred editorial cartoonists of all stripes. Some de-
spised President Roosevelt and the New Deal in no uncertain terms, yet
others found in him the salvation of the nation and could not praise him
enough. As the Depression waned and the war clouds gathered in the
later thirties, the editorial cartoonists were there; some were strongly
isolationist, urging the nation to avoid any impending war, just as many
of their comrades delighted in taking pokes at Hitler and the growing
Axis threat. Whatever the situation, these pen-and-ink artists have been

incisive visual commentators on the passing scene and have certainly contributed to ongoing popular culture.

Summary

Collectively, comic strips, Big Little Books, and comic books created a new national literature. They appealed to a broad audience, they played on basic American themes, and they were enormously successful. Annie and Dagwood made it through the Depression, and Superman and his super cohorts would see to it that the country made it through World War II.

In retrospect, the visual arts flourished during the 1930s. Although Modernist painting and sculpture lacked a large, significant following, realism and Regionalism had numerous proponents. Illustrators still found many outlets for their talents through books and magazines, and advertisers had not abandoned painting and drawing as a means of getting out their messages. Both comic strips and comic books boomed, providing simplistic solutions to complex problems. No arts exist in some aesthetic vacuum, isolated from the ongoing world, and never was this fact illustrated more forcefully than during the Depression years.

Cost of Products

When considering "what things cost back then," a number of important adjustments have to be made either to Depression-era prices or to contemporary ones. Dollars then do not equal dollars now. Adjusted for inflation and averaged over the decade, the Depression-era dollar is, in 2002, worth approximately $12.50. Conversely, a present-day dollar would be worth only about 12 cents if spent during the 1930s.

As an example of how conversion works, prime rib, the second item in the list below, can serve as an illustration. In the 1930s it averaged 35 cents a pound. Using a value of $1.00 (1930s) = $12.50 (2002), today the prime rib would cost (.35 × 12.50) about $4.38 a pound. Gasoline, also listed below, could be bought in the 1930s for around 15 to 20 cents a gallon. Again, using $1.00 = $12.50, 1930s gasoline cost the equivalent of $1.88 to $2.50 per gallon (.15 or .20 × 12.50) in today's dollars. Similar calculations can be made for any of the other products and services listed below.

All the figures given are approximations and averages for the decade, not precise, unchanging numbers. Prices tended to be lower during the worst years of the Depression (1930–1933), and slightly higher in other years.

FOOD

Chicken, 22 cents/pound

Prime rib, 35 cents/pound

Butter, 50 cents/pound

Eggs, 29 cents/dozen

Milk, 12 cents/quart

Bread, 7 cents/loaf

Cornflakes, 8 cents/box

Canned tomatoes, 9 cents/can

Oranges, 30 cents/dozen

Potatoes, 3 cents/pound

Jell-O (pudding), 4 packages for 15 cents

Coffee, 30 cents/pound

Restaurant breakfast, 25 cents; lunch, 40–50 cents; dinner, 75 cents–$1.75; dessert, 25 cents

Cocktail, 25 cents

Candy bar, 5 cents

CLOTHING

Quality man's suit, $60–$75

Good men's shoes, $4.00/pair

Necktie, 25 cents

Dresses, $1.00 and up

Cotton blouses, 50 cents and up

Women's fur coats (fox, lamb, leopard, pony), $125

Children's overalls, 50 cents

Sailor suit and cap, $1.75

Dress pattern, 15 cents

SHELTER AND FURNISHINGS

Rent, $35/month (a national average for all forms of housing, without respect to region)

Double bed, springs, and Mattress, $25

Bedroom suite (headboard, dresser and mirror, chest, wardrobe), $50

Dining room set (table, 5 chairs), $30

Living room suite (sofa, 2 chairs), $80

Electric stove (enameled), $50

Washing machine (electric agitator, hand wringer), $65

PERSONAL ITEMS

Haircut (men), 20 cents

Permanent (women), 30 cents

Hand soap, 12 bars for 49 cents

Hand cream, 75 cents/jar

Toilet tissue, 5 cents/roll

Tooth powder, 30 cents/can

Cigarettes, 10–15 cents/pack

Tobacco, 15 cents/tin

Wrist watches, $25 and up

TRANSPORTATION

Chevrolet (or Ford, Plymouth), $475 (1935, new)

Pierce-Arrow (luxury automobile), $2,000 (1935, new)

Cadillac V-16, $3,500 (1935, new)

In 1935, the average price paid for a new automobile was $580; the typical used car cost $250–$350

Gasoline, 15–20 cents/gallon

Automobile battery, $15

New bicycle, $10.95

MEDICAL COSTS

Hospital bed in ward, $4.00/day (no special care)

Single room, $6.50/day (no special care)

Chicken pox (full treatment), $1.82

Measles (full treatment), $5

Childbirth, $100

Aspirin (12-count), 15 cents

Prescription eyeglasses, $10/pair

ENTERTAINMENT AND LEISURE

Movie ticket (one), 10–50 cents

Ticket to symphony, $1.00–$2.50

Best-selling novel (hardcover), $2.00

Comic book, 10 cents

Mass magazine, 5 cents–20 cents/issue

Newspaper, 2–5 cents/copy

Baseball mitt and ball, $1.25

Yo-yo, 10 cents

Car radio, $35

Table radio, $30

Long-distance call, New York–California, $7.50 (3 minutes)

Postage: first-class letter, ground, 3 cents; airmail, 8 cents; postcard, 1 cent

Notes

CHAPTER 1

1. Two books that cover the New York World's Fair and its time capsule in considerable detail are David Gelernter, *1939: The Lost World of the Fair* (New York: Avon Books, 1995), 269–70, 353; and Alice G. Marquis, *Hopes and Ashes: The Birth of Modern Times, 1929–1939* (New York: The Free Press, 1986).

2. Elliott West, *Growing Up in Twentieth-Century America: A History and Reference Guide* (Westport, CT: Greenwood Press, 1996), 81–169.

3. Kennth T. Jackson, *The Crabgrass Frontier* (New York: Oxford University Press, 1985), 193.

4. T.H. Watkins, *The Hungry Years: America in an Age of Crisis, 1929–1939* (New York: Henry Holt, 1999), 60.

5. Maurice Horn, ed., *100 Years of American Newspaper Comics* (New York: Gramercy Books, 1996), 197–198.

6. Virtually any movie statistic can be found in Cobbett S. Steinberg, *Film Facts* (NY: Facts on File, 1980). Attendance figures from pp. 44–49.

7. Winona Morgan, *The Family Meets the Depression* (Minneapolis: University of Minnesota Press, 1939), 16–19.

8. Robert S. McElvaine, *The Great Depression: America, 1929–1941* (New York: Times Books, 1961), 189–190.

9. Agnes Rogers, *I Remember Distinctly: A Family Album of the American People in the Years of Peace, 1918 to Pearl Harbor* (New York: Harper & Brothers, 1947), 154.

10. Arthur P. Molella and Elsa M. Bruton, *FDR, the Intimate Presidency: Franklin Delano Roosevelt, Communication, and the Mass Media in the 1930s* (Washington, DC: National Museum of American History, 1982), 62.

CHAPTER 2

1. Elliott West, *Growing Up in Twentieth-Century America: A History and Reference Guide* (Westport, CT: Greenwood Press, 1996), 81–169.

2. Hal Draper, "The Student Movement of the Thirties," in *As We Saw the Thirties*, ed. Rita Simon (Urbana: University of Illinois Press, 1967), 155.

3. Errol Lincoln Uys, *Riding the Rails: Teenagers on the Move During the Depression* (New York: TV Books, 1999), 13–22.

4. Thomas Hine, *The Rise and Fall of the American Teenager* (New York: Avon Books [Bard], 1999), 206–207.

5. Lucy Rollin, *Twentieth-Century Teen Culture by the Decades: A Reference Guide* (Westport, CT: Greenwood Press, 1999), 81–84.

6. T.H. Watkins, *The Great Depression: America in the 1930s* (Boston: Little, Brown, 1993), 255–261.

7. Grace Palladino, *Teenagers: An American History* (New York: Basic Books, 1996), 5, 17–25.

8. All of these strips can be found in Maurice Horn, ed., *100 Years of American Newspaper Comics* (New York: Gramercy Books, 1996).

9. Steven M. Gelber, "A Job You Can't Lose: Work and Hobbies in the Great Depression," *Journal of Social History*, 24 (1991): 747–749.

10. Joseph J. Corn, *The Winged Gospel: America's Romance with Aviation, 1900–1950* (New York: Oxford University Press, 1983), 115–123.

11. Agnes Rogers, *I Remember Distinctly: A Family Album of the American People in the Years of Peace, 1918 to Pearl Harbor* (New York: Harper & Brothers, 1947), 191.

CHAPTER 3

1. Jackson Lears, *Fables of Abundance: A Cultural History of Advertising in America* (New York: Basic Books, 1994), 235–247.

2. Roland Marchand, *Advertising the American Dream: Making Way for Modernity, 1920–1940* (Los Angeles: University of California Press, 1985), 286–306.

3. Clarence P. Hornung and Fridolf Johnson, *200 Years of American Graphic Art* (New York: George Braziller, 1976), 149–174.

4. Stephen Fox, *The Mirror Makers: A History of American Advertising and Its Creators* (New York: William Morrow, 1984), 138–150.

5. Frank Rowsome, Jr., *They Laughed When I Sat Down* (New York: Bonanza Books, 1959), 151–152, 159.

6. For the story of Burma-Shave and many examples of their ads, see Frank Rowsome, Jr., *The Verse by the Side of the Road: The Story of Burma-Shave Signs and Jingles* (Lexington, MA: The Stephen Greene Press, 1965).

7. Dixon Wecter, *The Age of the Great Depression, 1929–1941* (Chicago: Quadrangle Books, 1948), 230–232.

8. Charles Goodrum and Helen Dalrymple, *Advertising in America: The First 200 Years* (New York: Harry N. Abrams, Inc., 1990), 38–40.

9. Marilyn Kern-Foxworth, *Aunt Jemima, Uncle Ben, and Rastus: Blacks in Ad-*

vertising, Yesterday, Today, and Tomorrow (Westport, CT: Greenwood Press, 1994), 113ff.

10. For more on attitudes about smoking, see Michael Schudson, *Advertising, the Uneasy Persuasion: Its Dubious Impact on American Society* (New York: Basic Books, 1984); and Jane Webb Smith, *Smoke Signals: Cigarettes, Advertising, and the American Way of Life* (Chapel Hill: University of North Carolina Press, 1990).

CHAPTER 4

1. Thomas Walton, "The Sky Was No Limit," *Portfolio* 1 (April/May 1979): 82–89.

2. David P. Handlin, *American Architecture* (New York: Thames and Hudson, 1985), 197ff.

3. William Peirce Randel, *The Evolution of American Taste* (New York: Crown Publishers, 1978), 183–185.

4. Clifford Edward Clark, Jr., *The American Home: 1800–1960* (Chapel Hill: University of North Carolina Press, 1986), 193–195.

5. Much more detailed information about the housing crisis can be found in chapters 6 and 7 of David M. Kennedy, *Freedom from Fear: The American People in Depression and War, 1929–1945* (New York: Oxford University Press, 1999), 160–217.

6. John A. Jakle and Keith A Sculle, *The Gas Station in America* (Baltimore: Johns Hopkins University Press, 1994), 144–150.

7. Carlton Jackson, *Hounds of the Road: A History of the Greyhound Bus Company* (Bowling Green, OH: Popular Press, 1984), 46–47.

8. Alice G. Marquis, *Hopes and Ashes: The Birth of Modern Times, 1929–1939* (New York: The Free Press, 1986), 187–231.

9. Michael Horsham, *'20s & '30s Style* (Secaucus, NJ: Chartwell Books, 1989), 24–31.

10. Helen A. Harrison, *Dawn of a New Day: The New York World's Fair, 1939/40* (New York: New York University Press, 1980), 30.

11. C. Ray Smith, *Interior Design in 20th-Century America: A History* (New York: Harper & Row, 1987), 124, 224–227.

CHAPTER 5

1. Ellie Laubner, *Collectible Fashions of the Turbulent Thirties* (Atglen, Pa.: Schiffer Publishing, 2000), 7.

2. Stella Blum, ed., *Everyday Fashions of the Thirties: As Pictured in Sears Catalogs* (New York: Dover Publications, 1986), 69.

3. For an overview of how the movie magazines influenced fashion, see Martin Levin, ed., *Hollywood and the Great Fan Magazines* (New York: Arbor House, 1970).

4. Kate Mulvey and Melissa Richards, *Decades of Beauty: The Changing Image of Women, 1890s–1990s* (New York: Checkmark Books, 1998), 82–97.

5. Laubner, 39–82.

6. Charles Panati, *Extraordinary Origins of Everyday Things* (New York: Harper & Row, 1987), 220.

7. Blum, 66, 110, 129.
8. Panati, 298.

CHAPTER 6

1. Dixon Wecter, *The Age of the Great Depression, 1929–1941* (Chicago: Quadrangle Books, 1948), 282–283.

2. An excellent introduction to the Americanization of the nation's eating habits is Harvey Levenstein's 2-volume study, *Revolution at the Table: The Transformation of the American Diet* (New York: Oxford University Press, 1988) and *Paradox of Plenty: A Social History of Eating in Modern America* (New York: Oxford University Press, 1993).

3. Richard J. Hooker, *Food and Drink in America: A History* (Indianapolis, IN: Bobbs-Merrill, 1981), 306.

4. Chester H. Liebs, *Main Street to Miracle Mile: American Roadside Architecture* (Baltimore: Johns Hopkins University Press, 1985), 124–125.

5. Sherrie A. Innes, *Dinner Roles: American Women and Culinary Culture* (Iowa City: University of Iowa Press, 2001), 110–115.

6. Various candy bars are discussed in Ray Broekel, *The Great American Candy Bar Book* (Boston: Houghton Mifflin, 1982).

7. David Powers Cleary, *Great American Brands* (New York: Fairchild Publications, 1981), 112–119.

8. Ruth Schwartz Cowan, *More Work for Mother* (New York: Basic Books, 1983), 133–139.

9. Many of the pamphlets distributed to homemakers are found throughout Bunny Crumpacker, *The Old-Time Brand-Name Cookbook* (New York: Smithmark, 1998).

10. Charles Panati, *Extraordinary Origins of Everyday Things* (New York: Harper & Row, 1987), 111–113.

11. A valuable study of American restaurants is Richard Pillsbury, *From Boarding House to Bistro: The American Restaurant Then and Now* (Boston: Unwin Hyman, 1990).

12. American drinking habits and cultural responses to them are covered in Andrew Barr, *Drink: A Social History of America* (New York: Carroll & Graf, 1999).

13. For more on the Pepsi-Cola and Coca-Cola competition, see Bob Stoddard, *Pepsi-Cola: 100 Years* (Los Angeles: General Publishing Group, 1997), and Pat Watters, *Coca-Cola: An Illustrated History* (Garden City, NY: Doubleday, 1978).

14. Stephen N. Tchudi, in *Soda Poppery: The History of Soft Drinks in America* (New York: Scribner's, 1986), describes a number of popular American soft drinks.

CHAPTER 7

1. For a broad overview of many different American fads, see Andrew Marum and Frank Parise, *Follies and Foibles: A View of 20th Century Fads* (New York: Facts on File, 1984); Charles Panati, *Panati's Parade of Fads, Follies, and Ma-*

nias (New York: HarperCollins, 1991); and Paul Sann, *Fads, Follies and Delusions of the American People* (New York: Crown Publishers, 1967).

2. Foster Rhea Dulles, *A History of Recreation: America Learns to Play* (Englewood Cliffs, NJ: Prentice-Hall, 1965), 378.

3. Marvin Kaye, *A Toy Is Born* (New York: Stein and Day, 1973), 51–59.

4. Frank W. Hoffmann and William G. Bailey, *Sports and Recreation Fads* (New York: Haworth Press, 1991), 289–291.

5. Ibid., 237–239.

6. John O'Dell, *The Great American Depression Book of Fun* (New York: Harper & Row, 1981), 2, 36–105.

7. Steven M. Gelber, "A Job You Can't Lose: Work and Hobbies in the Great Depression," *Journal of Social History*, 24 (1991): 741–742, 754.

8. Arthur P. Molella and Elsa M. Bruton, *FDR, the Intimate Presidency: Franklin Delano Roosevelt, Communication, and the Mass Media in the 1930s* (Washington, DC: National Museum of American History, 1982), 62.

9. G. Edward White, *Creating the National Pastime: Baseball Transforms Itself, 1903–1955* (Princeton, NJ: Princeton University Press, 1996), 118–123, 164–189.

10. Benjamin G. Rader, *American Sports: From the Age of Folk Games to the Age of Spectators* (Englewood Cliffs, NJ: Prentice-Hall, Inc., 1983), 196–215.

11. Paul Dickson, *The Worth Book of Softball: A Celebration of America's True National Pastime* (New York: Facts on File, 1994), 60–82.

12. Chester H. Liebs, *Main Street to Miracle Mile: American Roadside Architecture* (Baltimore: Johns Hopkins University Press, 1985), 137–145.

CHAPTER 8

1. A good introduction to the mystery genre is Julian Symons, *Bloody Murder: From the Detective Story to the Crime Novel* (New York: Penguin Books, 1972).

2. Elizabeth I. Hanson, *Margaret Mitchell* (Boston: Twayne, 1991), 90–102.

3. Margaret Mitchell, *Gone with the Wind* (Garden City, NY: Garden City Books, 1936), 689.

4. Two works that give a good overview of the FWP are Jerre Mangione, *The Dream and the Deal: The Federal Writers' Project, 1935–1943* (Boston: Little, Brown, 1972); and Monty Noam Penkower, *The Federal Writers' Project: A Study in Government Patronage and the Arts* (Urbana: University of Illinois Press, 1977).

5. Jan Cohn, *Creating America: George Horace Lorimer and the* Saturday Evening Post (Pittsburgh, PA: University of Pittsburgh Press, 1989), 218–267.

6. John Heidenry, *Theirs Was the Kingdom: Lila and DeWitt Wallace and the Story of the* Reader's Digest (New York: W.W. Norton, 1993), 59–149.

7. Loudon Wainwright, *The Great American Magazine: An Inside History of* Life (New York: Alfred A. Knopf, 1986), 69–120.

8. John Tebbel and Mary Ellen Zuckerman, *The Magazine in America: 1741–1990* (New York: Oxford University Press, 1991), 193–194.

9. Cabell Phillips, *The New York Times Chronicle of American Life. From the Crash to the Blitz: 1929–1939* (New York: The Macmillan, 1969), 472–473.

10. Frank Gruber provides an inside look at this side of magazine publishing in *The Pulp Jungle* (Los Angeles: Sherbourne Press, 1967).

11. A standard history of American newspapers is Frank Luther Mott, *American Journalism: A History, 1690–1960* (New York: Macmillan, 1962).

12. Edwin Emery, *The Press and America: An Interpretative History of Journalism* (Englewood Cliffs, NJ: Prentice-Hall, Inc., 1962), 513–579.

13. Details about all of the columnists cited can be found in John Dunning, *On the Air: The Encyclopedia of Old-Time Radio* (New York: Oxford University Press, 1998).

14. Emery, 621–650.

CHAPTER 9

1. Innumerable books exist about the big-band era; for thoroughness, one of the best is George T. Simon, *The Big Bands* (New York: Macmillan, 1967).

2. Russell Sanjek, *Pennies from Heaven: The American Popular Music Business in the Twentieth Century* (New York: Da Capo Press, 1988), 184ff.

3. Joseph Csida and June Bundy Csida, *American Entertainment: A Unique History of Popular Show Business* (New York: Watson-Guptill, 1978), 230–231.

4. Geoffrey C. Ward and Ken Burns, *Jazz: A History of America's Music* (New York: Alfred A. Knopf, 2000), 246.

5. David Ewen, *All the Years of American Popular Music* (Englewood Cliffs, NJ: Prentice-Hall, 1977), 413, 422.

6. Ian Whitcomb, *After the Ball: Pop Music from Rag to Rock* (Baltimore: Penguin Books, 1972), 149.

7. A good survey of the songwriter's art is Alec Wilder, *American Popular Song: The Great Innovators, 1900–1950* (New York: Oxford University Press, 1972).

8. Cabell Phillips, *The* New York Times *Chronicle of American Life. From the Crash to the Blitz: 1929–1939* (New York: Macmillan, 1969), 411–412.

9. Lewis A. Erenberg, *Swingin' the Dream: Big Band Jazz and the Rebirth of American Culture* (Chicago: University of Chicago Press, 1998), 41–43.

CHAPTER 10

1. Andrew Bergman's *We're in the Money: Depression America and Its Films* (New York: Harper & Row [Colophon], 1971) provides a good introduction to movie trends of the period, particularly gangster films.

2. An extensive survey of 1930s-era Westerns can be found in George N. Fenin and William K. Everson, *The Western: From Silents to Cinerama* (New York: Orion Press, 1962).

3. Jerome Delamater, *Dance in the Hollywood Musical* (Ann Arbor, MI: UMI Research Press, 1981), and John Springer, *All Talking! All Singing! All Dancing!* (Secaucus, NJ: Citadel Press, 1966), cover the musical well.

4. Arlene Croce, *The Fred Astaire & Ginger Rogers Book* (New York: Outerbridge & Lazard, 1972).

5. For more on the films of the Marx Brothers, see Richard J. Anobile, ed., *Why a Duck?* (New York: Darien House, 1971).

6. The screwball comedy, along with Hollywood comedy in general, is dis-

cussed in Ed Sikov, *Screwball: Hollywood's Madcap Romantic Comedies* (New York: Crown Publishers, 1985).

7. For a discussion of horror and fantasy pictures, see Carlos Clarens, *An Illustrated History of the Horror Film* (New York: Capricorn Books, 1967); for science fiction movies, see John Baxter, *Science Fiction in the Cinema* (New York: A.S. Barnes, 1970).

8. The phenomenon of youthful performers is treated in Norman J. Zierold, *The Child Stars* (New York: Coward-McCann, 1965).

9. A good overview of 1930s movies is given in John Baxter, *Hollywood in the Thirties* (New York: A.S. Barnes, 1968).

10. For more on *The Wizard of Oz* and *Gone with the Wind*, see Paul Trent, *Those Fabulous Movie Years: The 30s* (Barre, MA: Barre Publishing, 1975), 160–163.

11. The best general background study of American radio is Erik Barnouw's *A History of Broadcasting in the United States*, 3 vols. (New York: Oxford University Press, 1970).

12. For more on the racial issues surrounding the show, see Melvin Patrick Ely, *The Adventures of Amos 'n' Andy: A Social History of an American Phenomenon* (New York: The Free Press, 1991), 160–244.

13. An entertaining history of soap opera that includes the Hummerts is Mary Jane Higby's *Tune In Tomorrow* (New York: Cowles Education Corporation, 1968).

14. Arthur P. Molella and Elsa M. Bruton, *FDR, The Intimate Presidency: Franklin Delano Roosevelt, Communication, and the Mass Media in the 1930s* (Washington, DC: National Museum of American History, 1982), 46–53.

15. For more on Dr. Brinkley, see Gerald Carson, *The Roguish World of Dr. Brinkley* (New York: Holt, Rinehart & Winston, 1960).

16. T.H. Watkins, *The Hungry Years: America in an Age of Crisis, 1929-1939* (New York: Henry Holt and Company, 1999), 254.

17. John Dunning, *Tune in Yesterday: The Ultimate Encyclopedia of Old-Time Radio, 1925–1976* (Englewood Cliffs, NJ: Prentice-Hall, 1976), 448–455.

18. A good introduction to television's early years is Erik Barnouw, *Tube of Plenty: The Evolution of American Television* (New York: Oxford University Press, 1982), 1–96.

19. Stanley Green's *Ring Bells! Sing Songs! Broadway Musicals of the 1930's* (New Rochelle, NY: Arlington House, 1971) reviews the musicals of the decade.

20. For major plays of the period, see Gerald Bordman, *American Theatre: A Chronicle of Comedy & Drama, 1930–1969* (New York: Oxford University Press, 1996).

21. See Jane Dehart Mathews, *The Federal Theatre, 1935–1939: Plays, Relief, and Politics* (Princeton, NJ: Princeton University Press, 1967), and R. C. Reynolds, *Stage Left: The Development of the American Social Drama in the Thirties* (Troy, NY: Whitston, 1986), for more on the FTP and related subjects.

22. Marshall Stearns and Jean Stearns discuss the popularization of dance in *Jazz Dance: The Story of American Vernacular Dance* (New York: Schirmer Books, 1968).

23. John Culhane, *The American Circus* (New York: Henry Holt, 1990), covers circuses of the period.

CHAPTER 11

1. For statistics on automobiles during the 1930s, see Automobile Manufacturers Association, *Automobiles of America* (Detroit, MI: Wayne State University Press, 1968); for information about car ownership, see Robert Lynd and Helen Lynd, *Middletown in Transition: A Study in Cultural Conflicts* (New York: Harcourt Brace, 1937).

2. Maurice Horn, ed., *100 Years of American Newspaper Comics* (New York: Gramercy Books, 1996), 130–131.

3. Stephen W. Sears, *The American Heritage History of the Automobile in America* (New York: Simon and Schuster, 1977), 185–229.

4. Chester H. Liebs, *Main Street to Miracle Mile: American Roadside Architecture* (Baltimore: Johns Hopkins University Press, 1985), 16–37.

5. Two good surveys of highway lodging are John A. Jakle, Keith A. Sculle, and Jefferson S. Rogers, *The Motel in America* (Baltimore: Johns Hopkins University Press, 1996), and John Margolies, *Home Away from Home: Motels in America* (Boston: Little, Brown, 1995).

6. Warren James Belasco, *Americans on the Road: From Autocamp to Motel, 1910–1945* (Cambridge, MA: MIT Press, 1979), 143–144.

7. Keith A. Sculle, "Frank Redford's Wigwam Village Chain," in *Roadside America: The Automobile in Design and Culture*, ed. Jan Jennings (Ames: Iowa State University Press, 1990), 125–135.

8. Two studies that provide detail on this aspect of travel are Donald Olen Cowgill, *Mobile Homes: A Study of Trailer Life* (Washington, DC: American Council on Public Affairs, 1941); and David A. Thornburg, *Galloping Bungalows: The Rise and Demise of the American House Trailer* (Hamden, CT: Archon Books, 1991).

9. John Anderson Miller, *Fares, Please! A Popular History of Trolleys, Horse-Cars, Street-Cars, Buses, Elevateds, and Subways* (New York: Dover Publications, 1960), 109–117.

10. Carlton Jackson, *Hounds of the Road: A History of the Greyhound Bus Company* (Bowling Green, OH: Popular Press, 1984), offers a detailed history of the company.

11. Alfred Runte, *Trains of Discovery: Western Railroads and the National Parks* (Niwot, CO: Roberts Rinehart, 1990), 57.

12. John H. White, Jr., *The American Railroad Passenger Car* (Baltimore: Johns Hopkins University Press, 1978), 275–285.

13. G. Freeman Allen, *Railways: Past, Present, and Future* (New York: William Morrow, 1982), 183–193.

14. An introduction to this kind of air travel is Lennart Ege, *Balloons and Airships* (New York: Macmillan, 1974).

15. John Toland, *The Great Dirigibles: Their Triumphs and Disasters* (New York: Dover Publications, 1972), 309–339.

16. Introductions to the many daredevils of the era are given in American Heritage Editors, *The American Heritage History of Flight* (New York: Simon and Schuster, 1962).

17. Maurice Horn, ed., *The World Encyclopedia of Comics* (New York: Chelsea House, 1976), 624–625.

18. For more on the airplanes of the 1930s, see *The American Heritage History of Flight*.

19. Melvin Maddocks chronicles this area of maritime history in *The Great Liners* (Alexandria, VA: Time-Life Books, 1978).

CHAPTER 12

1. Benton's work can be found in Matthew Baigell, *Thomas Hart Benton* (New York: Harry N. Abrams, 1975); for Wood, see James Dennis, *Grant Wood: A Study in American Art and Culture* (Columbia: University of Missouri Press, 1986).

2. Hopper's work can be found in Lloyd Goodrich, *Edward Hopper* (New York: Harry N. Abrams, 1971); for Sheeler, see Martin Friedman, *Charles Sheeler* (New York: Watson-Guptill, 1975).

3. Marsh's work can be found in Lloyd Goodrich, *Reginald Marsh* (New York: Harry N. Abrams, 1972).

4. Richard D. McKinzie, *The New Deal for Artists* (Princeton, NJ: Princeton University Press, 1973), 8–12.

5. The popularity of murals is discussed in Karal Ann Marling, *Wall-to-Wall America: A Cultural History of Post Office Murals in the Great Depression* (Minneapolis: University of Minnesota Press, 1982).

6. William Stott, *Documentary Expression and Thirties America* (New York: Oxford University Press, 1973), 216–224, 261–314.

7. Ernie Pyle, "The Sculptor of Mount Rushmore," in *Ernie's America: The Best of Ernie Pyle's 1930s Travel Dispatches*, ed. David Nichols (New York: Random House, 1989), 100–102.

8. Wyeth's work can be found in Douglas Allen and Douglas Allen, Jr., *N.C. Wyeth: The Collected Paintings, Illustrations and Murals* (New York: Crown Publishers, 1972).

9. Rockwell's work can be found in Thomas S. Buechner, *Norman Rockwell: Artist and Illustrator* (New York: Harry N. Abrams, 1970); and Maureen Hart Hennessey and Anne Knutson, *Norman Rockwell: Pictures for the American People* (New York: Harry N. Abrams, 1999).

10. Thrasher's work can be found in Dorye Roettger, *Rivals of Rockwell* (New York: Crescent Books, 1992).

11. Arpi Ermoyan, *Famous American Illustrators* (New York: Society of Illustrators, 1997), 142–143.

12. Marc McCutcheon, *The Writer's Guide to Everyday Life from Prohibition through World War II* (Cincinnati, OH: Writer's Digest Books, 1995), 230.

13. *Little Orphan Annie* can be found in Harold Gray, *Arf! The Life and Hard Times of Little Orphan Annie, 1935–1945* (New Rochelle, NY: Arlington House, 1970).

14. *Dick Tracy* can be found in Chester Gould's *The Celebrated Cases of Dick Tracy, 1931–1951* (Secaucus, NJ: Wellfleet Press, 1990), and *Dick Tracy, the Thirties: Tommy Guns and Hard Times* (New York: Chelsea House, 1978).

15. *Blondie* can be found in Dean Young and Rick Marschall, *Blondie & Dagwood's America* (New York: Harper & Row, 1981).

16. Discussions of many popular newspaper strips can be found in Maurice

Horn's *100 Years of American Newspaper Comics* (New York: Gramercy Books, 1996), and his *The World Encyclopedia of Comics* (New York: Chelsea House, 1976).

17. For more on this kind of book, see Bill Borden and Steve Posner, *The Big Book of Big Little Books* (San Francisco: Chronicle Books, 1997).

18. The history of comic books is covered in Michael Barrier and Martin Williams, eds., *A Smithsonian Book of Comic-Book Comics* (Washington, DC: Smithsonian Institution Press, 1981), and Ron Goulart, *Over 50 Years of American Comic Books* (Lincolnwood, IL: Mallard Press, 1991).

Further Reading

Advertising Age Editors. *How It Was in Advertising: 1776–1976*. Chicago: Crain Books, 1976.

Agee, James, and Walker Evans. *Let Us Now Praise Famous Men*. Boston: Houghton Mifflin, 1941.

Allen, Douglas, and Douglas Allen, Jr. *N.C. Wyeth: The Collected Paintings, Illustrations and Murals*. New York: Crown Publishers, 1972.

Allen, Frederick. *Secret Formula*. New York: HarperCollins, 1994.

Allen, Frederick Lewis. *The Big Change*. New York: Bantam Books, 1952.

———. *Only Yesterday*. New York: Harper & Row, 1931.

———. *Since Yesterday*. New York: Bantam Books, 1940.

Allen, G. Freeman. *Railways: Past, Present, and Future*. New York: William Morrow, 1982.

Allen, Henry. *What It Felt Like: Living in the American Century*. New York: Pantheon Books, 2000.

Allen, Richard, and Bruce Hershenson. *The Illustrated History of Movies Through Posters*. Vol. 4: *Sports Movie Posters*. West Plains, MO: Bruce Hershenson, 1996.

American Heritage Editors. *The American Heritage History of Flight*. New York: Simon and Schuster, 1962.

———. *The American Heritage History of the 20's & 30's*. New York: American Heritage, 1970.

Andrews, Wayne. *Architecture, Ambition and Americans: A Social History of American Architecture*. New York: The Free Press, 1964.

———. *Architecture in New York: A Photographic History*. New York: Harper and Row, 1969.

Angelucci, Enzo. *World Encyclopedia of Civil Aircraft*. New York: Crown Publishers, 1981.

Anglo, Michael. *Nostalgia: Spotlight on the Thirties*. London: Jupiter Books, 1976.

Anobile, Richard J., ed. *Why a Duck?* New York: Darien House, 1971.

Appelbaum, Stanley. *The New York World's Fair, 1939/1940*. New York: Dover Publications, 1977.

Ardman, Harvey. *Normandie: Her Life and Times*. New York: Franklin Watts, 1985.

Armour, Richard. *Give Me Liberty*. New York: The World Publishing Company, 1969.

Armour, Robert A. *Film: A Reference Guide*. Westport, CT: Greenwood Press, 1980.

Art in America Editors. *The Artist in America*. New York: W.W. Norton, 1967.

Ashley, Bob. *The Study of Popular Fiction: A Source Book*. Philadelphia: University of Pennsylvania Press, 1989.

Associated Press Sports Staff. *A Century of Sports*. New York: The Associated Press, 1971.

Austin, James C., ed. *Popular Literature in America*. Bowling Green, OH: Popular Press, 1972.

Austin, Joe, and Michael Nevin Willard, eds. *Generations of Youth: Youth Cultures and History in Twentieth-Century America*. New York: New York University Press, 1998.

Automobile Manufacturers Association. *Automobiles of America*. Detroit, MI: Wayne State University Press, 1968.

Baeder, John. *Gas, Food, and Lodging*. New York: Abbeville Press, 1982.

Baigell, Matthew. *Thomas Hart Benton*. New York: Harry N. Abrams, 1975.

Baker, R.S., and P.L. Van Osdol. *The World on Wheels*. Boston: Allyn & Bacon, 1972.

Balio, Tino. *Grand Design: Hollywood as a Modern Business Enterprise, 1930–1939*. New York: Scribner's, 1993.

Barfield, Ray. *Listening to Radio, 1920–1950*. Westport, CT: Praeger, 1996.

Barnouw, Erik. *A History of Broadcasting in the United States*. Vol. 1: *A Tower in Babel*. New York: Oxford University Press, 1966.

———. *A History of Broadcasting in the United States*. Vol. 2: *The Golden Web*. New York: Oxford University Press, 1968.

———. *A History of Broadcasting in the United States*. Vol. 3: *The Image Empire*. New York: Oxford University Press, 1970.

———. *Tube of Plenty: The Evolution of American Television*. New York: Oxford University Press, 1982.

Barr, Andrew. *Drink: A Social History of America*. New York: Carroll and Graf, 1999.

Barrier, Michael, and Martin Williams, eds. *A Smithsonian Book of Comic-Book Comics*. Washington, DC: Smithsonian Institution Press, 1981.

Basinger, Jeanine. *A Woman's View: How Hollywood Spoke to Women, 1930–1960*. New York: Alfred A. Knopf, 1993.

Batterberry, Michael, and Ariane Batterberry. *Mirror Mirror: A Social History of Fashion*. New York: Holt, Rinehart and Winston, 1977.

Baughman, James L. *Henry R. Luce and the Rise of the American News Media*. Boston: Twayne, 1987.

Bawden, Liz-Anne. *The Oxford Companion to Film*. New York: Oxford University Press, 1976.

Baxter, John. *Hollywood in the Thirties*. New York: A.S. Barnes, 1968.

———. *Science Fiction in the Cinema*. New York: A.S. Barnes, 1970.

Beach, Joseph Warren. *American Fiction: 1920–1940*. New York: Russell and Russell, 1960.

Becker, Stephen. *Comic Art in America*. New York: Simon and Schuster, 1959.

Belasco, Warren James. *Americans on the Road: From Autocamp to Motel, 1910–1945*. Cambridge, MA: MIT Press, 1979.

Benton, Mike. *The Comic Book in America: An Illustrated History*. Dallas, TX: Taylor, 1989.

Bergman, Andrew. *We're in the Money: Depression America and Its Films*. New York: Harper and Row (Colophon), 1971.

Bessie, Simon Michael. *Jazz Journalism: The Story of Tabloid Newspapers*. New York: Russell and Russell, 1938.

Best, Gary Dean. *The Nickel and Dime Decade: American Popular Culture During the 1930s*. Westport, CT: Praeger, 1993.

Bigelow, Marybelle S. *Fashion in History: Western Dress, Prehistoric to Present*. Minneapolis, MN: Burgess, 1979.

Bilstein, Roger E. *Flight in America: From the Wrights to the Astronauts*. Baltimore: The Johns Hopkins University Press, 1984.

Binyon, T.J. *"Murder Will Out": The Detective in Fiction*. New York: Oxford University Press, 1989.

Bird, Caroline. *The Invisible Scar*. New York: David McKay, 1966.

Blackbeard, Bill, and Martin Williams. *The Smithsonian Collection of Newspaper Comics*. Washington, DC: Smithsonian Institution Press, 1977.

Bland, David. *A History of Book Illustration*. New York: World Publishing Company, 1958.

Blum, Daniel. *A Pictorial History of the American Theatre, 1860–1970*. New York: Crown Publishers, 1969.

Blum, Stella, ed. *Everyday Fashions of the Thirties: As Pictured in Sears Catalogs*. New York: Dover Publications, 1986.

Bode, Carl. *The Half-World of American Culture: A Miscellany*. Carbondale: Southern Illinois University Press, 1965.

Bolton, Theodore. *American Book Illustrators: Bibliographic Check Lists of 123 Artists*. New York: R.R. Bowker, 1938.

Bondi, Victor, ed. *American Decades: 1930–1939*. New York: Gale Research, 1995.

Bonn, Thomas L. *Under Cover: An Illustrated History of American Mass Market Paperbacks*. New York: Penguin Books, 1982.

Borden, Bill, and Steve Posner. *The Big Book of Big Little Books*. San Francisco: Chronicle Books, 1997.

Bordman, Gerald. *American Theatre: A Chronicle of Comedy & Drama, 1930–1969*. New York: Oxford University Press, 1996.

———. *Oxford Companion to American Theatre*. New York: Oxford University Press, 1984.

Bourke-White, Margaret, and Eskine Caldwell. *You Have Seen Their Faces*. New York: Modern Age Books, 1937.

Bradley, Carolyn. *Western World Costume: An Outline History*. New York: Appleton-Century-Crofts, 1954.

Brasch, R. *How Did Sports Begin? A Look at the Origins of Man at Play*. New York: David McKay, 1970.

Brendon, Piers. *The Dark Valley: A Panorama of the 1930s*. New York: Alfred A. Knopf, 2000.

Brenner, Joel Glenn. *The Emperors of Chocolate: Inside the Secret World of Hershey and Mars*. New York: Random House, 1999.

Breward, Christopher. *The Culture of Fashion: A New History of Fashionable Dress*. Manchester, UK: Manchester University Press, 1995.

Bridwell, E. Nelson, ed. *Superman: From the Thirties to the Seventies*. New York: Bonanza Books, 1971.

Brinkley, Douglas. *American Heritage History of the United States*. New York: Viking, 1998.

Broekel, Ray. *The Great American Candy Bar Book*. Boston: Houghton Mifflin, 1982.

Brosnan, John. *Movie Magic*. New York: St. Martin's Press, 1974.

Brown, Curtis F. *Star-Spangled Kitsch*. New York: Universe Books, 1975.

Brown, Milton, Sam Hunter, John Jacobus, Naomi Rosenblum, and David M. Sokol. *American Art*. Englewood Cliffs, NJ: Prentice-Hall, 1979.

Brunas, Michael, John Brunas, and Tom Weaver. *Universal Horrors: The Studio's Classic Films, 1931–1946*. Jefferson, NC: McFarland, 1990.

Buchanan, Lamont. *Ships of Steam*. New York: McGraw-Hill, 1956.

Buechner, Thomas S. *Norman Rockwell: Artist and Illustrator*. New York: Harry N. Abrams, 1970.

Bush, Donald J. *The Streamlined Decade*. New York: George Braziller, 1975.

Buxton, Frank, and Bill Owen. *The Big Broadcast: 1920–1950*. New York: The Viking Press, 1972.

Cahill, Holger, and Alfred H. Barr, Jr. *Art in America: A Complete Survey*. New York: Reynal and Hitchcock, 1934.

Calkins, Earnest Elmo. *Care and Feeding of Hobby Horses*. New York: Leisure League of America, 1934.

Cantor, Muriel G., and Suzanne Pingree. *The Soap Opera*. Beverly Hills, CA: Sage, 1983.

Caplow, Theodore, Louis Hicks, and Ben J. Wattenberg. *The First Measured Century: An Illustrated Guide to Trends in America, 1900–2000*. Washington, DC: AEI Press, 2001.

Capp, Al. *The Best of Li'l Abner*. New York: Holt, Rinehart and Winston, 1978.

Carlisle, Rodney P. *Hearst and the New Deal: The Progressive as Reactionary*. New York: Garland, 1979.

Carruth, Gordon, ed. *The Encyclopedia of American Facts and Dates*. New York: Thomas Y. Crowell, 1959.

Carson, Gerald. *The Roguish World of Dr. Brinkley*. New York: Holt, Rinehart & Winston, 1960.

Cassidy, Donna M. *Painting the Musical City: Jazz and Cultural Identity in American Art, 1910–1940*. Washington, DC: Smithsonian Institution Press, 1997.

Chandler, Lester V. *America's Greatest Depression, 1929–1941*. New York: Harper and Row, 1970.

Chenoweth, Lawrence. *The American Dream of Success: The Search for the Self in the Twentieth Century*. North Scituate, MA: Duxbury Press, 1974.

Churchill, Allen. *Remember When*. New York: Golden Press, 1967.

Clarens, Carlos. *Crime Movies: From Griffith to the Godfather and Beyond*. New York: W.W. Norton, 1980.

————. *An Illustrated History of the Horror Film*. New York: Capricorn Books, 1967.

Clark, Clifford Edward, Jr. *The American Home: 1800–1960*. Chapel Hill: University of North Carolina Press, 1986.

Clark, Eric. *The Want Makers: Inside the World of Advertising*. New York: Penguin Books, 1988.

Clarke, Donald. *The Rise and Fall of Popular Music*. New York: St. Martin's Press, 1995.

Cleary, David Powers. *Great American Brands*. New York: Fairchild Publications, 1981.

Cline, William C. *In the Nick of Time: Motion Picture Sound Serials*. Jefferson, NC: McFarland, 1984.

Clurman, Harold. *The Fervent Years: The Story of the Group Theatre and the Thirties*. New York: Hill and Wang, 1957.

Coffey, Frank, and Joseph Layden. *America on Wheels: The First 100 Years, 1896–1996*. Los Angeles: General Publishing Group, 1998.

Coffin, Tristram Potter. *The Old Ball Game: Baseball in Folklore and Fiction*. New York: Herder and Herder, 1971.

Cohen, Marilyn. *Reginald Marsh's New York: Paintings, Drawings, Prints and Photographs*. New York: Dover Publications, 1983.

Cohn, Jan. *Creating America: George Horace Lorimer and the Saturday Evening Post*. Pittsburgh, PA: University of Pittsburgh Press, 1989.

Collins, A. Frederick. *How to Ride Your Hobby*. New York: D. Appleton-Century Company, 1935.

————. *Money-Making Hobbies*. New York: World Publishing Company, 1938.

Colmer, Michael. *Pinball: An Illustrated History*. London: Pierrot Publishing, 1976.

Congdon, Don, ed. *The Thirties: A Time to Remember*. New York: Simon and Schuster, 1962.

Corn, Joseph J. *The Winged Gospel: America's Romance with Aviation, 1900–1950*. New York: Oxford University Press, 1983.

Corn, Wanda. *Grant Wood: The Regionalist Vision*. New Haven, CT: Yale University Press, 1983.

Couperie, Pierre, and Maurice C. Horn. *A History of the Comic Strip*. New York: Crown Publishers, 1968.

Cowan, Ruth Schwartz. *More Work for Mother*. New York: Basic Books, 1983.

Cowgill, Donald Olen. *Mobile Homes: A Study of Trailer Life*. Washington, DC: American Council on Public Affairs, 1941.

Crafton, Donald. *The Talkies: American Cinema's Transition to Sound, 1926–1931*. New York: Scribner's, 1997.

Craven, Wayne. *American Art: History and Culture*. New York: Harry N. Abrams, 1994.

Croce, Arlene. *The Fred Astaire & Ginger Rogers Book*. New York: Outerbridge and Lazard, 1972.

Crumpacker, Bunny. *The Old-Time Brand-Name Cookbook*. New York: Smithmark, 1998.

————. *The Old-Time Brand-Name Desserts*. New York: Abradale Press, 1999.

Csida, Joseph, and June Bundy Csida. *American Entertainment: A Unique History of Popular Show Business*. New York: Watson-Guptill, 1978.

Culhane, John. *The American Circus*. New York: Henry Holt, 1990.

Cummings, Paul. *Dictionary of Contemporary American Artists*. 6th ed. New York: St. Martin's Press, 1994.

Dale, Rodney. *The World of Jazz*. New York: Elsevier-Dutton, 1980.

Dance, Stanley. *The World of Count Basie*. New York: Scribner's, 1980.

———. *The World of Duke Ellington*. New York: Charles Scribner's, 1970.

Daniels, Les. *Comix: A History of Comic Books in America*. New York: Bonanza Books, 1971.

Davis, Maxine. *The Lost Generation: A Portrait of Youth Today*. New York: Macmillan, 1936.

Delamater, Jerome. *Dance in the Hollywood Musical*. Ann Arbor, MI: UMI Research Press, 1981.

Delong, Thomas A. *Radio Stars*. Jefferson, NC: McFarland, 1996.

Denison, Edward F. *Trends in American Economic Growth, 1929–1982*. Washington, DC: The Brookings Institution, 1985.

Dennis, James. *Grant Wood: A Study in American Art and Culture*. Columbia: University of Missouri Press, 1986.

Derks, Scott. *Working Americans, 1880–1999: Vol. 1: The Working Class*. Lakeville, CT: Grey House, 2000.

———. *Working Americans, 1880–1999. Vol. 2: The Middle Class*. Lakeville, CT: Grey House, 2001.

Dettelbach, Cynthia Golumb. *In the Driver's Seat: The Automobile in American Literature and Popular Culture*. Westport, CT: Greenwood Press, 1976.

Dickson, Paul. *The Worth Book of Softball: A Celebration of America's True National Pastime*. New York: Facts on File, 1994.

Dorner, Jane. *Fashion in the Twenties and Thirties*. New Rochelle, NY: Arlington House, 1973.

Douglas, George H. *All Aboard! The Railroad in American Life*. New York: Paragon House, 1992.

———. *The Smart Magazines*. Hamden, CT: Archon Books, 1991.

Draper, Hal. "The Student Movement of the Thirties." In *As We Saw the Thirties*. Edited by Rita Simon. Urbana: University of Illinois Press, 1967.

Driver, Tom F. *Romantic Quest and Modern Query: A History of the Modern Theater*. New York: Delacorte Press, 1980.

Dulles, Foster Rhea. *A History of Recreation: America Learns to Play*. Englewood Cliffs, NJ: Prentice-Hall, 1965.

Dunning, John. *On the Air: The Encyclopedia of Old-Time Radio*. New York: Oxford University Press, 1998.

———. *Tune in Yesterday: The Ultimate Encyclopedia of Old-Time Radio, 1925–1976*. Englewood Cliffs, NJ: Prentice-Hall, 1976.

Dupre, Judith. *Skyscrapers*. New York: Black Dog & Leventhal, 1996.

Durgnat, Raymond. *The Crazy Mirror: Hollywood Comedy and the American Image*. New York: Dell, 1969.

Ege, Lennart. *Balloons and Airships*. New York: Macmillan, 1974.

Elder, Glen H., Jr. *Children of the Great Depression*. Chicago: University of Chicago Press, 1974.

Ellis, C. Hamilton. *The Lore of the Train*. New York: Grosset & Dunlap, 1971.

Ellis, Edward Robb. *A Nation in Torment: The Great American Depression, 1929–1939*. New York: Kodansha America, 1995.

Ely, Melvin Patrick. *The Adventures of Amos 'n' Andy: A Social History of an American Phenomenon*. New York: The Free Press, 1991.

Emery, Edwin. *The Press and America: An Interpretative History of Journalism*. Englewood Cliffs, NJ: Prentice-Hall, 1962.

Erenberg, Lewis A. *Swingin' the Dream: Big Band Jazz and the Rebirth of American Culture*. Chicago: University of Chicago Press, 1998.

Ermoyan, Arpi. *Famous American Illustrators*. New York: Society of Illustrators, 1997.

Everson, William K. *The Art of W.C. Fields*. Indianapolis, IN: Bobbs-Merrill, 1967.

Ewen, David. *All the Years of American Popular Music*. Englewood Cliffs, NJ: Prentice-Hall, 1977.

Ewen, Stuart. *Captains of Consciousness: Advertising and the Social Roots of the Consumer Culture*. New York: McGraw-Hill, 1976.

Ewen, Stuart, and Elizabeth Ewen. *Channels of Desire: Mass Images and the Shaping of American Consciousness*. New York: McGraw-Hill, 1982.

Ewing, Elizabeth. *History of Twentieth Century Fashion*. London: B.T. Batsford, 1974.

Feather, Leonard. *The New Edition of the Encyclopedia of Jazz*. New York: Bonanza Books, 1962.

Fenin, George N., and William K. Everson. *The Western: From Silents to Cinerama*. New York: Orion Press, 1962.

Fenner, Mildred Sandison, and Wolcott Fenner. *The Circus: Lure and Legend*. Englewood Cliffs, NJ: Prentice-Hall, 1970.

Ferguson, James L. *General Foods Corporation: A Chronicle of Consumer Satisfaction*. New York: Newcomen Society of the United States, 1985.

Finch, Christopher. *The Art of Walt Disney: From Mickey Mouse to the Magic Kingdoms*. New York: Harry N. Abrams, 1975.

———. *Norman Rockwell's America*. New York: Harry N. Abrams, 1975.

Flexner, Stuart Berg. *Listening to America*. New York: Simon and Schuster, 1982.

Flink, James J. *The Car Culture*. Cambridge, MA: MIT Press, 1975.

Flusser, Alan. *Clothes and the Man: The Principles of Fine Men's Dress*. New York: Villard Books, 1989.

Foley, Mary Mix. *The American House*. New York: Harper and Row, 1980.

Ford, James L.C. *Magazines for Millions: The Story of Specialized Publications*. Carbondale: Southern Illinois University Press, 1969.

Forty, Adrian. *Objects of Desire: Design and Society Since 1750*. New York: Thames and Hudson, 1986.

Fowles, Jib. *Advertising and Popular Culture*. Thousand Oaks, CA: Sage, 1996.

Fox, Stephen. *The Mirror Makers: A History of American Advertising and Its Creators*. New York: William Morrow, 1984.

Fraser, Antonia. *A History of Toys*. New York: Delacorte Press, 1966.

Fraser, James. *The American Billboard: 100 Years*. New York: Harry N. Abrams, 1991.

Freeman, Larry, ed. *Yesterday's Games*. Watkins Glen, NY: Century House, 1970.

Friedman, Martin. *Charles Sheeler*. New York: Watson-Guptil, 1975.

Friedwald, Will. *Jazz Singing: America's Great Voices*. New York: Da Capo Press, 1996.

Gallo, Max. *The Poster in History*. New York: New American Library, 1972.

Gandt, Robert L. *China Clipper: The Age of the Great Flying Boats*. Annapolis, MD: Naval Institute Press, 1991.

Garraty, John A. *The Great Depression*. New York: Harcourt Brace Jovanovich, 1986.

Garwood, Darrell. *Artist in Iowa: A Life of Grant Wood*. New York: W.W. Norton, 1944.

Gebhard, David. *The National Trust Guide to Art Deco in America*. New York: John Wiley and Sons, 1996.

Geddes, Norman Bel. *Horizons*. Boston: Little, Brown, 1932.

Gehring, Wes D., ed. *Handbook of American Film Genres*. New York: Greenwood Press, 1988.

Gelber, Steven M. "A Job You Can't Lose: Work and Hobbies in the Great Depression." *Journal of Social History*, 24 (1991): 741–766.

Gelernter, David. *1939: The Lost World of the Fair*. New York: Avon Books, 1995.

Gleason, Ralph J., ed. *Jam Session: An Anthology of Jazz*. New York: G.P. Putnam's Sons, 1958.

Godfrey, Donald C., and Frederic A. Leigh, eds. *Historical Dictionary of American Radio*. Westport, CT: Greenwood Press, 1998.

Golden Age Radio. *101 Old Radio Commercials*. Plymouth, MN: Metacom, n.d. (CD).

Good Housekeeping. 10 representative issues: November 1930, November 1931, November 1932, November 1933, November 1934, November 1935, November 1936, November 1937, November 1938, November 1939.

Goodrich, Lloyd. *Edward Hopper*. New York: Harry N. Abrams, 1971.

———. *Reginald Marsh*. New York: Harry N. Abrams, 1972.

———. *Three Centuries of American Art*. New York: Frederick A. Praeger, 1966.

Goodrum, Charles, and Helen Dalrymple. *Advertising in America: The First 200 Years*. New York: Harry N. Abrams, 1990.

Gordon, Ian. *Comic Strips and Consumer Culture, 1890–1945*. Washington, DC: Smithsonian Institution Press, 1998.

Gordon, Lois, and Alan Gordon. *American Chronicle: Six Decades in American Life, 1920–1980*. New York: Atheneum, 1987.

Gottlieb, William P. *The Golden Age of Jazz*. New York: Simon and Schuster, 1979.

Goulart, Ron. *The Adventurous Decade: Comic Strips in the Thirties*. New Rochelle, NY: Arlington House, 1975.

———. *Cheap Thrills: An Informal History of the Pulp Magazines*. New Rochelle, NY: Arlington House, 1972.

———. *Over 50 Years of American Comic Books*. Lincolnwood, IL: Mallard Press, 1991.

———, ed. *The Encyclopedia of American Comics*. New York: Facts on File, 1990.

Gould, Chester. *The Celebrated Cases of Dick Tracy, 1931–1951*. Secaucus, NJ: Wellfleet Press, 1990.

———. *Dick Tracy, the Thirties: Tommy Guns and Hard Times*. New York: Chelsea House, 1978.

Gourse, Leslie. *Louis' Children: American Jazz Singers*. New York: Quill, 1984.

Gow, Gordon. *Suspense in the Cinema*. New York: A.S. Barnes, 1968.

Gray, Harold. *Arf! The Life and Hard Times of Little Orphan Annie, 1935–1945*. New Rochelle, NY: Arlington House, 1970.

————. *Little Orphan Annie in the Great Depression*. New York: Dover Publications, 1979.

Green, Harvey. *Fit for America: Health, Fitness, Sport, and American Society*. New York: Pantheon Books, 1986.

————. *The Uncertainty of Everyday Life: 1915–1945*. New York: HarperCollins, 1992.

Green, Stanley. *Encyclopaedia of the Musical Film*. New York: Oxford University Press, 1981.

————. *Ring Bells! Sing Songs! Broadway Musicals of the 1930's*. New Rochelle, NY: Arlington House, 1971.

Greene, Suzanne Ellery. *Books for Pleasure: Popular Fiction, 1914–1945*. Bowling Green, OH: Popular Press, 1974.

Greenfield, Thomas Allen. *Radio: A Reference Guide*. Westport, CT: Greenwood Press, 1989.

Greif, Martin. *Depression Modern: The Thirties Style in America*. New York: Universe Books, 1975.

Grier, Katherine C. *Culture and Comfort: Parlor Making and Middle-Class Identity, 1850–1930*. Washington, DC: Smithsonian Institution Press, 1988.

Griffith, Richard, and Arthur Mayer. *The Movies*. New York: Simon and Schuster, 1970.

Griffith, Sally Foreman. *Home Town News: William Allen White and the Emporia Gazette*. New York: Oxford University Press, 1989.

Gruber, Frank. *The Pulp Jungle*. Los Angeles: Sherbourne Press, 1967.

Gruskin, Alan D. *Painting in the U.S.A.* Garden City, NY: Doubleday, 1946.

Gurko, Leo. *The Angry Decade: American Literature and Thought from 1929 to Pearl Harbor*. New York: Harper & Row [Colophon], 1947.

Hackett, Alice Payne. *60 Years of Best Sellers, 1895–1955*. New York: R.R. Bowker, 1955.

Halpern, John. *New York/New York: An Architectural Portfolio*. New York: E.P. Dutton, 1978.

Hamm, Charles. "American Song During the Great Depression." Liner notes for *Brother, Can You Spare a Dime?* LP. New World Records, 1977.

————. *Yesterdays: Popular Song in America*. New York: W.W. Norton, 1979.

Handlin, David P. *American Architecture*. New York: Thames and Hudson, 1985.

Hanna, Linda. *The Jigsaw Book*. New York: The Dial Press, 1981.

Hanson, Elizabeth I. *Margaret Mitchell*. Boston: Twayne, 1991.

Harmon, Jim. *Jim Harmon's Nostalgia Catalogue*. Los Angeles: J.P. Tarcher, 1973.

Harris, Neil. *Cultural Excursions: Marketing Appetites and Cultural Tastes in Modern America*. Chicago: University of Chicago Press, 1990.

Harris, Rex. *Jazz*. New York: Penguin Books, 1952.

Harrison, Helen A. *Dawn of a New Day: The New York World's Fair, 1939/40*. New York: New York University Press, 1980.

Hart, James D. *The Popular Book: A History of America's Literary Taste*. Berkeley: University of California Press, 1950.

Harvey, Robert C. *The Art of the Comic Book: An Aesthetic History*. Jackson: University Press of Mississippi, 1996.

————. *The Art of the Funnies: An Aesthetic History*. Jackson: University Press of Mississippi, 1994.

————. *Children of the Yellow Kid: The Evolution of the American Comic Strip.* Seattle, WA: Frye Art Museum, 1998.

Haskell, Barbara. *The American Century: Art & Culture, 1900–1950.* New York: Whitney Museum of American Art, 1999.

Haskins, Jim. *The Cotton Club.* New York: New American Library [Plume], 1977.

Hastings, Robert J. *A Nickel's Worth of Skim Milk: A Boy's View of the Great Depression.* Carbondale: Southern Illinois University Press, 1972.

Hearn, Charles R. *The American Dream and the Great Depression.* Westport, CT: Greenwood Press, 1977.

Heide, Robert, and John Gilman. *Dime-Store Dream Parade: Popular Culture, 1925–1955.* New York: E.P. Dutton, 1979.

Heidenry, John. *Theirs Was the Kingdom: Lila and DeWitt Wallace and the Story of the Reader's Digest.* New York: W.W. Norton, 1993.

Held, John, Jr. *The Most of John Held, Jr.* Brattleboro, VT: Stephen Greene Press, 1972.

Heller, Nancy, and Julia Williams. *Painters of the American Scene.* New York: Galahad Books, 1976.

Heller, Steven, and Seymour Chwast. *Jackets Required: An Illustrated History of American Book Jacket Design, 1920–1950.* San Francisco: Chronicle Books, 1995.

Henderson, Amy, and Dwight Blocker Bowers. *Red, Hot & Blue: A Smithsonian Salute to the American Musical.* Washington, D.C.: Smithsonian Institution Press, 1996.

Henderson, Mary C. *Broadway Ballyhoo.* New York: Harry N. Abrams, 1989.

————. *Theater in America: 200 Years of Plays, Players, and Productions.* New York: Harry N. Abrams, 1986.

Henderson, Sally, and Robert Landau. *Billboard Art.* San Francisco: Chronicle Books, 1981.

Hennessey, Maureen Hart, and Anne Knutson. *Norman Rockwell: Pictures for the American People.* New York: Harry N. Abrams, 1999.

Hentoff, Nat, and Albert McCarthy, eds. *Jazz.* New York: Grove Press, 1959.

Hentoff, Nat, and Nat Shapiro, eds. *The Jazz Makers.* New York: Grove Press, 1957.

Higby, Mary Jane. *Tune In Tomorrow.* New York: Cowles Education Corporation, 1968.

Higham, Charles. *The Art of the American Film, 1900–1971.* Garden City, NY: Anchor Press, 1973.

Hilliard, Robert L., and Michael C. Keith. *The Broadcast Century: A Biography of American Broadcasting.* Boston: Focal Press, 1992.

Hillier, Bevis. *The Style of the Century: 1900–1980.* New York: E.P. Dutton, 1983.

Hilmes, Michele. *Radio Voices: American Broadcasting, 1922–1952.* Minneapolis: University of Minnesota Press, 1997.

Himelstein, Morgan Y. *Drama Was a Weapon: Left-Wing Theatre in New York, 1929–1941.* Westport, CT: Greenwood Press, 1963.

Hine, Thomas. *The Rise and Fall of the American Teenager.* New York: Avon Books (Bard), 1999.

Hirshhorn, Paul, and Steven Izenour. *White Towers.* Cambridge, MA: MIT Press, 1979.

History of the 20th Century: 1930–1939. Vol. 4. Dir. Richard A. Klein. Videocassette. ABC Video Enterprises, 1980.

Hitchcock, Henry-Russell, and Philip Johnson. *The International Style*. New York: W.W. Norton, 1932 [Revised 1966].

Hoffmann, Frank W., and William G. Bailey. *Sports and Recreation Fads*. New York: Haworth Press, 1991.

Hooker, Richard J. *Food and Drink in America: A History*. Indianapolis, IN: Bobbs-Merrill, 1981.

Horan, James D. *The Desperate Years*. New York: Bonanza Books, 1962.

Horn, Maurice. *Women in the Comics*. New York: Chelsea House, 1977.

———, ed. *100 Years of American Newspaper Comics*. New York: Gramercy Books, 1996.

———. *The World Encyclopedia of Comics*. New York: Chelsea House, 1976.

Hornung, Clarence P., and Fridolf Johnson. *200 Years of American Graphic Art*. New York: George Braziller, 1976.

Horsham, Michael. *'20s & '30s Style*. Secaucus, NJ: Chartwell Books, 1989.

Horwitz, Elinor Lander. *The Bird, the Banner, and Uncle Sam*. Philadelphia: J.B. Lippincott, 1976.

Howell, Georgina. *In Vogue: 75 Years of Style*. London: Conde Nast Books, 1991.

Hower, Ralph M. *The History of an Advertising Agency: N.W. Ayer & Son at Work, 1869–1939*. Cambridge, MA: Harvard University Press, 1939.

Hoyt, Edwin P. *The Tempering Years*. New York: Scribner's, 1963.

Hughes, Robert. *American Visions: The Epic History of Art in America*. New York: Alfred A. Knopf, 1997.

Huss, Roy, and T. J. Huss. *Focus on the Horror Film*. Englewood Cliffs, NJ: Prentice-Hall, 1972.

Ierley, Merritt. *Open House*. New York: Henry Holt, 1999.

Inge, M. Thomas. *Comics as Culture*. Jackson: University Press of Mississippi, 1990.

———, ed. *Concise Histories of American Popular Culture*. Westport, CT: Greenwood Press, 1982.

———. *Handbook of American Popular Culture*. 3 vols. Westport, CT: Greenwood Press, 1981.

Innes, Sherrie A. *Dinner Roles: American Women and Culinary Culture*. Iowa City: University of Iowa Press, 2001.

Jackson, Carlton. *Hounds of the Road: A History of the Greyhound Bus Company*. Bowling Green, OH: Popular Press, 1984.

Jackson, Kathy Merlock. *Images of Children in American Film*. Metuchen, NJ: Scarecrow Press, 1986.

Jackson, Kenneth T. *The Crabgrass Frontier*. New York: Oxford University Press, 1985.

Jakle, John A., and Keith A. Sculle. *The Gas Station in America*. Baltimore: Johns Hopkins University Press, 1994.

Jakle, John A., Keith A. Sculle, and Jefferson S. Rogers. *The Motel in America*. Baltimore: Johns Hopkins University Press, 1996.

Janello, Amy, and Brennon Jones. *The American Magazine*. New York: Harry N. Abrams, 1991.

Johnson, J. Stewart. *American Modern, 1925–1940: Design for a New Age*. New York: Harry N. Abrams, 2000.

———. *The Modern American Poster*. New York: Museum of Modern Art, 1983.

Jonas, Susan, and Marilyn Nissenson. *Going, Going, Gone: Vanishing Americana*. San Francisco: Chronicle Books, 1994.

Jones, Edgar R. *Those Were the Good Old Days: A Happy Look at American Advertising, 1880–1930*. New York: Simon and Schuster, 1959.

Jones, Max, and John Chilton. *Louis: The Louis Armstrong Story*. Boston: Little, Brown, 1971.

Jowett, Garth. *Film: The Democratic Art*. Boston: Little, Brown, 1976.

Jowett, Garth, Ian C. Jarvie, and Kathryn H. Fuller. *Children and the Movies: Media Influence and the Payne Fund Controversy*. Cambridge: Cambridge University Press, 1996.

Kammen, Michael. *American Culture, American Tastes: Social Change and the 20th Century*. New York: Alfred A. Knopf, 2000.

Kaplan, Donald, and Alan Bellink. *Classic Diners of the Northeast*. Boston: Faber and Faber, 1980.

Katz, Ephraim. *The Film Encyclopedia*. 2nd edition. New York: Harper and Row, 1994.

Kaye, Marvin. *A Toy Is Born*. New York: Stein and Day, 1973.

Kazin, Alfred. *On Native Grounds*. Garden City, NY: Doubleday, 1942.

Keepnews, Orrin, and Bill Grauer, Jr. *A Pictorial History of Jazz*. New York: Crown Publishers, 1955.

Kennedy, David M. *Freedom from Fear: The American People in Depression and War, 1929–1945*. New York: Oxford University Press, 1999.

Kern-Foxworth, Marilyn. *Aunt Jemima, Uncle Ben, and Rastus: Blacks in Advertising, Yesterday, Today, and Tomorrow*. Westport, CT: Greenwood Press, 1994.

Kidwell, Claudia B., and Margaret C. Christman. *Suiting Everyone: The Democratization of Clothing in America*. Washington, DC: Smithsonian Institution Press, 1974.

King, Constance Eileen. *The Collector's History of Dolls*. New York: St. Martin's Press, 1977.

Kisor, Henry. *Zephyr: Tracking a Dream Across America*. New York: Random House, 1994.

Kitahara, Teruhisa. *Yesterday's Toys*. Vol. 1: *Celluloid Dolls, Clowns, and Animals*. San Francisco: Chronicle Books, 1989.

———. *Yesterday's Toys*. Vol. 2: *Planes, Trains, Boats, and Cars*. San Francisco: Chronicle Books, 1989.

———. *Yesterday's Toys*. Vol. 3: *Robots, Spaceships, and Monsters*. San Francisco: Chronicle Books, 1989.

Koenigsberg, M. *King News: An Autobiography*. Philadelphia: F.A. Stokes, 1941.

Kostof, Spiro. *America by Design*. New York: Oxford University Press, 1987.

Kraus, Richard. *Recreation and Leisure in Modern Society*. Englewood Cliffs, NJ: Prentice-Hall, 1971.

Laforse, Martin W., and James A. Drake. *Popular Culture and American Life*. Chicago: Nelson-Hall, 1981.

Lahue, Kalton C. *Continued Next Week: A History of the Moving Picture Serial*, Norman: University of Oklahoma Press, 1964.

Landau, Robert, and James Phillippi. *Airstream*. Salt Lake City, UT: Peregrine Smith Books, 1984.

Laning, Edward. *The Sketchbooks of Reginald Marsh*. Greenwich, CT: New York Graphic Society, 1973.

Larkin, Oliver W. *Art and Life in America*. New York: Holt, Rinehart and Winston, 1960.

Larrabee, Eric, and Rolf Meyersohn, eds. *Mass Leisure*. Glencoe, IL: The Free Press, 1958.

Laubner, Ellie. *Collectible Fashions of the Turbulent Thirties*. Atglen, PA: Schiffer, 2000.

Lazo, Hector, and M.H. Bletz. *Who Gets Your Food Dollar?* New York: Harper and Brothers, 1938.

Lears, Jackson. *Fables of Abundance: A Cultural History of Advertising in America*. New York: Basic Books, 1994.

Lee, Alfred McClung. *The Daily Newspaper in America*. New York: Macmillan, 1937.

Leighton, Isabel, ed. *The Aspirin Age, 1919–1941*. New York: Simon and Schuster [Clarion], 1949.

Leonard, Thomas C. *News for All: America's Coming-of-Age with the Press*. New York: Oxford University Press, 1995.

Lesser, Robert. *A Celebration of Comic Art and Memorabilia*. New York: Hawthorn Books, 1975.

Levenstein, Harvey. *Paradox of Plenty: A Social History of Eating in Modern America*. New York: Oxford University Press, 1993.

———. *Revolution at the Table: The Transformation of the American Diet*. New York: Oxford University Press, 1988.

Levin, Gail. *Edward Hopper as Illustrator*. New York: W.W. Norton, 1979.

———. *Edward Hopper: The Art and the Artist*. New York: W.W. Norton, 1980.

Levin, Gail, and Judith Tick. *Aaron Copland's America: A Cultural Perspective*. New York: Watson-Guptill, 2000.

Levin, Martin, ed. *Hollywood and the Great Fan Magazines*. New York: Arbor House, 1970.

Lewine, Harris. *Good-Bye to All That*. New York: McGraw-Hill, 1970.

Lewis, Lucinda. *Roadside America: The Automobile and the American Dream*. New York: Harry N. Abrams, 2000.

Ley, Sandra. *Fashion for Everyone: The Story of Ready-to-Wear, 1870's–1970's*. New York: Scribner's, 1975.

Liebs, Chester H. *Main Street to Miracle Mile: American Roadside Architecture*. Baltimore: Johns Hopkins University Press, 1985.

Liesner, Thelma. *Economic Statistics, 1900–1983*. New York: Facts on File, 1985.

Life magazine. 4 representative issues: November 23, 1936; November 22, 1937; November 21, 1938; November 20, 1939.

Lifshey, Earl. *The Housewares Story*. Chicago: National Housewares Manufacturers Association, 1973.

Linton, Calvin D., ed. *The American Almanac*. New York: Thomas Nelson, 1977.

Lippa, Mario, and David Newton. *The World of Small Ads*. Secaucus, NJ: Chartwell Books, 1979.

Loney, Glenn. *20th Century Theatre*. Vol. 1. New York: Facts on File, 1983.

Love, Brian. *Play the Game*. Los Angeles: Reed Books, 1978.

Lovegren, Sylvia. *Fashionable Food: Seven Decades of Food Fads*. New York: Macmillan, 1995.

Lucie-Smith, Edward. *American Realism*. New York: Harry N. Abrams, 1994.

———. *Visual Arts in the Twentieth Century*. New York: Harry N. Abrams, 1996.

Lupoff, Dick, and Don Thompson, eds. *All in Color for a Dime*. New Rochelle, NY: Arlington House, 1970.

Lupton, Ellen. *Mechanical Brides: Women and Machines from Home to Office*. Princeton, NJ: Princeton Architectural Press, 1993.

Lynd, Robert, and Helen Lynd. *Middletown in Transition: A Study in Cultural Conflicts*. New York: Harcourt Brace, 1937.

Lynes, Russell. *The Lively Audience*. New York: Harper & Row, 1985.

MacDonald, J. Fred. *Don't Touch That Dial! Radio Programming in American Life, 1920–1960*. Chicago: Nelson-Hall, 1979.

Madden, David, ed. *Proletarian Writers of the Thirties*. Carbondale: Southern Illinois University Press, 1968.

Maddocks, Melvin. *The Great Liners*. Alexandria, VA: Time-Life Books, 1978.

Maltby, Richard. *Passing Parade: A History of Popular Culture in the Twentieth Century*. New York: Oxford University Press, 1989.

Manchester, William. *The Glory and the Dream: A Narrative History of America, 1932–1972*. 2 vols. Boston: Little, Brown, 1974.

Mandelbaum, Howard, and Eric Myers. *Screen Deco*. New York: St. Martin's Press, 1985.

Mangione, Jerre. *The Dream and the Deal: The Federal Writers' Project, 1935–1943*. Boston: Little, Brown, 1972.

Manring, M.M. *Slave in a Box: The Strange Career of Aunt Jemima*. Charlottesville: University Press of Virginia, 1998.

Marchand, Roland. *Advertising the American Dream: Making Way for Modernity, 1920–1940*. Los Angeles: University of California Press, 1985.

Margolies, John. *Home Away from Home: Motels in America*. Boston: Little, Brown, 1995.

———. *Pump and Circumstance: Glory Days of the Gas Station*. Boston: Little, Brown, 1993.

Margolies, John, and Emily Gwathmey. *Ticket to Paradise: American Movie Theaters and How We Had Fun*. Boston: Little, Brown, 1991.

Mariani, John F. *The Dictionary of American Food and Drink*. New York: Ticknor and Fields, 1983.

Marling, Karal Ann. *Wall-to-Wall America: A Cultural History of Post Office Murals in the Great Depression*. Minneapolis: University of Minnesota Press, 1982.

Marquette, Arthur F. *Brands, Trademarks and Goodwill*. New York: McGraw-Hill, 1967.

Marquis, Alice G. *Hopes and Ashes: The Birth of Modern Times, 1929–1939*. New York: The Free Press, 1986.

Marschall, Richard. *America's Great Comic-Strip Artists*. New York: Stewart, Tabori and Chang, 1997.

Martin, John. *John Martin's Book of the Dance*. New York: Tudor, 1963.

Marum, Andrew, and Frank Parise. *Follies and Foibles: A View of 20th Century Fads*. New York: Facts on File, 1984.

Marzulla, Elena, ed. *Pictorial Treasury of U.S. Stamps*. Omaha, NE: Collectors Institute, 1974.

Mathews, Jane Dehart. *The Federal Theatre, 1935–1939: Plays, Relief, and Politics*. Princeton, NJ: Princeton University Press, 1967.

Mathy, Francois. *American Realism: A Pictorial Survey from the Early Eighteenth Century to the 1970's*. New York: Skira, 1978.

Mattfeld, Julius. *Variety Music Cavalcade*. Englewood Cliffs, NJ: Prentice-Hall, 1962.

Matthew-Walker, Robert. *Broadway to Hollywood: The Musical and the Cinema*. London: Sanctuary Publishing, 1996.

Mazo, Joseph H. *Prime Movers: The Makers of Modern Dance in America*. New York: William Morrow, 1977.

McArthur, Colin. *Underworld U.S.A.* New York: Viking Press, 1972.

McClintock, Inez, and Marshall McClintock. *Toys in America*. Washington, DC: Public Affairs Press, 1961.

McCloud, Scott. *Understanding Comics: The Invisible Art*. Northampton, MA: Kitchen Sink Press, 1993.

McCutcheon, Marc. *The Writer's Guide to Everyday Life from Prohibition Through World War II*. Cincinnati, OH: Writer's Digest Books, 1995.

McDermott, Catherine. *Book of 20th Century Design*. New York: Overlook Press, 1998.

McElvaine, Robert S. *Down and Out in the Great Depression: Letters from the "Forgotten Man."* Chapel Hill: University of North Carolina Press, 1983.

———. *The Great Depression: America, 1929–1941*. New York: Times Books, 1961.

McKennon, Joe. *A Pictorial History of the American Carnival*. Sarasota, FL: Carnival Publishers, 1972.

McKinzie, Richard D. *The New Deal for Artists*. Princeton, NJ: Princeton University Press, 1973.

McLanathan, Richard. *The American Tradition in the Arts*. New York: Harcourt, Brace and World, Inc., 1968.

McShane, Clay. *Down the Asphalt Path: The Automobile and the American City*. New York: Columbia University Press, 1994.

Meeker, David. *Jazz in the Movies*. New York: Da Capo Press, Inc., 1981.

Meikle, Jeffrey L. *Twentieth Century Limited: Industrial Design in America, 1925–1939*. Philadelphia: Temple University Press, 1979.

Mergen, Bernard. *Play and Playthings: A Reference Guide*. Westport, CT: Greenwood Press, 1982.

Meyer, Susan E. *America's Great Illustrators*. New York: Galahad Books, 1978.

Milbank, Caroline Rennolds. *New York Fashion: The Evolution of American Style*. New York: Harry N. Abrams, 1989.

Miller, John Anderson. *Fares, Please! A Popular History of Trolleys, Horse-Cars, Street-Cars, Buses, Elevateds, and Subways*. New York: Dover Publications, 1960.

Miller, William H. *The Last Atlantic Liners*. London: Conway Maritime Press, 1985.

Mintz, Sidney W. *Sweetness and Power: The Place of Sugar in Modern History*. New York: Penguin Books, 1985.

Mintz, Steven, and Susan Kellogg. *Domestic Revolutions: A Social History of American Family Life*. New York: The Free Press, 1988.

Mitchell, Curtis. *Cavalcade of Broadcasting*. Chicago: Benjamin Company/Rutledge, 1970.

Mitchell, Margaret. *Gone with the Wind*. Garden City, NY: Garden City Books, 1936.

Modell, John. *Into One's Own: From Youth to Adulthood in the United States, 1920–1975*. Berkeley: University of California Press, 1989.

Molella, Arthur P., and Elsa M. Bruton. *FDR, the Intimate Presidency: Franklin Delano Roosevelt, Communication, and the Mass Media in the 1930s*. Washington, DC: National Museum of American History, 1982.

Moline, Mary. *Norman Rockwell Encyclopedia: A Chronological Catalog of the Artist's Work, 1910–1978*. Indianapolis, IN: Curtis Publishing Company, 1979.

Morgan, Hal, and Dan Symmes. *Amazing 3-D*. Boston: Little, Brown, 1982.

Morgan, Winona. *The Family Meets the Depression*. Minneapolis: University of Minnesota Press, 1939.

Morris, Ronald L. *Wait Until Dark: Jazz and the Underworld, 1880–1940*. Bowling Green, OH: Popular Press, 1980.

Mott, Frank Luther. *American Journalism: A History: 1690–1960*. New York: Macmillan, 1962.

———. *Golden Multitudes: The Story of Best Sellers in the United States*. New York: R.R. Bowker, 1947.

———. *A History of American Magazines*. Vol. 5: *Sketches of 21 Magazines, 1905–1930*. Cambridge, MA: Harvard University Press, 1968.

Mulvey, Kate, and Melissa Richards. *Decades of Beauty: The Changing Image of Women, 1890s–1990s*. New York: Checkmark Books, 1998.

Nachbar, Jack, and John L. Wright, eds. *The Popular Culture Reader*. Bowling Green, OH: Popular Press, 1977.

Nachman, Gerald. *Raised on Radio*. Berkeley: University of California Press, 1998.

Nasaw, David. *Going Out: The Rise and Fall of Public Amusements*. Cambridge, MA: Harvard University Press, 1993.

Nash, Anedith Jo Bond. *Death on the Highway: The Automobile Wreck in American Culture, 1920–40*. Ann Arbor, MI: University Microfilms International, 1985.

Naylor, David. *Great American Movie Theaters*. Washington, DC: Preservation Press, 1987.

Neuberg, Victor. *The Popular Press Companion to Popular Literature*. Bowling Green, OH: Popular Press, 1983.

Neumeyer, Martin H., and Esther S. Neumeyer. *Leisure and Recreation*. New York: Ronald Press, 1958.

Nye, David E. *American Technological Sublime*. Cambridge, MA: MIT Press, 1994.

Nye, Russel. *The Unembarrassed Muse: The Popular Arts in America*. New York: Dial Press, 1970.

———, ed. *New Dimensions in Popular Culture*. Bowling Green, OH: Popular Press, 1972.

O'Brien, Richard. *The Story of American Toys: From the Puritans to the Present*. New York: Abbeville Press, 1990.

O'Conner, Francis V., ed. *Art for the Millions*. Greenwich, CT: New York Graphic Society, 1973.

———. *The New Deal Art Projects: An Anthology of Memoirs*. Washington, DC: Smithsonian Institution Press, 1972.

O'Dell, John. *The Great American Depression Book of Fun*. New York: Harper and Row, 1981.

Optiz, Glenn B., ed. *Fielding's Dictionary of American Painters, Sculptors & Engravers*. Poughkeepsie, NY: Apollo Books, 1986.

O'Sullivan, Judith. *The Great American Comic Strip: One Hundred Years of Cartoon Art*. Boston: Little, Brown, 1990.

Outdoor Life Editors. Outdoor Life: *100 Years in Pictures*. Denver, CO: Cowles Creative Publishing, 1998.

Pack, Arthur Newton. *The Challenge of Leisure*. Washington, DC: National Recreation and Park Association, 1934.

Pagano, Grace. *Contemporary American Painting*. New York: Duell, Sloan and Pearce, 1945.

Palladino, Grace. *Teenagers: An American History*. New York: Basic Books, 1996.

Panati, Charles. *Extraordinary Origins of Everyday Things*. New York: Harper and Row, 1987.

———. *Panati's Parade of Fads, Follies, and Manias*. New York: HarperCollins, 1991.

Panschar, William G. *Baking in America: Economic Development*. Vol. 1. Evanston, IL: Northwestern University Press, 1956.

Parish, James Robert, and Michael R. Pitts. *The Great Gangster Pictures*. Metchuen, NJ: Scarecrow Press, 1976.

Pashko, Pearl, and Stanley Pashko. *American Girl's Treasury of Sports, Hobbies and Parties*. New York: Grosset & Dunlap, 1949.

Pashko, Stanley. *American Boy's Treasury of Sports, Hobbies and Games*. New York: Grosset & Dunlap, 1945.

Patton, Phil. *Open Road: A Celebration of the American Highway*. New York: Simon and Schuster, 1986.

Peacock, John. *Fashion Sketchbook: 1920–1960*. New York: Avon Books, 1977.

———. *20th-Century Fashion: The Complete Sourcebook*. London: Thames and Hudson, 1993.

Pease, Otis. *The Responsibilities of American Advertising: Private Control and Public Influence, 1920–1940*. New York: Arno Press, 1976.

Pendergast, Tom. *Creating the Modern Man: American Magazines and Consumer Culture, 1900–1950*. Columbia: University of Missouri Press, 2000.

Pendergrast, Mark. *For God, Country and Coca-Cola*. New York: Scribner's, 1993.

Penkower, Monty Noam. *The Federal Writers' Project: A Study in Government Patronage and the Arts*. Urbana: University of Illinois Press, 1977.

Peterson, Theodore. *Magazines in the Twentieth Century*. Urbana: University of Illinois Press, 1964.

Phillips, Cabell. *The* New York Times *Chronicle of American Life: From the Crash to the Blitz: 1929–1939*. New York: Macmillan, 1969.

Pillsbury, Richard. *From Boarding House to Bistro: The American Restaurant Then and Now*. Boston: Unwin Hyman, 1990.

Pitz, Henry. "N.C. Wyeth." *American Heritage*, 16, 6 (October 1965): 36–55.

———. *200 Years of American Illustration*. New York: Random House, 1977.

Pollay, Richard W., ed. *Information Sources in Advertising History*. Westport, CT: Greenwood Press, 1979.

Potter, David M. *People of Plenty: Economic Abundance and the American Character*. Chicago: University of Chicago Press, 1954.

Pyle, Ernie. "The Sculptor of Mount Rushmore." In *Ernie's America: The Best of Ernie Pyle's 1930s Travel Dispatches*. Edited by David Nichols. New York: Random House, 1989.

Pyron, Darden Asbury, ed. *Recasting:* Gone with the Wind *in American Culture*. Miami: University Presses of Florida, 1984.

Rader, Benjamin G. *American Sports: From the Age of Folk Games to the Age of Spectators*. Englewood Cliffs, NJ: Prentice-Hall, 1983.

Radio Flyer History. January, 11, 2001. *<http://www.radioflyer.com/history.html>*.

Rae, John B. *The Road and the Car in American Life*. Cambridge, MA: MIT Press, 1971.

Randel, William Peirce. *The Evolution of American Taste*. New York: Crown Publishers, 1978.

Raymond, Alex. *Flash Gordon: "Mongo, the Planet of Doom."* Princeton, WI: Kitchen Sink Press, 1990.

Reed, Walt, and Roger Reed. *The Illustrator in America, 1880–1980*. New York: The Society of Illustrators, 1984.

Reminisce Editors. *"We Had Everything But Money."* Greendale, WI: Reminisce Books, 1992.

Reynolds, Nancy, and Susan Reimer-Torn. *In Performance: A Companion to the Classics of the Dance*. New York: Harmony Books, 1980.

Reynolds, R.C. *Stage Left: The Development of the American Social Drama in the Thirties*. Troy, NY: Whitston, 1986.

Rhode, Eric. *A History of the Cinema from Its Origins to 1970*. New York: Hill and Wang, 1976.

Rideout, Walter B. *The Radical Novel in the United States: 1900–1954*. New York: Hill and Wang, 1956.

Riggs, Austen Fox. *Play: Recreation in a Balanced Life*. Garden City, NY: Doubleday, Doran, 1935.

Rives, Hallie Erminie. *The Modern and Complete Book of Etiquette*. Chicago: John C. Winston, 1939.

Roberts, Brady M., James M. Dennis, James S. Horns, and Helen Mar Parkin. *Grant Wood: An American Master Revealed*. San Francisco: Pomegranate Artbooks, 1995.

Roberts, Garyn G. *Dick Tracy and American Culture: Morality and Mythology, Text and Context*. Jefferson, NC: McFarland, 1993.

Robinson, Cervin, and Rosemarie Haag Bletter. *Skyscraper Style: Art Deco New York*. New York: Oxford University Press, 1975.

Robinson, Jerry. *The Comics: An Illustrated History of Comic Strip Art*. New York: G.P. Putnam's Sons, 1974.

Roettger, Dorye. *Rivals of Rockwell*. New York: Crescent Books, 1992.

Rogers, Agnes. *I Remember Distinctly: A Family Album of the American People in the Years of Peace, 1918 to Pearl Harbor*. New York: Harper & Brothers, 1947.

Rollin, Lucy. *Twentieth-Century Teen Culture by the Decades: A Reference Guide*. Westport, CT: Greenwood Press, 1999.

Rooker, Oliver E. *The Travel Bureau: Ghost Riders Network on Route 66 During the Great Depression*. Canton, OK: Memoir Publishing, 1994.

Rorty, James. *Our Master's Voice: Advertising*. New York: John Day, 1934.

Rose, Albert C. *Historic American Roads: From Frontier Trails to Superhighways*. New York: Crown Publishers, 1976.

Roth, Leland M. *A Concise History of American Architecture*. New York: Harper and Row, 1979.

Rothstein, Arthur. *The Depression Years*. New York: Dover Publications, 1978.

Rovin, Jeff. *Adventure Heroes: Legendary Characters from Odysseus to James Bond*. New York: Facts on File, 1994.

Rowsome, Frank, Jr. *The Verse by the Side of the Road: The Story of Burma-Shave Signs and Jingles*. Lexington, MA: Stephen Greene Press, 1965.

———. *They Laughed When I Sat Down*. New York: Bonanza Books, 1959.

Rubinstein, Ruth P. *Dress Codes: Meanings and Messages in American Culture*. Boulder, CO: Westview Press, 1995.

Ruehlmann, William. *Saint with a Gun: The Unlawful American Private Eye*. New York: New York University Press, 1984.

Runte, Alfred. *Trains of Discovery: Western Railroads and the National Parks*. Niwot, CO: Roberts Rinehart, 1990.

Sanderson, Dwight. *Research Memorandum on Rural Life in the Depression*. New York: Arno Press, 1972. (Reprint of 1937 edition, published by the Social Science Research Council.)

Sanjek, Russell. *Pennies from Heaven: The American Popular Music Business in the Twentieth Century*. New York: Da Capo Press, 1988.

Sann, Paul. *Fads, Follies and Delusions of the American People*. New York: Crown Publishers, 1967.

———. *The Lawless Decade*. New York: Crown Publishers, 1957.

Sasowsky, Norman. *The Prints of Reginald Marsh*. New York: Clarkson N. Potter, 1976.

Saturday Evening Post. 10 representative issues: November 22, 1930; November 21, 1931; November 19, 1932; November 25, 1933; November 24, 1934; November 23, 1935; November 21, 1936; November 20, 1937; November 26, 1938; November 25, 1939.

Scanlan, Tom. *The Joy of Jazz: The Swing Era, 1935–1947*. Golden, CO: Fulcrum, 1996.

Schlachter, Gail, ed. *The Great Depression: A Historical Bibliography*. Santa Barbara, CA: ABC-Clio, 1984.

Schnurnberger, Lynn. *Let There Be Clothes: 40,000 Years of Fashion*. New York: Workman, 1991.

Schreiner, Samuel A., Jr. *The Condensed World of the Reader's Digest*. New York: Stein and Day, 1977.

Schudson, Michael. *Advertising, the Uneasy Persuasion: Its Dubious Impact on American Society*. New York: Basic Books, 1984.

Schweitzer, Robert, and Michael W.R. Davis. *America's Favorite Homes: Mail-Order Catalogues as a Guide to Popular Early 20th-Century Houses*. Detroit, MI: Wayne State University Press, 1990.

Sculle, Keith A. "Frank Redford's Wigwam Village Chain." *In Roadside America:*

The Automobile in Design and Culture. Edited by Jan Jennings. Ames: Iowa State University Press, 1990.

Sears, Stephen W. *The American Heritage of the Automobile in America*. NY: Simon and Schuster, Inc., 1977.

Seidman, David. *All Gone: Things That Aren't There Anymore*. Los Angeles: General Publishing Group, 1998.

Settel, Irving. *A Pictorial History of Radio*. New York: Grosset & Dunlap, 1967.

Settel, Irving, and William Laas. *A Pictorial History of Television*. New York: Grosset & Dunlap, 1969.

Sexton, Richard. *American Style: Classic Product Design from Airstream to Zippo*. San Francisco: Chronicle Books, 1987.

Seymour, Harold. *Baseball: The Golden Age*. New York: Oxford University Press, 1971.

Shannon, David A. *Between the Wars: America, 1919–1941*. Boston: Houghton Mifflin, 1979.

————, ed. *The Great Depression*. Englewood Cliffs, N.J.: Prentice-Hall, 1960.

Sheridan, Martin. *Comics and Their Creators*. Westport, CT: Hyperion Press, 1942.

Sikov, Ed. *Screwball: Hollywood's Madcap Romantic Comedies*. New York: Crown Publishers, 1985.

Simon, George T. *The Big Bands*. New York: Macmillan, 1967.

Simon, Howard. *500 Years of Art in Illustration: From Albrecht Durer to Rockwell Kent*. Garden City, NY: Garden City Publishing, 1945.

Sinclair, Andrew. *Era of Excess: A Social History of the Prohibition Movement*. New York: Harper Colophon, 1962.

Sklar, Robert. *Movie-Made America*. New York: Vintage Books, 1975.

Slide, Anthony. *The American Film Industry*. New York: Greenwood Press, 1986.

————. *The Vaudevillians: A Dictionary of Vaudeville Performers*. Westport, CT: Arlington House, 1981.

Smith, Bradley. *The USA: A History in Art*. Garden City, NY: Doubleday, 1975.

Smith, C. Ray. *Interior Design in 20th-Century America: A History*. New York: Harper and Row, 1987.

Smith, Jane Webb. *Smoke Signals: Cigarettes, Advertising, and the American Way of Life*. Chapel Hill: University of North Carolina Press, 1990.

Smulyan, Susan. *Selling Radio: The Commercialization of American Broadcasting, 1920–1934*. Washington, DC: Smithsonian Institution Press, 1994.

Snyder, Robert W. *Voice of the City: Vaudeville and Popular Culture in New York*. New York: Oxford University Press, 1989.

Sorell, Walter. *The Dance Through the Ages*. New York: Grosset and Dunlap, 1967.

Spivey, Donald, ed. *Sport in America: New Historical Perspectives*. Westport, CT: Greenwood Press, 1985.

Springer, John. *All Talking! All Singing! All Dancing!* Secaucus, NJ: Citadel Press, 1966.

Stearns, Marshall. *The Story of Jazz*. New York: Oxford University Press, 1958.

Stearns, Marshall, and Jean Stearns. *Jazz Dance: The Story of American Vernacular Dance*. New York: Schirmer Books, 1968.

Stedman, Raymond William. *The Serials: Suspense and Drama by Installment*. Norman: University of Oklahoma Press, 1971.

Steinberg, Cobbett S. *Film Facts*. New York: Facts on File, 1980.

Steiner, Jesse F. *Research Memorandum on Recreation in the Depression*. New York: Arno Press, 1972. (Reprint of 1937 edition, published by the Social Science Research Council.)

Sterling, Christopher H., and John M. Kittross. *Stay Tuned: A Concise History of American Broadcasting*. Belmont, CA: Wadsworth, 1990.

Stern, Robert A.M. *Pride of Place: Building the American Dream*. Boston: Houghton Mifflin, 1986.

Sternau, Susan A. *Art Deco: Flights of Artistic Fancy*. New York: Todtri, 1997.

Stevenson, Katherine Cole, and H. Ward Jandl. *Houses by Mail: A Guide to Houses from Sears, Roebuck and Company*. Washington, DC: Preservation Press, 1986.

Stilgoe, John R. *Borderland: Origins of the American Suburb, 1820–1939*. New Haven, CT: Yale University Press, 1988.

———. *Metropolitan Corridor: Railroads and the American Scene*. New Haven, CT: Yale University Press, 1983.

Stoddard, Bob. *Pepsi-Cola: 100 Years*. Los Angeles: General Publishing Group, 1997.

Stoltz, Donald R., and Marshall L. Stoltz. *Norman Rockwell and* The Saturday Evening Post. Vol. 2: *The Middle Years, 1928–1943*. Philadelphia: The Saturday Evening Post Company, 1976.

Stott, William. *Documentary Expression and Thirties America*. New York: Oxford University Press, 1973.

Stover, John F. *The Life and Decline of the American Railroad*. New York: Oxford University Press, 1970.

Stowe, David W. *Swing Changes: Big-Band Jazz in New Deal America*. Cambridge, MA: Harvard University Press, 1994.

Strasser, Susan. *Never Done: A History of American Housework*. New York: Pantheon Books, 1982.

———. *Satisfaction Guaranteed: The Making of the American Mass Market*. Washington, DC: Smithsonian Institution Press, 1989.

Summers, Harrison B. *A Thirty-Year History of Programs Carried on National Radio Networks in the United States, 1926–1956*. Columbus: Ohio State University Press, 1958.

Swados, Harvey, ed. *The American Writer and the Great Depression*. Indianapolis, IN: Bobbs-Merrill, 1966.

Swanberg, W.A. *Citizen Hearst: A Biography of William Randolph Hearst*. New York: Scribner's, 1961.

———. *Luce and His Empire*. New York: Scribner's, 1972.

Sweeney, Russell C. *Coming Next Week: A Pictorial History of Film Advertising*. New York: Castle Books, 1973.

Symons, Julian. *Bloody Murder: From the Detective Story to the Crime Novel*. New York: Penguin Books, 1972.

Tannahill, Reay. *Food in History*. New York: Stein and Day, 1973.

Taylor, John W.R., and Kenneth Munson. *History of Aviation*. New York: Crown Publishers, 1972.

Taylor, Joshua. *America as Art*. Washington, DC: Smithsonian Institution Press, 1976.

Tchudi, Stephen N. *Soda Poppery: The History of Soft Drinks in America*. New York: Charles Scribner's, 1986.

Tebbel, John. *The American Magazine: A Compact History*. New York: Hawthorn Books, 1969.

Tebbel, John, and Mary Ellen Zuckerman. *The Magazine in America: 1741–1990*. New York: Oxford University Press, 1991.

Terkel, Studs. *Hard Times: An Oral History of the Great Depression*. New York: Random House (Pantheon), 1970.

Thompson, Don, and Dick Lupoff, eds. *The Comic-Book Book*. New Rochelle, NY: Arlington House, 1973.

Thornburg, David A. *Galloping Bungalows: The Rise and Demise of the American House Trailer*. Hamden, CT: Archon Books, 1991.

Thurber, James. *The Years with Ross*. Boston: Little, Brown, 1959.

Tierney, Tom. *American Family of the 1930s: Paper Dolls in Full Color*. New York: Dover Publications, 1991.

———. *Great Fashion Designs of the Thirties: Paper Dolls in Full Color*. New York: Dover Publications, 1984.

TIME-LIFE Books. *This Fabulous Century*. Vol. 3: *1920–1930*. New York: Time-Life Books, 1969.

———. *This Fabulous Century*. Vol. 4: *1930–1940*. New York: Time-Life Books, 1969.

Toland, John. *The Great Dirigibles: Their Triumphs and Disasters*. New York: Dover Publications, 1972.

Toll, Robert C. *The Entertainment Machine: American Show Business in the Twentieth Century*. New York: Oxford University Press, 1982.

———. *On with the Show: The First Century of Show Business in America*. New York: Oxford University Press, 1976.

Trent, Paul. *Those Fabulous Movie Years: The 30s*. Barre, MA: Barre Publishing, 1975.

Tsujimoto, Karen. *Images of America: Precisionist Painting and Modern Photography*. Seattle: University of Washington Press, 1982.

Twitchell, James B. *Adcult USA: The Triumph of Advertising in American Culture*. New York: Columbia University Press, 1996.

———. *Lead Us into Temptation: The Triumph of American Materialism*. New York: Columbia University Press, 1999.

———. *Twenty Ads That Shook the World*. New York: Crown Publishers, 2000.

Ulanov, Barry. *A History of Jazz in America*. New York: Da Capo Press, 1952.

Unstead, R.J. *The Thirties: An Illustrated History in Colour, 1930–1939*. London: Macdonald Educational, 1974.

Uys, Errol Lincoln. *Riding the Rails: Teenagers on the Move During the Depression*. New York: TV Books, 1999.

Van Dover, J. Kenneth. *Murder in the Millions: Erle Stanley Gardner, Mickey Spillane, & Ian Fleming*. New York: Frederick Ungar, 1984.

Variety Books. *The Variety History of Show Business*. New York: Harry N. Abrams, 1993.

Vermyle, Jerry. *The Films of the Thirties*. Secaucus, NJ: Citadel Press, 1982.

Visser, Margaret. *Much Depends on Dinner*. New York: Grove Press, 1986.

Wainwright, Loudon. *The Great American Magazine: An Inside History of* Life. New York: Alfred A. Knopf, 1986.

Wald, Carol. *Myth America: Picturing American Women, 1865–1945*. New York: Pantheon Books, 1975.

Waldau, Roy S. *Vintage Years of the Theatre Guild, 1928–1939*. Cleveland, OH: Press of Case Western Reserve University, 1972.

Wallechinsky, David. *The People's Almanac Presents the Twentieth Century: The Definitive Compendium of Astonishing Events, Amazing People, and Strange-but-True Facts*. Boston: Little, Brown, 1995.

Wallis, Michael. *Route 66: The Mother Road*. New York: St. Martin's Press, 1990.

Walton, Thomas. "The Sky Was No Limit." *Portfolio* Vol 1 (April/May 1979): 82–89.

Ward, Geoffrey C., and Ken Burns. *Jazz: A History of America's Music*. New York: Alfred A. Knopf, 2000.

Ware, Susan. *Holding Their Own: American Women in the 1930s*. Boston: Twayne, 1982.

Washburne, Carolyn Kott. *America in the Twentieth Century: 1930–1939*. New York: Marshall Cavendish, 1995.

Watkins, Julius Lewis. *The 100 Greatest Advertisements: Who Wrote Them and What They Did*. New York: Dover Publications, 1959.

Watkins, T.H. *The Great Depression: America in the 1930s*. Boston: Little, Brown, 1993.

———. *The Hungry Years: America in an Age of Crisis, 1929–1939*. New York: Henry Holt, 1999.

Watters, Pat. *Coca-Cola: An Illustrated History*. Garden City, New York: Doubleday, 1978.

Waugh, Coulton. *The Comics*. New York: Luna Press, 1947.

Wecter, Dixon. *The Age of the Great Depression, 1929–1941*. Chicago: Quadrangle Books, 1948.

Weibel, Kathryn. *Mirror Mirror: Images of Women Reflected in Popular Culture*. Garden City, NY: Anchor Books, 1977.

Weisberger, Bernard A., ed. *The WPA Guide to America*. New York: Pantheon Books, 1985.

West, Elliott. *Growing Up in Twentieth-Century America: A History and Reference Guide*. Westport, CT: Greenwood Press, 1996.

West, Nancy Martha. *Kodak and the Lens of Nostalgia*. Charlottesville: University Press of Virginia, 2000.

Whitcomb, Ian. *After the Ball: Pop Music from Rag to Rock*. Baltimore: Penguin Books, 1972.

White, David Manning, and Robert H. Abel, eds. *The Funnies: An American Idiom*. New York: The Free Press, 1963.

White, G. Edward. *Creating the National Pastime: Baseball Transforms Itself, 1903–1955*. Princeton, NJ: Princeton University Press, 1996.

White, John H., Jr. *The American Railroad Passenger Car*. Baltimore: Johns Hopkins University Press, 1978.

Wigmore, Deedee. *American Scene Painting and Sculpture: Dominant Style of the 1930's and 1940's*. New York: D. Wigmore Fine Art, 1988.

Wilder, Alec. *American Popular Song: The Great Innovators, 1900–1950*. New York: Oxford University Press, 1972.

Williams, Martin T. *The Jazz Tradition*. New York: Oxford University Press, 1983.

Williams, Martin T., ed. *The Art of Jazz*. New York: Oxford University Press, 1959.

Wilson, Elizabeth. *Adorned in Dreams: Fashion and Modernity*. Berkeley: University of California Press, 1985.

Wilson, Richard Guy, Dianne H. Pilgrim, and Dickran Tashjian. *The Machine Age in America: 1918–1941*. New York: Harry N. Abrams, 1986.

Winship, Michael. *Television*. New York: Random House, 1988.

Witzel, Michael Karl. *The American Gas Station*. New York: Barnes and Noble, 1999.

Wood, James Playsted. *Magazines in the United States*. New York: Ronald Press, 1956.

———. *The Story of Advertising*. New York: Ronald Press, 1958.

Woodham, Jonathan M. *Twentieth-Century Design*. New York: Oxford University Press, 1997.

Wulffson, Don. *Toys: Amazing Stories Behind Some Great Inventions*. New York: Henry Holt, 2000.

Yaquinto, Marilyn. *Pump'em Full of Lead: A Look at Gangsters on Film*. New York: Twayne, 1998.

Young, Dean, and Rick Marschall. *Blondie & Dagwood's America*. New York: Harper & Row, 1981.

Young, William H. "The Serious Funnies: Adventure Comics During the Depression." *Journal of Popular Culture*, 3 (Winter 1969): 404–427.

———. "That Indomitable Redhead: Little Orphan Annie." *Journal of Popular Culture*, 6 (Fall 1974): 309–316.

Zierold, Norman J. *The Child Stars*. New York: Coward-McCann, 1965.

Zuckerman, Mary Ellen. *A History of Popular Women's Magazines in the United States, 1792–1995*. Westport, CT: Greenwood Press, 1998.

Index

Note: *Italic type* indicates a page reference to an illustration.

A&P (The Great Atlantic and Pacific Tea Company), 99; and self-service meat departments, 101
A&W Root Beer, 111
"Abe Lincoln" (Robinson), 176
Academy Award statuette ("Oscar") (Gibbons), 77
Ace Drummond (Knight), 248–249
Action Comics, xix, 275
Action Stories, 31
Adams, Franklin P., 165
Adventures in Good Eating (Hines), 111
advertising, 37–56; of automobiles, 51–54; blacks in, 54–55; of breakfast cereals, 53–54; cartoons and, 43; and consumerism, 38–41; Depression and, 38, 39, 50; goals of, 37–38; illustration in, 52; in 1920s , 37; jingles in, 41, 46; in magazines, 49–51; modernism and, 41–42, 44; and movies, 44; newspaper, 162; outdoor, 44–46; photography in, 52; radio, 30, 46–48, 162, 209; and smoking, 55–56; suspicion of, 38; target marketing and, 157–158;

teenage culture and, 25; and trademarks, 48
Advertising Age, 153
aerial racing, 247–248
African-Americans. *See* blacks
Agee, James, *Let Us Now Praise Famous Men*, 262
Ager, Milton, "Happy Days Are Here Again," 176
Air Cadets of America, 33
air travel, xv, xviii, 244–252
Airflow, Chrysler, xvii, 74–75, 129, *234*
Airmail, 250
airships, 244–247
Airstream Trailer Company, 239
Akron, 245
Alamo Plaza, 236
Albers Super Mkts., 99
alcoholic beverages, 113–116; advertising of, 52
Aldrich Family, The, 30
All American, 137
All-Star Game (baseball), xvii, 134
Allen, Gracie, 213

Allen, Hervey, *Anthony Adverse*, xvii, 149

Allen, Robert S., 165

Alsberg, Henry, 152

Amazing Stories, 159

American Basketball League (ABL), 137

American Boy, 26

American Flyer (Radio Flyer) wagon, 128–129

American Girl, 27

American Gothic (Wood), xv, 3, 258, 259

American Guide series (books), 152

American Institute of Interior Decorators (now American Society of Interior Decorators), 65–66

American Legion, 33

American Magazine, 237

American Ping-Pong Association, 126

American Tobacco Company, 265

Amos 'n' Andy, 30, 47, 55, 103, 211–212

Anderson, Eddie, 55, 214

Anderson, Marian, xx

Anderson, Maxwell, *Winterset*, 225

Andy Hardy movies, xix, 202

Angels with Dirty Faces, 28

Animal Crackers, 197

Anna Christie, xv, 114

announcers, radio, 47–48

Anthony Adverse (Allen), xvii, 149

antiquing, 66

Apple Mary and Dennie, 9

Apple Mary (Orr), 9

apple-selling movement, xv, 8–9

appliances, kitchen, 105–110

Aquacade, 72, 143

architecture and design, 57–79; Art Deco in, 57–58; fairs and expositions, 69–74; gas stations, 68–69; interior decoration, 66, 67–68; International Style, 60–62; mass housing, 64–65; modernism in, 57–58; movies and, 66–67; period revivals, 65–66; skyscrapers, 59; Streamline Moderne in, 57–58; survey of, 261

"Are You Makin' Any Money?" (Hupfield), 176

Argosy, 31

Argosy Weekly, 159

Arlen, Harold, 178, 205

Armour food company, Treet, 105

Armstrong, Henry, 142

Armstrong, Louis, 171, *172*

Art Deco: in advertising, 41; in architecture, 57–58; at Chicago World's Fair, *70*; in Chrysler Building, 59, 61; in costume jewelry, 87; in Empire State Building, 59; in interior decoration, 67, 68; in movie set design, 76, 205–206; in musicals, 193; on ocean liners, 253; in science fiction movies, 202

Art Institute of Chicago, 258

As Thousands Cheer, 85, 224

As You Desire Me, 85

Associated Press (A.P.), 164

Asta (Powell's and Loy's terrier), 87, 207

Astaire, Fred, xviii, 67, 193–194, 202, 228, 251, 253, 254

Astounding Stories, 159

AT&T, 76

athletics (*see also* sports): and youth, 23

Atlantic City Game, 128

Atlas, Charles, 43

Atwater Kent electronics company, 207

Aunt Jemima, 54, 68

auto camps, 236

auto racing, 143; movies and, 143

automobiles (*see also under specific makes*), 12; advertising of, 51–54; cost of, 281; equipment on, 235; and food shopping, 100; roads for, 232–233; travel by, 232–239

Autry, Gene, 180, 191

aviation, 244–252; aerial racing, 247–248; movies and, 249–252

aviators, 247–249

Awake and Sing! (Odets), 225

Awful Truth, The, 198

B. Altman department store, 66
"B" movies, 141, 186, 191
Babes in Arms, 202, 223
Babies, Just Babies, 158
Baby Brownie camera, 77, 262
baby food, 105
Backstage Wife, 215
Baer, Max, 141
Bakelite, 67, 68
"Ballad for Americans" (Robinson), 176–177
Ballyhoo, 38
Barker, "Ma," 188
Barnet, Charlie, 172
Barney Baxter in the Air (Miller), 249
Barney Google (DeBeck), 272
Barrymore, John, 244
Barrymore, Lionel, 202
Barthelmess, Richard, 250
baseball, 133–135; All-Star Game, 134; movies and, 135; night games, xviii, 134; radio and, 134–135; television and, 221
Basie, Count, 170, 172, 175
basketball, 137
Bat, The, 159
Batman, 31, 275
Baugh, Sammy, 136
Baum, L. Frank, "The Wizard of Oz," 205
Beach, Rex, 159
Beatty, Clyde, 229–230
Becky Sharp, 187
Beech-Nut gum, 54
beer: canned, 115; near, 114; needle, 114; 3.2 , 115
Beery, Wallace, 141
"Begin the Beguine" (Porter), xviii
Bel Geddes, Norman, 74–76; and Chrysler Airflow, 74–75; "Futurama," 72; gas station designs of, 69; set designs of, 254
Bendix Home Laundries, 52
Bendix Trophy (aerial racing), 248
Benny, Jack, 165, 213–214, 253
Benson, Mildred Wirt (pseud. Carolyn Keene), *The Secret of the Old Clock*, 31

Benton, Thomas Hart, 258, 259
Bergen, Edgar, xix
Berkeley, Busby, 84, 193, 228
Berlin, Irving, 178, 224; "Easter Parade," 85
Berryman, C. K., 276
Better Homes and Gardens, 66, 153
Better Little Books, 274
Betty Crocker, 48
Betty Crocker (radio show), 48
bicycle races, 121
Big Bad Wolf (Disney character), 130
Big Bear Super Market, 99
Big Big Books, 274
Big Broadcast of 1938, The, 195, 254
Big Cage, The, 229–230
Big City, The, 241
Big Fight, The, 141
Big Game, The, 137
Big Little Books, xvi, 274–275
Biggers, Earl Derr, 190
billboards, 45
Billy the Kid (Copland), 181
bingo, 124, *125*
Birds Eye frozen foods, xvi, 102
Birdseye, Clarence, 102
Bisquick, 104
Black Cat, The, 200
Black Mask Magazine, 159
blacks: in advertising, 54–55; as musicians, 170–173, 175, 182, 227; segregation and, 171; stereotyping of, 54–55, 141; wages and, 11; and youth unemployment, 18
Blanc, Mel, 214
blimps. *See* airships
Block, Martin, 182
Blockade, 204
Blondell, Joan, 192
Blondie (Young), 67, 267, 271–272; marketing of, 271; movies, 271; radio comedy, 271
Blosser, Merrill, *Freckles and His Friends*, 31
Blue Ribbon Books, 274
board games, xviii, 128
bobby-soxers, 25
Bogart, Humphrey, 28, 251

Bolger, Ray, 228
Bonnie and Clyde, xvii, 188
book clubs, 151
Book-of-the-Month Club, 151
books (*see also under specific titles*), 147–
    152; cost of, 282; paperback, 148
Border Legion, The, 191
Borglum, Gutzon, 263
Born to Dance, 253
Boston Symphony, 180
Bourke-White, Margaret, *You Have
    Seen Their Faces*, 262
Bovril, 54
bowling, 143–144
boxing, xix, 140–142; movies and, 141–
    142; radio and, 141
Boy Scouts of America, 24, 31, 266
Boyd, William (pseud. Hopalong Cas-
    sidy), 191
Boy's Life, 26, 266
Braddock, Jim, 141
breadlines, *8*, 95
breakfast foods, 53–54
Breck, John, 89
Breck's Shampoo, 89
Breen, Joseph I., 189
Breen Office. *See* Production Code
    Administration
Bride of Frankenstein, The, 200
Bride's Magazine, 153, 160
bridge, contract, xvii, 126–128
Bringing Up Baby, 198
Bringing Up Father (McManus), 268
Brinkley, John R., 217–218
Broadcasting, 153
Broadway. *See* theater
Broadway Gondolier, 192
Broadway Limited, 76
Broadway Melody of 1936, 165, 228
Brooklyn Bridge (New York), *8*
"Brother, Can You Spare a Dime?"
    (Gormey/Harburg), xvi, 176
Brown, Joe E., 121, 141
Brown, Johnny Mack, 107
Brown, Lew, "Life Is Just a Bowl of
    Cherries," 176
Brown, Nacio Herb, "You Are My
    Lucky Star," 165

Brownies, 24
Browning, Tod, 199
Brunswick record label, 173
Buck, Pearl S., *The Good Earth*, xvi,
    149
Buck Rogers, 71, 143, 207, 254
Buck Rogers (Nowlan and Calkins),
    272, 274
Buck Rogers (radio serial), xvi, 30
Budge, Don, 138
Buffalo Indian Head nickel, 264
Buick company, 143
Bullets or Ballots, 190
Bumstead, Dagwood, 67
Bunyan, Paul, 48
Burlington Line, 243; *Pioneer Zephyr*,
    69–70
Burma-Shave, 45–46
Burns, George, 213
Burton, David, 9
buses, 239–241
"But Not for Me" (Gershwin and
    Gershwin), 169
Butterick sewing pattern books, 83
Byam, Wally, 239
Byrd, Admiral Richard E., 14–15, 133

Cagney, James "Jimmy," 28, 114, 141,
    143, 188, 190, 192, 241
Cain and Mabel, 141
Caldwell, Erskine: *God's Little Acre*,
    148, 149; *Journeyman*, 148; *Tobacco
    Road*, 148; *You Have Seen Their
    Faces*, 262
California-Pacific International Exposi-
    tion (San Diego, 1935), 71
California Zephyr, 243
Calkins, Dick, *Buck Rogers*, 272
Camel cigarettes, 55
Campbell's food company, 97, 104
Campbell's Soup, 211
Campus Confessions, 137
candy, 103
Caniff, Milton, *Terry and the Pirates*,
    31
Cantor, Eddie, 210
capitalism, and *Little Orphan Annie*,
    269–270

Capone, Al, 157, 270
Capp, Al, *Li'l Abner*, 269, 272
Capra, Frank, xvii, 9, 197–198, 235
Captain Midnight, 30
Caray, Harry, 135
Carefree, 194
Carle, Frankie, 172
Carmichael, Hoagy, 178; "Georgia on My Mind," 178
Carnegie, Dale, *How to Win Friends and Influence People*, xix, 151
Carnera, Primo, 141
Carroll, Madeleine, 204
Carter, Garnet, 139
cartoons (*see also* comic books; comic strips), editorial, 275–277
Case of the Black Cat, The, 149
Case of the Curious Bride, The, 148
Case of the Howling Dog, The, 148
Case of the Lucky Legs, The, 148
Case of the Stuttering Bishop, The, 149
Case of the Velvet Claws, The, xvii, 148–149
Cassidy, Hopalong. *See* Boyd, William
Catholic Church, 218–219
CBS: radio network, xx, 135–136, 174, 209, 213, 218; television network, 220
CCC. *See* Civilian Conservation Corps
cellar clubs, 21
Century of Progress Exposition. *See* Chicago World's Fair (1933)
Century, The (Scribner's), 153
Cermak, Anton, 4–5
chain businesses: food stores, 99; motels, 236–237; newspapers, 161–162; restaurants, 110–111
chain letters, 122–123
Chained, 253
Champ, The, 141, 203
Charlie Chan, 190
Chase and Sanborn Hour, The, xix, 47, 210
Chasing Rainbows, 176
Check and Double Check, 212
Cheerios, 54
Chesterfields cigarettes, 56

Chesterfield Time, 180
Chevrolet automobiles, 52
Chicago Cubs, 135
Chicago Tribune, 157
Chicago World's Fair (1933), xvii, 69–71, 135, 246; futuristic homes in, 65
child actors, 203–204
child labor, 17; *Little Orphan Annie* and, 269–270
China Clipper, 251
Chinese Orange Mystery, The (Queen), 148
Christy Brothers circus, 229
chromed tubular steel, 67
Chrysler Building (Van Alen), xv, 59, 60, 61, 234
Chrysler company, 72, 143; Airflow automobile, xvii, 74–75, 129, 234
Cincinnati Reds, 134
circuses, 229–230
City of Salina, 69, 243
City, The (Copland), 181
Civilian Conservation Corps (CCC), 19–21, 233
classical music, xix, 180–181
Cleveland Symphony, 181
Click, 158
"Clifton, The" (television set), 221
Clinton, Larry, 172
clothing (*see also* fashion), cost of, 280
Coca-Cola, 116–117, 265, 266, 267
Cocomalt, 30
Code restrictions (Hollywood), 67, 189, 190, 193, 196, 197
coffee, 117–118
Colbert, Claudette, 84, 90, 197–198, 235
Coldspot refrigerator, Loewy design of, 77, 107
Cole Brothers-Clyde Beatty Combined Circus, 229
colleges, 18
Collier's, 153, 157
Colonial Williamsburg, 66
Columbia Broadcasting System. *See* CBS
Columbia record label, 173, 175

Columbo, Russ, 177
comedy: in movies, 195–199; on radio, 211–214; screwball, xvii, 197–199; situation, 214
comic books (see also under specific titles), 274–275; radio and, 29; and youth, 31
comic strips (see also under specific titles), 9, 268–274; and advertising, 43; animals in, 272–273; and aviation, 248–249; compared to movies, 269; hillbillies, 272; popularity of, 164; radio and, 29; science fiction, 272; youth and, 31
Comics, The, 275
commercial roadside strips, 233
Communism, 227
concrete, reinforced, 67
Confessions of a Nazi Spy, 204–205
Consumer Reports, 153
consumerism, 38–41; and advertising, 51
Consumers Research, 38
Consumers Union, 38
contract bridge, xvii, 126–128
Cooper, Gary, 191, 213, 266
Cooper, Jackie, 141, 203, 274
Coors Brewing Company, Adolph, 115
Copland, Aaron: Billy the Kid, 181; The City, 181; El Salon Mexico, 181; Of Mice and Men, 181; Music for Radio (Prairie Journal), 181
Coppertone, 87
Correll, Charles, 211–212
Corrigan, "Wrong Way," xix
Cosmopolitan, 153
costs, of products, 279–282; clothing, 280; entertainment and leisure, 282; food, 280; medical costs, 281; personal items, 281; shelter and furnishings, 280–281; transportation, 281
Cotton Bowl (football), 136
Coughlin, Rev. Charles E., 218–219
country music, 261
country swing music, 179
Cowboy Quarterback, 137

Cowles, Gardner, Jr., 156
Cox newspapers, 162
Crabbe, Clarence "Buster," 143, 207
Crawford, Joan, xv, 82, 253
Cream of Wheat, 54
Cresta Blanca Carnival (Gould), 180
Crosby, Bing, xvi, 47, 129, 171, 176, 177, 194, 195
Crosley electronics company, 207
Cross Country Cruise, 240
Crowd Roars, The, 143
"Crystal House" (Keck), 65
Cub Scouts, 24
Cuban Overture (Gershwin), 180
Cugat, Xavier, 174
Cukor, George, 206
Culbertson, Ely, 126–128
Cunard Lines, 252
curtain walls, glass, 67

Dagwood Sandwich, 271
Dairy Queen, 111
Daisy air rifles, 26
Dana Girls, 32
dance, 177, 227–229; modern, 227–228; popular, 228–229; theatrical, 228
dance marathons, 121, 122, 229
Daniel, Daniel M., 134
Daniels, Bebe, 192
Dannay, Frederic (pseud. Ellery Queen): The Chinese Orange Mystery, 148; The Dutch Shoe Mystery, 148; The Egyptian Cross Mystery, 148
Darrow, Charles, 128
Daughters of the American Revolution, xx
David, Elmer, 217
David Harum, 138
Davies, Marion, 141
Davis, Bette, 84
"Dawn of a New Day" (Gershwin and Gershwin), 72
Dawn Patrol, The, 250
Day at the Races, A, 138, 197
Day the Bookies Wept, The, 138
"Day You Came Along, The," 194
Daylight, 243
Daytona 250 (auto racing), 143

DC-3, xviii, 249, *250*
De Mille, Cecil B., xviii, 198, 216, 245
Dead End, 28
Dead End Kids, 28
Dean, Dizzy, 134
DeBeck, Billy, *Barney Google*, 272
Decca record label, 175
Decorator's Digest, The, 66
Del Rio, Delores, 193
Dell Publishing, 274, 275
Deluxe Motor Courts, 237
"Democracity" (Dreyfuss), 73
Democratic Party, 176
Dentist, The, 195
department stores, 39, 66
Depression, 6–13; music and, 175–178;
    naming of, xii
Depression Glass, 68
Depression Years, The (Rothstein), 262
Des Moines Register and Tribune, 156
design. *See* architecture and design
Detective Comics, 31
Devil Dogs of the Air, 250
Diamond, "Legs," 188
Dick Tracy, xvi, 274
Dick Tracy (Gould), xvi, 268, 269, 270–
    271, 272, 274; marketing of, 271;
    movies, 271; radio serials, 271
Dietrich, Marlene, xv, 213
diets (*see also* food, American diet),
    82, 96
Dillinger, John, xvii, 270
Dimaggio, Joe, 134
diners, 110
Dionne quintuplets, xvii, 15
Dirigible, 245
dirigibles. *See* airships
disc jockeys, 181–182
Disney, Walt (*see also* Walt Disney
    Studios), xvi
Dix, Dorothy. *See* Gilmer, Elizabeth
    M.
Doc Savage, 31
documentary movies, 107
documentary photography (*see also*
    journalistic photography), xii, 261–
    262
Dodge City, 191

Dodsworth, 254
Don Winslow of the Navy, 30
Donald Duck, 130, 273
Doolittle, Jimmy, 248
Dos Passos, John, *USA*, 150
Dougherty, Dan, "There's No Depres-
    sion in Love," 176
Douglas aircraft, DC-3, xviii, 249, *250*
Downbeat, 175
Dr Pepper, 117
Dracula , xvi
Dracula, 199
Dracula's Daughter, 200
Dreyfuss, Henry: *20th Century Limited*,
    76; "Democracity," 73; telephone
    design of, 76
drink, 113–118; alcoholic beverages,
    113–116; coffee and tea, 117–118;
    soft drinks, 116–117
Drums Along the Mohawk (Edmonds),
    149
Drunkard, The, 195
Dubin, Al, "We're in the Money," 192
Duchin, Eddie, 172
Duck Soup, 197
Dumont, Allen B., 220–221
Dumont, Margaret, 196, 197
Dupree, Elmer, 121
Durbin, Deanna, 202
Dust Bowl, 7, 176, 231, 262
Dutch Shoe Mystery, The (Queen), 148
Dvorak, Ann, 241
Dyer, Bill, 135

Earhart, Amelia, xix, 32, 248, 249
Early American style, 65
"Easter Parade" (Berlin), 85
Eastman-Kodak, 77, 262
Easy Living, 198
Eat Drink and Be Wary, 38
Ebsen, Buddy, 228
Ed, Carl, *Harold Teen*, 31
Eddie Cantor, 47
Eddy, Nelson, 194
Edison Mazda (General Electric), 266
Edison record label, 173
editorial cartoons, 275–277

Edmonds, Walter D., *Drums Along the Mohawk*, 149
Edson, Gus, *The Gumps*, 268
education, 18
Edward VIII (king of England), xviii, 15–16
Egyptian Cross Mystery, The (Queen), 148
Eighteenth Amendment (Volstead Act), 113
8-pagers, 27
electric razors, 91
Elizabeth Arden, 87
Elizabeth, Princess, 92
Ella Cinders, 239
Ellington, Duke, 170, 172, 175, 178; "It Don't Mean a Thing (If It Ain't Got That Swing)," 169
"Embraceable You" (Gershwin and Gershwin), 178
Empire State Building, xv, 200, 250
Empire State Building (Shreve, Lamb & Harmon), 40, 59
employment (*see also* unemployment): during Depression, 11; and hours worked, 119; women's, 11
End of the Trail (Fraser), 264
Esquire, 27, 153, 157
Evans, Walker, *Let Us Now Praise Famous Men*, 262
Everygirls, 27
Everything Happens at Night, 167
Exposition Internationale des Arts Decoratifs et Industriels Modernes (Paris), 57
expositions. See architecture and design, fairs and expositions

fads, 120–124
Fair, A. A.. *See* Gardner, Erle Stanley
Fair Labor Standards Act (1938), 17
Fairbanks, Douglas, Jr., 250
Fairfax, Beatrice. *See* Manning, Marie
Fairyland, Tennessee, 139
Fala (Roosevelt's terrier), 4, 87
"Fallingwater." *See* Kaufmann House ("Fallingwater"), Bear Run, Pennsylvania (Wright)
Family Affair, A, 202

Family Circle, 153
Famous Funnies, 275
fan magazines, 83, 206
fantasy and horror movies, 199–201
F.A.O. Schwarz, 128
Farley, James A., 132
Farm Security Administration, xii
Farrell, Glenda, 251
Farrell, James T., *Studs Lonigan* trilogy, 150
fascism, 22, 204, 218, 226
fashion, 81–93; accessories, 87; children's, 92; fan magazines and, 83–84; hair, 88–89; men's, 89–91; movies and, xv, 83–84, 90–91; new products and, 101–102; personal grooming, 91–92; sportwear, 85–87; women's, 82–85
Fashions of 1934, 84
Fawcett Publications, 274
Federal Arts Project (FAP), xviii, 23, 42, 260–261
Federal Home Loan Bank Act (1932), 65
Federal Housing Act (1934), 65
Federal Music Project (FMP), 181
Federal Radio Commission, 218
Federal Rural Electrification Program, 136
Federal Theater Project (FTP), 226–227
Federal Trade Commission, 38
Federal Writers Project (FWP), 152
Felix the Cat (Sullivan), 273
Fetchit, Stepin, 141
Fibber McGee and Molly, xviii, 30, 47, 214
Fields, Dorothy, 178
Fields, Shep, 172
Fields, W. C., 195, 196, 254
Fiesta Ware, 68
Fighting Caravans, 191
Fireside Chats, xvii, 4, 5, 16, 164, 216–217, 218
First Nighter, 216
Fisher, Ham, *Joe Palooka*, 141, 269
Fisk Tires, 266
Fitch Shampoo, 47
five-and-dimes (stores), 42

Flanagan, Hallie, 226
Flash Gordon, 143, 207, 254
Flash Gordon (Raymond), 272, 274
"Flat Foot Floogie," 3
Fleischmann Hour, The, 210
Fleischmann's Yeast, 25
Fleming, Victor, 205, 206
Floyd, "Pretty Boy," xvii, 188
fluorescent lighting, 71
Fly-Away Baby, 251
Flying Down to Rio, 193, 228, 251
Flynn, Errol, 191, 250
Follow the Fleet, 194, 253
Fonda, Henry, 191, 204
food, 95–113; American diet, 97; ap-
    pliances for, 105–110; baby, 105;
    breakfast, 53–54; candy, 103; cost of,
    280; eating out, 110–113; frozen, 101–
    102, 108; prepackaged, 102–103;
    preparation of, 103–105; refrigera-
    tion, 105–108; stores for, 98–101
football, 136–137; movies and, 136–
    137
Football Thrills, 137
Footlight Parade, 192, 193
For the Love o' Lil, 267
For the Love of Pete, 142
Ford company, 52, 53, 72, 143, 221
Ford, Corey, 159
Ford, John, 191
Fortune, 153, 155, 157–158, 204
42nd Street, xiii, xvii, 192, 193, 244
Forum, 155
Foster, Hal, *Prince Valiant*, 31
4-H clubs , 24
Frankenstein, xvi, 199–200
Frankfort Distilleries, 265
Franklin, Ben, 151
Fraser, James Earle: *End of the Trail*,
    264; *George Washington*, 264
Freckles and His Friends (Blosser), 31
Fred Allen Show, The, xvi
Freed, Arthur, "You Are My Lucky
    Star," 165
Fremont Canning Company, 105
French Line, 252
Frigidaire, 107; pamphlets on, 108
Friml, Rudolph, 194

Fritos Corn Chips, 105
Front Page, The, 167
frozen foods, xv, 101–102, 108
Fugitive Lovers, 240
Fuller Brush Company, 10
Funnies on Parade, 275
Funnies, The, 275
furnishings, cost of, 280–281
"Futurama" (Kahn and Bel Geddes),
    72

"G" Men, 190
Gable, Clark, 90, 138, 141, 197–198,
    206, 225, 235, 252, 253
Gallant Fox (horse), 138
Gallico, Paul, 134
Gallup, George, 42
gambling, 124–126
games, 124–128
Gang Busters, 274
gangster movies, 114, 188
Gannett newspapers, 162
Garbo, Greta, xv, 85, 114
Gardner, Erle Stanley (pseud. A. A.
    Fair), 148; *Case of the Velvet Claws,
    The*, xvii
Garfield, 273
Garfield, John, 142
Gargantua, 230
Garland, Judy, 137, 202, 205
gas stations, 68–69
Gasoline Alley (King), 232
Gay Divorcee, The, 194
GE. *See* General Electric
Gehrig, Lou, xvi, 134
gender roles, teenagers and, 26
General Electric (GE), 52, 68, 87, 207,
    265, 266; Electric Sink, 108; pam-
    phlets, 108; refrigerators, 107; and
    television, 221
General Foods, 117
General Mills, 47, 48
General Motors company, 72
Gennett record label, 173
*George Burns and Gracie Allen Show,
    The*, 213
George Washington (Fraser), 264
George White's Scandals of 1931, 176

George White's Scandals of 1935, 228
"Georgia on My Mind" (Carmichael), 178
Gerber Baby Foods, 105
Gershwin, George, 178; "But Not for Me," 166; *Cuban Overture*, 180; "Dawn of a New Day," 72; "Embraceable You," 178; "I Got Rhythm," 224; *Rhapsody in Blue*, 180–181, 223–224; *Second Rhapsody*, 180; *Variations on I Got Rhythm*, 180
Gershwin, Ira, 178, 223–224; "But Not for Me," 166; "Dawn of a New Day," 72; "Embraceable You," 178; "I Got Plenty of Nothin'," 180; "I Got Rhythm," 224; "It Ain't Necessarily So," 180; "Summertime," 180
Ghoul, The, 200
Gibbons, Cedric: movie set design of, 76; "Oscar" design of, 77
Gibson, Hoot, 191
Gilbert and Sullivan, 227
Gilmer, Elizabeth M. (pseud. Dorothy Dix), 166
Girl Crazy, 224
Girl Scouts of America, 24; annual cookie sale of, 24
Glamour, 153
glass curtain walls, 67
God's Little Acre (Caldwell), 148, 149
Godwin, Frank, *Roy Powers, Eagle Scout*, 31
Gold Diggers of 1933, xvii, 192, 193
Gold Medal Flour, 48
Gold Star Mothers of Future Wars, 23
Golden Boy (movie), 225–226
Golden Boy (Odets), 142, 225
goldfish swallowing, xx, 33–34
golf, 138–140; miniature, xv, 139–140; traditional, xv, 138–139
Gone with the Wind (book) (Mitchell), xviii, xix, 3, 149
Gone with the Wind (movie), xx, 149, 206
Good Earth, The (Buck), xvi, 149
Good Housekeeping, 49–52, 53, 54, 55, 153, 265

Goodman, Benny, xvii, xix, 25, 170, 171, 172, 174–175, 177
Goodyear Tire and Rubber Company, 245
Goofy, 130
Gorcey, Leo, 28
Goren, Charles, 128
Gormey, Jay, "Brother, Can You Spare a Dime?," 176
Gosden, Freeman, 211–212
Gould, Chester: *Dick Tracy*, 268, 270–271
Gould, Chester, *Dick Tracy*, xvi
Gould, Morton, *Cresta Blanca Carnival*, 180
Grable, Betty, 138
Graham, Martha, 228
Grainger, Ralph, "Thanks for the Memory," 195
Grand Canyon Suite, The (Grofé), 181
Grand Central Rail Road, 243
Grand Slam (golf), xv, 139
Grand Slam (tennis), 138
Grand Union, 99
Graney, Jack, 135
Grant, Cary, 196, 198
Grape Nuts, 43, 54
Grapes of Wrath, The (Steinbeck), 149, 150–151, 231
Gray, Glen, 174
Gray, Harold, *Little Orphan Annie*, 268, 269–270
Great Depression. *See* Depression
Great Lakes Exposition (Cleveland, 1936), 71
Great Train Robbery, The, 191
Great Ziegfeld, The, 228
Green Hornet, The, 274
Green, Paul, *The Lost Colony*, 227
greenbelt towns, 64
Grey, Zane, 191
Greyhound Bus Lines, 70, 71, 240–241
grocery stores. *See* food, stores for
Grofé, Ferde, 180–181; *The Grand Canyon Suite*, 181
Guest, Edgar, 166
Gumps, The (Smith; Edson), 268, 274

Guthrie, Woody, "So Long, It's Been Good to Know Ya," 176
Guys and Dolls (Runyon), 9
Gypsy Rose Lee. *See* Hovick, Louise

hair fashions, 88–89
Hall, Huntz, 28
Hall, James Norman, *Mutiny on the Bounty*, 149
Hamilton Beach Company, 109
Hammond, John, 175
Hampton, Lionel, 175
"Happy Days Are Here Again" (Yellen and Ager), xiii, 176
Happy Landing, 142
Harburg, E. Y., 205; "Brother, Can You Spare a Dime?," 176
Hardy, Oliver, 207
Harlow, Jean, xv, 84, 89, 114, 167, 266
Harold Teen (Ed), 31
Harper's, 239
Harris, Phil, 214
Hart, Lorenz, 178, 223; "Little Girl Blue," 223; "My Funny Valentine," 223; "Ten Cents a Dance," 178, 223
Hart, Moss, 224
Harvard University, 33
Hauptmann, Bruno, xvii, xviii, 13–14
Havoc, June. *See* Hovick, June
Hawks, Frank "Meteor Man," 248
Hawks, Howard, 250
Hay, William, 96
Hays Code (*see also* Code restrictions [Hollywood]), 67
Hays Office. *See* Motion Picture Producers and Distributors of America
Hays, Will, 189
Hearst newspapers, 162
Hearst, William Randolph, 32
Heatter, Gabriel, 217
Hecht, Ben, 167
Hedda Hopper Show, The, 165
Heinz food company, 72, 96
Held, John, Jr., 81
Hell's Angels, 245, 250
Henderson, Fletcher, 171, 172
Henderson, Ray, "Life Is Just a Bowl of Cherries," 176

Henie, Sonja, 142, 167
Hepburn, Katharine, 84, 198
Herbert, Victor, 194
Here Is My Heart, 194
Herlihy, Ed, 47
Heroes for Sale, 189
Hershey's, 103
Heyward, Dorothy: "I Got Plenty of Nothin'," 180; "It Ain't Necessarily So," 180; "Summertime," 180
Heyward, DuBose: "I Got Plenty of Nothin'," 180; "It Ain't Necessarily So," 180; "Summertime," 180
Hiawatha, 243
Hindenburg, xix, 246
Hine, Lewis, 262
Hines, Duncan, 111–112; *Adventures in Good Eating*, 111
His Girl Friday, 167
Historical American Buildings Survey, The, 261
Hitchcock, Henry-Russell, 61
Hitler, Adolf, xviii, 144–145, 204, 276
HMV record label, 173
Hobbies, 131
hobbies, 32–33, 131–133; gardening, 131; jigsaw puzzles, 132; model airplane building, 32–33; stamp collecting, 32, 33, 132–133
"Hobby Lobby," 131–132
Hoey, Fred, 135
Hold 'em Jail, 137
Hold Everything, 141
Holden, William, 142, 225
Holgate building blocks, 130
Holiday, 198
Hollywood, 83, 158
Hollywood Hotel, 165
Hollywood studios (*see also under specific names*), 187
Holm, Hanya, 228
Holt, Jack, 191
Hoover, Herbert, xii, xvi, 4, 134, 216, 224; ridicule of, 123
Hoover, J. Edgar, 237
Hoover vacuum cleaners, 52
"Hooverette" dresses, 83
Hop Harrigan, 30

Hope, Bob, 47, 195, 254
Hopper, Edward, 259–260
Hopper, Hedda, 107, 165
Hormel food company, Spam, 104
horror movies. *See* fantasy and horror movies
Horse Feathers, 137, 197
horse racing, 138; movies and, 138
Hostess Twinkies, xvi, 102
Hot Mikado, The, 227
Hot Shoppes, 111
House and Garden, 66
House Beautiful, 153
"House of Tomorrow" (Keck), 65
House Un-American Activities Committee, 227
Hovick, June (pseud. June Havoc), 121
Hovick, Louise (pseud. Gypsy Rose Lee), 121
How to Always Be Well, 96
How to Win Friends and Influence People (Carnegie), xix, 151
Howard Johnson's, xix, 111
Howe, George, 61
huckster wagons, 99
Hudson company, 143
Hughes, Howard, xix, 245, 248, 250
Hughes Special, 248
Hummert, Anne, 215
Hummert, Frank, 215
Humphrey, Doris, 228
Hunt, Marshall, 134
Hupfield, Herman, "Are You Makin' Any Money?," 176
Husing, Ted, 135

I Am a Fugitive from a Chain Gang, 158–159, 189
"I Got Plenty of Nothin'" (Gershwin, Gershwin, Heyward, and Heyward), 180
"I Got Rhythm" (Gershwin and Gershwin), 224
ice-skating, 142–143; movies and, 142
Idiot's Delight (movie), 225
Idiot's Delight (Sherwood), 225

IGA (Independent Grocers' Alliance), 99
Île de France, 252
ILGWU. *See* International Ladies Garment Workers' Union
illustration, 264–268; in advertising, 52
"I'm Just a Vagabond Lover," 210
In Dubious Battle (Steinbeck), 150
"In the Mood," xx
Index of American Design, The, 261
"Indian Love Song," 194
Indianapolis 500 (auto racing), 143
Indianapolis Speedway, 143
Indians (travel trailer), 238
interior decoration, 66, 67–68
Interior Decorator, The, 66
Internal Revenue Service, 38
International Apple Shippers' Association, 8
International Harvester, 265
International Ladies Garment Workers' Union (ILGWU), 222
International Style, 60–62, 78; in gas stations, 69; and housing, 64; in PSFS building, 61
Interwoven Socks, 266
Invisible Man, The, xvii
"It Ain't Necessarily So" (Gershwin, Gershwin, Heyward, and Heyward), 180
It Can't Happen Here (Lewis), 226
"It Don't Mean a Thing (If It Ain't Got That Swing)" (Ellington), 169
It Happened One Night, xvii, 90, 197–198, 235, 240
It's a Gift, 195
It's in the Air, 250

Jack Armstrong, the All-American Boy, 29–30, 47, 274
Jack Benny Program, The, xvi, 47, 55, 213–214
Jack Straws, 126
James, Harry, 25, 172, 177
Japanese-made goods, 129
Jarvis, Al, 181
jazz music, 170

Jefferson Memorial (Pope), 60
Jell-O, 43, 47, 266
Jergens Journal, The, 165
Jesse James, 191
jigsaw puzzles, 132
Jimmie Allen Club, The, 32–33
jingles: advertising, 41, 46; on radio, 46
jitterbug, xix, 177
Jockey underwear, 90
"Joe Hill" (Robinson), 176
Joe Palooka (Fisher), 141, 269
Johnson, Philip, 61
Johnson Wax, 47
Johnson Wax offices (Wright), 64
jokes, knock-knock, 123–124
Jolly Green Giant, 48
Jones, Bobby, xv, 138–139
Jones, Buck, 143, 191
Jordan, Jim, 214
Jordan, Marian, 214
journalistic photography, 16, 163, 261–262
Journeyman (Caldwell), 148
Joy of Living, 198
Judge, 266
Judge Hardy's Children, 202
Judy Bolton, 32
jukeboxes, 182
Jumbo, 223
Junior Birdmen of America, 32
Just Imagine, 201–202, 206
Just Plain Bill, 215
juvenile delinquency, 27–28

Kahn, Albert, 72
Kallet, Arthur, 102–103
Kaltenborn, H. V., 217
Karloff, Boris, xvi, 199–200
Kaufmann House ("Fallingwater"), Bear Run, Pennsylvania (Wright), 62–64
Kay Tracey, 32
Kaye, Sammy, 172
Keck, George Fred, 65
Keeler, Ruby, 192–193, 228
Keene, Carolyn. *See* Benson, Mildred Wirt

Keep Punching, 142
Kellogg food company, 96
Kelly, "Machine Gun," 188
Kelly, Paul, 143
Kelly the Second, 141
Kelvinator, 107
Kemp, Hal, 172
Kentucky Blue Streak, 138
Kern, Jerome, 178
Kid Comes Back, The, 141
King Comics, 275
King, Frank, *Gasoline Alley*, 232
King Kong, xvii, 200, *201*, 230, 250–251
King Kullen Market, 99
King of the Jungle, 143
King, Wayne, 172
Kingsley, Sidney, 28
KitchenAid, 109
Knight, Clayton, *Ace Drummond*, 248–249
knock-knock jokes, 123–124
"Knock-Knock Song, The," 124
Kostelanetz, André, 180
Kozy Coaches (travel trailer), 238
Kraft Foods, 47, 103; macaroni and cheese, 105
Kraft Music Hall, The, 47
Krazy Kat, 273
Kresge's, 173
Kroger food stores, 99–100; as self-service supermarket, 101
Krystal, 111

labor, child. *See* child labor
labor unions, 5
Ladies' Home Journal, 27, 265, 266
Lady by Choice, 9
Lady for a Day, 9
Laides' Home Journal, 153
Lake, Arthur, 271
Lamour, Dorothy, 254
Landlord's Game, The, 128
Landon, Alf, xviii
Lange, Dorothea, 262
Lardner, Ring, 134
Lastex, 84, 86, 90
Laurel, Stan, 207
Lay's potato chips, 105

Lee, Manfred B. (pseud. Ellery Queen): *The Chinese Orange Mystery*, 148; *The Dutch Shoe Mystery*, 148; *The Egyptian Cross Mystery*, 148
Legion of Decency, 189
leisure activities, 119–145; cost of, 282; fads, 120–124; games, 124–128; hobbies, 131–133; sports, 133–145; toys, 128–131
LeRoy, Mervyn, 189
Lescaze, William, 61
Leslie's, 266
Let 'Em Eat Cake, 224
Let Us Now Praise Famous Men (Agee and Evans), 262
"Let Yourself Go," xviii
Let's Dance, xvii, 174
"Let's Face the Music and Dance," xviii
Lewis, Sinclair: *Dodsworth*, 254; *It Can't Happen Here*, 226
Libeled Lady, 167
Liberty, 157–159, 266, 267
Liberty Coaster Company, 128–129
Library of Congress, 261
Life, 49–51, 53, 54, 55, 64, 153, 155–156, 158, 204, 239, 262
Life Begins in College, 137
"Life Is Just a Bowl of Cherries" (Henderson and Brown), xvi, 176
Lifebuoy Soap, 43, 91
Li'l Abner (Capp), 269, 272
Lindbergh, Anne Morrow, xvi; *Listen! The Wind*, 247; *North to the Orient*, 247
Lindbergh, Charles, xvi, 13, *14*, 92, 247
Lindbergh kidnapping, xvi, xvii, xviii, 13–14
Lionel Corporation, 130
liquor. *See* alcoholic beverages
Listen! The Wind (Morrow), 247
Literary Digest, 153, 266
Literary Guild, 151
literature, 147–167; books, 147–152; magazines, 152–160; newspapers, 160–167
"Little Brown Jug," xx

Little Caesar, xv, 114, 188
"Little Girl Blue" (Rodgers and Hart), 223
Little Miss Marker, 203
Little Orphan Annie (Gray), 268, 269–270, 272, 273, 274; marketing of, 270; movies, 270; radio serial, xvi, 270
"Living Newspaper, The," 227
lodging: auto camps, 236; motels, 236–237; travel, 235–237
Loewy, Raymond, 77; *Broadway Limited*, 76; gas station designs of, 69; Greyhound bus designs of, 71; refrigerator design of, 77, 107
Lombard, Carole, 9, 244, 253
Lombardo, Guy, 172, 213
Lone Ranger, The, 30, 274
Long, Huey, 157
Long Island Rail Road, 71
Longines Symphonette, The, 180
Look, 153, 156
Lopez Orchestra, Vincent, 124
Lord & Taylor department store, 66
Lorenzo Jones, 215
Lorimer, George Horace, 154, 155
Lost Colony, The (Green), 227
Louis, Joe, xix, 141, 142
Love Finds Andy Hardy, 202
"Love for Sale" (Porter), 223
"Love Is Just Around the Corner," 194
Lowe, Edwin S., 124
Loy, Myrna, 207; and Asta, 87
Luce, Henry R., 155–156
Lucky Devils, 250
Lucky Strike cigarettes, 47, 56, 265; package design of, 77
Lugosi, Bela, xvi, 199, 200
Luisetti, Hank, 137
Lunceford, Jimmy, 172, 177
Lux Radio Theatre, xviii, 216

Ma Perkins, 215
MacArthur, Charles, 167
MacDonald, Jeanette, 194
Macfadden, Bernarr, 43, 157, 158
machine aesthetic, 58
MacKinlay, Kantor, 159

Macon, 245

Macy's department store, 66

Macy's Thanksgiving Parade, 221

Madam Satan, 245

"Made in Japan," 129

Mademoiselle, 153

Madison Square Garden, 137

magazines (*see also under specific titles*), 152–160; advertising in, 49–51; audience for, 152; confessional, 158–159; cost of, 282; fan, 83, 206; and fashion, 83–84; pulp, 31, 159–160; for youth, 26–27

Magnavox, 207

Maidenform bra company, 84

mail order businesses, 43

"Maine Stein Song, The," 210

Major Bowes and His Original Amateur Hour, xiii

malnutrition (*see also* nutrition), 95

Manning, Marie (pseud. Beatrice Fairfax), 166

Manning, Tom, 135

Manship, Paul, 263–264; *Prometheus*, 62, 264

marathons, dance. *See* dance marathons

March of Time, The, 47, 204

Margaret, Princess, 92

marketing, target, 157–158

Marlboro cigarettes, 55–56

Marokko, 126

Mars food company, 103

Marsh, Reginald, 260

Marshall Field department store, 66

Marx Brothers, xviii, 137, 138, 196–197

Marxism, 22, 150

Mary Worth's Family, 9

Massachusetts Institute of Technology (MIT), 34

Master Detective, 158

Master's Golf Tournament, 139

Max Factor, 87

Maxwell House, 117

Maybelline, 87

Maynard, Ken, 180, 191

Maytime, 194

MBS. *See* Mutual Broadcastng System

McCall's, 265

McCall's sewing pattern books, 83

McCarthy, Charlie, xix

McClure's, 155

McCoy, Horace, *They Shoot Horses, Don't They?*, 121

McCoy, Tim, 191

McCrea, Joel, 191

McDonald, Arch, 135

McHugh, Jimmy, 178

McIntyre, O. O., 165

McManus, George, *Bringing Up Father*, 268

medical costs, 281

Menzies, William Cameron, 251, 253

Mercury , 243

Mercury Theatre on the Air, 219

Meredith, Burgess, 225

Merman, Ethel, 176, 224

Messmer, Otto, *Felix the Cat*, 273

Metro-Goldwyn-Mayer (MGM), 76, 144, 165, 202, 205, 206, 245, 253

Metronome, 175

Mickey Mouse, xvi, 3, 129–130, 273

Mickey's Stampede, 136

Midsummer Night's Dream, A, 274

Miller, Ann, 228

Miller, Frank, *Barney Baxter in the Air*, 249

Miller, Glenn, xx, 172

miniature golf, xv, 139–140

Minnesota Valley Canning Company, 48

Minnie Mouse, 130, 273

Miracle Whip, 47

MIT. *See* Massachusetts Institute of Technology

Mitchell, Margaret, *Gone with the Wind*, xviii, xix, 149, *150*, 206

Mitchell, Thomas, 191

Mix, Tom, 191, 275

Mixmaster, 109

Mobilgas, 69

Moby Dick (Melville), 274

model airplane building, 32–33

Model Airplane Club of the Air, 32

Modern Marriage, 158

Modern Screen, 83, 158

Moderne. *See* Streamline Moderne
modernism: in advertising, 41–42, 44; in appliance design, 77; in architecture, 57–58, 59; in art, 257; and housing, 65; in Kaufmann House, 63; in movie set design, 76, 205–206; in nightclubs, 67; 1932 exhibition of, 61
Monkey Business, 197
Monopoly, xviii, 128
Montgomery, Robert, 240–241
Montgomery Ward department store, 239
Moon Mullins (Willard), 269
Morrison, Herb, 246–247
Mosley, Zack, *Smilin' Jack*, 30, 249
motels, 236–237
Motion Picture, 158
Motion Picture Producers and Distributors of America ("Hays Office") (*see also* Code restrictions [Hollywood]), 189
Mount Rushmore, 263
movie cameras, 262
Movie Classic, 158
Movie Mirror, 83
movies (*see also under specific titles*), xii–xiii, 185–207; admission attractions at, 68, 186; admission prices of, 186, 282; for adolescents, 202–203; advertising and, 44; architecture and, 66–67; auto racing and, 143; and aviation, 249–252; "B" movies, 186, 191; baseball and, 135; boxing and, 141–142; censorship of, 188–189; child actors in, 203–204; comedies, 195–199; compared to comic strips, 269; "Dish Night," 68; documentary, 107; family and, 11; fantasy and horror, 199–201; and fashion, xv, 83–84, 90–91; football and, 136–137; gangster movies, 188; home, 262; horse racing and, 138; ice-skating and, 142; law enforcement and, 190; musicals, 192–195; newsreels, 204–205; and ocean liners, 252–254; and radio, 29, 216; science fiction, 201–202; screwball comedies, xvii, 197–

199; serials, 29, 207; set design for, 67, 76, 253; special effects in, 200, 245, 251; technical advances of, 187–188; and theater, 226; and trains, 244; Westerns, 190–191; and youth, 27–28
Moxie, 117
Mr. Deeds Goes to Town, 198
Mr. Smith Goes to Washington, 198
Mummy, The, 200
murals, xviii, 260, 261
Murray, Ken, 174
Murrow, Edward R., xx, 217
Museum of Modern Art, New York, 61
music, 169–183; audience for, 179–180; classical, xix, 180–181; and Depression, 175–178; jazz, 170; recordings of, 173, 175; sheet, 173; sweet, 172–173; swing, 169–170, 171–173, 174–175; swing dancing/music, xix
Music for Radio (Prairie Journal) (Copland), 181
musicals: in movies, 192–195; in theater, 222–224
Mutiny on the Bounty (Nordhoff and Hall), 149
Mutual Broadcastng System (MBS), 166, 209
Muzak, 182
"My Funny Valentine" (Rodgers and Hart), 223
My Man Godfrey, 198
Mydans, Carl, 262

NAACP. *See* National Association for the Advancement of Colored People
Nabisco Ritz Crackers, 105
Nancy Drew and the Hidden Staircase, 32
Nancy Drew, Detective, 32
Nancy Drew mysteries, 31–32
Nancy Drew, Reporter, 32
Nancy Drew, Troubleshooter, 32
Nast, Thomas, 276
National Air Races, 248
National Association for the Advance-

ment of Colored People (NAACP), 212

National Basketball Association (NBA), 137

National Basketball League (NBL), 137

National Broadcasting Company. *See* NBC

National Gallery of Art (Pope), 60

National Invitational Tournament (NIT), 137

National Recovery Administration (NRA), xvii, 11, *12*, 13, 119

National Socialist party. *See* Nazism

National Tom Thumb Open Championship (miniature golf), 139

National Trailways, 240

National Youth Administration (NYA), 21, *22*, 136

nationalism, and *Little Orphan Annie*, 269–270

Naughty Marietta, 194

Navy, U.S., 245, *246*

Nazism, 22, 144, 204

NBC: radio network, xviii, xix, 32, 135–136, 174, 182, 209, 210, 211, 213, 220, 246, 270; television network, 220, 221

NBC Symphony Orchestra, xix

near beer, 114

needle beer, 114

Nelson, "Baby Face," xvii, 188

Nestle's food company, 103

networks, radio (*see also* CBS; Mutual Broadcastng System; NBC)

New Americana, 176

New Faces of 1937, 228

New York Daily News, 157

New York Evening Graphic, 158

New York Table Tennis Association, 126

New York World's Fair (1939), xi, xx, 71–74, 77, 143, 177, 181, 206, 221, 227, 264; time capsule from, 3

New Yorkers, The, 223

news, radio, 216

newspapers, 160–167; advertising in, 162; chain ownership of, 161–162;

columnists for, 164–166; cost of, 282; decline of, 162–163; photography and, 163; radio and, 163; reporting for, 166–167; syndication and, 164

newsreels, 204–205

Newsweek, 153, 158

Nick Carter, 159

Nielsen, A. C., 42

Night After Night, 196

Night at the Opera, A, xviii, 197

night baseball, xviii, 134

Niven, David, 250

Nordhoff, Charles, *Mutiny on the Bounty*, 149

Normandie, 252

Norris, Kathleen, 159

North American Review, The, 153, 155

North to the Orient (Morrow), 247

Northwest Passage (Roberts), 149

Nothing Sacred, 167

Novachords, 181

Now and Forever, 203

Nowlan, Phil, *Buck Rogers*, 272

NRA. *See* National Recovery Administration

nutrition (*see also* malnutrition), 96, 102–103

NYA. *See* National Youth Administration

nylon stockings, xx

O'Brien, Pat, 143, 251

ocean liners, 252–254

Odets, Clifford: *Awake and Sing!*, 225; *Golden Boy*, 142, 225; *Paradise Lost*, 225; *Rocket to the Moon*, 225; *Till the Day I Die*, 225; *Waiting for Lefty*, 225

Of Mice and Men (Copland), 181

Of Thee I Sing, 224

Okeh record label, 173

Oland, Warner, 190

Old-Fashioned Way, The, 195

Oliver, Sy, "Tain't Wha'cha Do (It's the Way That You Do It)," 177

Olympics, 142; 1932 Winter, xvi, 142; 1936 Summer, xviii, 144–145

Omaha (horse), 138

On Your Toes, 180

100,000,000 Guinea Pigs, 102–103
One in a Million, 142
One Man's Family, 215
One-Third of a Nation, 227
opera, xviii, 180, 224
Orange Bowl (football), 136
Orange Crush, 266
organs, electronic, 181
Orr, Martha, *Apple Mary*, 9
"Oscar" (Academy Award statuette) (Gibbons), 77
Our Gal Sunday, 215
Our Gang, 207
Out West with the Hardys, 202
Ovaltine, 30, 47, 54, 270
Overland automobiles, 266
Owens, Jesse, xviii, *144*, 145
Oxford Pledge Movement, 22

Pabst Blue Ribbon Beer, 47
Pack Up Your Troubles, 203
Packard company, 143
Page, Dorothy, 191
Page, Ruth, 228
painting (*see also under specific works*): realism in, 259–260; Regionalism in, 258–259
paperback books, 148
Paradise Lost (Odets), 225
Paramount on Parade, 187
Paramount record label, 173
Parents, 27
Parker Brothers company, 126, 128
parking meters, 233–234
Parsons, Louella, 165
Partners in Plunder, 38
Paul Jones whiskey, 265
Peanuts, 273
Pearson, Drew, 165
Pennies from Heaven, 171
Pennsylvania Railroad, 76, 243
Pep, 54
Pepper Young's Family, 215
Pepsi-Cola, 47, 116–117
Pepsodent, 47, 211
Pepsodent Show Starring Bob Hope, The, 47
Perfect record label, 173

Perry Mason, xvii, 148–149
personal items, cost of, 281
Phantom Empire, The, 180
Philadelphia Savings Fund Society (PSFS) (Howe and Lescaze), 61
philately. *See* stamp collecting
Philco electronics company, 207
Philip Morris cigarettes, 56, 181
Phillips oil company, 68
photography: in advertising, 52; documentary, xii, 261–262; journalistic, 16, 163, 261–262; movie cameras, 262; and newspapers, 163
photojournalism. *See* journalistic photography
Photoplay, 83, 158
Physical Culture, 157
Pick-Up Sticks, 126
"Pick Yourself Up," xviii
Piggly Wiggly, as self-service supermarket, 99, 100–101
Pigskin Parade, 137
Pigskin Skill, 137
pinball, 126
ping-pong, 126
Pins and Needles, 222–223
Pioneer Zephyr, 69–70
Pitkin, Walter B., 151
Plainsman, The, 191
planned obsolescence, 75–76
Planter's peanuts, 25
Platinum Blonde, 114, 167
Playskool Manufacturing Company, 130
Pluto, 130
Plymouth atutomobiles, 52
Pocket Books, 148
Polglase, Van Nest, 194
Police Call, 141
Pop-Up Books, 274
Pope, John Russell, 60
Popeye (*Thimble Theater*) (Segar), 268
Popular Comics, 275
Popular Mechanics, 236, 239
Popular Photography, 153
Popular Practice of Fraud, The, 38
Popular Science, 266
Porgy and Bess, xviii, 180, 224

Porter, Cole, 178, 223, 253; "Begin the Beguine," xviii; "Love for Sale," 223; "What Is This Thing Called Love?," 178
Porter, Edwin S., 191
Post, Emily, 166
Post food company, 96
Post, Wiley, 92, 247, 249
postage, cost of, 282
Postum, 25
Powell, Dick, 192, 241
Powell, Eleanor, 228, 253
Powell, William, 84, 207; and Asta, 87
Power, 227
Power, Tyrone, 191
Prince Valiant (Foster), 31
Princess Comes Across, The, 253
Pro Football, 137
Proctor Company (later Proctor-Silex), 109
product costs, 279–282; clothing, 280; entertainment and leisure, 282; food, 280; medical costs, 281; personal items, 281; shelter and furnishings, 280–281; transportation, 281
Production Code Administration ("Breen Office") (*see also* Code restrictions [Hollywood]), 189, 193, 196
Prohibition, xvi, 52, 67, 113–115, 182, 270
Prometheus (Manship), 62, 264
PSFS bulding. *See* Philadelphia Savings Fund Society (PSFS) (Howe and Lescaze)
public assistance, 18; *Little Orphan Annie* and, 269–270
Public Enemy, 114, 188
public transportation, 239–241
Public Works Administration (PWA), 64
Public Works of Art Project, 260
Publishers' Syndicate, 9
Pullman Company, 76
pulp magazines, 159–160; and youth, 31

punchboards, 124–125
Pure Food and Drugs Act (1938), 103
Pure Food, Drug, and Cosmetic Act (1938), 38
Pure oil company, 68
"Puttin' on the Ritz," 225
PWA. *See* Public Works Administration (PWA)

Queen, Ellery. *See* Dannay, Frederic; Lee, Manfred B.
Queen Mary, 252, 254
quintuplets, Dionne, xvii, 15

Racing Strain, The, 143
Rackety Rax, 137
radio (*see also under specific titles*), 207–219; advertising on, 46–48, 162, 208, 209; announcers on, 47–48; baseball and, 134–135; boxing and, 141; comedies, 211–214; cost of, 282; drama, 216; family and, 11; and movies, 29, 216; news, 216; newspapers and, 163; receiver design, 207, *208*; serials, xvi, 29, 30, 31; soap operas, 214–216, 239; sound effects on, 214; on trains, 242; variety shows, 209–210; and youth, 28–31, 32–33
Radio City Music Hall, xvi, 62, 221
Radio Corporation of America, 220
Radio Flyer (American Flyer) wagon, 128–129
Radio Steel and Manufacturing, 129
Raft, George, 196
Ragú, 105
Ralston, 30
Rand, Sally, 71, 72
Rathbone, Basil, 250
Raye, Martha, 254
Raymond, Alex, *Flash Gordon*, 272
razors, electric, 91
RCA, 207, 220, 221
RCA Victor. *See* Victor record label
Reaching for the Moon, 253
Reader's Digest, 151, 153, 154–155
ready-to-wear clothing, 82
Ready, Willing, and Able, 193

Reagan, Ronald "Dutch," 135
realism, in painting, 259–260
records (music), 173, 175
Red Cross, 266
Redbook, 153, 159, 265
refrigerators, 105–108
Regionalism, in painting, 258–259
Reid, Wallace, 143
reinforced concrete, 67
"Remember My Forgotten Man," 192
Remington firearms, 26
rent, cost of, 280
Repeal (of Prohibition), xvi, 113–115, 116, 182
restaurants, 110–112
Revlon, 87
Rhapsody in Blue (Gershwin), 180
Rice, Elmer, 227
Rice, Grantland, 134
Rickenbacker, Eddie, 249
Ride 'Em Cowboy!, 143
Riders of the Purple Sage, 191
Rinehart, Mary Roberts, 159
Ringling Brothers and Barnum & Bailey circus, 229, 230
Rinso, 43
Ritter, Tex, 191
Ritz Brothers, 137, 138
RKO Pictures, 200, 225, 254
roads, automobile, 232–233
Robber's Roost, 191
Robert Burns Panatela Program, The, 213
Roberta, 194
Roberts, Kenneth, *Northwest Passage*, 149
Robin, Leo, 178; "Thanks for the Memory," 195
Robinson, Earl: "Abe Lincoln," 176; "Ballad for Americans," 176–177; "Joe Hill," 176
Robinson, Edward G., xv, 114, 190, 204–205
Robson, May, 9
Rochester, 55
Rockefeller Center (Reinhard and Hofmeister; Corbett, Harrison and

MacMurray; Hood and Fouilhoux), xvi, 62, 264
Rockefeller, John D., 224
Rocket to the Moon (Odets), 225
Rockne, Knute, 136
Rockwell, Norman, 43–44, 153, 158, 265–267, 267–268
Rodgers, Richard, 178, 223; "Little Girl Blue," 223; "My Funny Valentine," 223; *Slaughter on Tenth Avenue*, 180; "Ten Cents a Dance," 178, 223
Rogers, Ginger, xviii, 67, 192, 193–194, 202, 228, 251, 253, 254
Rogers, Roy, 191
Rogers, Will, xii, 138, 166, 275
Roller Derby, 121
roller-skating, 121
Roman, Charles, 43
Romance, 85
Romance of Helen Trent, The, 215
Romberg, Sigmund, 194
Rooney, Mickey, xix, 33, 202, 229
Roosevelt, Eleanor, 4, 158, 166, 203
Roosevelt, Franklin D., 4–6, 216–217; assassination attempt on, 4; editorial cartoons on, 276; and Fala, 4, 87; Fireside Chats, xvii, 4, 5, 16, 164, 216–217, 218; and "Happy Days Are Here Again," 176; and housing financing, 64; Lorimer and, 154; Macfadden and, 157; national conditions on inauguration of, xvii; and "new deal" campaign, xvi; newspapers and, 164–165; and public assistance, 18; satire of, 224; and softball, 136; and stamp collecting, 32, 132; as stamp designer, 15; and television, 221; trailer campaign for, 239
Rose, Billy, 72, 143
Rose Bowl, 137
Rose Marie, 194
Ross, Shirley, 195
Rothstein, Arthur, *The Depression Years*, 262
rotogravure, 85
Roventini, Johnny, 56

Roy Powers, Eagle Scout (Godwin), 31
Royal Gelatin Hour, The, 210
runaways, 19
Runyon, Damon, 159; *Guys and Dolls*,
    9
rural areas: as depicted in advertising,
    51; Depression hardships of, 7
Ruth, Babe, xvi, 134

Saalfield Publishing Company, 274
Sabatini, Raphael, 159
Sacco-Venzetti case, 225
Sadie Hawkins Day, 272
Safeway food stores, 99
Salon Mexico, El (Copland), 181
San Francisco-Golden Gate Interna-
    tional Exposition (1939), 71
Sandburg, Carl, 69
Sanka, 117
Santa Claus, 267–268
Santa Fe Rail Road, 243
Saraka (laxative), 72
Sarnoff, David, 220
Saturday Evening Post, 49–51, 53, 54,
    55, 153, 153–154, 155, 157, 159, 239,
    240, 265, 266, 267
Saturday Night Swing Session, 174
Scarface, 188
Schick Corporation, 91
Schlink, F. J., 102–103
Schmeling, Max, xix, 141
science fiction: in comic strips, 272; in
    movies, 201–202
Scorchy Smith, 249
Screen Romances, 158, 165
Screenland, 83, 158
screwball comedies, xvii, 197–199
Scribner's (*The Century*), 153
Scripps-Howard newspapers, 162
sculpture (*see also under specific works*),
    262–264
Sears, Roebuck and Company, 68, 77;
    catalog, 3; refrigerators, 107; and
    sewing supplies, 83
Second Fiddle, 142
Second Rhapsody (Gershwin), 180
Securities and Exchange Commission,
    38

Segar, Elzie, 268; *Popeye*, 268
segregation, 171
self-service supermarkets, 39, 100–101
Sells-Floto circus, 229
Selznick, David O., 206
serials: movie, 143, 207; radio, 29, 30,
    31
70,000 Witnesses , 137
7-Up , 117
sexuality, youth and, 27
Shadow, The, 31
Shall We Dance?, 194, 254
Shape of Things to Come, The, 251
Sharkey, Jack, 141
Shaw, Artie, xviii, 172
She Done Him Wrong, 196
Shearer, Norma, 225
Sheeler, Charles, 259–260
sheet music, 173
Shell oil company, 69
Shelley, Mary, "Frankenstein," 199
Sheridan, Ann, 143
Sherman, Arthur, 238
Sherman Covered Wagon (travel
    trailer), 238
Sherwood, Robert, *Idiot's Delight*, 225
shopping centers, 233
Shreve, Lamb & Harmon, 59
Shriek in the Night, 167
"Shuffle Off to Buffalo," 244
Shuster, Joe, *Superman*, 275
Siciliano, Charles. *See* Atlas, Charles
Siegel, Jerry, *Superman*, 275
Silver Domes (travel trailer), 238
Silver Screen, 83, 158, 165
Silver Streak, The, 244
Simple Simon, 223
Simpson, Wallis Warfield, xviii, 16
Sinatra, Frank, xix, 25, 177
"Sing Me a Song of Social Signifi-
    cance," 223
singing commercials, 46
singing cowboys, 180, 191
Singing Cowgirl, The, 191
Singleton, Penny, 271
situation comedy, 214
6 Day Bike Rider, 121
skiing, xvi, 142

Skin Deep, 38
Sky Devils, 250
Sky King, 30
Skyscraper Wilderness, 241
skyscrapers, xv, 59; as design motif, 78
slang, 25–26
Slaughter on Tenth Avenue (Rodgers), 180
Smackout—The Crossroads of the Air, 214
Smart Set, The, 153
Smilin' Jack (Mosley), 30, 249
Smith, Dorothy Hope, 105
Smith, Kate, xvi
Smith, Pete: "Oddities," 137, 144; "Specialties," 137
Smith, Red, 134
Smith, Sydney, *The Gumps*, 268
smoking, advertising and, 55–56
Snickers candy bars, xvi
Snow White, xix, 207
"So Long, It's Been Good to Know Ya" (Guthrie), 176
soap operas, 214–216, 239
Society Girl, 141
soft drinks, 116–117
softball, 135–136
Sokoloff, Nikolai, 181
soldiers, toy, 130
Some Like It Hot, 195
Son of Kong, 200–201
songwriting, 178–179
Sothern, Ann, 84
sound effects, on radio, 214
Southern Pacific Railroad, *243*
Spalding sporting goods company, 139
Spam, 104–105
Spanish Civil War, 204
Sparks circus, 229
special effects (movies), 200, 245, 251
Speed Devils, 143
Spicy Detective, 27
Spider, The, 159
Spirit of Notre Dame, The, 136
Spirit of Youth, 142
Split-Coaches (travel trailer), 238
Sporting Blood, 138

Sporting News, The, 134
sports, 133–145; auto racing, 143; baseball, 133–135; basketball, 137; bowling, 143–144; boxing, xix, 140–142; football, 136–137; golf, 138–140; horse racing, 138; ice-skating, 142–143; skiing, xvi, 142; softball, 135–136; swimming, 143; television and, 133; tennis, 138
sportwear, 85–87
square dancing, 261
Stagecoach, 191
stamp collecting, 32, *33*, 132–133, 245–246
Stand Up and Cheer, 203
Stanford University, 137
Stanwyck, Barbara, 84
Steamboat Willie, 130
Steele, Bob, 191
Steele, Dudley, 33
Steinbeck, John: *In Dubious Battle*, 150; *The Grapes of Wrath*, 149, 150–151, 231
Stella Dallas, 215
stereotyping: of blacks, 54–55, 141, 211–212; gender, 215; of Italians, 197; in screwball comedies, 198
stewardesses, xv
Stone, Lewis, 202
Story of Vernon and Irene Castle, The, 194
Stout, Wesley W., 154
Straight, Place and Show, 138
Strand, Paul, 262
Stratemeyer Syndicate, 32
Streak-O-Lite wagon, 129
Streamline Moderne, 62, 78; in appliance design, 77, 107, 109, 254; in architecture, 57–58; in automobile design, xvii, 75, 129; Bel Geddes and, 74; in *Flash Gordon*, 272; in interior decoration, 67, 68; in Johnson Wax offices, 64; meaning of, 76; in movie set design, 76, 244; in musicals, 193; at New York World's Fair, 72, 73; on ocean liners, 253; in science fiction movies, 202; in train

design, 243; in "The Wizard of Oz,"
205
Strike Up the Band, 224
Striker, Fran, 30
Strikes and Spares, 144
Studebaker company, 143
Studs Lonigan trilogy (Farrell), 150
subsistence homesteads, 64
Sugar Bowl (football), 136
Sullivan, Pat, *Felix the Cat*, 273
"Summertime" (Gershwin, Gershwin,
Heyward, and Heyward), 180
Sun Bowl (football), 136
Sun-Maid Raisins, 266
Sunbeam Corporation, Mixmaster, 109
Sunday Drive, 234–235
Sundblom, Haddon, 267–268
"Sunrise Serenade," xx
suntans, 87
Super Chief, 243
Super Comics, 275
Superman, xix, 31
Superman (Siegel and Shuster), 275
supermarkets, 99–100; self-service, 39
Susan and God, 221
sweepstakes, 125
sweet music, 172–173
Sweet Music, 244
Sweethearts, 194
swimming, 143
swing dancing/music, xix, 25, 169–
170, 171–173, 174–175, 227, 228;
youth and, 177–178
Swing Mikado, The, 227
Swing, Raymond Gram, 217
Swing Time, 67
Swingtime, 194
syndication, of news, 164

table tennis, 126
Tailspin Tommy, 249
"Tain't Wha'cha Do (It's the Way
That You Do It)" (Oliver and
Young), 177
Taking the Count, 142
tank glass, 68
target marketing, 157–158
Tarzan (comic strip), 274

Tarzan movies, 72, 90, 143, 207; *Tarzan
and His Mate*, 143; *Tarzan the Ape
Man*, 90, 143; *Tarzan the Fearless*, 143
Taxi!, 241
taxis, 241
Taylor, Robert, 266
tea, 117–118
Teague, Walter Dorwin: Baby
Brownie camera casing design of,
77; gas station designs of, 69; and
New York World's Fair, 77
tearooms, 112–113
Technicolor, 187, 205
teenagers, xix, 17, 24–26; advertising
and, 25; comic strips and, 31; culture of, 25–26; and dating, 26; gender roles and, 26; as life stage, 17,
24, 28; and movies, 202–203; slang
of, 25–26
telephone call, cost of, 282
television, xx, 220–222; baseball and,
221; naming of, 220; sports and, 133;
television sets, 221
Temple, Shirley, xvi, 33, 84, 92, 203–
204, 229–230, 274; marketing of, 203
"Ten Cents a Dance" (Rodgers and
Hart), 178, 223
tennis, 138
terriers, 87
Terry and the Pirates (Caniff), 31
Test Pilot, 252
Texaco oil company, 69
Texas Centennial Exposition (Dallas,
1936), 71
Texas Christian University, 136
Texas swing music, 179
Thanks a Million, 241
Thanks for the Memory, 195
"Thanks for the Memory" (Robin and
Grainger), 195
That Certain Age, 203
"That Silver-Haired Daddy of Mine,"
180
That's My Boy, 137
The Camel Caravan, 174
"The Music Goes 'Round and
'Round" (Hodgson/Farley & Riley),
182

theater (*see also under specific titles*),
222–227; audience for, 222; drama,
225–226; Federal Theater Project,
226–227; and movies, 226; musicals,
222–224
"There's No Depression in Love"
(Dougherty/Yellen), 176
They Made Me a Criminal, 142
They Shoot Horses, Don't They? (Mc-
Coy), 121
Thin Ice, 142
Thin Man movies, 87, 207
Things to Come, 251
Thirteenth Man, The, 167
This Is the Life, 203
Thomas, Lowell, 217
Thompson Trophy (aerial racing), 248
Thoroughbreds Don't Cry, 202
Thrasher, Leslie, 267
Three Little Pigs, xvii, 66
Three Little Pigs (Disney characters),
130
Three Smart Girls, 202
Three Stooges, 241
3.2 beer, 115
Three Women, 107
Thrilling Detective, 159
Tijuana Bibles, 27
Tilden, "Big Bill," 138
Till the Day I Die (Odets), 225
Tillie and Gus, 195
Tillie the Toiler (Westover), 269
Time, 47, 153, 155, 158, 204, 230, 239,
259
Tip Top Comics, 275
Tobacco Road (Caldwell), 148
Toddle House, 111
Toler, Sidney, 190
Tom Mix, 30
Too Hot to Handle, 167
Too Much Harmony, 194
Top Hat, 194
top ten song charts, xviii, 182
Torchy Blaine movies, 251–252
Toscanini, Arturo, xix
tour packages, 240
toys, 128–131; homemade, 130; sol-
diers, 130

Tracy, Spencer, 141, 241, 252
trademarks, 48
Trail of the Lonesome Pine, The, 191
trailer camps, 239
trailers, travel. *See* travel trailers
trains: and air-conditioning, 242; movies and, 244; and radio, 242; travel
by, 241–244
Transatlantic, 253
Transatlantic Merry-Go-Round, 253
transportation, cost of, 281
travel, 231–255; by air, xv, xviii, 244–
252; automobile, 232–239; bus, 239–
241; lodging, 235–237; ocean, 252–
254; public transportation, 239–241;
taxis, 241; tour packages, 240; train,
241–244; travel trailers, 237–239
travel trailers, 237–239; camps for, 239
TraveLodge, 237
Treasure Island (Stevenson), 274
Trevor, Claire, 191
Triple-A Plowed Under, 227
Triple Crown (horse racing), 138
True Detective Mysteries, 158, 159
True Experiences, 158
True Ghost Stories, 158
True Lovers, 158
True Romances, 158
True Story, 157
tubular steel, chromed, 67
Turner, Roscoe, 92, 247, 248, 249
Twentieth Century, 244
20th Century Limited, 76
Twenty-first Amendment, xvi, 113
Two Minutes to Play, 137

Uncle Ben, 54
unemployment (*see also* employment),
xv, xvi, xvii, xviii, xix, xx, 6; and
leisure, 119; and youth, 17–19
Union oil company, 69
Union Pacific Railroad, 142, 243; *City
of Salina*, 69
Union Party, 218
unions, labor, 5
United Airlines, xv
United Artists, 204
United Motor Courts, 237

United Press (U.P.), 164
United States Rubber Company, 84
Universal Studios, 199
universities, 18
urban areas: as depicted in advertising, 51; Depression hardships of, 8–11
U.S. Camera, 153
U.S. Navy, 245, *246*
U.S. News & World Report, 153, 158
U.S. Post Office Department, 38
U.S. Table Tennis Association, 126
USA (Dos Passos), 150
Usonian houses (Wright), 64

Vagabonds (travel trailer), 238
Vallee, Rudy, xii, 177, 209–210, 244
Van Alen, William, 59
Van Voorhis, Westbrook, 47
Vanity Fair, 153
Variations on I Got Rhythm (Gershwin), 180
variety shows, on radio, 209–210
Varipupa, Andy, 144
Vassar College, 226
vaudeville, 209–210
Veterans of Future Wars, 22–23
Victor record label (RCA Victor), 171, 173, 175
vigilantism, *Dick Tracy* and, 271
visual arts, 257–277; cartoons, 268–277; illustration, 264–268; painting, 258–260; photography, 261–262; sculpture, 262–264
Vitaglass, 67
vitamins, 96
Vitriolite, 67
Vocalion record label, 173
Vogue, 77, 82, 153
Voice of Firestone, The, 180
Volstead Act, 114
Volstead Act (Eighteenth Amendment), 113
Von Zell, Harry, 47

wagons, 128–129
Waiting for Lefty (Odets), 225
Wallace, DeWitt, 154, 155

Wallace, Lila, 154, 155
Waller, Fats, 169
Walt Disney Studios, xix, 66, 129–130, 207; cartoon characters, 68, 130, 272–273, 274
Wanamaker's department store, 66, 128
war (*see also* World War II), 22–23
War Admiral (horse), 138
War of the Worlds, The, xix, 219
Waring Blendor, 109–110
Waring, Fred, 109–110, 172
Warner Brothers studio, 192, 204, 206, 230, 251
Warners bra company, 84
Warren, Harry, 192; "We're in the Money," 178
Washington, George, 133
"Washington Merry-Go-Round," 165–166
Washington Redskins, 136
Water Rustlers, 191
"Way You Look Tonight, The," xviii
Wayne, John, 191
Weavers (singing group), 176
Webb, Chick, 172, 177
Weber, Rex, 176
Weidman, Charles, 228
Weissmuller, Johnny, 72, 90, 143, 207
Welch's food company, 103
Welles, Orson, xix, 219
Wellman, William, 189
Wells Fargo, 191
Wells, H. G., 251; *The War of the Worlds*, xix, 219
"We're in the Money" (Warren/Dubin), xiii, 192
West, Mae, 195–196
western swing music, 179
Westerns (movies), 190–191
Westinghouse, 3, 77, 221; pamphlets, 108
Westover, Russ, *Tillie the Toiler*, 269
Whale, James, 199–200
"What Is This Thing Called Love?" (Porter), 178
Wheaties, 30, 47, 54

When a Girl Marries, 215
"When the Moon Comes Over the Mountain," xvi
"Where the Blue of the Night Meets the Gold of the Day," xvi
"Whiffenpoof Song, The," 210
White Castle, 111
White House Purgers (softball team), 136
White Tower, 111
White Zombie, The, 200
Whiteman, Paul, 170, 180, 241
Whitman Publishing Company, 274
"Who's Afraid of the Big Bad Wolf?," xiii, xvii
Wigwam Village, 237
Wilcox, Harlow, 47
Wilder, Alec, 178
Willard, Frank, *Moon Mullins*, 269
Willis, Edwin B., 205
Wills, Bob, 179
Wilson, Don, 47, 214
Wilson, Teddy, 175
Winchell, Walter, 165, 217
Windsor: duchess of, xviii, 16; duke of, xviii, 15–16
Wine, Women and Horses, 138
Wings in the Dark, 250
Wings of the Navy, 252
Winner Take All, 141
Winnie Mae, 247
Winter Carnival, 142
Winterset (Anderson), 225
Withers, Jane, 203, 275
Wizard of Oz, 69, 202, 205–206
Wodehouse, P. G., 159
Woman's Day, 153, 160, 265
Woman's Home Companion, 266
women (*see also* gender roles): alcoholic beverages and, 115; as consumers in advertising, 51; and diets, 82; employment of, 11; excluded from CCC, 19; and fashion, 82–85; soap operas and, 214–215; time for activities of, 104; vocational training for, 22

Wonder Bread, 43
Wonder Stories, 159
Wood, Grant: *American Gothic*, xv, 3, 258, 259
Wood, Sam, 206
Woolworth Building (Gilbert), 59
Woolworth's, 3, 173
Works Progress Administration (WPA), 13, 21, 23, 78, 226, 233, 260
"World of Tomorrow, The," 206
World War II, xi, xx, 30, 33, 73, 156, 205, 217, 225, 249
world's fairs. *See* Chicago World's Fair; New York World's Fair
WPA. *See* Works Progress Administration
Wray, Fay, 84, 200
Wright, Frank Lloyd, 62–64; Johnson Wax offices, 64; Kaufmann House ("Fallingwater"), 62–64; Usonian houses, 64
Wright, Russel, 77–78
Wyeth, N. C., 264–265, 267

Yankee, 153
Yellen, Jack: "Happy Days Are Here Again," 176; "There's No Depression in Love," 176
Yellowstone Park, 242
yo-yo, 129; cost of, 282
"You Are My Lucky Star" (Brown and Freed), 165
You Can't Cheat an Honest Man, 195
You Can't Take It with You, 198
You Have Seen Their Faces (Bourke-White and Caldwell), 262
Young Communists, 22
Young, Loretta, 84
Young, Murat "Chic," *Blondie*, 67, 267, 268, 271–272
Young Socialists, 22
Young, Trummy, "Tain't Wha'cha Do (It's the Way That You Do It)," 177
Your Hit Parade, xviii
Your Lucky Strike Hit Parade, 182
Your Money's Worth, 38

You're Only Young Once, 202
youth (*see also* teenagers), 17–34; and
    athletics, 23; comic strips and, 31;
    culture of, 30–31; education and, 18;
    and juvenile delinquency, 27–28;
    magazines for, 26–27; movies and,
    27–28; and politics, 22–24; popular
    entertainment and, 26–32; programs
    for, 19–21; and radio, 32–33; radio

and, 28–31; runaway, 19; sexuality
    and, 27; and swing, 177–178; unem-
    ployment and, 17–19

Zangara, Giuseppe, 4–5
Zenith, 52
Zep wagon, 129
Zeppelin, Count Ferdinand von, 244
zeppelins. *See* airships

About the Author

WILLIAM H. YOUNG is a freelance writer and independent scholar. He has recently retired from teaching English, American Studies, and popular culture at Lynchburg College in Virginia for 36 years. Young has published books and articles on various subjects of popular culture.